Domestic Violence in the Lives of Children

Domestic Violence in the Lives of Children

The Future of Research, Intervention, and Social Policy

Edited by
Sandra A. Graham-Bermann
and Jeffrey L. Edleson

American Psychological Association
Washington, DC

First printing April 2001
Second printing March 2002

Published by
American Psychological Association
750 First Street, NE
Washington, DC 20002
www.apa.org

To order
APA Order Department
P.O. Box 92984
Washington, DC 20090-2984
Tel: (800) 374-2721,
   Direct: (202) 336-5510
Fax: (202) 336-5502,
   TDD/TTY: (202) 336-6123
Online: www.apa.org/books
Email: order@apa.org

In the U.K., Europe, Africa, and the
   Middle East, copies may be ordered from
American Psychological Association
3 Henrietta Street
Covent Garden, London
WC2E 8LU England

Typeset in Goudy by World Composition Services, Inc., Sterling, VA

Printer: Data Reproductions, Auburn Hills, MI
Dust jacket designer: Naylor Design, Washington, DC
Technical/Production Editor: Amy J. Clarke

The opinions and statements published are the responsibility of the authors, and such opinions and statements do not necessarily represent the policies of the American Psychological Association.

Library of Congress Cataloging-in-Publication Data

Domestic violence in the lives of children : the future of research, intervention, and social policy / edited by Sandra A. Graham-Bermann and Jeffrey L. Edleson.—1st ed.
   p.   cm.
Includes bibliographical references and indexes.
ISBN 1-55798-799-3 (cb : acid-free paper)
1. Children and violence—Congresses. 2. Children and violence—Research—Congresses. 3. Children of abused wives—Congresses. 4. Family violence—Psychological aspects—Congresses. 5. Family violence—Research—Congresses.
I. Graham-Bermann, Sandra A. II. Edleson, Jeffrey L.
HQ784.V55 D65 2001
362.82'923—dc21   00-069972

British Library Cataloguing-in-Publication Data
A CIP record is available from the British Library.

Printed in the United States of America

CONTENTS

Contributors vii

Preface ix

Introduction 3
Sandra A. Graham-Bermann and Jeffrey L. Edleson

I. Understanding Children's Exposure to Domestic Violence 11

Chapter 1. Issues and Controversies in Documenting
the Prevalence of Children's Exposure
to Domestic Violence 13
*Ernest N. Jouriles, Renee McDonald,
William D. Norwood, and Elizabeth Ezell*

Chapter 2. Longer Term Effects of Children's Exposure
to Domestic Violence 35
B. B. Robbie Rossman

Chapter 3. Resilience in Children Exposed to Domestic
Violence 67
*Honore M. Hughes, Sandra A. Graham-Bermann,
and Gabrielle Gruber*

Chapter 4. Studying the Co-Occurrence of Child Maltreatment
and Domestic Violence in Families 91
Jeffrey L. Edleson

Chapter 5. Ethically Sound Research on Children's Exposure
to Domestic Violence: A Proposal 111
Einat Peled

II. Providing Context: The Role of Families and Social Support...... 133

Chapter 6. Overcoming Mother Blaming? Future
Directions for Research on Mothering
and Domestic Violence 135
Lorraine Radford and Marianne Hester

Chapter 7. Fatherhood and Domestic Violence: Exploring
the Role of Men Who Batter in the Lives
of Their Children 157
*Oliver J. Williams, Jacquelyn L. Boggess,
and Janet Carter*

Chapter 8. Domestic Violence and High-Conflict Divorce:
Developing a New Generation of Research
for Children 189
*Peter G. Jaffe, Samantha E. Poisson,
and Alison Cunningham*

Chapter 9. Researching Children's Experience of
Interparental Violence: Toward a
Multidimensional Conceptualization 203
Zvi Eisikovits and Zeev Winstok

Chapter 10. Critical Issues in Research on Social Networks
and Social Supports of Children Exposed
to Domestic Violence 219
Sandra K. Beeman

III. Preventive Intervention Initiatives and Evaluations 235

Chapter 11. Designing Intervention Evaluations for Children
Exposed to Domestic Violence: Applications of
Research and Theory 237
Sandra A. Graham-Bermann

Chapter 12. Evaluating Coordinated Community Responses
for Abused Women and Their Children 269
Cris M. Sullivan and Nicole E. Allen

Chapter 13. Prevention of Domestic Violence:
Emerging Initiatives 283
David A. Wolfe and Peter G. Jaffe

Author Index 299

Subject Index 311

About the Editors 331

CONTRIBUTORS

Nicole E. Allen, PhD, Department of Psychology, University of Illinois, Urbana–Champaign

Sandra K. Beeman, PhD, School of Social Work, University of Minnesota, St. Paul

Jacquelyn L. Boggess, JD, Center on Fathers, Families, and Policy, Madison, WI

Janet Carter, MA, Family Violence Prevention Fund, San Francisco, CA

Alison Cunningham, MA, Centre for Research on Violence Against Women and Children, University of Western Ontario, London, Ontario, Canada

Jeffrey L. Edleson, PhD, School of Social Work, University of Minnesota, St. Paul

Zvi Eisikovits, PhD, School of Social Work, University of Haifa, Haifa, Israel

Elizabeth Ezell, MA, Department of Psychology, University of Houston, Houston, TX

Sandra A. Graham-Bermann, PhD, Department of Psychology, University of Michigan, Ann Arbor

Gabrielle Gruber, MA, Department of Psychology, University of Michigan, Ann Arbor

Marianne Hester, PhD, School of Humanities and Social Sciences, University of Sunderland, Sunderland, England

Honore M. Hughes, PhD, Department of Psychology, St. Louis University, St. Louis, MO

Peter G. Jaffe, PhD, CPsych, Centre for Children and Families in the Justice System, London Family Court Clinic, and Departments of Psychiatry and of Psychology, University of Western Ontario, London, Ontario, Canada

Ernest N. Jouriles, PhD, Department of Psychology, University of Houston, Houston, TX

Renee McDonald, PhD, Department of Psychology, University of Houston, Houston, TX

William D. Norwood, PhD, Department of Psychology, University of Houston, Houston, TX

Einat Peled, PhD, Bob Shapell School of Social Work, Tel Aviv University, Tel Aviv, Israel

Samantha E. Poisson, MEd, Centre for Children and Families in the Justice System, London Family Court Clinic, London, Ontario, Canada

Lorraine Radford, PhD, School of Sociology and Social Policy, University of Surrey Roehampton, London, England

B. B. Robbie Rossman, PhD, Psychology Department, University of Denver, Denver, CO

Cris M. Sullivan, PhD, Department of Psychology, Michigan State University, East Lansing

Oliver J. Williams, PhD, School of Social Work, University of Minnesota, St. Paul

Zeev Winstok, MA, School of Social Work, and research associate, Minerva Center for Youth Studies, University of Haifa, Haifa, Israel

David A. Wolfe, PhD, Department of Psychology, University of Western Ontario, London, Ontario, Canada

PREFACE

As researchers, we have learned that exposure to family violence affects many children in multiple aspects of their lives—from how they act to how they think. We know from our clinical work that some children are severely affected by exposure to violence, yet others appear to be relatively unaffected by these events. For example, a 12-year-old boy testified in court that he witnessed his father kill his mother on the front lawn of their house. The police arrived just as neighbors came out of their houses and watched the grisly scene. This child's adjustment was further complicated by a series of family disputes over his custody. Yet a year later, this child appeared to be coping adequately with these seemingly overwhelming events. Another boy was 14 years old when he intervened to break up a domestic fight by threatening to retaliate against his father. He went on to become president of the United States. However, not all children exposed to family violence are left unaffected by their experiences. For example, a 4-year-old girl was expelled from her preschool for repeatedly biting and verbally threatening other children. The girl had watched her father abuse her mother on many occasions. In another family, a 2-year-old boy clung to his mother in fear and stopped speaking for more than 6 months after witnessing severe acts of violence against her. He had been traumatized by what he saw. These examples raise a host of questions about the range of behaviors children exhibit following violence exposure and what is needed to help them.

Research is just beginning to address the questions of who is most at risk for negative outcomes following violence exposure, what protects children in these families, and how the larger community and social systems impede or enhance adjustment for their mothers. Given that the most informed clinical practice for children exposed to family violence is based on theory and research, it is clear that we need many more studies to discover what these children need and what are the optimal ways to help them. As both researchers and practitioners, our clinical work with women and children exposed to domestic violence has given us a unique view of the daily challenges and coping strengths of these families. The resulting questions are complex and push us as researchers to go beyond what is known to expand the way violence is commonly understood and studied as well as to develop new measures and to design new interventions to be helpful to these children and their families. There are many controversial issues and debates as to who should be included in these studies, what questions are permissible to ask of children and parents, and whose story should be told. The contributors to this volume have had numerous conversations about the challenges and limitations of research on children's exposure to violence. This book represents an effort to highlight, from multiple perspectives, some of the important gains and remaining gaps in this emerging field.

We conceptualized this book as the next logical step to follow two volumes recently published by the American Psychological Association: *Children Exposed to Marital Violence: Theory, Research, and Applied Issues* (1998), edited by George Holden, Robert Geffner, and Ernest Jouriles, and *Violence Against Children in the Family and the Community* (1998), edited by Penelope Trickett and Cynthia Schellenbach. Both of these books successfully captured the array of published research specific to children living in violent families. The Trickett and Schellenbach book followed a conference held at the University of Southern California in 1995. The Holden et al. book derived its material from the Second International Conference on Children Exposed to Family Violence held in Austin, Texas, in June 1996. Whereas these volumes focused on what is (or was) already known, the current book is intended not only to update and to extend this conversation but also to chart directions for the future. Thus, we hope to suggest what is needed to facilitate progress in this area and to advance research and public policy for children who experience family violence. Accordingly, most of the chapters begin with a brief, critical, and updated review of the salient research in a specific area and proceed to a discussion of future directions and policy implications.

The impetus for this volume began with a 2½-day working meeting that was specifically engineered to provide a group of researchers from around the world with the time and opportunity to explore the state of the art research on the impact of domestic violence on the lives of children, to discuss the adequacy of intervention programs and their evaluations, and to discuss policy implications that flow from this body of work. Some members of this group had met at international conferences over the years to share information, to compare interventions, and to collaborate. For the most part, these meetings had been unplanned, haphazard, and fleeting (and therefore, intellectually energizing but frustrating). We were joined by legal experts, public policymakers, and child development specialists for 2½ days at the Asilomar Conference Center in Pacific Grove, California, in February 1999. Generous support for these meetings was provided by the David and Lucile Packard Foundation and the National Institute of Justice. We would especially like to thank and acknowledge the assistance of Carol Stevenson and Lucy Salcido Carter from the David and Lucile Packard Foundation and Bernie Auchter from the Office of Justice Programs at the National Institute of Justice, which is part of the Department of Justice, in this endeavor.

This working conference was instrumental in helping us to identify what is needed in the future in defining central research constructs, in setting standards for conducting this research with this population of children, and in determining what steps are needed next to ensure that quality interventions can be identified and implemented for children who experience abuse to themselves and to their mothers. Our current efforts to compare the efficacy of various interventions are considerably impaired by the many differences between research studies on the effects of family violence on children. The chapters of this book originated as working papers presented at the small group conference and address these salient issues. Each chapter was revised on the basis of this discussion and the feedback provided at the meeting.

We would like to thank editors Margaret Schlegel and Judy Nemes at the American Psychological Association for their timely editorial assistance in bringing this volume to publication. A number of people provided essential support and editorial comments and otherwise aided in the development of this book. We thank Eric Bermann, Sandra Beeman, and Einat Peled.

Domestic Violence
in the Lives of Children

INTRODUCTION

SANDRA A. GRAHAM-BERMANN
AND JEFFREY L. EDLESON

Violence in the lives of children has been considered the number one public health problem in the United States for some time (Shalala, 1994; Reno, 1999). Current rates of both woman abuse and child maltreatment remain high, and children are exposed to increasing rates of violence in some areas. It is estimated that approximately 12% of American women experience intimate partner violence and that 3% are severely beaten by their intimate partners each year (Straus & Gelles, 1990). Surveys reveal that an estimated 10 million children witness this violence each year (Straus, 1992). The third National Incidence Studies of Child Abuse and Neglect (NIS), which surveys a range of professionals each year, estimates that approximately 2.8 million American children were maltreated in the year of the survey, a doubling of the rate found in the first NIS study (NIS-3; Sedlack & Broadhurst, 1996). It is often difficult to tease out the effects of better reporting mechanisms, increased recognition of the problem, and actual increases in incidence. However, given that reports of the numbers of child abuse and neglect cases have risen 41% since 1988 (Wang & Daro, 1998) and that the number of severe abuse cases has increased from 1986 to 1993, it is highly likely that a real increase in serious abuse to children has occurred (Emery & Laumann-Billings, 1998).

Witnessing domestic violence and being a victim of child maltreatment both have the potential for negative outcomes in a child's development. Studies comparing children who have witnessed domestic violence with those who have been maltreated have found each to produce unique negative outcomes for the children involved (see Edleson, 1999a). In addition, in the majority of studies on the co-occurrence of child maltreatment and domestic violence in the same families, it has been found that these forms of violence co-occur from 30% to 60% of the time, with a median of a 40% overlap (Appel & Holden, 1998; Edleson, 1999b). These findings have alarmed child safety advocates and policy makers and have resulted in a

3

variety of new legislative and policy initiatives across America (see National Council of Juvenile and Family Court Judges, 1999).

Yet violence in the family is often only one aspect of an atmosphere of violence in the lives of American children. Children are routinely exposed to acts of violence on television, in the movies, in many communities, and far too often in many school settings (Graham-Bermann & Bermann, 2000). For example, by age 13, the average American child has witnessed more than 8,000 murders on television and 100,000 acts of television violence (Huston & Wright, 1996). Since 1993, murder has been on the increase in elementary and high schools, involving younger and younger children as perpetrators, growing from single-target to multiple-victim crimes, and usually having boys as the perpetrators and girls as the targets of violence (Sleek, 1998). In other countries, children are exposed to the violence of war, to ethnic and racial hatred, and to violence associated with political persecution.

THIS VOLUME

Given the urgent need to understand the role of domestic violence and child maltreatment in the lives of children, there is, in turn, a compelling need to identify the best ways of studying families in which violence and violence exposure occur and for selecting the most effective interventions for this population of children. When considering a child's concurrent exposure to domestic violence and child maltreatment, issues are raised that challenge what have been, until recently, the work of entirely separate domains. In this volume, we intend to review studies in each area, to suggest the next steps for researchers, to present models for intervention evaluation, and suggest implications for creating public policy in this area. A number of consequential elements are carefully presented, including differences between studies in the ways in which both kinds of violence are measured, the focus of research study, the reporter of events, and the link between this emerging field of research and intervention strategies that meet the needs of these children.

In this volume, we not only highlight the best available measures, methods of analyzing data, and advances in intervention but also suggest improved strategies and minimum standards for coordinating such work in the future. In most chapters, the authors extend the results of their work into the public arena by taking into account implications for public policy, legislation, and funding priorities. The voices in this book are diverse and do not always present a consensus on the issues addressed or the best ways to define them. (For example, a number of terms are used to refer to adult domestic violence, including *woman abuse*, *intimate partner violence*, and *violence against women*. Wherever possible, we have elected to use the term *domestic violence* to refer to this often broadly construed construct.) Although we do not agree with all the statements made in the following chapters, we know that they have been carefully thought out and represent some of the best thinking in this field of study.

Thinking Ahead: Understanding Children's Exposure to Domestic Violence

The book is divided into three parts, beginning with an understanding of the requisite future research and policy needs concerning the implications of children's exposure to intimate violence. In chapter 1, Ernest Jouriles, Renee McDonald, William Norwood, and Elizabeth Ezell focus on issues and controversies in documenting the incidence and prevalence of children's exposure to domestic violence. They begin with a presentation of existing problems in defining and measuring violence and highlight some of the controversies and shortcomings in this area. Next, they address the prevalence of children's exposure to such violence and review research pertaining to this issue. They conclude with a discussion of gaps in the existing knowledge base and offer suggestions for future research to develop policy and practice for this population of children.

Although we know that many children witness domestic violence each year, a brief review of existing studies shows that relatively little is known about its long-term developmental consequences. In chapter 2, B. B. Robbie Rossman considers a number of ways or processes through which a child's development can be affected. The relevant areas of learning, nurturing, and trauma processes are all considered as possible conduits of negative long-term effects. Rossman notes that as more studies track children exposed to interparental violence over time, the long-term course of violence exposure and the consequences of violence exposure to the child should be documented in these significant and interrelated domains.

Honore Hughes, Sandra Graham-Bermann, and Gabrielle Gruber describe in chapter 3 a number of ways of defining and assessing resiliency in children who are exposed to adult domestic violence. They note that at present, there is little information available regarding what factors play a role in how children in violent families actually cope with the violence and abuse around them. The authors consider those children exposed to domestic violence who do not appear to demonstrate significant negative effects in the face of the domestic violence—those successful "copers," the adaptable or seemingly resilient children. After a brief review of the various definitions and key studies of resilience in children exposed to family violence, data from two studies of resilient children of battered women are briefly examined. Many questions are raised about resilience in the context of family violence, with a careful eye toward understanding its possible implications for future study and public policy.

Policy makers and practitioners are increasingly concerned about the welfare of children who live in homes where woman battering is occurring. These concerns have increased as the results of research on problems associated with children's witnessing of violence and the co-occurrence of child maltreatment and woman battering have become more widely distributed. Chapter 4 by Jeffrey Edleson focuses on a series of research issues that require attention if researchers are to understand child abuse, children's exposure to adult domestic violence, and the unique contribution of such abuse and exposure to a child's development problems. He also addresses the need for efforts to intervene with these children and their families. Suggestions for necessary changes in future research agendas are raised throughout this chapter.

Einat Peled then completes this part by tackling the question of ethical issues in research with children exposed to intimate family violence in chapter 5. The general assumption underlying this chapter is that a study cannot be done well unless proper ethical standards have been maintained throughout the research process. A review of reported research procedures in the domain of children's exposure to domestic violence raises questions as to the meaning of the phrase "proper ethical standards" and the extent to which these assumptions are shared by researchers and journal editors. Peled suggests a definition for ethical research in the domain of children's exposure to domestic violence and then critically reviews the body of reported research practices aimed at maintaining ethical standards in studies on children's exposure. She concludes with an outline of tentative guidelines for implementing ethically sound research in this domain.

Providing Context: The Role of Families and Social Support

The second part weighs the role of families and social support in the adjustment of children in maltreating families. First, Lorraine Radford and Marianne Hester address in chapter 6 ways to overcome mother blaming and future directions for theory and research in this domain. This chapter reviews and develops four themes within the existing research and theoretical debates on mothering and domestic violence. Taking the issue of child contact as the main focus, Radford and Hester consider (a) the impact and effects that abuse has on mothering, health costs, parenting stress, and relationship between mothering and gender entrapment or survival; (b) the institutional responses, ideological, legal, and policy frameworks, and particularly the reconstitution of parenting, notions of equality, children's rights, and fatherhood; (c) mothering, violence, and identity and the negotiation and construction of the maternal identities of "battered women" in feminist, academic, and therapeutic discourses; and (d) social support for abusive and nonabusing mothers and their children.

Oliver Williams, Jacqueline Boggess, and Janet Carter write about fathering in the context of domestic violence. Although most fathers continue to have contact with their children even after separating from their partners, many fathers' rights groups complain that men are unfairly excluded from contact with children because of charges of domestic violence against them. In chapter 7, they review existing research and emerging issues regarding fathers who batter. Several research issues that should be addressed in the coming years are outlined and include ensuring that fathers are present in studies of the effects of family violence on children and using measures sensitive to the unique contributions of fathers to their families. Questions of how the perspectives of the various stakeholders (battered women's advocates, fathers' rights advocates, and father involvement supporters) affect this issue also are considered.

Recent high-profile child custody cases and government hearings have made child custody and domestic violence a major issue for public debate and professional training, policy and service development, and legislation. Peter Jaffe, Samantha Poisson, and Alison Cunningham argue that social scientists need to inform this debate with a new generation of research that can address the impact of witnessing violence and separation on children. In chapter 8, they identify future research needs, including capturing critical variables to explore the historical and ongoing nature of the violence, risk and protective factors, poverty and access to legal and counseling resources, and adjustment for boys and girls across different developmental stages.

The purpose of chapter 9 by Zvi Eisikovits and Zeev Winstok is to suggest a conceptual framework for including children's own perceptions in future empirical study of exposure to adult domestic violence. Some ethical and methodological problems with using standardized existing measures, such as the Child Behavior Checklist and others, are suggested. The authors argue that in families in which adult conflicts escalate to violence, several central themes affect the way family members perceive and interact with each other and then report on the violence-ridden environment of the child. They maintain that to acquire a holistic picture of a child's experience of domestic violence, researchers need to examine the dimensions of mutual influence between the child and parents in terms of the extent of acknowledgment of the violence and their respective levels of perceived competence, mastery, and self-perception.

Critical issues in research on social networks and social supports of children exposed to domestic violence are raised by Sandra Beeman in chapter 10. A growing body of literature examines the ways in which supportive resources may protect children exposed to family violence. In this chapter, social support is considered to influence a child's well-being both directly (through the child's own network) and indirectly (through the influence of the parent's network on his or her parenting ability). This chapter focuses on the social networks of children and the types of support children receive through them.

Identifying and Evaluating Preventive Intervention Efforts

The third part is devoted to exploring and evaluating current intervention initiatives and outcome studies. Growing interest by researchers and clinicians in the field of domestic violence has begun to establish a scientific foundation for implementing prevention and treatment initiatives and public policy to end domestic violence. In chapter 11 on evaluating intervention efforts, Sandra Graham-Bermann maintains that research consistently shows that approximately half of all children exposed to domestic violence have emotional and behavioral problems in the clinical range—that is, they are in need of direct intervention. Yet just at the time that many shelters, communities, and even schools have initiated direct intervention programs for children exposed to adult domestic violence, there are only a handful of outcome studies to document the potential, efficacy, and limitations of such programs. These existing research studies are carefully reviewed and compared with evaluation studies in related fields. Standards for intervention outcome evaluation studies and future research requirements in this area are offered to stress the pressing need for doing this difficult and important job in the best possible manner.

Cris Sullivan and Nicole Allen examine in chapter 12 the larger system evaluations and interventions. They begin with a review of existing studies and move to consider questions pertinent to this developing field. They ask the following questions: What are the important outcomes to measure? How should researchers go about measuring these outcomes? How should researchers test the strengths of community-wide interventions? Which aspects of larger systems can and should be included as the focus of the work? The challenges and rewards of coordinating multiple services across systems to both abused women and their children are debated. Recommendations and caveats to the best ways of implementing and then evaluating such approaches are made.

In chapter 13, David Wolfe and Peter Jaffe present an overview of theoretical approaches to preventing domestic violence at a primary level and describe alternatives to violence that can be activated in each community in a manner that stimulates interest, informs choices, and promotes action to decrease violence and abuse in the lives of children, youth, and families. Promising approaches to prevention with children and adults are discussed in relation to school-based curricula, neighborhood-based health and social services, and family-based child and health care.

Cross-Cutting Themes

Numerous cross-cutting themes can be identified in this volume. They include (a) the variability of definitions of key constructs, particularly violence variables; (b) the problem of relying on measures that are not culturally heterogeneous; (c) the ethical concerns about who frames the questions and therefore sets the research (or intervention or public policy) agenda; and (d) the emphasis on setting standards and selecting criteria that are the best for evaluating the efficacy of interventions. This volume addresses issues that may have serious implications for the well-being of children and their families. As new policies and interventions develop around the witnessing of domestic violence and co-occurring violence in families, it will be critical for all involved to have clear, accurate, and helpful information on which to base decisions. We hope that this volume will assist in raising the quality of information available to researchers, policy makers, and practitioners in the future.

REFERENCES

Appel, A. E., & Holden, G. W. (1998). The co-occurrence of spouse and physical child abuse: A review and appraisal. *Journal of Family Psychology, 12,* 578–599.

Edleson, J. L. (1999a). Children's witnessing of adult domestic violence. *Journal of Interpersonal Violence, 14,* 839–870.

Edleson, J. L. (1999b). The overlap between child maltreatment and woman battering. *Violence Against Women, 5,* 134–154.

Emery, R. E., & Laumann-Billings, L. (1998). An overview of the nature, causes, and consequences of abusive family relationships: Toward differentiating maltreatment and violence. *American Psychologist, 53,* 121–135.

Graham-Bermann, S. A., & Bermann, E. A. (2000, August). *An ecological approach to assessing violence in preschoolers' lives.* Symposium presented at the 108th Annual Convention of the American Psychological Association, Washington, DC.

Huston, A. C., & Wright, J. C. (1996). Television and socialization of young children. In T. M. Macbeth (Ed.), *Tuning in to young viewers: Social science perspectives on television* (pp. 37–60). Thousand Oaks, CA: Sage.

National Council of Juvenile and Family Court Judges. (1999). *Effective intervention in domestic violence and child maltreatment cases: Guidelines for policy and practice.* Reno, NV: Author.

Reno, J. (1999, June 24). *Safe from the start: The national summit on children exposed to violence.* Washington, DC: U.S. Department of Justice, Office of Juvenile Justice and Delinquency Prevention.

Sedlack, A., & Broadhurst, D. (1996). *Third national incidence study of child abuse and neglect, final report.* Washington, DC: U.S. Department of Health and Human Services.

Shalala, D. (1994, March). *Domestic terrorism: An unacknowledged epidemic.* Keynote presentation at the national conference of the American Medical Association, Washington, DC.

Sleek, S. (1998, August). Experts scrambling on school shootings: The recent homicides in rural schools represent a violence puzzling to psychologists. *APA Monitor, 29*(8), 1, 35.

Straus, M. A. (1992). *Children as witnesses to marital violence: A risk factor for lifelong problems among a nationally representative sample of American men and women* (Report of the Twenty-Third Ross Roundtable). Columbus, OH: Ross Laboratories.

Straus, M. A., & Gelles, R. J. (Eds.). (1990). *Physical violence in American families.* New Brunswick, NJ: Transaction.

Wang, C.-T., & Daro, D. (1998). *Current trends in child abuse reporting and fatalities: The results of the 1997 Annual Fifty State Survey.* Chicago, IL: Center for Child Abuse Prevention Research. Retrieved on June 12, 1998, from the World Wide Web http://www.childabuse.org/50data97.htm/6/12/98

I

UNDERSTANDING CHILDREN'S EXPOSURE TO DOMESTIC VIOLENCE

1

ISSUES AND CONTROVERSIES IN DOCUMENTING THE PREVALENCE OF CHILDREN'S EXPOSURE TO DOMESTIC VIOLENCE

ERNEST N. JOURILES, RENEE MCDONALD,
WILLIAM D. NORWOOD, AND ELIZABETH EZELL

Domestic violence has been recognized as an important health and social problem that can have devastating short- and long-term consequences for families. Although women are the most obvious victims, it has become increasingly clear that the impact of such violence extends to the children in these families as well. The study of children's exposure to domestic violence, however, is hampered by several conceptual, methodological, and practical difficulties. In this chapter, we focus on problems associated with documenting the prevalence of children's exposure to domestic violence (i.e., the number of children exposed to such violence), beginning with a brief discussion of the importance of such documentation. We then follow with a detailed discussion of associated issues and controversies, many of which are relevant to the study of domestic violence in general but several are unique to the study of children in domestically violent families. Next we present some rough estimates of the prevalence of children's exposure to domestic violence and illustrate the problems in deriving such estimates on the basis of existing data. We conclude with a brief discussion of gaps in the existing knowledge and offer suggestions for future research to inform policy and practice in this area.

DOCUMENTATION OF THE PREVALENCE OF CHILDREN'S EXPOSURE TO DOMESTIC VIOLENCE

As many others have noted (e.g., Gelles, 2000), it is important to have accurate estimates of the prevalence of domestic violence. Documenting that many people are affected by a particular phenomenon is often necessary to convince policymakers that the phenomenon is a significant social problem and that resources should be allocated to address the problem. Also prevalence estimates can help inform the development of cost-effective and targeted interventions. In other words, the number and characteristics of people likely to be affected by a particular problem can influence the efforts taken to prevent and treat the problem.

Exposure to domestic violence is believed to place children at risk for maladjustment. Thus, the reasons for documenting the prevalence of domestic violence are also applicable to documenting the prevalence of children's exposure to that violence. It should be clear, however, that documenting prevalence of exposure to violence is different from and is arguably much more complicated than documenting the prevalence of the violence itself. This is due, in part, to the conceptualization and measurement of "exposure" and the lack of knowledge about how domestic violence operates as a risk factor for children. In this chapter, we present several important issues in documenting the prevalence of children's exposure to domestic violence. We believe that their careful consideration is required if researchers are to develop socially and clinically useful information regarding children's exposure to such violence.

ISSUES AND CONTROVERSIES IN CONCEPTUALIZATION AND OPERATIONALIZATION

Wife Abuse Versus Marital Violence

The conceptualization and operationalization of wife abuse or marital violence is both complex and controversial. In fact, a close inspection of the research literature (the literature on children's exposure to domestic violence and the broader literatures of violence against women and violence within the family) suggests that there is no clear consensus about the construct of interest across studies. For example, terms such as *wife abuse*, *battered women*, and *husband-to-wife violence* are often used synonymously with the terms *marital violence*, *spouse abuse*, and *physically aggressive couples*. Interchanging such terms may appear trivial to some; however, it is not uncommon to see the use of the latter group of terms criticized harshly in this literature (e.g., McMahon & Pence, 1996). Specifically, using the terms *marital violence* and *spouse abuse* is thought to detract from what many view as the real problem or construct of interest: violence against women, not violence between intimates. This distinction has implications for how the existing research is construed and for the design of future studies in this area.

The above discussion implies that there are at least two different violence constructs. The first is "violence between intimates," regardless of perpetrator, and the second is "violence toward women" by a male intimate partner. Researchers and advocates have compellingly argued that male-to-female violence differs greatly from female-to-male violence and that the two should not be equated (e.g., Dobash, Dobash, Wilson, & Daly, 1992; Holtzworth-Munroe, Smutzler, & Stuart, 1998). However, both forms of violence may be important from the perspective of a witnessing child. In fact, it is possible that husband-to-wife violence and wife-to-husband violence—although different from one another in form, function, and consequence—both influence child adjustment (Straus, 1993).

This controversy (wife abuse vs. marital violence) has implications for documenting the prevalence of children's exposure to violence and for addressing many other questions pertaining to children and domestic violence. Furthermore, this issue provides a backdrop against which we consider other conceptual and definitional issues that plague research in this area. Although some of these issues have been debated extensively, others have not yet captured the attention they deserve. Unless otherwise noted, we use the term *marital violence* to refer to physical aggression between intimate partners without respect to perpetrator gender. We use *wife abuse* or *violence toward women* to refer to acts of physical aggression directed toward women by a male intimate partner. We use *violence* and *domestic violence* in reference to both marital violence and violence toward women. For brevity, we use the terms *wife* and *marital* even though we refer to adult intimate relationships in general, regardless of legal marital status.

Narrow Versus Broad Definitions of Violence

One issue that has received attention in the literature is the breadth of the definition of *violence*. As noted in the National Research Council (1996) report *Understanding Violence Against Women*, many researchers have relied on a narrow conceptualization and definition of violence and use as their criterion for violence the occurrence of specific acts of physical aggression. For example, the physical aggression items from a version of the Conflict Tactics Scales (CTS; Straus, 1979; Straus, Hamby, Finkelhor, & Runyan, 1995) are often used to classify families as "violent" or "nonviolent." These acts include threw something; pushed, grabbed, or shoved; slapped; kicked, bit, or hit with a fist; hit or tried to hit with something; beat up; threatened with a knife or gun; and used a knife or gun. Some researchers classify families as violent if at least one such act has occurred within a given time period, most commonly the year before assessment. Others require the occurrence of multiple acts within a given time period or have used multiple criteria (e.g., the occurrence of an act of physical aggression during the past year and current residence at a battered women's shelter) for classifying families.

In contrast to the above conceptualization and definition of violence, other researchers argue that the construct of violence is much broader and that its measurement should not be limited to acts of physical aggression. The working definition used by the American Psychological Association Task Force on Male Violence Against Women provided examples of the domains of behavior encompassed by this broader view of violence: "physical, visual, verbal, or sexual acts that are experienced by a woman or girl as a threat, invasion, or assault and that have the effect of hurting her or degrading her and/or taking away her ability to control contact (intimate and otherwise) with another individual" (Koss et al., 1994, p. xvi). Those taking this broader view of violence believe that researchers should broaden their measurement approaches accordingly. For example, a tenet of feminist theory is that violence against women is perpetrated by men in efforts to maintain socially sanctioned power and "coercive control" of women (Yllö, 1993). Measurement of violence based on this precept would include the specific physically violent acts described above and other acts, such as the denial of resources, stalking, verbal abuse, and sexual violence. Although most researchers in this area would likely agree that such activities are common in the context of wife abuse, published research reports are typified by measurement only of physically aggressive acts.

We would like to raise three additional points that are pertinent to this issue. First, researchers and policymakers have been admonished for focusing their efforts solely on the physical violence, in spite of arguments that victims of wife abuse perceive other aspects of their treatment to be equally and sometimes more harmful and abusive (e.g., Kelly, 1988; Schwartz, 2000). In essence, it is argued that researchers have imposed their own value systems on the research, defining and operationalizing the construct of violence toward women without regard to the beliefs and experiences vis-à-vis violence of the women who are the victims of that violence. There is also little data on the meaning of violent acts to the children exposed to it. Obviously, these issues warrant greater attention.

Second, measuring violence more broadly could improve clinicians' and researchers' ability to predict child behavior problems. In a study on children in families characterized by marital violence, Jouriles, Norwood, McDonald, Vincent, and Mahoney (1996) found that forms of marital aggression other than physical violence toward a partner (e.g., verbal threats, throwing objects) relate to children's behavior problems, even after accounting for the frequency of physical violence in these families. Should these findings be interpreted to suggest that the other forms of aggression be included in the conceptualization and definition of violence? The answer is not necessarily, but it does suggest that such acts are important to child adjustment (at least in the context of physical violence) and deserve consideration.

Third, this chapter is primarily concerned with children's exposure to violence between their parents, but children's exposure to "family" violence is certainly not limited to this type of violence. Children may witness many other forms of violence between family members, such as violence between a father and a stepfather or between a grandparent and a parent. Straus and Gelles (1990) found that sibling abuse (fighting between siblings) was the most prevalent type of violence in American families. Similarly, children may witness parental violence toward other children in the family or children attacking their parents. In short, many forms of family violence exist, and little is known about the impact of these forms.

Conflict Versus Violence

Another conceptual issue that has received little attention is the distinction between marital conflict (a term whose definition is also controversial) and the phenomena that are the focus of this chapter: marital violence and wife abuse. In fact, given that many researchers of children of battered women have also published in the area of marital conflict and child adjustment, it is somewhat surprising that so little attention has been devoted to this distinction. It might be inferred from some of the published research that marital violence falls within the construct of marital conflict; it is sometimes conceptualized as an "intense" form of marital conflict. That is, marital conflict is conceptualized as multidimensional, with the intensity of conflict being one of several dimensions and marital violence representing a high level of intensity (e.g., Grych & Fincham, 1990). Others appear to conceptualize violence and conflict as separate constructs (e.g., Hershorn & Rosenbaum, 1985; Jouriles, Murphy, & O'Leary, 1989; Rossman & Rosenberg, 1992), but this distinction is seldom articulated in published reports.

Both marital violence and marital conflict (at least certain manifestations of marital conflict) can be components of a destructive home environment for children. Furthermore, if one conceptualized a continuum of destructive marital conflict, there would probably be little argument that families characterized by violence toward women or frequent, heated, poorly resolved marital disputes would lie on the destructive end of this continuum. However, several important conceptual distinctions can be made between wife abuse and marital conflict, distinctions that suggest that they are not part of the same construct. For example, conflict is often thought to be synonymous with disagreement, and it is sometimes operationalized as the frequency of certain types of disagreements (as in the commonly used

O'Leary–Porter Scale; Porter & O'Leary, 1980). Violence, however, does not always occur in the context of marital conflict (although the most commonly used measures often situate violence in the context of conflict).

As noted earlier, feminist theorists maintain that much violence toward women is spurred by the motive to control one's partner rather than to resolve a conflict, and some marital violence comes from "out of the blue," with no conflict immediately preceding the violence (DeKeseredy & Schwartz, 1998). A second conceptual distinction is that some marital conflict may be considered constructive, and a number of scholars believe that children can benefit from exposure to constructive conflict resolution (e.g., where spouses jointly problem solve and seek mutually acceptable resolutions to disagreements; Cummings & Davies, 1994; Fincham, 1994). Although this notion of constructive conflict is not yet well developed, it certainly does not include the use of violence. In other words, it is unlikely that any scholars in the area of child development believe that exposing children to domestic violence can have any short- or long-term positive effects. A third conceptual distinction is that conflict is ubiquitous in marriage, particularly when it is defined in ways that are synonymous with disagreement; wife abuse is not.

Ordinary or Common Violence Versus Wife Abuse

An important but often overlooked issue, with respect to the prevalence of children's exposure to violence, is that many couples are domestically violent at certain stages of their relationships. For example, O'Leary et al. (1989) found that 31% of the men and 44% of the women in their sample reported that they had engaged in physical aggression against their partners in the year before their marriage. Similarly, prevalence estimates based on large representative samples of young couples (the time in marriage when many have children) suggest that a high percentage of these couples (again, at times, over 40%) engage in physical aggression (see Magdol et al., 1997, for a review). In studies such as these, most violent couples are reporting pushes, grabs, or shoves that occur, on average, six times a year or less often, and women are reported to engage in violent acts as frequently as men. This level of violence has been called "ordinary" (Straus, 1990) or "common couple" violence (Johnson, 1995).

In an important conceptual article, Johnson (1995) reviewed evidence from studies using women's shelter samples and community survey samples to support a distinction between "common couple" violence and "patriarchal terrorism." He argued that common couple violence is prevalent across marriages. It is characterized by low-frequency, low-severity violence that involves both partners initiating violent acts. Furthermore, this type of violence often dissipates over the course of a relationship. In contrast, the patriarchal terrorism that characterizes shelter samples consists of more frequent and severe violence that is primarily unidirectional (man to woman) and is intended to subjugate or harm the woman. This type of violence often escalates in frequency and severity over the course of a relationship. This distinction is important in understanding both domestic violence and the effects of domestic violence on children.

It is also interesting to note that there are many inconsistencies in the literature with respect to this phenomenon that has been called "ordinary" or "common couple" violence. For example, in some studies, families in which one or two incidents of physical marital aggression have occurred are labeled as "violent" and compared with "nonviolent" groups, in which no act of aggression between partners has occurred over a given time period (e.g., Rossman & Rosenberg, 1992). In other studies, families reporting "minor" acts of physical aggression between partners (e.g., pushes, slaps) have been explicitly included in "nonviolent" comparison groups (e.g., Graham-Bermann, 1996; Hughes, 1988). Such inconsistencies highlight the need to carefully conceptualize and specify what is meant by "violent" and "nonviolent."

Conceptual Issues Unique to Children's Exposure to Violence

Many other conceptual issues still need to be addressed in the study of children's exposure to violence. In fact, what is meant by a child's "exposure" to violence is often not well articulated. Children's exposure can be conceptualized several ways, including (a) observing violence, (b) hearing parents fighting and "knowing" that their mother is being hit but not directly observing the violence, (c) observing outcomes of the violence (e.g., bruises on their mother, broken furniture) but not necessarily observing or hearing the violence directly, (d) becoming aware of the violence (e.g., their mother or a sibling tells them about it) but not necessarily observing or hearing evidence of it, or (e) living in a household in which the violence occurs but not being aware of it. Although empirical data on different types of exposure are sparse, some data support the argument that a child does not have to observe wife abuse (or at least certain types of wife abuse) to be affected by it. For example, in a study on children in families characterized by the threat or use of knife or gun violence, Jouriles, McDonald, Norwood, et al. (1998) found that the occurrence of knife or gun violence, not necessarily children's witnessing of this type of violence, was associated with an increased risk for child behavior problems.

There are other related conceptual issues, some of which can also be considered measurement issues with respect to estimating the prevalence of children's exposure to violence. For example, how much time can or should elapse after an incident of violence before the child is no longer considered exposed to it (e.g., 1 month, 6 months, 1 year)? Should a child be considered exposed to violence if the violence occurred before the birth of the child? It is not untenable to argue that violence occurring before the birth of a child might have an influence on that child (e.g., by virtue of changing the way the parents interact with each other). Furthermore, violence toward women during pregnancy is often directed at the woman's abdomen and can adversely affect the child's health and development (McFarlane, Parker, & Soeken, 1995). In short, the concept of children's exposure to domestic violence requires systematic theoretical and empirical attention.

PROCEDURAL ISSUES INVOLVED IN MEASUREMENT

The measurement of violence, although less controversial than its conceptualization, is still complex. Furthermore, measurement issues are central to any study attempting to document the prevalence of violence. Because individuals are often reluctant to disclose violent experiences for several reasons, including embarrassment and fear of reprisal (DeKeseredy, 2000), such factors need to be considered in the selection of methods to assess violence. Many researchers believe that a measure of trust needs to be built between the interviewer and study participant before many participants will disclose an episode of violence (Koss, 1993; Schwartz, 2000). Other researchers, again because of the sensitivity of the subject, have argued that violence needs to be assessed several times during the course of an interview (Schwartz, 2000; Smith, 1987). Smith, for example, found that many women who failed to disclose violence the first time they were asked did so when asked again later during their assessment. In summary, the influence on prevalence rates of interview methods (e.g., telephone, face to face) and format (e.g., questionnaire, interview with one vs. multiple opportunities to disclose violence) require consideration.

Related to the above discussion, wives and husbands often do not agree with each other about the occurrence of violence (e.g., Arias & Beach, 1987; Edleson & Brygger, 1986; Jouriles & O'Leary, 1985; Szinovacz, 1983) or whether children in the family have seen or heard acts of violence (O'Brien, John, Margolin, & Erel, 1994). This lack of concordance might be expected and suggests that one family member's report of violence cannot be used as a proxy for the report of all family members (see Moffitt et al., 1997, for an alternative point of view). Thus, although the measurement of violence from multiple perspectives can yield much richer data than the reliance on a single informant (Sternberg, Lamb, & Dawud-Noursi, 1998), it is not yet clear how to interpret the differences among informants. Collecting violence data from multiple informants is also complicated. For example, collecting data from male partners may be unethical because it could lead to further violence under certain circumstances. This is particularly true when women are trying to escape or hide from their partners, as is often the case among women seeking help from agencies who provide services to victims of wife abuse.

It is also unclear how accurately children can report on wife abuse or marital violence. Numerous researchers have documented discrepancies between children and parents in reports of violence and aggression within the family (e.g., Jouriles, Mehta, McDonald, & Francis, 1997; Sternberg et al., 1993), but the reasons for these discrepancies are again not understood. Furthermore, although children may see or hear some of the violence that occurs in a marriage, they are unlikely to witness all such incidents. It is also likely to be extremely difficult to collect data on exposure to violence from very young children.

Obtaining more than one person's report of marital violence or wife abuse may be helpful for answering some research questions but less so for others. For example, it could be argued that children's perception of the violence is the variable of interest for certain questions (e.g., questions dealing with children's interpretation and processing of violence), regardless of the actual violence that takes place. In such cases, it may be sufficient to measure only the child's view of domestic violence. Alternatively, when trying to determine whether violence actually occurred in a particular family, it may be necessary to collect reports from multiple sources (e.g., family members, police records, hospital or service agency records). Again, the investigator's question dictates which sources of information should be used.

Other measurement issues need to be explored as well. For example, the words used to describe specific acts of violence (e.g., "pushed, grabbed, or shoved") are likely to be interpreted differently by different individuals. In some work on the measurement of parental aggression toward children, Jouriles et al. (1997) found that children ages 7–9 years are much more liberal in their conception of "beaten up" than are their mothers. Furthermore, the prevalence rates for this act are higher when children, rather than mothers, are the reporters (Jouriles et al., 1997). The context in which the questions are asked (e.g., children queried in contexts in which they believe that their parents may get in trouble on the basis of their reports) is likely to make a difference, as might certain interviewer characteristics (e.g., gender, ethnicity). Also the research literature on violence and child adjustment relies heavily on the CTS (or idiosyncratically modified versions of the CTS), often in combination with other indicators, to select participants for violent and nonviolent groups. It is unclear how reliance on this measure has influenced the knowledge on this topic.

Despite the many challenging issues inherent in measuring children's exposure to domestic violence, researchers continue to document strong, consistent relations between such violence (wife abuse, in particular) and children's adjustment. Improved measures might allow for even stronger prediction of child adjustment and could facilitate the development and refinement of theory in this area. Measures are needed that will improve the understanding of the phenomenon of domestic violence, and a series of studies focused on measurement of domestic violence would serve this goal well. Attention should be given to the items constituting these measures, the response formats used, the context in which violent acts occur, and the meaning of violent acts to the respondents.

PREVALENCE ESTIMATES OF CHILDREN'S EXPOSURE TO VIOLENCE

Given the issues raised in the previous sections, providing an accurate, agreed-on estimate of the number of children who have been exposed to wife abuse or marital violence during a given time period presents a daunting challenge. Moreover, to our knowledge, a large, scientifically sound study of children's exposure to violence in which the complex issues of defining exposure are considered has not yet been conducted. However, on the basis of census data and existing prevalence estimates of violence, several projections have been offered. For example, based on the first National Family Violence Survey (Straus, Gelles, & Steinmetz, 1980), Carlson (1984) estimated that at least 3.3 million American children between the ages of 3 and 17 years are exposed to marital violence each year. On the basis of the second National Family Violence Survey (Straus & Gelles, 1990), Straus (1992) projected that 10 million American children are exposed. Holden (1998) used Silvern et al.'s (1995) survey of undergraduate students as the basis for his estimate that 17.8 million children may be exposed to domestic violence during childhood. Although the range of these estimates is somewhat broad, most would agree that many children are exposed to domestic violence.

In this chapter, we review results from four national surveys (Greenfeld et al., 1998; Schafer, Caetano, & Clark, 1998; Straus & Gelles, 1990; Tjaden & Thoennes, 1998), each of which uses different measurement strategies and criteria for defining domestic violence and determining its prevalence. Table 1.1 presents the annual prevalence estimates obtained from these surveys. Although several other studies report prevalence rates for domestic violence, the four we review nicely serve our purpose of illustrating the complexity involved in estimating the prevalence of violence, arguably a necessary step in estimating children's exposure to such violence.

The National Crime Victimization Survey (Greenfeld et al., 1998), conducted by the U.S. Department of Justice, provides estimates of criminal victimization from a nationally representative sample of U.S. residents ages

TABLE 1.1
Annual Prevalence of Domestic Violence in the United States

Sample type	Violence type	National Crime Victimization Survey (%)	National Violence Against Women Survey (%)
Individual	Male to female	0.75	1.50
	Female to male	0.14	0.90
		National Family Violence Survey (%)	National Alcohol Survey (%)
Couple	Any intimate partner	16.00	21.00
	Wife to husband	12.00	18.00
	Husband to wife	12.00	14.00
	Husband to wife (severe)	3.40	na

Note. "Husband to wife (severe)" is a subset of "husband to wife"; the subset concerns the level of violence reported, namely, severe husband-to-wife violence or any husband-to-wife domestic violence.

12 and older. Approximately 43,000 households comprising more than 80,000 people are sampled annually. The survey defines *intimates* as spouses, ex-spouses, boyfriends, girlfriends, and former boyfriends and girlfriends. Violent victimization is indexed by the occurrence of any of the following crimes: rape and nonrape sexual assault, coerced sexual contact that involves threat or attempt to harm, robbery, aggravated assault, and simple assault (whether the crimes were reported or not). Single-year estimates for the prevalence of violence by intimates vary, but for 1996, the most recent year for which data were available, the rate of violence toward women was 7.5 per 1,000 women (0.75%). The rate of violence toward men was 1.4 per 1,000 (0.14%).

Tjaden and Thoennes (1998) reported survey results from the National Violence Against Women Survey, issued jointly by the National Institutes of Justice and the Centers for Disease Control and Prevention. A total of 8,000 women and 8,005 men older than age 18, identified by random-digit dialing across the country, were interviewed using a computer-assisted telephone interviewing system. For the analyses of intimate partner violence, *intimates* were defined as current or former spouses, opposite- or same-sex cohabiting partners, dates, or boyfriends or girlfriends. The criterion for partner violence was any instance of rape (attempted or completed anal, oral, or vaginal penetration by penis, mouth, digit, or object) or physical assault as measured by a 12-item modified version of the Physical Aggression scale of the CTS. The items on this scale include throw something at you that could hurt; push, grab, or shove you; slap or hit you; kick or bite you; choke or attempt to drown you; hit you with some object; beat you up; threaten you with a gun; threaten you with a knife or other weapon; use a gun on you; and use a knife or other weapon on you. Tjaden and Thoennes also reported annual and lifetime prevalence rates of rape, physical assault, and either rape or physical assault by intimate partners for both men and women. The annual rate of rape or physical assault of women was 1.5% (rape = 0.2%, physical assault = 1.3%). The annual rate of intimate partner rape of men was too small to be considered reliable and was not reported, and the annual rate of physical assault of men by an intimate partner was reported to be 0.9%.

In contrast to the two surveys reviewed above, family violence researchers have assessed intimate partner violence and wife abuse in samples of couples, arriving at much higher estimates of prevalence. Straus and Gelles (1990) surveyed a nationally representative sample ($N = 6,002$) that included married and cohabiting heterosexual couples, individuals who had been divorced or separated within the past 2 years, and single-parent households in which a minor child resided in their National Family Violence Resurvey. A telephone interview was conducted with one adult from each household. Violence was measured with the CTS, and data were collected on both male-to-female violence and female-to-male violence. The criterion for violence was the endorsement of at least one occurrence of any of the acts of violence on the Physical Aggression scale of the CTS during the year before the survey. According to this survey, approximately 16% of American families were marked by an incident of marital violence during the year before the survey. Approximately 12% were marked by an incident of husband-to-wife violence, and 12% were marked by an incident of wife-to-husband violence. When only the "more severe" items were used to define "wife beating" (kicked, bit, hit with fist; hit or tried to hit with something; beat up; choked; threatened with a knife or gun; used a knife or fired a gun), approximately 3% of families met this criterion.

Schafer et al. (1998) also surveyed a nationally representative sample ($N = 1,599$) of married and cohabiting heterosexual couples in their National Alcohol Survey. Face-to-face interviews were conducted, and both partners were interviewed privately. Violence was measured with an expanded version of the Physical Aggression scale of the CTS (which includes "burned or scalded" and "forced sex"), and data were collected on both male-to-female violence and female-to-male violence. The criterion for violence was an indication by either partner that at least one of the CTS Physical Violence scale items occurred during the year before the survey. According to this survey, approximately 21% of the surveyed families were marked by an incident of marital violence during the year before the survey. Approximately 14% were marked by an incident of husband-to-wife violence, and approximately 18% were marked by an incident of wife-to-husband violence.

This brief review greatly simplifies the data collected as part of these surveys and overlooks nontrivial differences across studies in sampling and survey methodology. However, it does serve a useful function because it highlights the differences in prevalence estimates of domestic violence yielded by different national surveys. A quick glance at the results of these surveys, presented in Table 1.1, suggests that characteristics of the sample surveyed (e.g., individuals vs. couples) can greatly affect prevalence estimates of domestic violence. Rates based on samples of individuals are reduced to the extent that they include women at no risk for domestic violence or partner assault because they have not had a partner during the time period covered by the assessment. It should also be noted that the highest rates for domestic violence are from the survey that collected domestic violence data from both members of the couple (Schafer et al., 1998). Other researchers have found that the collection of data from both members of a couple substantially increases estimates of the prevalence of domestic violence, relative to the collection of data from a single partner (McDonald, Jouriles, Norwood, Ware, & Ezell, 2000; O'Leary et al., 1989).

Although data from the four studies above have been used to derive estimates of the numbers of children exposed to domestic violence, we have little confidence in those extrapolations (except perhaps as a rough estimate) because the populations from which they are derived are not the population of interest for the question of children's exposure to violence. That is, the existing data address two questions with respect to violence: (a) What is the prevalence of domestic violence in American households? (b) What is the prevalence of violence in American households in which couples reside? These questions provide a larger context in which children's exposure to domestic violence can be understood. However, the specific questions of interest with respect to the prevalence of children's exposure to domestic violence are the following: What is the prevalence of domestic violence in American households in which children reside? What is the extent of children's exposure to that violence? These are different questions than those that can be answered from sampling households on the basis of adults. Answering them requires a nationally representative sample of U.S. households that include at least one minor child. Within those households then, one can assess the prevalence of domestic violence and variations of children's exposure to such violence.

FUTURE DIRECTIONS FOR RESEARCH, POLICY, AND PRACTICE

Clarification of Concepts and Definitions

As we noted at the beginning of this chapter, there are several important reasons to understand the extent of children's exposure to violence.

Rough estimates extrapolated from existing data suggest that many American children are exposed to domestic violence, irrespective of the definitions or criteria used. However, we do not really know whether the magnitude of the problem of children's exposure to domestic violence is truly at epidemic proportions, as might be suggested from such rough estimates.

When thinking about the prevalence of children's exposure to domestic violence, we believe that it is important to keep in mind why this information is valuable: Exposure to domestic violence appears to place children at risk for maladjustment. In the sections above, we offered many ways to conceptualize violence (e.g., wife abuse vs. marital violence, narrow vs. broad definitions of violence, common couple violence vs. patriarchal terrorism). We also offered several ways to think about children's exposure to violence (e.g., observing violence directly, not observing the violence but seeing the aftermath) and highlighted issues in the measurement of violence exposure. Unfortunately, we still lack data on the criterion validity of the various conceptualizations and definitions of children's exposure to violence (i.e., which conceptualizations of violence and exposure are associated with an increased risk for child maladjustment). It is necessary to consider that certain definitions of children's exposure to violence, and more precisely definitions that some of the current prevalence estimates are based on, may not be associated with an increased risk for children. For example, it is possible that children from families in which infrequent violence occurs may not be at greater risk for problems than children from nonviolent families. Greater attention to variations in the definition of children's exposure to violence is necessary for a better understanding of how domestic violence influences children.

At this point, it is important to note that the majority of studies indicating that exposure to domestic violence is a risk factor for children are based on a restricted group of children and an equally restricted definition of violence (i.e., samples of children who have been exposed to frequent and severe violence and who have been exposed to many additional risk factors for child problems). Specifically, the majority of studies on children of battered women recruit their violent samples from women's shelters. These samples represent a small proportion of American children exposed to violence and are at the extreme of the distribution of violence frequency and intensity (Ware et al., in press). Although gaining a better understanding of the children who are brought to women's shelters is important, it tells researchers little about the effects of children's exposure to violence between intimates or wife abuse as it most often occurs in society.

Straus (1990) reported that 13 of the 622 women who were victims of violence in the National Family Violence Resurvey used the services of a shelter. It is unclear from the report if shelter services were used during the year before the survey or during the lifetime of the respondent. These data suggest that approximately 2% of the female victims of domestic violence (as defined by Straus, 1990) at some point become residents at battered women's shelters. Straus further reported that the average number of violent acts experienced by these women (15.3 per year) was three times greater than the number of violent acts experienced by those women who did not use the services of a shelter. Moreover, Straus acknowledged that this estimate is much lower than those provided by other researchers who have studied shelter samples (Giles-Sims, 1983, reported an average of 68.7 assaults during the year before a shelter stay; Okun, 1986, reported an average of 65.0 assaults per year). It is also worth noting that the type of violence experienced by women in battered women's shelters is likely to be different than the type of violence experienced by women in community surveys who do not seek shelter services. For example, Jouriles, McDonald, Norwood, et al. (1998) found that more than half of a sample of women seeking shelter services in the greater Houston area had been threatened or attacked with a knife or a gun (also see Jouriles, Spiller, Stephens, McDonald, & Swank, 2000). However, less than 1% of the women who were participants in community surveys reported such violence (Schafer et al., 1998; Straus & Gelles, 1990).

In short, most of the knowledge on children's exposure to violence is based on a small subgroup of children (those at battered women's shelters) and is therefore not representative of most children who live in families that are characterized by violence. As a result, we do not know if domestic violence as it most often occurs in society is associated with an increased risk for problematic child behavior. These issues need to be addressed if researchers are to develop socially and clinically useful information regarding the prevalence of children's exposure to violence.

Violence in Combination With Other Factors

Researchers also need to be careful in their interpretation of data linking children's exposure to violence with increased risk for problematic child outcomes. Wife abuse and marital violence do not occur in isolation; they are part of a package of factors known to adversely affect child development. For example, there is substantial evidence from shelter families that wife abuse often co-occurs with child abuse (e.g., Jouriles & Norwood, 1995; Moore & Pepler, 1998; O'Keefe, 1995). In fact, Appel and Holden (1998) reported a median co-occurrence rate of 41% in such samples. When attempting to document the prevalence of any one risk factor, it is necessary to document other related risk factors. For example, it may be a combination of factors rather than the one of principal interest that is responsible for any increased risk observed. In fact, one could make a compelling argument on the basis of the existing literature that child physical abuse plays a large role in the problems experienced by children in families characterized by wife abuse or marital violence (Jouriles, Barling, & O'Leary, 1987; O'Keefe, 1994). To understand the specific role of violence, researchers need to make a special effort to measure and document the most relevant related phenomena.

Ethnicity

Another gap in the literature is the dearth of information on ethnicity and domestic violence. Public opinion surveys offer preliminary evidence that differences exist in the conceptualization of domestic violence across ethnic groups (Klein, Campbell, Soler, & Ghez, 1997). There is also some indication that the prevalence of specific acts of violence varies across ethnic groups (Straus & Gelles, 1990). However, many researchers neglect to consider ethnicity and differences across ethnic groups. For example, of the four national surveys reviewed in this chapter, in one data were not analyzed according to ethnicity, and the remaining three present limited data regarding ethnicity, usually without controlling for related factors such as socioeconomic status. More careful attention is needed with regard to ethnic differences in prevalence of domestic violence, individuals' concept of violence, individuals' willingness to disclose domestic violence, and the consideration of additional factors related to ethnicity such as socioeconomic status.

Special Populations

Methods also need to be developed to document the prevalence of children's exposure to wife abuse in families that come into contact with social service and criminal justice agencies as a result of violence. This includes children in families of court-referred batterers, in families requiring police intervention for a domestic disturbance, and in families seeking a court order of protection because of wife abuse. Thus, it could be determined whether children's exposure to violence is associated with child maladjustment in these populations. Although fraught with ethical dilemmas, this information is valuable from a public health perspective because the criminal justice and social services systems offer convenient points of entry into service delivery systems for children and their families (e.g., Jouriles, McDonald, Stephens, et al., 1998; Sullivan & Davidson, 1991). Presently, we know that children who are brought to battered women's shelters are much more likely to have any number of adjustment problems than are children in community comparison families (Jouriles, Norwood, McDonald, & Peters, in press). Moreover, a substantial proportion of the children in these shelters score in the clinical range on standard measures of child problems. In fact, in an early review of this literature, McDonald and Jouriles (1991) found that across various shelter samples, the number of children with problems at clinical levels varied from 25% to 70%. This could be interpreted to suggest that children's exposure to certain levels or types of violence between intimates or wife abuse does represent an important risk factor for a variety of childhood problems. Unfortunately, with the exception of a few studies (e.g., Fantuzzo, Boruch, Beriama, Atkins, & Marcus, 1997), we have little information on the children in other clinical or criminal justice populations.

CONCLUSION

We have covered a broad range of issues pertinent to estimating the prevalence of children's exposure to domestic violence, each of which is relevant to research and policy in this area. The issues we described address broad concepts related to the definition of violence and children's exposure to it. The issues also bring to the forefront more specific and technical questions about when, how, and from which informants is it best to obtain reports of violence; what other variables are important to consider in understanding the impact of exposure to domestic violence on children; and which population is appropriate to sample to obtain accurate estimates of children's exposure to violence. These are thorny issues that cannot readily be resolved by simple appeals to existing data or theory. We believe, however, that they can provide a point of departure from which researchers can begin to focus clearly and work systematically on how best to assess the magnitude and limits of the problem of children's exposure to domestic violence.

REFERENCES

Appel, A. E., & Holden, G. W. (1998). The co-occurrence of spouse and physical child abuse: A review and appraisal. *Journal of Family Psychology, 12*, 578–599.

Arias, I., & Beach, S. (1987). Validity of self-reports of marital violence. *Journal of Family Violence, 2*, 139–149.

Carlson, B. E. (1984). Children's observations of interpersonal violence. In A. Roberts (Ed.), *Battered women and their families* (pp. 147–167). New York: Springer.

Cummings, E. M., & Davies, P. T. (1994). *Children and marital conflict: The impact of family dispute and resolution.* New York: Guilford Press.

DeKeseredy, W. S. (2000). Current controversies on defining non-lethal violence against women in intimate, heterosexual relationships: Empirical implications. *Violence Against Women, 6*, 728–746.

DeKeseredy, W. S., & Schwartz, M. D. (1998). *Measuring the extent of woman abuse in intimate heterosexual relationships: A critique of the Conflict Tactics Scales.* U.S.

Department of Justice, Violence Against Women Office. Retrieved on January 23, 2001 from the World Wide Web http://www.vaw.umn.edu/vawnet/ctscrit.htm

Dobash, R. P., Dobash, R. E., Wilson, M., & Daly, M. (1992). The myth of sexual symmetry in marital violence. *Social Problems, 39,* 71–91.

Edleson, J. L., & Brygger, M. P. (1986). Gender differences in reporting of battering incidences. *Family Relations, 35,* 377–382.

Fantuzzo, J. W., Boruch, R., Beriama, A., Atkins, M., & Marcus, S. (1997). Domestic violence and children: Prevalence and risk in five major U.S. cities. *Journal of the American Academy of Child and Adolescent Psychiatry, 36,* 116–122.

Fincham, F. D. (1994). Understanding the association between marital conflict and child adjustment: Overview. *Journal of Family Psychology, 8,* 123–127.

Gelles, R. J. (2000). Estimating the incidence and prevalence of violence against women: National data system and sources. *Violence Against Women, 6,* 784–804.

Giles-Sims, J. (1983). *Wife battering: A systems theory approach.* New York: Guilford Press.

Graham-Bermann, S. A. (1996). Family worries: The assessment of interpersonal anxiety in children from violent and nonviolent families. *Journal of Clinical Child Psychology, 25,* 280–287.

Greenfeld, L. A., Rand, M. R., Craven, D., Klaus, P. A., Perkins, C. A., Ringel, C., Warchol, G., Maston, C., & Fox, J. A. (1998). *Violence by intimates: Analysis of data on crimes by current or former spouses, boyfriends, and girlfriends.* Washington, DC: U.S. Department of Justice, Bureau of Justice Statistics.

Grych, J. H., & Fincham, F. D. (1990). Marital conflict and children's adjustment: A cognitive–contextual framework. *Psychological Bulletin, 108,* 267–290.

Hershorn, M., & Rosenbaum, A. (1985). Children of marital violence: A closer look at the unintended victims. *American Journal of Orthopsychiatry, 55,* 260–266.

Holden, G. W. (1998). Introduction: The development of research into another consequence of family violence. In G. W. Holden, R. Geffner, & E. N. Jouriles (Eds.), *Children exposed to marital violence: Theory, research, and applied issues* (pp. 1–18). Washington, DC: American Psychological Association.

Holtzworth-Munroe, A., Smutzler, N., & Stuart, G. L. (1998). Demand and withdraw communication among couples experiencing husband violence. *Journal of Consulting and Clinical Psychology, 66,* 731–743.

Hughes, H. M. (1988). Psychological and behavioral correlates of family violence in child witnesses and victims. *American Journal of Orthopsychiatry, 58,* 77–90.

Johnson, M. P. (1995). Patriarchal terrorism and common couple violence: Two forms of violence against women. *Journal of Marriage and the Family, 57,* 283–294.

Jouriles, E. N., Barling, J., & O'Leary, K. D. (1987). Predicting child behavior problems in maritally violent families. *Journal of Abnormal Child Psychology, 15,* 167–173.

Jouriles, E. N., McDonald, R., Norwood, W. D., Ware, H. S., Spiller, L. C., & Swank, P. R. (1998). Knives, guns, and interparent violence: Relations with child behavior problems. *Journal of Family Psychology, 12,* 178–194.

Jouriles, E. N., McDonald, R., Stephens, N., Norwood, W., Spiller, L. C., & Ware, H. S. (1998). Breaking the cycle of violence: Helping families departing from battered women's shelters. In G. W. Holden, R. Geffner, & E. N. Jouriles (Eds.), *Children exposed to marital violence: Theory, research, and applied issues* (pp. 337–369). Washington, DC: American Psychological Association.

Jouriles, E. N., Mehta, P., McDonald, R., & Francis, D. J. (1997). Psychometric properties of family members' reports of parental physical aggression toward clinic-referred children. *Journal of Consulting and Clinical Psychology, 65,* 309–318.

Jouriles, E. N., Murphy, C. M., & O'Leary, K. D. (1989). Interspousal aggression, marital discord, and child problems. *Journal of Consulting and Clinical Psychology, 57,* 453–455.

Jouriles, E. N., & Norwood, W. D. (1995). Physical aggression toward boys and girls in families characterized by the battering of women. *Journal of Family Psychology, 9,* 69–78.

Jouriles, E. N., Norwood, W. D., McDonald, R., & Peters, B. R. (in press). Conflict and violence in the family. In J. Grych & F. Fincham (Eds.), *Child development and interparental conflict.* Cambridge, England: Cambridge University Press.

Jouriles, E. N., Norwood, W. D., McDonald, R., Vincent, J. P., & Mahoney, A. (1996). Physical violence and other forms of marital aggression: Links with children's behavior problems. *Journal of Family Psychology, 10,* 223–234.

Jouriles, E. N., & O'Leary, K. D. (1985). Interspousal reliability of reports of marital violence. *Journal of Consulting and Clinical Psychology, 53,* 419–421.

Jouriles, E. N., Spiller, L. C., Stephens, N., McDonald, R., & Swank, P. (2000). Variability in adjustment of children of battered women: The role of child appraisals of interparent conflict. *Cognitive Therapy and Research, 24,* 233–249.

Kelly, L. (1988). *Surviving sexual violence.* Minneapolis: University of Minnesota Press.

Klein, E., Campbell, J., Soler, E., & Ghez, M. (1997). *Ending domestic violence: Changing public perceptions/halting the epidemic.* Thousand Oaks, CA: Sage.

Koss, M. P. (1993). Detecting the scope of rape: A review of prevalence research methods. *Journal of Interpersonal Violence, 8,* 198–222.

Koss, M. P., Goodman, L., Browne, A., Fitzgerald, L. Keita, G. P., & Russon, N. F. (1994). *No safe haven: Male violence against women at home, at work, and in the community.* Washington, DC: American Psychological Association.

Magdol, L., Moffitt, T. E., Capsi, A., Newman, D. L., Fagan, J., & Silva, P. A. (1997). Gender differences in partner violence in a birth cohort of 21-year-olds: Bridging the gap between clinical and epidemiological approaches. *Journal of Consulting and Clinical Psychology, 65,* 68–78.

McDonald, R., & Jouriles, E. N. (1991). Marital aggression and child behavior problems: Research findings, mechanisms, and intervention strategies. *The Behavior Therapist, 14*, 189–192.

McDonald, R., Jouriles, E. N., Norwood, W., Ware, H. S., & Ezell, E. (2000). Husbands' marital violence and the adjustment problems of clinic-referred children. *Behavior Therapy, 31*, 649–665.

McFarlane, J., Parker, B., & Soeken, K. (1995). Abuse during pregnancy: Frequency, severity, perpetrator, and risk factors of homicide. *Public Health Nursing, 12*, 284–289.

McMahon, M., & Pence, E. (1996). Replying to Dan O'Leary. *Journal of Interpersonal Violence, 11*, 452–455.

Moffitt, T. E., Caspi, A., Kruger, R., Magdol, L., Margolin, G., Silva, P., & Sydney, R. (1997). Do partners agree about abuse in the relationship? A psychometric evaluation of interpartner agreement. *Psychological Assessment, 9*, 47–56.

Moore, T. E., & Pepler, D. J. (1998). Correlates of adjustment in children at risk. In G. W. Holden, R. Geffner, & E. N. Jouriles (Eds.), *Children exposed to marital violence: Theory, research, and applied issues* (pp. 157–184). Washington, DC: American Psychological Association.

National Research Council. (1996). Introduction. In N. A. Crowell & A. W. Burgess (Eds.), *Understanding violence against women* (pp. 7–21). Washington, DC: National Academy Press.

O'Brien, M., John, R. S., Margolin, G., & Erel, O. (1994). Reliability and diagnostic efficacy of parents' reports regarding children's exposure to marital aggression. *Violence and Victims, 9*, 45–62.

O'Keefe, M. (1994). Linking marital violence, mother–child/father–child aggression, and child behavior problems. *Journal of Family Violence, 9*, 63–78.

O'Keefe, M. (1995). Predictors of child abuse in maritally violent families. *Journal of Interpersonal Violence, 10*, 3–25.

Okun, L. (1986). *Woman abuse: Facts replacing myths.* Albany: State University of New York Press.

O'Leary, K. D., Barling, J., Arias, I., Rosenbaum, A., Malone, J., & Tyree, A. (1989). Prevalence and stability of physical aggression between spouses: A longitudinal analysis. *Journal of Consulting and Clinical Psychology, 57*, 263–268.

Porter, B. K., & O'Leary, K. D. (1980). Marital discord and childhood behavior problems. *Journal of Abnormal Child Psychology, 8*, 287–295.

Rossman, B. B. R., & Rosenberg, M. (1992). Family stress and functioning in children: The moderating effects of children's beliefs about their control over parental conflict. *Journal of Child Psychology and Psychiatry, 33*, 699–715.

Schafer, J., Caetano, R., & Clark, C. (1998). Rates of intimate partner violence in the United States. *American Journal of Public Health, 88*, 1701–1704.

Schwartz, M. D. (2000). Methodological issues in the use of survey data for measuring and characterizing violence against women. *Violence Against Women, 6*, 815–838.

Silvern, L., Karyl, J., Waelde, L., Hodges, W. F., Starek, J., Heidt, E., & Min, K. (1995). Retrospective reports of parental partner abuse: Relationships to depression, trauma symptoms and self-esteem among college students. *Journal of Family Violence, 10,* 177–201.

Smith, M. D. (1987). The incidence and prevalence of woman abuse in Toronto. *Violence and Victims, 2,* 33–47.

Sternberg, K. J., Lamb, M. E., & Dawud-Noursi, S. (1998). Using multiple informants to understand domestic violence and its effects. In G. W. Holden, R. Geffner, & E. N. Jouriles (Eds.), *Children exposed to marital violence: Theory, research, and applied issues* (pp. 121–156). Washington, DC: American Psychological Association.

Sternberg, K. J., Lamb, M. E., Greenbaum, C., Cicchetti, D., Dawud, S., Cortes, R. M., Krispin, O., & Lorey, F. (1993). Effects of domestic violence on children's behavior problems and depression. *Developmental Psychology, 29,* 44–52.

Straus, M. A. (1979). Measuring intrafamily conflict and violence: The Conflict Tactics (CT) Scales. *Journal of Marriage and the Family, 41,* 75–88.

Straus, M. A. (1990). Injury and frequency of assault and the "representative sample fallacy" in measuring wife beating and child abuse. In M. A. Straus & R. J. Gelles, (Eds.), *Physical violence in American families: Risk factors and adaptations to violence in 8,145 families* (pp. 75–91). New Brunswick, NJ: Transaction.

Straus, M. A. (1992). Children as witness to marital violence: A risk factor for lifelong problems among a nationally representative sample of American men and women. In D. F. Schwarz (Ed.), *Children and violence* (Report of the 23rd Ross Roundtable on Critical Approaches to Common Pediatric Problems). Columbus, OH: Ross Laboratories.

Straus, M. A. (1993). Physical assaults by wives: A major social problem. In R. J. Gelles & D. R. Loseke (Eds.), *Current controversies on family violence* (pp. 67–87). Newbury Park, CA: Sage.

Straus, M. A., & Gelles, R. J. (1990). *Physical violence in American families: Risk factors and adaptations to violence in 8,145 families.* New Brunswick, NJ: Transaction.

Straus, M. A., Gelles, R. J., & Steinmetz, S. K. (1980). *Behind closed doors: Violence in the American family.* Garden City, NJ: Doubleday Press.

Straus, M. A., Hamby, S. L., Finkelhor, D., & Runyan, D. (1995). *The Parent–Child Conflict Tactics Scales (PCCTS).* Durham: University of New Hampshire, Family Research Laboratory.

Sullivan, C. M., & Davidson, W. S. (1991). The provision of advocacy services to women leaving abusive partners: An examination of short-term effects. *American Journal of Community Psychology, 19,* 953–960.

Szinovacz, M. E. (1983). Using couple data as a methodological tool: The case of marital violence. *Journal of Marriage and the Family, 45,* 633–644.

Tjaden, P., & Thoennes, N. (1998). *Prevalence, incidence, and consequences of violence against women: Findings from the National Violence Against Women Survey* [Research in brief]. Washington, DC: National Institutes of Justice and Centers for Disease Control and Prevention.

Ware, H. S., Jouriles, E. N., Spiller, L. C., McDonald, R., Swank, P. R., & Norwood, W. D. (in press). Conduct problems among children at battered women's shelters: Prevalence and stability of maternal reports. *Journal of Family Violence*.

Yllö, K. A. (1993). Through a feminist lens: Gender, power, and violence. In R. J. Gelles & D. R. Loseke (Eds.), *Current controversies on family violence* (pp. 47–62). Newbury Park, CA: Sage.

2

LONGER TERM EFFECTS OF CHILDREN'S EXPOSURE TO DOMESTIC VIOLENCE

B. B. ROBBIE ROSSMAN

As the world enters the 21st century after the "decade of the brain," researchers are being afforded the opportunity to think about longer term effects of children's exposure to domestic violence in terms of trauma and brain–body conceptualizations. This is made possible by a growing understanding of the brain under stress and the trauma experienced by children, including exposure to adult domestic violence. Other theoretical mechanisms that offer additional explanatory power for understanding this impact are observational learning (Bandura, 1977), parent–child dynamics, and the family and societal legitimization of violence (Straus, Gelles, & Steinmetz, 1980; Straus & Smith, 1990). Because nontrauma mechanisms have been explicated in other work, a trauma perspective is emphasized here.

Long-term impact of exposure is taken to mean impact that could be in the areas of an individual's cognitive, social, emotional, or behavioral functioning and is assessed when time has passed (i.e., beyond the assessment done at initial contact). This is an artificial definition because by the time an individual is first seen, he or she may have experienced years of exposure. However, it is not possible to know that individual's pre-exposure state. Thus, either an initial measurement of functioning and exposure needs to be made and the individual followed over time or a retrospective account of past exposure needs to accompany measurement of current functioning.

This work was made possible through the financial support of the Frost Foundation and with the collaboration and tireless efforts of a number of battered women's shelters, school districts, community agencies, mothers and children, and members of our research team, namely, Karen Mallah, M. Sachi Kimura, Jennifer West, Michelle Acker, Joyce Ho, Emily Millikan, and Kim Shipman as well as many volunteer and work–study research assistants. Huette Thompson is owed special thanks for her scholarly research for the completion of this chapter. I also thank Sandra Graham-Bermann, Jennifer West, and Emily Milikan for their helpful comments on this chapter.

Prospective longitudinal and retrospective studies are consistent with this definition, with long-term (e.g., over years of a child's life) prospective studies being the most satisfactory in an empirical sense.

Still another way of defining long-term impact—that is not consistent with this definition—is in terms of developmental projection or estimation. This means that when one determines the developmental skill level for an exposed child, it is sometimes possible to discern a likely developmental trajectory. This method of estimating impact is less satisfactory and relies on the notion that an exposed child who has completed developmental tasks poorly, say, in the area of social relationships, will be at risk for difficulty with later similar developmental tasks.

Four types of definitions and literatures are reviewed in this chapter because there is little prospective information about long-term effects of interparental violence exposure: (a) retrospective accounts of adults experiencing childhood trauma, (b) long-term prospective studies of individuals traumatized as children, (c) short-term prospective studies of children exposed to spousal violence, and (d) studies of exposed children that bear on the accomplishment of developmental tasks. The goal of this chapter is not to comprehensively review these literatures but rather to build a framework for understanding the effects of violence exposure for the development of children and thereby offer speculation about long-term effects and needed research and policy efforts. Before this review is a brief presentation of trauma mechanisms and research to set the stage for considering these long-term effects.

EXPOSURE, TRAUMA, AND BIOBEHAVIORAL EVIDENCE

The aims of this section are to examine the link between repetitive exposure to adult domestic violence and the development of posttraumatic stress disorder (PTSD) and traumatic stress symptoms as well as to consider research on biobehavioral effects of chronic trauma exposure. Although little work has been done in either of these areas for children, existing adult research is informative.

Studies of both natural disasters and violent trauma have shown that children do experience PTSD symptoms and reactions following exposure. Incidence of PTSD for children exposed to natural disasters is variable, ranging around 30% (Rossman & Ho, 2000). For violent trauma, a substantial proportion of children have also been found to meet diagnostic criteria. Pynoos et al. (1987) found 40% of children with PTSD following exposure to a sniper attack on their school grounds. Saigh (1991) studied children exposed to war violence and found 27% with PTSD. These incidence rates were calculated based on interviews done within a month or so following the event, and results were considered indicative of PTSD following earlier versions of the *Diagnostic and Statistical Manual of Mental Disorders* (*DSM–III*, American Psychiatric Association, 1980; *DMS–III–R*, American Psychiatric Association, 1987). The diagnosis of acute stress disorder would probably be used today to describe these results because it is not known that the children's symptoms persisted for longer than 1 month (*DSM–IV*, American Psychiatric Association, 1994). In *DSM–IV*, it is required that symptoms persist for longer than 1 month but less than 3 or 3 months or longer to meet diagnostic criteria for acute PTSD or chronic PTSD, respectively. For children exposed to adult domestic violence, estimates have ranged from 13% in a community sample (Graham-Bermann & Levendosky, 1998b) to about 20% in a community and clinical sample, with substantial symptoms remaining after a year (Rossman, 1999), to 51% derived from a clinical sample (Devoe & Graham-Bermann, 1997). These estimates are based on the assumption that the children experienced symptoms for longer than 3 months because they generally experienced years of exposure. These data suggest that a substantial portion of children exposed to interpersonal violence develop posttraumatic symptomatology.

Trauma approaches posit that the dysregulated behaviors of children exposed to violence, their difficulties with cognitive functioning, and their fears may be accounted for in part by their natural reactions to the trauma. These reactions, which are assessed by *DSM–IV* as PTSD symptoms, may have been part of the impact commonly assessed as behavior problems. For example, PTSD symptoms include aggressiveness, irritability, and high arousal, which also are measured using the Child Behavior Checklist (CBCL; Achenbach & Edelbrock, 1983) as externalizing behavior problems. Additional somatic symptoms include anxiety and social disengagement, which are measured by CBCL as internalizing problems. Furthermore, all of these problems or symptoms could be linked to the reported difficulties in social competence of children exposed to violence.

There is the possibility that these trauma symptoms could be carried into longer term behavior patterns following initial and interim reactions to trauma (Briere, 1992). In the short term, substantial correlations have been noted between problem behavior scores and PTSD symptom scores (Rossman, 1994). Thus, a trauma view of behavior problems of children exposed to violence would allow for the possibility that the problems in part reflected the trauma or over time had solidified into more enduring patterns characterized by often received diagnoses of conduct disorder, anxiety, or depression. This conceptualization would suggest that initially their problems might be treated with trauma interventions. If a certain form of problem persisted (e.g., conduct disorder), the need for more traditional interventions should be evaluated.

The link of PTSD symptomatology with the possibility of more lasting changes in neurotransmitter function has been examined in adults but not in children. However, Pynoos and colleagues (e.g., Pynoos, Steinberg, & Goenjian, 1996; Pynoos, Steinberg, & Wraith, 1995) have posited that children may show similar changes because these changes appear physiologically connected to the PTSD symptomatology that children also experience. Several researchers have contributed to the knowledge of adult chronic PTSD and changes in neurotransmitter function (Charney et al., 1994; Foa, Riggs, & Gershuny, 1995; van der Kolk, 1994, 1996) on the basis of their study of combat veterans and assault victims. With combat veterans, the exposure was that of both witnessing attacks on others and experiencing them. For assault victims, the exposure was to personal attack. It should be noted that, initially, the neurotransmitter reactions described were normal responses to prepare the body for self-protection.

Studying combat veterans with PTSD, van der Kolk (1994, 1996) has noted that the output of several neurotransmitters increases: adrenalin and noradrenalin, glucocorticoids such as cortisol, dopamine, and endogenous opiates. Serotonin output is lowered. These neurotransmitter changes are thought to underlie behavioral symptoms of PTSD, including difficulties with attention, concentration, and memory consolidation; greater irritability; exaggerated startle; and greater fluctuation in mood. It is interesting to note that some of these problems are consistent with those reported for school-age children exposed to adult domestic violence, such as higher levels of externalizing behaviors (e.g., hyperactivity, aggressiveness; Emery, 1996) or lower school achievement (Pepler & Moore, 1989). It is the prolongation of these responses beyond their immediate function and context that may create problems for individuals.

The association of these psychobiological sequelae with early adversity is now being examined. Kaufman et al. (1997) studied the serotonergic functioning in depressed abused, depressed nonabused, and control children ages 7–18 years. In particular, they studied prolactin secretion following administration of L-5-HTP, a serotonin precursor that is expected to be elevated for both depressed groups. Primate and preliminary human studies suggest that early problematic parent–child relationships were associated with serotonergic system dysregulation and with depression, suicidality, and impulsive aggression. Kaufman et al. found greater serotonergic system dysregulation in the abused depressed children than in the control or depressed-only groups.

Using the same sample, these researchers (Kaufman et al., in press) also examined hypothalamic pituitary adrenal axis (HPA) regulation by administering a corticotropin-releasing hormone challenge because HPA disturbances have been associated with abuse. As expected, abused depressed children appeared to show sensitization (defined as evidencing a significantly greater cortisol response to the challenge than other groups) but returned to initial levels postchallenge. The sensitization of response appeared greatest in combination with increased family–genetic risk and ongoing family adversity, meaning it was greatest for the children who both witnessed parental violence and were personally abused. Of particular interest is the finding of a bimodal distribution among abused children, wherein some children's responses were similar to those of the nonabused groups. Other abused children, those with greater cortisol response, were exposed to more ongoing life adversity in the form of poverty, poorer caregiver relationships, and greater emotional abuse and adult domestic violence.

These types of evidence support the notion that children's responses to repetitive trauma may be accompanied by sensitization (i.e., an increased magnitude of response following repeated administration of a stimulus or presentation of a different but stronger stimulus), similar to that found in some adult work (Charney et al., 1994). Thus, children exposed to violence do show PTSD, and their behavior problems mimic some of the effects cataloged to accompany neurotransmitter changes with chronic adult PTSD.

There is also speculation that prolonged traumatic stress from an early age could be associated with differences in aspects of brain development. At present, this is only speculation. Perry (1994, 1997) has proposed that two types of brain development could register environmental influence: (a) the pruning of excess neuronal branches that takes place after birth and (b) the continuing myelination of neuronal pathways. These two processes could allow brain development to be use dependent. For example, when a baby experiences frequent positive caregiver interaction during feeding, pathways to support the expectation of interpersonal warmth and caring could be strengthened through use. Alternately, chronic violence exposure could strengthen fear pathways. These are interesting notions that await empirical validation.

RESEARCH BEARING ON LONGER TERM EXPOSURE

In this section, I consider different windows that the literature provides for tracing violence exposure effects on longer term development. Mechanisms such as direct instruction, modeling, family dynamics, societal value structures, and traumatic stress exposure are all likely contributors to these effects. The review of this research is limited mainly to the study of disadvantaged families and youths because those populations have more often come to the attention of researchers. This means that most children studied have been exposed to a package of adversity rather than just to family or interpersonal violence. Researchers are only beginning to untangle these myriad risks.

Retrospective Studies

It should be noted that studies using a retrospective design to understand later effects of early trauma tend to demonstrate stronger relationships than actually exist (Malinosky-Rummell & Hansen, 1993; Widom, 1989). In part, this is because retrospective work relies on participants' memories of childhood experiences, which may vary in accuracy, and, in part, because when looking backward, the starting population often has selected characteristics (e.g., depression). The question then becomes what percentage of that population (e.g., depressed adults) experienced the childhood trauma of interest? The study population is limited to those with the later outcome. In prospective work, the target population is all who have experienced a childhood trauma who are then followed forward to determine what percentage also experience the outcome of interest. Thus, the beginning research population is broader in prospective work, meaning that the incidence of outcome in this broader population will likely be smaller than when working backward: Not all childhood targets will experience the selected outcome. Furthermore, several different experiences have been associated with the same outcome. This phenomenon has been discussed by Cicchetti (1989) as one of *equifinality*, meaning many paths may lead to the same outcome. The accompanying principal of *multifinality* is often demonstrated in prospective studies in which a single antecedent experience may be associated with different outcomes.

In retrospective studies of childhood trauma exposure, researchers have examined primarily the association of child physical abuse or neglect or sexual abuse with various types of later functioning. Note that this review begins with studies in which the documented violence exposure is personal abuse. The discussion includes evidence concerning the witnessing of parental violence interspersed with that of experiencing personal abuse. One of the most comprehensive reviews of prospective and retrospective research of physical abuse and later outcome was conducted by Malinosky-Rummell and Hansen (1993).

The main finding from the retrospective studies is that later physically aggressive and violent behavior is associated with earlier physical abuse experience. The later violent behavior includes adolescent violence, adult extrafamilial violence, physical abuse of one's children, and adult aggression toward dating partners and spouses. Some of these studies also note that childhood neglect and exposure to adult domestic violence, in addition to physical abuse, are related to later violent behavior. Kalmuss (1984) reported that early marital violence was more strongly predictive of the child's later marital violence than was the child's physical abuse during adolescence, but earlier abuse was not assessed. Early marital conflict and physical abuse also have been linked to self-injurious behaviors, such as suicide attempts and substance abuse (Malinosky-Rummell & Hansen, 1993); factors such as parental substance abuse have not usually been controlled, although Widom (1998) suggested that parental substance abuse was not uniquely predictive. Other forms of emotional and social distress, such as anxiety, depression, and social discomfort, have also been found to be positively related to childhood physical abuse.

Research on the relationship of childhood sexual abuse with concurrent and later outcome was reviewed by Kendall-Tackett, Williams, and Finkelhor (1993). Concurrently, although about 20% of sexually abused children appear asymptomatic, remaining children evidence a variety of problems, including greater fears, PTSD diagnoses, behavior problems, sexualized behaviors, and self-esteem deficits, than do their nonabused peers. Retrospective studies of abuse survivors note similar findings, with abuse history associated with higher incidence of emotional and relationship problems among adults (e.g., Bryer, Nelson, Miller, & Kroll, 1987).

Several retrospective studies of multiple forms of youth victimization have been carried out. Boney-McCoy and Finkelhor (1995) conducted telephone surveys with a nationally representative probability sample of 2,000 youths ages 10–16 years or their parents regarding earlier exposure to or experience of intra- or extrafamilial violent and sexual victimization experiences and current functioning. Most of the families were intact, were White, and had annual incomes of $20,000 or more. Over one third reported at least one victimization incident. In a comparison of assaulted and nonassaulted youths, findings show that PTSD-related symptomatology was elevated for boys and girls who had experienced sexual or aggravated assault, attempted kidnapping, and exposure to parental violence. In general, victimized youths had greater PTSD symptomatology, sad mood, and trouble with teachers than did nonvictimized youths.

A similar type of study was carried out by Langhinrichsen-Rohling and Neidig (1995). Their initial study pool was 474 disadvantaged youths (n = 137 girls, n = 337 boys), average age 18 years, who were participating in an Adolescent Job Corps program. Participants were asked if they had ever seen, heard, received, or perpetrated any of the nine Conflict Tactics Scale (Straus, 1979) conflict behaviors with reference to different perpetrators (e.g., parents, siblings, friends, adult strangers). Past victimization by parents was significantly associated with perpetrating aggression toward parents and friends, and victimization by all except strangers contributed to the prediction of perpetration of aggression against parents by both boys and girls. Surprisingly, witnessing parental violence was a significant, negative predictor of girls' perpetration of violence toward parents; the same trend was shown for boys. The authors suggested that watching parental aggression may teach children to avoid aggression with parents.

As a counterpoint to these types of findings, Simons and Johnson (1998) used a partially retrospective study with 3 years of prospective data to investigate relationships among antisocial behaviors; marital conflict; and harsh parenting in grandparent, parent, and child generations in rural communities. Structural equations suggest that it was the antisocial behaviors and beliefs across generations that predicted marital conflict, harsh parenting, and further antisocial behaviors. Intergenerational behaviors and beliefs also appeared to mediate the intergenerational transmission of violence rather than strict modeling or legitimization of violence transmitted in specific roles (e.g., spouse or parent). In one sense, these researchers were simply modeling the adversity package mentioned above. It will, however, be important to monitor their later follow-up findings because, as they noted, interventions that target only child abuse or only marital violence could be inadequate if they do not attempt to change a general familial antisocial orientation.

Another retrospective community study was carried out by Felitti et al. (1998), who examined the relationship of adverse childhood experiences (e.g., all types of child abuse; wife abuse; living with household members who were abusing substances, mentally ill or suicidal, or had spent time in jail) to adult health problems. In a large sample of health maintenance organization service receivers, they found that receivers who had been exposed to wife abuse had an 86% chance that they had been exposed to one additional risk category and a 62% chance that they had been exposed to two additional categories. With exposure to three risks, the likelihood of ischemic heart disease, stroke, diabetes mellitus, and other major medical problems increased. Again, exposure to family violence appears to be part of a lethal package for development. Finally, Weeks and Widom (1998) studied a group of incarcerated men. Interestingly, they did not find self-reported childhood physical abuse to discriminate between violent and nonviolent offenders, but neglect did discriminate such.

Some of the retrospective studies targeting childhood exposure to adult domestic violence have involved college students. Forsstrom-Cohen and Rosenbaum (1985) found that college women exposed to family violence reported higher levels of depressive symptomatology than did nonexposed women. Straus (1992) found that exposed men and women reported higher levels of depressive and stress symptoms.

Henning, Leitenberg, Coffey, Turner, and Bennett (1996) attempted to account for aspects of the adversity package mentioned above by controlling for physical abuse or parental verbal conflict when they examined differences between women exposed to adult domestic violence and nonexposed women. They still found that exposed women demonstrated greater psychological distress symptoms and poorer social adjustment than did non-exposed women.

Maker, Kemmelmeier, and Peterson (1998) went further toward untangling the adversity package by retrospectively assessing exposure to interparental verbal and physical conflict before age 16 among community college women as well as exposure to sexual and physical abuse and parental drug and alcohol abuse. They also obtained current functioning on a broad set of measures: violence in intimate relationships, trauma symptoms, depression, antisocial behaviors, and suicide attempts. They found a tendency for current depression and PTSD symptomatology to increase as the severity of exposure to parental violence increased. The more severely exposed women also experienced greater violence in their intimate relationships and exhibited more antisocial behaviors. The most interesting finding was that when the researchers controlled for all adversity factors except exposure to adult domestic violence, exposure was still predictive of bidirectional violence in current dating relationships.

Cantrell, MacIntyre, Sharkey, and Thompson (1995) assessed college students' self-reports of adult domestic violence in their family of origin as related to current violence in same- and opposite-sex peer relationships. Milder forms of physical aggression from father to mother or vice versa were predictive of milder aggression in the college students' same- and opposite-sex relationships. However, only father-to-mother severe physical aggression was predictive of mild and severe aggression in student relationships. In contrast, Langhinrichsen-Rohling, Monson, Meyer, Caster, and Sanders (1998) found that the depression, hopelessness, and suicidal behaviors of college students were not related to adult domestic violence exposure. However, these behaviors were related to reports of psychological and physical abuse by parents.

Overall, retrospective studies show the clearest relationship of a child's exposure to adult domestic violence to later crime and violence, but there is also evidence to suggest that witnessing such violence may be associated particularly with violence in later interpersonal relationships. In addition, both abuse and exposure experiences appear to be linked to current trauma, psychiatric symptoms and distress, self-injurious behaviors, and poorer health.

Prospective Studies

Few long-term prospective studies have been undertaken, and most have been of physical child abuse, neglect, or sexual abuse. McCord (1983) followed a large group of boys involved in her juvenile delinquency prevention study over 30 years using archival data. The boys originally had been divided into abused, neglected, rejected, and loved groups, depending on social work counselors' observations of the boys and their treatment by their families. Controlling for socioeconomic differences, McCord found no differences among the groups in overall rate of adult crimes or divorce. Her regression analyses show that lack of supervision, marital conflict, and parental aggression (including abuse) accounted for significant variance in the commission of "personal crimes" and involved assault, rape, and murder. Surprisingly, given research suggesting that physically abused and neglected children show cognitive delays or deficits (e.g., Fish-Murray, Kolby, & van der Kolk, 1987; Hansen, Conaway, & Christopher, 1990), McCord's data did not show group differences in adult occupational status or men returning to school for further education.

Widom (1992) reported results from two follow-ups of a large group of individuals with documented childhood physical abuse, neglect, or sexual abuse and a matched nonabused group into late adolescence and early adulthood. At the first follow-up, abused–neglected children had been involved in more crimes than had been nonabused children. However, the differences were most striking for physically abused children who had been involved in more crimes, both violent and nonviolent. Approximately 5 years later, Widom (1998) was able to re-interview 76% of the original sample. The abused–neglected group still showed signs of dysfunction compared with the control group: They had significantly lower IQ scores; were less likely to have completed high school; were more likely to be unemployed and if employed, to be employed in lower status occupations (e.g., menial or semiskilled); and were less likely to report a stable marriage, with more reporting a history of multiple divorces and separations. Abused–neglected individuals were more likely to report suicide attempts and to have a diagnosis of antisocial personality disorder, which implies greater criminal behavior, although crime rates were not reported. However, they were not more likely to report receiving a diagnosis of alcohol abuse or dependence, except for the neglected women. In the total sample, alcohol problems were more likely in the context of similar parental problems, but antisocial personality diagnosis was associated with the childhood abuse, irrespective of parental characteristics.

In contrast to these findings, an examination of the relationship between abuse and nonviolent crime produced mixed results (Malinosky-Rummell & Hansen, 1993; Silverman, Reinherz, & Giaconia, 1996). Although physically abused children appear to have more trouble in the area of relationship violence and violent crime and to show elevated levels of externalizing behaviors, nonviolent crime and general externalizing behaviors seem to be as predictable from other family variables such as lack of supervision (McCord, 1979) and marital violence.

Once again, a positive relationship was demonstrated, particularly between parental aggression and later violent crime. Although parental conflict also played a role, it was not possible to determine its unique importance. Mixed findings regarding the relationship between physical neglect–abuse or exposure to adult domestic violence and future occupational status or educational attainment suggest the need for further research.

Prospective studies of sexually abused children provide a slightly more positive perspective than those of physically abused children; however, these have all been shorter term studies (Kendall-Tackett et al., 1993). About half of the children evidenced fewer symptoms at follow-up. However, more than 10% appeared to experience greater symptoms. There was a pattern in which anxiety symptoms seemed most likely to abate, whereas problems with sexual preoccupation and aggression (Ernst, Angst, & Foldenyi, 1993) tended to remain or worsen.

Taken together, prospective studies show parent-to-child aggression to be most consistently predictive of adult criminality, psychiatric distress, lower educational or occupational attainment, and greater difficulty with intimate relationships. The unique role of adult domestic violence exposure remains unclear.

Short-Term Prospective Studies

Several groups of researchers have attempted to follow exposed children and battered mothers over time. In an assessment after exposure, Wolfe, Zak, Wilson, and Jaffe (1986) found that children of former residents of a battered women's shelter did not have levels of problem behaviors above those of a community sample. Giles-Sims (1985) found that mother-to-child aggression had decreased during the 6 months following shelter residence. However, Andres and Moore (1995) reported that exposed children's academic problems were still present several months after the mothers had left the shelter. Emery (1996) noted that in the first year following initial contact, children whose mothers had left the violent home had fewer behavior problems and their mothers had fewer depressive symptoms, whereas children and mothers who had returned to the violent setting remained about the same.

Holden, Stein, Ritchie, Harris, and Jouriles (1998) followed battered mothers and their children for 6 months after they left the shelter, with about one third of those followed returning to the violent home. They noted a decline in maternal depressive symptoms and parenting stress but no change in mother-to-child aggressive disciplinary behaviors. Mother-to-child aggression and children's behavior problems had decreased, but children with the highest scores initially retained them. However, the absolute level of problems was lower, such that fewer children met clinical cutoff score criteria. Thus, it appears that time away from the violent home has positive benefits for mothers and children.

Results from the above studies were replicated in the work of Rossman (1998, 1999) and her colleagues. For almost a year, they followed more than 100 children ages 5–14 years from disadvantaged shelter and community families characterized by different levels of adult conflict and domestic violence. More than 90% of exposed children had been in violent homes since age 2 or younger. Researchers assessed initial and ongoing levels of poverty; adult domestic violence; family life stressors; and the children's PTSD symptomatology, behavior problems, and school performance. In general, trauma symptoms and behavior problems decreased across follow-up for all children exposed to violence. However, although school performance ratings improved slightly for nonexposed children during follow-up, those for exposed children declined.

Three factors were associated with greater declines in symptoms and problems and lesser declines in school performance: the absence of ongoing adult domestic violence, the fact that children attended 6–12 treatment sessions, and being male (because boys showed a greater decline in PTSD symptoms). The positive influence of the first two factors may actually be the result of other unmeasured factors. Battered mothers living in violence-free homes who took their children to treatment could also have been more responsive to their children's other needs. These mothers might also have been more likely to see their children as doing better. This could make a difference because mothers provided all outcome ratings except children's self-ratings of PTSD symptoms. However, these results may not be simply a function of maternal biases because even the exposed children who were doing better were not doing as well as the nonexposed children. In addition, the positive role of both a violence-free home and treatment was noted in the research by Emery (1996) and Jouriles et al. (1998).

In summary, mainly on the basis of the study of children recruited from shelters, it appears that there is a decrease in exposed children's behavior problems over relatively short periods of time. However, exposed children's behavior problems and trauma symptoms do not seem to reach the lower levels shown by nonexposed peers. In addition, positive functioning, such as school performance, may continue to decline. Fortunately, factors such as being in a nonviolent household and treatment seem to be obvious candidates for enhancing the positive effects of the passage of time.

Studies of Exposure and Development

A final window for understanding longer term effects comes from the research of the relationship between traumatization and children's abilities to carry out developmental tasks. If one knows that certain developmental tasks (e.g., regulatory capacity represented by consistent sleep cycles, communication capacity as represented by language development) need to be accomplished for a child to progress toward later adaptive functioning, then knowledge that certain types of developmental tasks are poorly accomplished by traumatized children can help predict where difficulties may occur in longer term adjustment. The point is that children continue to try to accomplish developmental tasks in the face of fairly severe adversity and that exposed children often do this in the context of the multiple risk factors (e.g., poverty, community violence, parental substance abuse, personal victimization). These children may evidence atypical developmental trajectories.

Although children are usually targeted for attention in research because of their membership in a single risk factor group, the existence of multiple risk is critical to consider (Rossman & Rosenberg, 1998). Evidence from Rutter, Mauthan, Mortimore, Ouston, and Smith's (1979) work; Sameroff's (Sameroff & Fiese, 1990; Sameroff & Seifer, 1983) Rochester Longitudinal Study; Masten's Project Competence (1989); Erickson, Egeland, and Pianta's (1989) Mother–Child Interaction Project; and Werner and Smith's (1982, 1992) Hawaiian Longitudinal Study suggests that risk factors accumulate and, for some outcomes, appear to multiply each other's adverse effects. This maybe due in part to the problems encountered because poorly accomplished developmental tasks set the stage for the next set of developmental hurdles.

The review of the longer term prospective and retrospective impact studies highlights certain areas of dysfunction for abused–neglected and exposed children: later underemployment and poorer educational attainment; later psychiatric distress, trauma symptoms, depression, and self-injurious behaviors; and later interpersonal violence, crime, and relationship difficulties. Therefore, findings regarding the developmental status of traumatized children in several areas are considered: perception, attention, and cognition; emotional development; and interpersonal relationships. Many fine books, articles, and papers not reviewed here are also relevant (e.g., Cicchetti & Carlson, 1989; Cicchetti & Cohen, 1995; Osofsky, 1997; Pynoos et al., 1996; Rossman & Rosenberg, 1998). Most of the work reviewed in the following sections is derived from the study of abused children because it constitutes the focus of the majority of developmentally oriented studies.

Perception, Attention, and Cognition

A developmental question awaiting more research attention is the extent to which basic perceptual, attentional, and cognitive processes are affected by traumatic exposure. Several types of studies are informative. Regarding perception, Zwiney and Nash (1988) administered the Rorschach projective test to girls ages 11–13 years who had been sexually abused before or after age 9. Those with earlier onset of abuse produced significantly more distorted perceptions (e.g., lower adequate perceptions; higher schizophrenia index scores; and the reflection of primitive needs for food, clothing, and relatedness) than did those with a later onset of abuse. As consistent with the formation of poorer perceptions, Harwicke and Hochstadt (1986) found that physically abused children ages 5–16 years made significantly more errors on the Bender–Gestalt Test than did a chronically ill control group comprised mostly of children with asthma. Further analyses led them to interpret this finding as indicating an immaturity or delay in visual–motor performance on the part of the abused children.

Medina and Margolin (1998) addressed the relationship between attentional capacities and exposure to marital violence in a community sample of children ages 8–13 years. Children's attentional capacities were assessed in terms of the learning and recall of sequences of letters, numbers, and words. This assessment took place both before and after the children listened to a brief audiotape of a man and woman engaging in a verbally and physically aggressive interaction. Before the audiotape exposure, the witnessing of greater violence was associated with poorer overall attentional performance. After the audiotape, greater violence exposure was related to better immediate attention and learning but to poorer delayed recall. The authors suggested that this change in immediate attentional capacity reflected greater immediate vigilance triggered by the audiotape for the more exposed children but poorer actual processing because they did not retain the information well for delayed recall.

The findings of greater distortion of perceptions and immediate vigilance but later poorer encoding lead into a discussion of the four conceptual approaches that have been used to examine the cognitive functioning of traumatized children. These rely to some extent on the notion that the heightened arousal or distress that often accompanies trauma can shape cognitive processing. First, LeDoux (1996) with evidence suggested that there are dual tracks for processing survival information, with the fast track more likely to produce distorted perceptions because cortical sensory stimulus interpretation mechanisms are not involved. Given a violence history, this mechanism, plus fear conditioning, could be likely to produce an immediate vigilance to the stimulus array that could interfere with accurate interpretation and consolidation of stimulus information.

A second conceptualization, social information processing theory (Crick & Dodge, 1994), was developed on the basis of findings that aggressive and harshly punished boys tend to misread benign social cues as hostile. Crick and Dodge hypothesized that when a child is highly emotionally aroused, he or she is likely to pre-emptively process situational information. By this, they meant that the child relies more on old scripts and takes in less new information, making the child more likely to make a mistake in interpreting benign social situations as dangerous. They called this tendency a "hostile aggressive bias." Price and Van Slyke (1991), working with physically maltreated and nonmaltreated preschoolers, found that physically abused children were significantly less accurate than nonphysically abused children in encoding both hostile and nonhostile cues in videotaped peer group entry situations and generated a higher proportion of physically aggressive responses to peer rebuffs and provocation situations. They also were less likely to seek an adult's help with these situations. Children exposed to adult domestic violence also have shown a greater expectation of aggressive endings to videotaped peer and male–female adult ambiguous or neutral dyadic interaction situations (Mallah & Rossman, 1998; Rossman, 1999; West, 1997).

From a trauma perspective, if an exposed child is fear conditioned to link a raised voice with a coming violent encounter when entering a rowdy peer group, then that child could respond with aggression or another preparation for danger, not noticing that the peers were only joking around. This could quickly earn the child a reputation of being socially different and lead to rejection. Such rejection could interfere with the successful completion of developmental tasks carried out with peers, such as the development of accurate social comparison skills or moving from earlier developmental egocentrism to learn accurate empathy and perspective taking.

A third perspective, using a Piagetian (1952) approach, is represented in the work of Fish-Murray et al. (1987). They examined the accommodation skills of physically abused and nonabused school-age children. They did not specifically posit higher arousal as an interfering factor on the part of abused children, but a later discussion by Murray and Son (1998) suggests that traumatic arousal may be part of the formulation. Accommodation skills are those in which new information is taken in and existing schemas are changed to incorporate new information. In contrast, assimilation occurs when the information is changed or distorted to fit existing schemas. Piaget felt that both processes were needed for the growth of intelligence. Fish-Murray et al. found that abused children had weaker accommodation skills than did nonabused children. Children exposed to violence would be at risk for delays in intellectual growth, given this approach. This factor may be partially involved in the lower intelligence scores and educational or occupational attainment reported for adult victims of childhood abuse.

Finally, Santostefano's (1985) cognitive control theory suggests that people unconsciously use their perceptual and cognitive systems to keep arousal levels manageable. One of the unconscious arousal control cognitive styles or mechanisms posited is leveling or sharpening. At the leveling end of the dimension, people are protecting themselves from new information by taking it in more slowly or less accurately. At the sharpening end, a person is seeking protection through the preparedness provided by quick or accurate processing of new information. Typical preschoolers start more on the leveling side and move with development to a midpoint on this continuum. The key here is thought to be the flexibility of operation on the continuum, wherein a person can move back and forth around that midpoint given the demands of the current situation. Difficulties are created when an individual's style is fixed toward one end or the other. Rieder and Cicchetti (1989) found that abused preschoolers leveled all information relative to nonabused preschoolers. Rogosch, Cicchetti, and Aber (1995) found that leveling assessed at age 6 acted as a mediator of the relationship between earlier abuse experience and poor social effectiveness at age 8 as measured by teacher ratings of social acceptance and social competence and peer ratings of sociability–leadership.

Studies of exposed children in my lab also assessed leveling and sharpening. This research tends to show, relative to that involving nonexposed control children, greater leveling of aggressive information and equal leveling of nonaggressive cues in young abused, exposed children (ages 5–7) as well as greater leveling of nonaggressive cues by all older exposed children who perform similarly to nonexposed children with aggressive cues. In addition, in a recent study, Rossman (1999) found that abused, exposed school-age children made fewer errors but also had longer response times on the Matching Familiar Figures Task of attentional capacity and tended toward fewer errors on the Stroop inference task's color-word section than did their nonexposed peers. These results also suggest a type of immediate carefulness or vigilance on the part of older exposed children, particularly those who also have experienced direct victimization. These findings are consistent with the emotional development research reported below (Pollak, Cicchetti, Klorman, & Brumaghim, 1997).

In summary, it appears that violence exposure may change how children use information. Older school-age exposed children appear to adopt a more vigilant strategy, with neutral information following a reminding trigger and with aggressive information relative to nonaggressive cues in the context of a reminder perhaps showing a fast track or pre-emptive strategy. However, this does not appear to represent age-appropriate processing in the sense that this information is not recalled well later, is not accommodated into existing schemas, and is attended to at the expense of attention to nonaggressive information. Younger abused and exposed children appear likely to be decreasing their attention to processing all information relative to nonabused, exposed peers; this is heightened when aggressive information is involved.

Exposure to abuse and spousal violence may have an impact on a child's ability to attend to and use new information as flexibly or completely as nonexposed peers. This could make a number of learning tasks, or merely the following of instructions, more difficult for exposed children. In fact, Fox, Long, and Langlois (1988) reported significantly greater language comprehension deficits for a group of severely neglected children ages 3–8 years than for control children. Comprehension deficits of physically abused children were almost as severe as those of the neglected children. If these attentional or perceptual styles and information-processing strategies are carried forward, they could create lifelong difficulties for exposed children in interpersonal, educational, and occupational arenas.

Emotional Development

The work presented here is all based on physically abused children because no researcher has specifically examined how children exposed to family violence accomplish different tasks needed for emotional development. These tasks include emotion expression, recognition, understanding, and regulation. However, one might infer that the greater problems with aggression or depression of exposed children reflect poorer emotion regulation skills.

In general, abused children appear more prone to negative emotion in a number of ways. Gaensbauer and Hiatt (1984) found that abused infants show expressions of negative emotion earlier than nonabused infants. Abused toddlers show more negative or neutral emotional reactions to the self-recognition task, where rouge is put on a child's nose and then he or she is placed in front of a mirror (Schneider-Rosen & Cicchetti, 1991). Generally, toddlers show surprise or delight in this self-recognition. Beeghly and Cicchetti (1994) found that abused children use fewer emotion-specific words and references to negative emotion. In addition, preschool and early school-age abused children made more mistakes in recognizing emotions than nonabused peers (Camras et al., 1990). Thus, physically abused children appear to be delayed or less competent in certain aspects of emotional development and perhaps precocious in others.

Pollak et al. (1997) argued that the differential emotional competence of abused children may have a physiological underpinning in their attention to, processing the significance of, and intensity of emotional reaction to the emotions conveyed in the faces of others. Using P300 potentials that indicate attention and alertness to specific stimuli, Pollak et al. studied the P300 frequency evoked response potentials of abused and nonabused children ages 7–11 years to standardized pictures of angry and happy faces. With a methodologically elegant design, they found that whereas nonabused children showed equal P300 responses to happy and angry faces, maltreated children showed significantly lower P300 responses to the smiling faces than to the angry faces. Their response to angry faces was not significantly different from those of nonabused children. The authors felt these findings reflected the greater significance of an angry face for an abused child because it could signal impending danger.

This result is intriguing in light of the results showing that older abused exposed children sharpen equally to nonexposed peers for aggressive cues (i.e., are equally quick to see their omission) but level more than nonexposed peers with nonaggressive information (i.e., are slower to see their omission) and in light of the social cognitive research cited showing a tendency toward aggressive bias. Children exposed to violence appeared more likely to ignore or misinterpret benign social information. The age-appropriate accomplishment of emotional development tasks appears to be at risk for exposed children, perhaps being carried forward to create more emotion-related and interpersonal difficulties in adulthood.

Interpersonal Relationships

There is a great deal of information available in the literature about how abused children accomplish relational developmental tasks. In general, physically abused and neglected children were found to have less secure attachments to their caregivers and problematic social relationships compared with nonabused peers (e.g., Cicchetti & Carlson, 1989). One important finding (George & Main, 1979; Main, Kaplan, & Cassidy, 1985) has been that abused children's attachments tend to be more disorganized, meaning that they do not have even a stable insecure interpersonal schema, such as hostile or anxious insecure attachments, to use in interpersonal interactions. Thus, the developmental task of forming a consistent working model of others that can support growth may not have been accomplished.

Three studies of attachment status have been conducted with children exposed to adult domestic violence. Posada, Waters, Liu, and Johnson (in press) worked with community preschoolers exposed to a range of marital conflict, including low-level violence. Using the Q set maternal rating methodology, they found less secure attachment to be associated with greater exposure to violence, especially for girls. Ritchie and Miller (1996), working with children ages 3–8 years, used observation and the story-telling methodology, "the bears' picnic," to assess attachment security in exposed children. Exposed children showed less secure attachment than nonexposed homeless or community children. Although not studying attachment per se, Graham-Bermann and Levendosky (1998a) found children ages 3–5 years of battered mothers to show both more positive and more negative emotion in interacting with their mothers than did children of nonbattered mothers. This may suggest greater ambivalence on the part of the exposed children.

Finally, Wolfe, Wekerle, Reitzel-Jaffe, and Lefebvre (1998) studied violence exposure factors associated with interpersonal uneasiness and hostility, negative attitudes, and verbal and physical aggression in the friendship and dating relationships of 15-year-old high school students who reported maltreatment experiences that occurred before age 12. They found that physical abuse and adult domestic violence exposure were significantly related to interpersonal wariness and hostility and to more negative attitudes toward others and greater aggressive tendencies in relationships. These factors, as well as sexual abuse, were related to avoidant and anxious or ambivalent attachment styles but not to secure attachment. In addition, adult domestic violence exposure and sexual abuse were substantially related to abusive and coercive behaviors both toward and from a current partner. These abused youths appear to have remaining wariness and difficulty in establishing close interpersonal relationships; the authors note that they also appear to be on a maladaptive interpersonal trajectory.

This type of trajectory is demonstrated in the work of Elicker, Englund, and Sroufe (1992) who followed high-risk children participating in the Mother–Child Interaction Project. They found children characterized by secure attachments to show greater social competence and self-confidence 10 years later in a summer camp setting. This was reflected in making friends, maintaining appropriate cross-gender boundaries, and spending more time in peer groups than with counselors or alone. Anxious-avoidant (A) children had lower levels of interpersonal sensitivity than anxious-resistant (C) or secure (B) children. Both A and C children showed more negative biases in their evaluation of their camp peer group, relative to a standard reference group, than did B children who showed a bias in positive direction. The successful negotiation of early mother–child interactions, threatened by marital violence, appears to have lasting effects on interpersonal competence.

Other studies of abused children provide additional ideas regarding the interpersonal problems faced by them. Haviland, Sonne, and Woods (1995) found both relationship and reality testing problems among adolescents who had experienced physical, sexual, or multiple abuse, starting on average around age 6. More than half of the abused adolescents had clinically severe problems with insecure attachment and uncertainty of perception. They evidenced problems with egocentricity, alienation, and reality distortion. These types of problems were significantly correlated with children's self-ratings of PTSD symptoms. Cicchetti and Rogosch (1997) did three years of assessment of maltreated and nonmaltreated children ages 6–11 years attending a summer camp for disadvantaged children. Most maltreated children had experienced multiple forms of abuse (i.e., physical, sexual, emotional abuse; neglect), and all differed from nonabused children on the adaptive composite made of indices of school risk; behavior problems; and low prosocial, disruptive, and withdrawn behaviors.

Although the pattern of results changed some during the year of assessment, in the third year maltreated children remained higher on internalizing problems and school risk and lower on prosocial behaviors. In the previous years, they also had been higher on disruptive and externalizing behaviors. This is a pattern that could interfere with the development of social competence and completion of relational tasks. In addition, Fonagy,

Target, Steele, and Steele (1997) presented evidence supporting the connection of both insecure and distorted attachment–relationship strategies with exposure to family violence and exposure with later violent criminal behavior. In summary, it would appear that exposed children are at risk for maladaptive accomplishment of relational tasks. This could carry forward and be reflected in some of the interpersonal difficulties and violence reported earlier in longitudinal studies.

CONCLUSION AND RECOMMENDATIONS

Overall, it appears that a key problem is disruption in the development of the affiliative system and internal representations of others when children are exposed to chronic violence and abuse. This is certainly consistent with the social cognitive findings regarding aggressive interpersonal biases of children exposed to violence and abuse and with the findings of social incompetence of insecurely attached children. It is normally within the context of safe parental and family relationships that cognitive processes and schemas, behavior and emotion regulation strategies, and expectations for help from others are learned. This context also provides buffering from fear and adversity. Thus, it is not surprising that dysregulation is seen in perceptual, cognitive, emotional, and interpersonal domains for children exposed to violence at home. All of these areas of outcome represent development that may cascade into the greater emotional, educational, and behavioral problems among adult survivors noted in longer term prospective studies. Although there are counterexamples (e.g., the unique role of marital violence remains undifferentiated, not all victimized children show poor outcome), the message seems clear that early repetitive exposure to or experience of violence, particularly physical violence, may start a child on a different trajectory for developmental tasks. These findings are clearest for disadvantaged families and children. There simply is not much research regarding the plight of exposed or abused middle- and upper-class children.

These examples of atypical development for children exposed to violence reflect several factors. The first factor is the influence of severe and repetitive traumatic exposure with accompanying PTSD symptomatology that could include neurophysiological traumatic stress responses and use-dependent development. Posttraumatic symptoms, such as high arousal and difficulty in attending, could interfere with the exploration, experimentation, and openness of learning needed to accomplish developmental tasks. As the second factor, what is learned, in or out of awareness, in a violent home about the availability of safety, comfort, predictability, and the reliable support of others, in addition to family dynamics, introduces another set of critical features for development. As the third factor, society teaches further lessons about the acceptability of interpersonal violence to achieve goals.

The following recommendations echo comments by Emery and Laumann-Billings (1998) in reference to physical maltreatment. Researchers need to gain greater clarity regarding the role of risk factors colinear with spousal violence exposure and examine exposure in understudied groups, such as less disadvantaged families, very young children, and adolescents. There needs to be more attention paid to the role of exposure-related traumatic responding and to the characteristics of the exposure, child, and environment that are associated with greater risk or protection. A multifinality principle needs to guide this work, so that researchers equip themselves to examine multiple growth pathways. For example, one might posit that a trauma-based trajectory with an overrepresentation of fear-related behaviors and vigilance could characterize several groups of children: those with very early and severe exposure, those in which exposure was taking place in the context of much additional adversity, or those who were temperamentally more prone to fearfulness. These children might also be strong candidates for modeling learning, given their increased attention to cues for aggression.

Conversely, a previously nonexposed adolescent, who had more resources than a young child, might respond to adult domestic violence by attempting revenge or alienating him- or herself from the family. This could interfere with adolescent emancipation tasks. Thus, it may be useful to ask such questions as why would a child of this age and gender be likely to become aggressive or depressed? Is this adolescent demonstrating traumatic arousal, poor emotion regulation skills, poor social problem-solving skills, disrupted needs for affiliation, attempts at self- or other protection, temperamental predisposition, learned strategies for gaining control or desired outcomes, or attempts at revenge? Attention to individual differences within a developmental orientation is critical, both methodologically and conceptually. Researchers need to study processes and process models that explicate long-term developmental trajectories. These models need to consider protective and risk factors. Little is known about the role of a child's relationship with a battering father or father figure, the circumstances under which sibling relationships could be protective or destructive, the implications of the existence of multiple types of abuse within a violent family, or the impact of violence in the community in which the family resides.

There is a clear need for sizable, possibly multisite prospective studies of children exposed to different levels of adult domestic violence from both community and sheltered families. The sheltered families form an important part of such an effort because those children usually experience the longest and most severe exposure and have the fewest individual or family resources available for buffering. A model for this work comes from Widom (1998), who carefully matched target children with nonvictimized children on a number of dimensions. Future studies need to be developmentally oriented and to incorporate models of trauma, learning, and interpersonal processes. Priority should be given to funding research of this type.

In addition, a large prospective study of ethnically and socioeconomically diverse community families in which children are studied from birth would be useful. Even existing prospective research, excepting work such as the Mother–Child Interaction Project, has not been designed to examine changes for nonexposed children who remain nonexposed versus becoming exposed. This would provide the most sensitive reading on developmental trajectories. This type of research could also investigate the development of children whose parents had been exposed but there was no direct exposure of the children. Social referencing and learning of the interpersonal fears, emotion regulation, and coping strategies could lead nonexposed children of exposed parents to different developmental trajectories. Research of this type integrates community and public health perspectives and would have related policy implications.

A third area of need is for multidomain developmental assessment of children exposed to severe and repetitive spousal violence, in addition to assessment of health, behavior problems, and trauma symptomatology. The needs of individual children and their mothers vary, and interventions need to be more tailored to those needs. It is highly likely that multisystem interventions will be needed for these children in families, given the suggestion that an intergenerational antisocial orientation may be a factor and the positive results of the multifaceted intervention programs. This recommendation is not meant to overpathologize these children or battered mothers but simply to accurately reflect the potential physical and psychological injuries they may have sustained over many years of life adversity, violence, lack of access to health and educational resources, and poverty. Multidomain child assessment could provide clearer guidelines for what different community response systems could best contribute at what stage for which families (e.g., crisis shelter, health and mental health services, police protection, court and child protective systems that are sensitive to not punishing victims, single-parent low-cost housing, public education) and how to coordinate these efforts.

A need related to those identified above is for research dedicated to the development and validation of instruments to assess which violence-supporting mechanisms are most critical in different families and how to intervene when single or multiple mechanisms are involved. Because trauma, family dynamics, learning, and social legitimization mechanisms all appear capable of supporting what appears to be a strong tendency for physical violence to beget physical violence, this area of inquiry seems critical and could be incorporated into the types of research recommended above. In addition, these instruments need to be capable of assessing potential family strengths, such as indications of good parenting, a helpful social support network, useful resources in the neighborhood or community, and belief systems that can reinforce a nonviolent lifestyle.

Little is known about the role of trauma mechanisms. The incidence data for children exposed to parental violence suggest that valid trauma symptom screening devices for children of all ages are needed. These instruments need to be appropriate for administration in many types of community agencies by professionals with different training backgrounds. In addition, such instruments need to be researched with a broad segment of children from diverse economic and cultural backgrounds, so that appropriate norms are available. These screening instruments would serve as red flags regarding the need for further trauma evaluation. Briere's (1995) Revised Trauma Symptom Checklist for Children could serve this function for school-age children and youths, but currently it does not address the potential need for separate norms for diverse groups.

Initial trauma research also suggests that physiological, cognitive neurological, and imaging studies for children exposed to repetitive and severe parental violence are badly needed. If the types of results cited earlier (e.g., sensitization of the cortisol response to a challenge) were replicated and further evidence was gathered, it might be possible to design interventions that could better help exposed children deal with potential traumatic sources of dysregulation.

Research of the type described above takes time. However, there are current needs that could be more adequately addressed. For example, given the likely involvement of trauma with many exposed children and battered mothers as well as the need for longer term support and help with developing violence-free and independent lifestyles, there should be more funding for community efforts to develop and sustain longer term safe residences with programs for battered mothers and their children. An adjunct to this effort would be to provide funding for research to determine the feasibility and usefulness of early home-based intervention to support battered mothers with infants and toddlers. This would be an ideal point at which to intervene to prevent cascading difficulties in child and adult development.

Pediatric clinics could constitute strong intervention sites for identifying battered mothers and their young children. A clinic- or home-visitor program (e.g., David Olds's HV2000; Olds, Kitzman, Cole, & Robinson, 1997) could be based in pediatric clinics to provide medical, developmental, and other support for these mothers. This type of effort would be assisted by the development of policy that would make inquiry into adult domestic violence exposure a standard part of medical and mental health intake and assessment procedures, with information regarding pragmatic help and treatment easily available. Policy would need to be developed to guard the confidentiality of this type of historical information to protect the victims' safety.

In the advocating of a more universal screening for the occurrence of adult domestic violence, it becomes critical to also advocate for policy to mandate the use and evaluation of training modules for any personnel involved regarding trauma, adult domestic violence, and likely effects of exposure on adults and children. This would include training personnel at multiple potential points of contact, such as those involved with health and mental health services, child protective services, protective and legal services and adjudication, and educational services. These and other professionals may be the first community contact people for battered mothers and children. One such program is currently offered through the Massachusetts Attorney General's Office. In connection with this type of effort and given the likely effects of severe adult domestic violence history, it is important that policy be developed so that attention to this history during legal proceedings (e.g., the penalty phase in trials of exposed defendants, adults, and children) would be more commonplace.

In summary, a useful way of thinking about the longer term effects of adult domestic violence exposure may be this: Exposure at any age can create disruptions that can interfere with the accomplishment of development tasks, and early exposure may create more severe disruptions by affecting the subsequent chain of developmental tasks. Earlier prevention and intervention, through incorporation of screening and assessment into highly used services and guided by multidomain prospective research, may be able to save children and adults years of pain and developmental disappointment, making the intervention task, if needed, easier and the outcomes brighter.

REFERENCES

Achenbach, T. M., & Edelbrock, C. S. (1983). *Manual for the Child Behavior Checklist and Revised Child Behavioral Profile*. Burlington: University of Vermont.

American Psychiatric Association. (1980). *Diagnostic and statistical manual of mental disorders* (3rd ed.). Washington, DC: Author.

American Psychiatric Association. (1987). *Diagnostic and statistical manual of mental disorders* (3rd ed. rev.). Washington, DC: Author

American Psychiatric Association. (1994). *Diagnostic and statistical manual of mental disorders* (4th ed.).Washington, DC: Author.

Andres, J., & Moore, T. E. (1995, March). *The adjustment of child witnesses to spousal abuse: A follow-up study*. Poster session presented at the meeting of the Society for Research in Child Development, Indianapolis, IN.

Bandura, A. (1977). *Social learning theory*. Englewood Cliffs, NJ: Prentice-Hall.

Beeghly, M., & Cicchetti, D. (1994). Child maltreatment, attachment, and the self-system: Emergence of an internal state lexicon in toddlers at high social risk. *Development and Psychopathology, 6,* 5–30.

Boney-McCoy, S., & Finkelhor, D. (1995). Psychosocial sequelae of violent victimization in a national youth sample. *Journal of Consulting and Clinical Psychology, 63,* 726–736.

Briere, J. N. (1992). *Child abuse trauma: Theory and treatment of the lasting effects.* Newbury Park, CA: Sage.

Briere, J. N. (1995). *Trauma Symptom Checklist for Children (TSCC–A).* Odessa, FL: Psychological Assessment Resources.

Bryer, J. B., Nelson, B. A., Miller, J. B., & Kroll, P. A. (1987). Childhood sexual and physical abuse as factors in adult psychiatric illness. *American Journal of Psychiatry, 44,* 1426–1430.

Camras, L. A., Ribordy, S., Hill, J., Martino, S., Sachs, V., Spaccarelli, S., & Stefani, R. (1990). Maternal facial behavior and the recognition and production of emotional expression by maltreated and nonmaltreated children. *Developmental Psychology, 25,* 394–402.

Cantrell, P. J., MacIntyre, D. I., Sharkey, K. J., & Thompson, V. (1995). Violence in the marital dyad as a predictor of violence in peer relationships of older adolescents/young adults. *Violence and Victims, 10,* 35–41.

Charney, D. S., Southwick, S. M., Krystal, J. H., Deutch, A. Y., Murburg, M. M., & Davis, M. (1994). Neurobiological mechanisms of PTSD. In M. M. Murburg (Ed.), *Catecholamine function in PTSD: Emerging concepts* (pp. 131–158). Washington, DC: American Psychiatric Association.

Cicchetti, D. (1989). How research on child maltreatment has informed the study of child development: Perspectives from developmental psychopathology. In D. Cicchetti & V. Carlson (Eds.), *Child maltreatment: Theory and research on the causes and consequences of child abuse and neglect* (pp. 377–431). New York: Cambridge University Press.

Cicchetti, D., & Carlson, V. (1989). *Child maltreatment: Theory and research on the causes and consequences of child abuse and neglect.* New York: Cambridge University Press.

Cicchetti, D., & Cohen, D. J. (1995). *Developmental psychopathology.* New York: Wiley.

Cicchetti, D., & Rogosch, F. A. (1997). The role of self-organization in the promotion of resilience in maltreated children. *Development and Psychopathology, 9,* 797–815.

Crick, N. R., & Dodge, K. A. (1994). A review and reformulation of social information-processing mechanisms in children's social adjustment. *Psychological Bulletin, 115,* 74–101.

Devoe, E., & Graham-Bermann, S. (1997, June). *Predictors of posttraumatic stress symptoms in battered women and their children.* Poster session presented at the Second International Conference on Children Exposed to Family Violence, London, Ontario, Canada.

Elicker, J., Englund, M., & Sroufe, L. A. (1992). Predicting peer competence and peer relationships in childhood from early parent–child relationships. In R. D. Parke & G. W. Ladd (Eds.), *Family–peer relationships: Modes of linkage* (pp. 77–106). Hillsdale, NJ: Erlbaum.

Emery, R. E. (1996, June). *A longitudinal study of battered women and their children: One year following shelter residence.* Paper presented at the First International Conference on Children Exposed to Family Violence, Austin, TX.

Emery, R. E., & Laumann-Billings, L. (1998). An overview of the nature, causes, and consequences of abusive family relationships: Toward differentiating maltreatment and violence. *American Psychologist, 53,* 121–135.

Erickson, M. F., Egeland, B., & Pianta, R. (1989). The effects of maltreatment on the development of young children. In D. Cicchetti & V. Carlson (Eds.), *Child maltreatment: Theory and research on the causes and consequences of child abuse and neglect* (pp. 647–684). New York: Cambridge University Press.

Ernst, G., Angst, J., & Foldenyi, M. (1993). The Zurich Study: Sexual abuse in childhood, frequency and relevance for adult morbidity data of a longitudinal epidemiological study. *European Archives of Psychiatry and Clinical Neuroscience, 242,* 293–300.

Felitti, V. J., Anada, R. F., Nordenberg, D., Williamson, D. F., Spitz, A. M., Edwards, V., Koss, M. P., & Marks, J. S. (1998). Relationship of childhood abuse and household dysfunction to many of the leading causes of death in adults. *American Journal of Preventive Medicine, 14,* 245–258.

Fish-Murray, C. C., Koby, E. V., & van der Kolk, B. A. (1987). Evolving ideas: The effect of abuse on children's thought. In B. A. van der Kolk (Ed.), *Psychological trauma* (pp. 89–100). Washington, DC: American Psychiatric Association.

Foa, E. B., Riggs, D. S., & Gershuny, B. S. (1995). Arousal, numbing, and intrusion: Symptom structure of PTSD following assault. *American Journal of Psychiatry, 152,* 116–120.

Fonagy, P., Target, M., Steele, M., & Steele, H. (1997). The development of violence and crime as it relates to security of attachment. In J. D. Osofsky (Ed.), *Children in a violent society* (pp. 150–182). New York: Guilford Press.

Forsstrom-Cohen, B., & Rosenbaum, A. (1985). The effects of parental marital violence on young adults: An exploratory investigation. *Journal of Marriage and the Family, 47,* 467–472.

Fox, L., Long, S. H., & Langlois, A. (1988). Patterns of language comprehension deficit in abused and neglected children. *Journal of Speech and Hearing Disorders, 53,* 239–244.

Gaensbauer, T. J., & Hiatt, S. (1984). Facial communication of emotion in early infancy. In N. Fox & R. Davidson (Eds.), *The psychobiology of affective development* (pp. 207–230). Hillsdale, NJ: Erlbaum.

George, C., & Main, M. (1979). Social interactions of young abused children: Approach, avoidance, and aggression. *Child Development, 50,* 306–318.

Giles-Sims, J. (1985). A longitudinal study of battered children of battered wives. *Family Relations, 34*, 205–210.

Graham-Bermann, S. A., & Levendosky, A. A. (1998a). The social functioning of preschool-age children whose mothers are emotionally and physically abused. *Journal of Emotional Abuse, 1*, 57–80.

Graham-Bermann, S. A., & Levendosky, A. A. (1998b). Traumatic stress symptoms in children of battered women. *Journal of Interpersonal Violence, 14*, 111–128.

Hansen, D. J., Conaway, L. P., & Christopher, J. S. (1990). Victims of child physical abuse. In R. Ammerman & M. Hersen (Eds.), *Treatment of family violence: A sourcebook* (pp. 17–49). New York: Wiley.

Harwicke, N. J., & Hochstadt, N. J. (1986). Intellectual functioning in abused–neglected children. *Education, 107*, 76–82.

Haviland, M. G., Sonne, J. L., & Woods, L. R. (1995). Beyond posttraumatic stress disorder: Object relations and reality disturbances in physically and sexually abused adolescents. *Journal of the American Academy of Child and Adolescent Psychiatry, 34*, 1054–1059.

Henning, K., Leitenberg, H., Coffey, P., Turner, T., & Bennett, R. T. (1996). Long-term psychological and social impact of witnessing physical conflict between parents. *Journal of Interpersonal Violence, 11*, 35–51.

Holden, G. W., Stein, J. D., Ritchie, K. L., Harris, S. D., & Jouriles, E. N. (1998). Parenting behaviors and beliefs of battered women. In G. W. Holden, R. Geffner, & E. N. Jouriles (Eds.), *Children exposed to marital violence: Theory, research, and applied issues* (pp. 289–334). Washington, DC: American Psychological Association.

Jouriles, E. N., McDonald, R., Stephens, N., Norwood, W., Spiller, L. C., & Ware, H. S. (1998). Breaking the cycle of violence: Helping families departing from battered women's shelters. In G. W. Holden, R. Geffner, & E. N. Jouriles (Eds.), *Children exposed to marital violence: Theory, research, and applied issues* (pp. 337–369). Washington, DC: American Psychological Association.

Kalmuss, D. (1984). The intergenerational transmission of marital aggression. *Journal of Marriage and the Family, 46*, 11–19.

Kaufman, J., Birmaher, B., Dahl, N., Ryan, N., Perel, J., & Nelson, B. (1997, April). *Psychobiological sequelae of abuse*. Poster session presented at the meeting of the Society for Research in Child Development, Washington, DC.

Kaufman, J., Birmaher, B., Perel, J., Dahl, R., Moreci, P., Nelson, B., Wells, W., & Ryan, N. (in press). The corticotrophin releasing hormone challenge in depressed, abused, depressed non-abused and normal control children. *Biological Psychiatry*.

Kendall-Tackett, K. A., Williams, L. M., & Finkelhor, D. (1993). Impact of sexual abuse on children: A review and synthesis of recent empirical studies. *Psychological Bulletin, 113*, 164–180.

Langhinrichsen-Rohling, J., Monson, C. M., Meyer, K. A., Caster, J., & Sanders, A. (1998). The associations among family-of-origin violence and young adults' current depressed, hopeless, suicidal, and life-threatening behavior. *Journal of Family Violence, 13*, 243–261.

Langhinrichsen-Rohling, J., & Neidig, P. (1995). Violent backgrounds of economically disadvantaged youth: Risk factors for perpetrating violence? *Journal of Family Violence, 10*, 379–397.

LeDoux, J. E. (1996). *The emotional brain.* New York: Simon & Schuster.

Main, M., Kaplan, N., & Cassidy, J. (1985). Security in infancy, childhood, and adulthood: A move to the level of representation. *Monographs of the Society for Research in Child Development, 50*(1–2, Serial No. 209).

Maker, A. H., Kemmelmeier, M., & Peterson, C. (1998). Long-term psychological consequences in women of witnessing parental physical conflict and experiencing abuse in childhood. *Journal of Interpersonal Violence, 13*, 574–589.

Malinosky-Rummell, R., & Hansen, D. J. (1993). Long-term consequences of childhood physical abuse. *Psychological Bulletin, 114*, 68–79.

Mallah, K., & Rossman, B. B. R. (1998). *Information processing for children exposed to family violence.* Manuscript submitted for review, University of Denver, Denver, CO.

Masten, A. (1989). Resilience in development: Implications of the study of successful adaptation for developmental psychopathology. In D. Cicchetti (Ed.), *Rochester Symposium on Developmental Psychopathology: Vol. I. The emergence of discipline* (pp. 251–294). Hillsdale, NJ: Erlbaum.

McCord, J. (1979). Some child-rearing antecedents of criminal behavior in adult men. *Journal of Personality and Social Psychology, 37*, 1477–1486.

McCord, J. (1983). A forty-year perspective on the effects of child abuse and neglect. *Child Abuse & Neglect, 7*, 265–270.

Medina, J., & Margolin, G. (1998, October). *Subtle effects of marital violence on parent–child relations, children's behavior and cognition.* Paper presented at the Fourth International Conference on Children Exposed to Family Violence, San Diego, CA.

Murray, C. C., & Son, L. (1998). The effect of multiple victimization on children's cognition: Variations in response. In B. B. R. Rossman & M. S. Rosenberg (Eds.), *Multiple victimization of children: Conceptual, developmental, research, and treatment issues* (pp. 131–146). Binghamton, NY: Haworth Press.

Olds, D., Kitzman, H., Cole, R., & Robinson, J. (1997). Theoretical foundations of a program of home visitation for pregnant women and parents of young children. *Journal of Community Psychology, 25*, 9–25.

Osofsky, J. D. (1997). The violence intervention project for children and families. In J. D. Osofsky (Ed.), *Children in a violent society* (pp. 256–260). New York: Guilford Press.

Pepler, D. J., & Moore, T. E. (1989, March). *Children exposed to family violence: Home environments and cognitive functioning.* Paper presented at the meeting of the Society for Research in Child Development, Kansas City, MO.

Perry, B. D. (1994). Neurobiological sequelae of childhood trauma: PTSD in children. In M. M. Murburg (Ed.), *Catecholamine function in PTSD: Emerging concepts* (pp. 233–255). Washington, DC: American Psychiatric Association.

Perry, B. D. (1997). Incubated in terror: Neurodevelopmental factors in the "cycle of violence." In J. D. Osofsky (Ed.), *Children in a violent society* (pp. 124–149). New York: Guilford Press.

Piaget, J. (1952). *The origins of intelligence in children.* New York: International Universities Press.

Pollak, S. D., Cicchetti, D., Klorman, R., & Brumaghim, J. T. (1997). Cognitive brain event-related potentials and emotion processing in maltreated children. *Child Development, 68,* 773–787.

Posada, G., Waters, E., Liu, X. D., & Johnson, S. (in press). Specific domains of marital discord and attachment security: Girls and boys. In E. Waters, B. Vaughn, G. Posada, & D. Teti (Eds.), *Patterns of secure base behavior: Q-sort perspectives on attachment and caregiving in infancy and childhood.* Hillsdale, NJ: Erlbaum.

Price, J. M., & Van Slyke, D. (1991, March). *Social information processing patterns and social adjustment of maltreated children.* Paper presented at the meeting of the Society for Research in Child Development, Seattle, WA.

Pynoos, R. S., Frederick, C., Nader, K., Arroyo, W., Steinberg, A., Eth, S., Nunez, F., & Fairbanks, L. (1987). Life threat and posttraumatic stress in school age children. *Archives of General Psychiatry, 44,* 1057–1063.

Pynoos, R. S., Steinberg, A. M., & Goenjian, A. (1996). Traumatic stress in childhood and adolescence: Recent developments and current controversies. In B. A. van der Kolk, A. C. McFarlane, & L. Weisaeth (Eds.), *Traumatic stress: The effects of overwhelming experience on mind, body, and society* (pp. 331–358). New York: Guilford Press.

Pynoos, R. S., Steinberg, A. M., & Wraith, R. (1995). A developmental model of childhood traumatic stress. In D. Cicchetti & D. J. Cohen (Eds.), *Developmental psychopathology* (Vol. 2, pp. 72–95). New York: Wiley.

Rieder, C., & Cicchetti, D. (1989). Organizational perspective on cognitive control functioning and cognitive–affective balance in maltreated children. *Developmental Psychology, 25,* 382–393.

Ritchie, K. L., & Miller, G. (1996, June). *Familial conceptualizations and attachment in 3- to 8-year-old children of battered women.* Paper presented at the First International Conference on Children Exposed to Family Violence, Austin, TX.

Rogosch, F. J., Cicchetti, D., & Aber, J. L. (1995). The role of child maltreatment in early deviations in cognitive and affective processing abilities and later peer relationship problems. *Development and Psychopathology, 7,* 591–609.

Rossman, B. B. R. (1994). Children in violent families: Current diagnostic and treatment considerations. *Family Violence and Sexual Assault Bulletin, 10,* 29–34.

Rossman, B. B. R. (1998, October). *Time heals all: How much and for whom?* Paper presented at the Fourth International Conference on Children Exposed to Family Violence, San Diego, CA.

Rossman, B. B. R. (1999). *Frost Foundation project final report.* Unpublished manuscript, University of Denver, Denver, CO.

Rossman, B. B. R., & Ho, J. (2000). Posttraumatic response and children exposed to parental violence. In R. A. Geffner, P. G. Jaffe, & M. Suderman (Eds.), *Children exposed to domestic violence: Current issues in research, intervention, prevention and policy development* (pp. 85–106). Binghamton, NY: Haworth Press.

Rossman, B. B. R., & Rosenberg, M. S. (1998). *Multiple victimization of children: Conceptual, developmental, research, and treatment issues.* Binghamton, NY: Haworth Press.

Rutter, M., Mauthan, B., Mortimore, P., Ouston, J., & Smith, A. (1979). *Fifteen thousand hours: Secondary schools and their effects on children.* Cambridge, MA: Harvard University Press.

Saigh, P. A. (1991). The development of posttraumatic stress disorder following four different types of traumatization. *British Research & Therapy, 29,* 213–218.

Sameroff, A. J., & Fiese, B. H. (1990). Transactional regulation and early intervention. In S. J. Meisels & J. P. Shonkoff (Eds.), *Handbook of early childhood intervention* (pp. 119–149). Cambridge, England: Cambridge University Press.

Sameroff, A. J., & Seifer, R. (1983). Familial risk and child competence. *Child Development, 54,* 1254–1268.

Santostefano, S. (1985). *Cognitive control therapy with children and adolescents.* New York: Pergamon Press.

Schneider-Rosen, K., & Cicchetti, D. (1991). Early self-knowledge and emotional development: Visual self-recognition and affective reactions to mirror self-image in maltreated and nonmaltreated toddlers. *Developmental Psychology, 27,* 481–488.

Silverman, A., Reinherz, H., & Giaconia, R. (1996). The long-term sequelae of child and adolescent abuse: A longitudinal community study. *Child Abuse & Neglect, 20,* 709–723.

Simons, R. L., & Johnson, C. (1998). An examination of competing explanations for the intergenerational transmission of domestic violence. In Y. Danieli (Ed.), *International handbook of multigenerational legacies of trauma* (pp. 553–570). New York: Plenum Press.

Straus, M. A. (1979, February). Measuring intrafamily conflict and violence: The Conflict Tactics (CT) Scales. *Journal of Marriage and the Family,* pp. 75–88.

Straus, M. A. (1992). Children as witnesses to marital violence: A risk factor for lifelong problems among a nationally representative sample of American men and women. In D. F. Schwarz (Ed.), *Children and violence: Report on the 23rd Ross Roundtable on Critical Approaches to Common Pediatric Problems* (pp. 98–104). Columbus, OH: Ross Laboratories.

Straus, M. A., Gelles, R. J., & Steinmetz, S. K. (1980). *Behind closed doors: Violence in the American family.* Beverly Hills, CA: Sage.

Straus, M. A., & Smith, C. (1990). Family patterns and primary prevention of family violence. In M. A. Straus & R. J. Gelles (Eds.), *Physical violence in American families* (pp. 507–528). New Brunswick, NJ: Transaction.

van der Kolk, B. A. (1994). The body keeps score: Memory and the evolving psychobiology of posttraumatic stress. *Harvard Review of Psychiatry, 1*, 253–265.

van der Kolk, B. A. (1996). The body keeps score: Approaches to the psychobiology of posttraumatic stress disorder. In B. A. van der Kolk, A. C. McFarlane, & L. Weisaeth (Eds.), *Traumatic stress: The effects of overwhelming experience on mind, body, and society* (pp. 214–241). New York: Guilford Press.

Weeks, R., & Widom, C. S. (1998). Self-reports of early childhood victimization among incarcerated adult male felons. *Journal of Interpersonal Violence, 13*, 346–361.

Werner, E. E., & Smith, R. S. (1982). *Vulnerable but invincible: A longitudinal study of resilient children and youth.* New York: Adams, Banister, Cox.

Werner, E. E., & Smith, R. S. (1992). *Overcoming the odds: High risk children from birth to adulthood.* Ithaca, NY: Cornell University Press.

West, J. C. (1997). *Exposure to interparental violence and children's social functioning.* Unpublished master's thesis, University of Denver, Denver, CO.

Widom, C. S. (1989). Does violence beget violence? A critical examination of the literature. *Psychological Bulletin, 106*, 3–28.

Widom, C. S. (1992, October). *The cycle of violence* [Research in brief] (NJC 136607). U.S. Department of Justice, National Institute of Justice.

Widom, C. S. (1998). Childhood victimization: Early adversity and subsequent psychopathology. In B. P. Dohrenwend (Ed.), *Adversity, stress and psychopathology* (pp. 81–95). New York: Oxford University Press.

Wolfe, D. A., Wekerle, C., Reitzel-Jaffe, D., & Lefebvre, L. (1998). Factors associated with abusive relationships among maltreated and nonmaltreated youth. *Development and Psychopathology, 10*, 61–85.

Wolfe, D. A., Zak, L., Wilson, S., & Jaffe, P. (1986). Child witnesses to violence between parents: Critical issues in behavioral and social adjustment. *Journal of Abnormal Child Psychology, 14*, 95–104.

Zwiney, O. A., & Nash, M. R. (1988). Sexual abuse in early versus late childhood: Differing patterns of pathology as revealed on the Rorschach. *Psychotherapy, 25*, 99–106.

3

RESILIENCE IN CHILDREN EXPOSED TO DOMESTIC VIOLENCE

HONORE M. HUGHES, SANDRA A. GRAHAM-BERMANN, AND GABRIELLE GRUBER

Most investigations of the impact of domestic violence on children focus on various aspects of child psychopathology such as anxiety, depression, and conduct disorder or other pathological outcomes (e.g., low self-esteem; Graham-Bermann, 1998; Hughes, 1988; Hughes & Graham-Bermann, 1998). More recent studies focus on posttraumatic stress disorder in children exposed to domestic violence (Graham-Bermann & Levendosky, 1998; Rossman, 1998; Wolfe, Gentile, & Wolfe, 1989). Reviews indicate that children exposed to domestic violence often show symptoms in the areas of behavioral and emotional functioning, cognitive and school problems, and social relationships (Hughes & Graham-Bermann, 1998; Kolbo, Blakely, & Engelman, 1996; Margolin, 1998). Moreover, on average, approximately 35–45% of children studied receive scores in the clinical problem range on standardized measures of psychopathology (Hughes, 1997). Conversely, this means that approximately 55–65% of children do not appear to be severely affected by such violence, at least at the time of evaluation.

For more than 20 years, researchers have studied resilient children—those children who seem to adapt despite exposure to stressful and high-risk environments (Garmezy, 1983; Rutter, 1979, 1985). Numerous populations have been assessed for these qualities, including children living in foster care (Festinger, 1983; Folman, 1995), those living in poverty (Elder, 1974; Radke-Yarrow & Sherman, 1990), those with parental psychopathology (Garmezy, 1991; Sameroff & Seifer, 1990), those born premature or with low birthweight (Werner, 1989), homeless children (Masten, Miliotis, Graham-Bermann, & Neeman, 1993), and children of divorce (Hetherington, Bridges, & Insabella, 1998). Interest in resilience grew out of studies of children at risk (Masten & Coatsworth, 1998), yet to date there are no investigations of resilience in children exposed to domestic violence.

DEFINING RESILIENCE IN CHILDREN

Before applying the resiliency construct to the study of children exposed to domestic violence and before describing two studies of resilient outcomes for these children, we offer a brief review of definitions that have been used to describe resiliency. In doing so, we open a discussion of the limits and parameters of what may or may not be resilience in this population of children.

Originally, children who did not develop expected problems in reaction to stressful circumstances were characterized as invulnerable (Anthony & Kohler, 1987) and stress resistant (Garmezy, 1985). Resilient children also have been described in terms of their behavior as children who function adequately (Garmezy, 1991) or who recover from trauma and have a capacity for self-repair (Murphy & Moriarty, 1976). A more recent and likely more apt term for such children is "survivors of adversity" because the lack of obvious psychopathology does not necessarily indicate that all is well or that the same children will not show deficits later.

Over the years, researchers have been in somewhat of a quandary regarding the use of the term *resilience*. For example, in 1993, Luthar noted the confusion surrounding the terms *risk, resilience, protective factors, ameliorative effects,* and *compensatory factors*. Researchers who are known in the area of resilience have also used the term differently at different times. Masten, Best, and Garmezy (1990) defined resilience as "the process of, capacity for, or outcome of successful adaptation despite challenging or threatening circumstance" (p. 426). Later, Masten, and Coatsworth (1998) stated that the study of resilience is usually considered to be an examination of "how children overcome adversity to achieve good developmental outcomes" (p. 205). Nevertheless, although it remains unclear whether resiliency is a goal, a process, or a characteristic within an individual child, clearly there are desirable developmental outcomes for all children; those who attain these goals under adverse circumstances can be considered resilient. Furthermore, by studying the processes through which a child overcomes adversity or prevails in the face of severe stress, we can learn about both normal and abnormal development (Cicchetti & Lynch, 1993). To that end, when planning interventions for children, it is essential not only to be cognizant of psychopathology but also to have a firm understanding of the potential strengths and protective features in the child's environment.

It is also important to note a clarification of the common practices and criteria used to identify resilience. Masten and Coatsworth (1998) suggested that to distinguish resilience from other kinds of circumstances, two questions need to be addressed: (a) Has there been a significant threat to the individual, with that threat usually considered to be exposure to severe adversity or trauma (e.g., family violence, death of a parent) or a circumstance that imbues high-risk status (e.g., poverty)? and (b) As an outcome, is the quality of adaptation or development positive? Moreover, although standards for evaluating risk outcomes have not been formally established, researchers often use as criteria the ability to reach desired levels of competence or lack of symptoms of psychopathology (Masten & Coatsworth, 1995).

RISK AND PROTECTIVE FACTORS

Several developmental psychopathologists have studied the risk factors that contribute to vulnerability and the protective factors that work to ameliorate the expected negative consequences to the child (Luthar & Zigler, 1991; Masten & Coatsworth, 1995; Sameroff, Seifer, & Bartko, 1997). In their overview, Masten and Coatsworth concluded that current data were consistent with key risk or protective factors having generalized influences. These authors listed stressors, parenting qualities, intellectual functioning, and socioeconomic status variables as being generally involved as predictors, correlates, and moderators of both competence and psychopathology. Masten and Coatsworth (1998) then took a step further, stating that the "same powerful adaptive systems protect development in both favorable and unfavorable environments" (p. 205).

Regarding risk factors, in the early studies of children exposed to domestic abuse, the assessment of risk was often limited to documenting the presence of physical assault to the mother (Hughes, 1988; Rosenberg, 1987). Other studies include multiple risks to the child in addition to witnessing domestic violence, for example, child abuse (Hughes, Parkinson, & Vargo, 1989; Rossman, Hughes, & Hanson, 1998; Sternberg et al., 1993); emotional maltreatment (Graham-Bermann, 1998); moving to a shelter (Fantuzzo et al., 1991); or parental substance abuse, poverty, single-female-headed household, and low educational level of a care provider (Fantuzzo & Boruch, 1997). To date, few studies exist of cumulative risk factors in the child's environment for this population of children exposed to domestic violence. Furthermore, it is difficult to capture the sequence of causality in attributing specific outcomes to specific risk factors (e.g., being traumatized by an exposure to violence, failing in school, becoming depressed) because as Rossman points out in the previous chapter, there are no prospective studies of the impact of domestic violence on children.

Protective factors specifically associated with overcoming adversity for children exposed to domestic violence include those particular to the child, the parent, and the environment. Only a few studies are available in which the authors examined protective factors in this population. One characteristic of the child that has been associated with lower risk of negative outcome is an age older than 5 years (Fantuzzo & Boruch, 1997; Holden, Stein, Ritchie, Harris, & Jouriles, 1998). Parental factors found to provide a protective function for children in families with domestic violence are parental competence (Graham-Bermann & Levendosky, 1998) and mother's mental health (Hughes & Luke, 1998; Jaffe, Wolfe, & Wilson, 1990). Protective factors associated with the broader environmental context include the availability and strength of social support (Graham-Bermann, Levendosky, Porterfield, & Okun, 2000).

PHYSICALLY ABUSED CHILDREN AND RESILIENCE

Because so few studies specifically examine resilience in children exposed to domestic violence, the literature on physically abused children and resilience can inform this review. Factors associated with risk and resilience for physically abused children can elucidate several issues regarding possible risk and protective factors for children exposed to domestic violence.

Several studies identify important mediators and moderators of adjustment among children who have been physically abused. (Essentially, a mediator variable is one that is positioned between two other variables in a model that explains a certain amount of variance in outcome; a moderator variable is considered to have a linear effect on one variable in accounting for a portion of the outcome.) These variables range in the breadth of their focus from the individual to the societal level, yet the variables that received the most research attention are at the individual level, that is, parental characteristics associated with abuse (Wolfe, 1985). Several studies identify personality traits associated with abusive behaviors. Perpetrators of child physical abuse are more likely to report anger and have anger control problems relative to nonphysically abusive adults. Researchers have identified links in adults who abuse children to traits, including low frustration tolerance, low self-esteem, rigidity, deficits in empathy, substance abuse or dependence, depression, physical health problems, and physiological reactivity (Barnett, Miller-Perrin, & Perrin, 1997). However, subsequent studies indicate that parents' thoughts and feelings about caretaking may be more directly linked to parenting skills than to static personality traits.

Using this model, several researchers have demonstrated that when compared with their nonmaltreating counterparts, abusive parents have less understanding about the complexity of social relationships, in particular parenting, and their feelings about meeting the needs of another person (Brunnquell, Crichton, & Egeland, 1981; Newberger, 1980; Newberger & Cook, 1983; Pianta, Egeland, & Erickson, 1989). Moreover, maltreating parents have unrealistic expectations and negative perceptions of their children, consider their role of parent as stressful, and interact with their children less than do nonabusive parents (Azar, Barnes, & Twentyman, 1988; Bauer & Twentyman, 1985; Bousha & Twentyman, 1984; Mash, Johnston, & Kovitz, 1983; Trickett & Kuczynski, 1986).

At the individual level, several characteristics within the child have been linked to increased vulnerability to abuse. For example, as found in the literature on children of battered women, young age is a predictor of child physical abuse, specifically, the majority of child victims are younger than age 5 (American Association for Protecting Children, 1989; U.S. Department of Health and Human Services, 1994). These reports also suggest that adolescence is a dangerous time because the highest rates of physical injury occur to infants and adolescents. Mirroring research on children's exposure to domestic violence, the link between gender and physical abuse of children at this point is equivocal (Barnett, Miller-Perrin, & Perrin, 1997). Birth complications, physical and mental disabilities, and difficult child behaviors have also been shown to be associated with victimization of children (Ammerman, Van Hasselt, Hersen, McGonigle, & Lubetsky, 1989; Friedrich & Boriskin, 1976).

Researchers who have investigated these factors make the assumption that children who are difficult to care for may elicit abuse from parents who would otherwise not maltreat their children (Pianta et al., 1989). An abused child "may become the victim of maltreatment, not because of its own behavior, but because the child places added burdens upon an already stressed or incapable family system, resulting in a breakdown in the processes of good parenting" (Pianta et al., 1989, p. 209). According to Ammerman (1990), the majority of studies provide some support, although quite weak, for the role of the child in child abuse and neglect. Ammerman concluded that although prospective studies identify several child behavioral characteristics that can contribute to maltreatment, the explanatory power of these variables is minor compared with other causative factors.

Several relationship variables have been linked with increased likelihood of abuse. Living in a household with domestic violence or marital discord, for example, places children at risk to be physically abused themselves; also at risk are children from families with intergenerational histories of abuse (Barnett et al., 1997; Hughes et al., 1989). Social and economic conditions that are also thought to place additional strain on families and that, in turn, may contribute to the likelihood of child physical abuse include having a low socioeconomic status, living in a single-parent household, and receiving public assistance (Belsky, 1980; Rutter, 1979; Straus, 1983). These authors have found that children are also at risk if their caregivers are employed in a blue-collar job, are unemployed, or hold part-time employment, there is inadequate social support in their environments and additional family stressors are present (e.g., large family size). Finally, several societal factors have been linked with a risk to children being physically abused:

societal approval of violence in a broad sense, approval of corporal punishment, and unequal distribution of power in society and in the family (Gelles & Cornell, 1990).

CHILDREN OF BATTERED WOMEN AND RESILIENCE

In terms of the psychological adjustment of children exposed to domestic violence, rarely have researchers taken an in depth look at the children who seem to be functioning reasonably well and studied resilience in these children. That is, little research specifically focuses on identifying children who may be coping well, or even coping adequately, in the face of exposure to such violence. Two studies are briefly described to illustrate one way to investigate resilience in children who have witnessed this form of family violence. We are interested in examining characteristics associated with positive, as opposed to problematic, functioning in groups of children.

Heterogeneity in Psychological Adjustment

In two studies of children of battered women, researchers found that the children could be separated empirically into subgroups as a function of their psychological adjustment; these clusters of children could then be described on the basis of characteristics that differed among the clusters (Hughes & Luke, 1998; Hughes, Luke, Cangiano, & Peterson, 1998). Although these studies were not designed specifically to investigate resilience, those factors found to be associated with good rather than poor adjustment could be explored for their potential as protective factors.

Overview of the Methodology

Participants. In the first study (Hughes & Luke, 1998), participants consisted of 58 mother–child pairs: Mothers were residing in a shelter for battered women, and their oldest child was between the ages of 4 and 12 years. The majority of the families were European American (85%); the rest of the families were primarily African American. In the second study (Hughes et al., 1998), there were 59 mother–child pairs, with the children's ages again ranging from 4 to 12 years. These families were predominantly African American (85%), with the rest European American.

Variables. For both studies, the variables investigated were made up of four conceptually distinct types of factors. The first group of variables consisted of family demographics; the second group of factors was composed of violence variables. Measures of the children's psychological functioning were included in the third group of factors. The mothers reported on externalizing-type behavior problems, and the internalizing-type distress (anxiety, depression) was assessed through child report. Children also reported on their self-esteem. The fourth group of variables for the first study consisted of the measures of the mother's psychological functioning. In the second study, the fourth and fifth categories of variables were also obtained from the women. Each mother's psychological functioning was assessed through measures of depression, anxiety, and a symptom checklist. Parenting indicators was the new category added for the second study; these included instruments measuring parenting stress and parenting behaviors.

Cluster Analysis. Cluster analysis is especially useful for clinical samples and service provisions because it allows one to focus on individuals and the diversity within larger groups (Aldenderfer & Blashfield, 1984). Mean scores and group averages often obscure important individual differences in adjustment or in other characteristics. Cluster analysis is frequently used to identify subgroups within larger samples on the basis of differences and similarities among those subgroups and allows researchers to investigate the heterogeneity among participants (Borgen & Barnett, 1987).

Conceptually, cluster analysis helps to identify patterns or profiles based on scores of individual participants on particular measures. With this method, it is possible to investigate more than one score at a time, thereby obtaining profiles of individuals (Rapkin & Luke, 1993). For example, one child might be high on one measure, medium on another, and low on a third, with other children showing diverse combinations of scores. The cluster analysis procedure basically groups children together on the basis of similarities and differences in the profile of scores. Thus, subgroups or clusters are identified, wherein there are differences between the clusters formed and similarities within the clusters. This statistical procedure follows certain empirical rules for putting children into subgroups; one can then examine the profile patterns to describe the children's adjustment in each cluster.

For both studies, three types of child adjustment variables were selected from the third group of factors mentioned above to conduct the cluster analysis: (a) externalizing-type behavior problems, (b) anxiety, and (c) self-esteem. Other variables in the three groups of factors listed above were used to describe and validate the clusters obtained.

Resiliency Results of the First Study

On the basis of the scree plot, dendogram, and overall interpretability, a five-cluster solution for the cluster analysis was chosen as the best fit for the data in both studies, with five clearly different patterns of distress and problems evident. In the first study, a subgroup of children in the first cluster identified those who were not experiencing many difficulties. A second subgroup of children emerged who reported being only very mildly distressed.

The last three clusters contained children for whom either the child or the mother indicated emotional or behavioral problems for the child.

The five-cluster solution for the first study showed that the children in the first cluster (one that could be labeled Hanging in There), had an average number of problems, some mild anxiety symptoms, and an average level of self-esteem. This was the largest cluster, containing approximately 36% of the children. Children in the second largest cluster (named Doing Well) had few behavior problems, experienced no anxiety, and had rather high levels of self-esteem—hence the name chosen for this group. This group contained 26% of the children, and together these first two groups made up 62% of the sample. These findings suggest that some children in shelters may not experience substantial amounts of distress and might, therefore, be considered resilient or at least "survivors" of traumatic exposure to domestic violence.

Additional characteristics other than the clustering variables that described and differentiated the two resilient clusters (i.e., Hanging in There and Doing Well) from the distressed clusters included the mothers' scores on depressive symptoms and their verbal aggressiveness. Mothers in these two survivor or resiliency clusters had anxiety and depression scores at the mild-to-moderate level and were among the three lowest clusters on verbal aggressiveness toward their male partners. Regarding environmental factors, although duration of the mothers' abuse did not make a substantial difference in distinguishing among clusters, there was a trend toward an association of length of abuse with poor functioning when the abuse had taken place over the course of a child's lifetime.

Overall, the children in this first study who were considered to be resilient had been exposed to a relatively less stressful family situation than children in the other clusters, although it should be noted that this is in the context of chronic physical abuse of their mothers. The factors that seemed to contribute to the resilience of the children included mothers who did not engage in substantial verbal abuse of their partners and mothers who were less depressed and less anxious than mothers in the other clusters. (It should be also noted that the partners' mental health was not assessed here.) Thus, the particular characteristics of the violent situation and of the mothers' mental health both seemed to be associated with resilience outcomes for the child.

Resiliency Results of the Second Study

For the second study, child psychological adjustment again was selected for clustering. Four scores were used in this cluster analysis, similar to the first one: externalizing and internalizing scores from the mothers' reports of their children, plus anxiety and self-esteem scores from the children. Other variables were used to describe similarities and differences among the clusters that emerged. The same clustering method and distance measure were used in this study as in the previous one.

Results indicate that as noted above, a five-cluster solution fit the data, with one cluster of children clearly having fewer problems (32%), three clusters of children with evident difficulties (47%), and one cluster (20%) that might be managing, although that is open to debate (see Hughes, Etzel, & Luke, 2001). Regarding the clearly resilient children, the Doing Well children (32%) in general showed few problems. They reported having low levels of anxiety, few depressive symptoms, and moderately high self-esteem. In addition, they were not seen by their mothers to have internalizing or externalizing types of problems.

In terms of parenting stress and behaviors and a violent environment, several features were associated with good adjustment and distinguished significantly among the clusters. Mothers of the resilient children indicated that they felt they were able to continue to parent in a reasonable fashion, despite the violence they endured. In contrast, women in the other four clusters indicated more parenting difficulties and had scores on both of the parenting subscales at the 80th percentile and higher.

Moreover, the resilient children's environment seemed to contain less stressful and fewer stressful interactions, with the lowest psychological maltreatment scores among all the clusters, both to the child (from either the mother or father figure) and between the adults. Thus, once again, several factors seem to contribute to outcomes associated with resilience for these children. In this sample, attributes of parenting and the level of psychological abuse in the family appear to distinguish the emotional climate that the resilient children experienced.

Discussion of Studies

Resilience on the part of some European American children in shelters was associated with their mothers' mental health. Specifically, these resilient children's mothers did not experience moderate or severe depressive symptoms. For the African American children, more positive functioning was associated with mothers who, even if they were quite distressed, had low levels of expression of hostile feelings toward their children and were able to maintain their competent parenting. Essentially, African American children were more likely to be in the resilient cluster if their mother felt that they were not difficult to parent (e.g., did not make a lot of demands).

In addition, characteristics of the abusive family environment associated with resilience and better adjustment of children included relatively low levels of verbal and psychological maltreatment between the mothers and their partners as well as low levels of psychological maltreatment of the children from both parenting figures. For both European American and African American children, not being exposed to verbal or psychological maltreatment within the family appeared to be a crucial component in their resilience. Clearly, children's adjustment is better when there is less stress, when the emotional climate is less negative, and when parenting is competent.

These results may provide a start toward elucidating factors that contribute to resilience in children of battered women. Yet much additional research needs to be conducted. For example, little is known regarding the quality of parenting that the children in these families receive. To obtain a comprehensive picture regarding risk and protective factors, researchers need to initiate more in-depth studies of the influence of the men in these families, including male parental competence, and to investigate in more detail the quality of the parenting provided by the women.

Issues in the Assessment of Resilience

Several questions are raised when one applies concepts and knowledge regarding resilience to children who have been exposed to domestic violence. Basically, they are all related to definitional issues.

Is Resilience Developmentally and Culturally Defined?

In the study of resilience, the aspects of functioning considered the most salient are likely to be age related and life-span dependent. Masten and Coatsworth (1998) listed the four broad domains of conduct, academic achievement, social relationships, and self as important to consider at each stage of development; they also pointed out that competence includes developmentally appropriate tasks at each stage. Thus, for infants, an evaluation of competence early in development would include attachment systems and self-regulation. Therefore, very young children exposed to domestic violence may respond with disturbances in attachment, whereas those children in the same circumstances who maintain secure attachments may be considered resilient. The resilient coping of preschool-age children exposed to violence has been described in terms of the regulation of emotion and of social interaction with siblings, peers, and caretakers (Graham-Bermann & Follett, 2000). For school-age children, the four domains of social competence, academic achievement, socially appropriate conduct, and emotional regulation would be salient areas for defining competence and resilience. School-age children who are able to do well academically and who have good friendships may be seen as resilient. For teenagers, resilience may be developmentally defined in terms of showing positive social, academic, and work adjustment in the face of severe domestic violence and not engaging in specific high-risk activities (e.g., drinking, abuse in dating relationships).

Similarly, there are also issues related to development over the life course. According to Masten and Coatsworth (1998), at various points in children's and adolescents' lives, there are likely to be different vulnerability and protective factors operating. These need to be specified more clearly for children of battered women, in particular. For example, one can ask whether social relationships will function in adolescence in the same protective manner for girls who have been exposed to domestic violence as they seem to for girls who have not been exposed to such family violence.

Cultural factors are also clearly important to consider. Cohler, Stott, and Musick (1995) and Masten and Coatsworth (1998) have discussed the importance of considering context when establishing whether a child is thought to have a positive outcome; this is especially true if the child's cultural background differs from the mainstream. Any sort of judgment regarding what would be considered competent or positive behavior and functioning must be made within the context of the children's culture. It is important to keep in mind, for example, when assessing resilience in the four broad domains of social functioning, academic achievement, socially appropriate conduct, and emotional regulation that children from Asian backgrounds are considered more socially reticent and more emotionally restrained than children from Latino families (Paniagua, 1998).

Is Resilience General or Domain Specific?

Some researchers have focused on the lack of obvious symptoms of psychopathology as an index of resilience (Anthony & Kohler, 1987). However, it may be helpful to think of resilience in relation to particular areas of functioning rather than a general lack of obvious symptoms. Related to this, one might ask whether resilience is domain specific and, if so, what domains should be studied? Initially, some researchers argued that social competence should be the primary index of resiliency (Garmezy, Masten, & Tellegen, 1984). More recently, as noted above, Masten and Coatsworth (1998) included several other broad domains (viz., conduct, academic achievement plus the self) and manifested appropriately for each developmental stage.

Thus, when it comes to exposure to domestic violence, children who are able to maintain relationships with friends and peers and who do not develop social interaction styles similar to those they have observed at home (e.g., use of violence, emotional lability, abuse of power) may be considered socially resilient. Other areas of competence and resilience that could be considered features of successful adaptation specific to children in families with domestic violence could include keeping good grades despite a chaotic home situation, being able to maintain a job after school, or being successful in sports.

How Much Resilience Is Enough?

Two questions can be asked in this context: To what extent should a characteristic be present to count as resilience? and Does a child need to be symptom or problem free in all domains mentioned above to be considered truly resilient ? If a child is symptom free (i.e., not in the clinical range of psychological or emotional problems) but not especially happy, would that child be thought of as resilient? Would the child need to be happy or have high self-esteem to be considered to have a positive outcome under adversity? Even if a child is problem free in three of the four developmentally appropriate areas, is that enough? Are one or two of the domains more important for adjustment and therefore more crucial to being considered resilient?

According to Masten and Coatsworth's (1998) overview, there are some suggestions that resilient children may feel distress, and they think it important to examine whether children pay a price psychologically for achieving competence under adversity. The authors distinguished this area as important for research: Specifically, one should ask, What are the long-term consequences of adversity for children who are exposed to domestic violence? Under what circumstances might there be long-term consequences, even if the child appears competent in the short run?

However, it is possible that there are short-term and long-term costs of being resilient. Cohler et al. (1995) pointed out that personal costs in different areas may accompany enhanced resilience in response to adversity. They gave the example of someone whose career might be a success but who might have difficulties establishing and maintaining close interpersonal relationships. Other features of this personal cost might indicate that the child or adolescent's adaptiveness is actually an overcompensation rather than resiliency because the latter may be harder to detect. These examples could include avoidance of emotions, fewer friends, and few extracurricular activities. Furthermore, the types of compensating mechanisms that maintain short-term functioning may not be the kinds of variables typically studied (e.g., the apparently resilient child may develop physical symptoms and illnesses that would not be captured under the social competence and psychopathology umbrella).

How Long Is Long Enough?

In this same vein, it is currently not clear that children who do well initially in the face of adversity will be able to maintain their high levels of functioning in the future. To that end, researchers need to study resilience over the life course. In studying resiliency over time, one can ask whether there are different patterns of resilience (Graham-Bermann, 1998). For example, there may be early adapters who never go on to develop symptoms of psychopathology or deficits in social competence as compared with those children who do well initially, do not exhibit problems in the immediate aftermath of distress, but may develop significant symptoms later on. Furthermore, some children who initially express their difficulties may then get their needs met or find ways to cope with the stress and show reduced psychopathology over time.

To give but one example, a 6-year-old child interviewed in a shelter for battered women said that she did not plan to get married when she grew up because she did not think she would be able to pick the right husband. The child may appear to be functioning adequately currently but may be missing out on developmental activities that are critical to later success in selecting a partner. The long-term personal costs of such strategies may be high. A similar pattern has been noted in some long-term studies of children (especially girls) who have experienced the divorce of their parents (Hetherington et al., 1998).

What Is Needed in Future Studies of Children and Domestic Violence

The following are some suggestions regarding areas where obtaining additional information would be especially productive. These include expanding the range of outcome variables now used in studying children exposed to domestic violence, using more diverse samples, trying new methodologies to capture and to better describe the variability within groups of children, looking for a range of risk and protective elements in the child's life, and using more comprehensive models to test theories.

Outcomes

In terms of outcomes, measures of strength and resilience specific to the populations of children who experience family violence need to be developed and included in studies. Once definitions of resilience are clearer, it will be easier to assess the construct. Scales to measure resilience and protective factors need to be designed that are developmentally and culturally appropriate, taking into account expectations for competence, broadly defined, at each stage of a child's life. These outcome measures would include how children are actually doing on their developmental tasks at each appropriate stage and should take into account the appropriate expectations given the child's cultural background. Optimally, researchers need measurement methods or devices that would be usable across the child's life span.

Investigating multiple domains to more fruitfully assess competence, well-being, and lack of psychopathology would also be helpful. In addition to the areas of social competence and appropriate conduct that are typically studied, researchers need more evidence gathered regarding academic achievement and self-regulation. For example, investigators could adopt more complex criteria for resilience that would encompass evidence that the child handles emotions well and appropriately, is achieving successfully in school, is not adopting negative patterns of relating, is able to talk about problems, engages in extracurricular activities, and has and maintains high-quality friendships.

Diversity in Samples

Studies that do not include shelter populations are needed because of the many potential confounds that exist when evaluating outcomes for children who have had both a shelter move and exposure to domestic violence (Fantuzzo et al., 1991). In addition, the socioeconomic status of families within shelters is likely to be low; therefore, investigations of families who have more resources would shed light on the functioning of family members not also dealing with the impact of poverty. Samples of families that are non-European American would also be helpful for understanding resilience within a cultural context.

Diversity in Methodologies

In a related vein, there is a need to take advantage of methodologies tied to ethnography, especially in the investigation of families from out of the mainstream context. Cohler et al. (1995) emphasized that in their view, the next stage in the study of culture and resilience is to use qualitative methodologies and to take advantage of the emerging narrative perspectives regarding culture. Such methods allow understudied groups a voice in investigations, one that is not biased by the assumptions of researchers imposing structure on oppressed groups based on mainstream culture. For example, grounded theory (Strauss & Corbin, 1990) has been used to obtain particular and individualized explanations of people and settings based on their unique circumstances. Combining the benefits of both quantitative and qualitative approaches would allow researchers to gather information from women and children in their own words from their unique perspectives and, at the same time, develop measures that are targeted and standardized for this population.

Full Consideration of Risk Factors

Masten and Coatsworth (1995) mentioned that simply having a better outcome because one was exposed to fewer hazards or challenges is, in their opinion, usually not considered resilience. They pointed out that it is currently not clear whether good outcomes are the result of less exposure to hazards or of lower vulnerability rather than of the specific characteristics of an individual or the operation of protective processes that buffer the individual in some way. They stated that the number of risk factors appears to be more important for prediction than the precise nature of any one variable. Therefore, there is a need to study the degree to which this is true and why. Along those same lines, a more comprehensive assessment of what Masten and Coatsworth (1998) called differential net risk among members of the same group would be helpful, keeping track of the degree of exposure to hazards and taking into account the number of risk and protective factors.

A full accounting of risk factors in studies should include individual and relationship factors as well as those beyond the immediate violence events (e.g., poverty, child abuse, child sexual abuse, sibling violence, community violence, exposure to other traumatic events). Moreover, there are other stresses specifically related to domestic violence, such as having the police come to the home, having a parent arrested, having a mother stalked, moving into a shelter, or changing schools, that would be helpful if included in models.

Full Consideration of Protective Factors

Several features of the child and the child's context should be included in the study of protective factors that can moderate the negative effects of family violence on the child (e.g., measurement of the sources of support, quality of sibling and peer relationships, involvement in school or sports activities, mentors and role models outside the family). In addition, studies show that what differentiates resilient children from high-risk children in other populations includes social skills and high intelligence (Luthar & Zigler, 1991). It would be helpful to see if these variables also differentiated children of battered women.

Both social and cognitive problems have been identified as common difficulties noted in children exposed to domestic violence (Hughes & Graham-Bermann, 1998; Margolin, 1998). However, this illustrates the difficulty in defining and distinguishing protective factors from factors considered as outcomes of development. For example, Rossman et al. (1998) found that children of battered women were more likely to engage in the cognitive process of "leveling" as a result of the violence to which they were exposed; this in turn led to decreased academic success. Or in regard to social skills, there may be a crucial age by which one would need to have acquired good social skills for them to serve as a protective factor. These hypotheses must still be tested.

Individual Differences

Resilience may be based on individual characteristics over the life span. Factors such as age, gender, and their interaction might provide protection at one point in life but not at another (Cohler et al., 1995). As an example, Cohler et al. noted that vulnerability and risk reverses at adolescence: Boys are especially at risk for difficulties early in life because of neurodevelopmental factors; at adolescence, this changes, with girls more likely to have psychological problems due to increasing strain and burden confronting women in society.

In addition, Werner (1990) suggested that among boys, innate individual differences may be the most important determinant of resilience, whereas among girls, the impact of early life within the family may be the primary factor determining resilience. Moreover, Werner and Smith (1992) noted that events during the school-age period seemed to have the most substantial impact on women, especially family disputation and discord, whereas for boys, their later adjustment as adults was more tied to their physiological and physical status as infants and children. Similarly, Luthar, Doernberger, and Zigler (1993) suggested a need to consider issues of risk, vulnerability, and resilience separately for boys and girls of different ages and over different periods in their lives.

Investigation of Causal Factors

In every area, there is the need for more comprehensive, longitudinal studies focused on investigations of risk and resilience mechanisms to answer questions of causation. Basically, little is known about the processes underlying resilience. Yet understanding these causal processes is essential for creating and implementing interventions that actually foster resilience and lead to better functioning. For example, it is currently not clear whether children who feel more self-efficacious can cope better with adversity, thus reflecting a process leading to a positive outcome.

Comprehensive Models

Recently, questions have been raised about the utility of global approaches to resilience. Masten and Coatsworth (1998) noted that researchers are beginning to take a closer look at the many influences on resilience and apply more fine-grained strategies, an approach that they feel is more likely to lead to identifying risk and protective processes underlying resilience in specific situations. Thus, it is apparent that there is a need to build and test models that include both risk and protective factors with all their intricacies in accounting for resiliency in children.

Clearly, researchers need to be able to appreciate the complexities of this area and plan investigations that are both comprehensive and detailed. Children typically have multiple risk factors and multiple resources contributing to their lives; therefore, cumulative protection efforts are needed to address cumulative risk. Several authors have pointed out that prevention and intervention efforts will be more effective if they target multiple risks for amelioration and boost multiple protection factors. However, this would be a huge undertaking and would require commitments of expertise, time, and money. Research in this area will not move forward unless there is adequate funding for these types of investigations.

Implications for Intervention and Policy

Strategies for intervention fruitful to consider are those Masten and Coatsworth (1998) considered to be risk focused, resource focused, and process focused.

Risk-Focused Strategies

In this approach, the task is to prevent or eliminate risk factors. For example, poverty is a risk factor, as is being a single mother without a high school education; both can be prevented. Growing up in a home where there is family violence is also a clear risk factor, and with appropriate efforts, this experience can also be eliminated. These risk-focused types of approaches would be amenable to social and educational interventions as well as to prevention efforts. Public policy efforts would need to be made on a grand scale to eliminate some of these primary risk factors. However, according to Luthar (1993), it is not entirely clear whether the focus should be on factors that provide enhanced vulnerability to adversity, such as living in poverty or conflict, or on factors that reduce the impact of adversity or provide enhanced coping at times of increased vulnerability. This would be important for a research agenda and needs to be attended to through public policy efforts as well.

Resource-Focused Strategies

There are several ways to approach these resource-focused strategies. For example, resources could be directed toward preventing stressors, such as by establishing mandatory arrest and treatment for batterers or by implementing a communication skills program that prevents violence among teenage couples. If particular stressors have already taken place, reducing their impact would be a focus. One could provide support to children who have experienced a trauma, such as is provided by children's groups in shelters for battered women. In addition, efforts could be made to add resources to a child's life or improve the child's access to resources. For example, children could be provided with scholarships to local girls' or boys' clubs for afterschool activities. Resources should focus on adaptation systems that seem to be most closely tied to competence, such as attachment, self-efficacy, and self-regulation. In addition, these efforts would need to be started early to be the most effective. Thus, children of battered women need to be identified and helped early in the course of their exposure.

Process-Focused Strategies

Process-focused strategies to promote resilience would enhance efforts to improve parent–child relationships and foster mentoring relationships of children with supportive adults, such as teachers or coaches. Parenting programs could be available to assist parents with dealing both with normal bumps in the road when their children are negotiating their developmental tasks and with issues related to violence. Also programs that build self-efficacy through skill and mastery experiences or assist a child in developing her or his talents, as well as programs to help open doors to new opportunities, would be helpful.

Public Policy Strategies That Enhance Protective Factors

Risk-focused, resource-focused, and process-focused strategies all lend themselves to implementation through public policy efforts. Public policies need to be considered on individual, family, and social levels. Policymakers need to focus on enhancing the development of individual protective qualities, such as good intellectual functioning; self-efficacy, self-confidence, and high self-esteem; faith; and an appealing, sociable, easy-going disposition. At this level, improving the quality of life for individual children would be the focus. The protective characteristics that need to be enhanced at the family level include a close relationship with a caring parent figure; authoritative parenting (e.g., warmth, structure, high expectations); socioeconomic advantages; and connection to extended, supportive family networks. Public policy efforts are needed to help build the supports that families must have to function optimally and to promote the secure parent–child bond and positive emotional climate that foster physical and emotional growth.

At the extrafamilial contextual level, the child's bonds to prosocial adults outside the family, connections to prosocial organizations, and effective schools would help in promoting resilience. Thus, the focus of public policy efforts would be to implement policies that enhance the probability that schools will be positive and empowering, that organizations will be available for children to be a part of, and that caring adults will have time in their lives to give to others.

CONCLUSION

The concept of resilience could be useful for understanding the functioning of children who have experienced family violence. A focus on the seemingly resilient child and on those children who show significant levels of difficulties can provide a more complete picture of the heterogeneity in adjustment among these children. When researchers have a better idea of which factors contribute to children's functioning as risk factors and which serve as protective factors, appropriate actions can be taken to intervene with the former and to enhance the latter.

Much work remains to be done. Based on the foregoing discussion, it appears that several general questions related to the definitions of resilience, risk, vulnerability, and protective factors need to be answered. Then, those concepts can be applied more clearly to children of battered women. Little is known specifically about resilience in children exposed to domestic violence, although the few studies to date that were reviewed here show findings consistent with the results from other child populations. Recommendations for future studies include the use of both quantitative and qualitative approaches. Only when public policies are established to support research in this area can researchers provide for intervention based on risk-focused, resource-focused, and process-focused strategies.

REFERENCES

Aldenderfer, M. S., & Blashfield, R. K. (1984). *Cluster analysis*. Beverly Hills, CA: Sage.

American Association for Protecting Children. (1989). *Highlights of official child neglect and abuse reporting, 1987*. Denver, CO: American Humane Association.

Ammerman, R. T. (1990). Predisposing child factors. In R. T. Ammerman & M. Hersen (Eds.), *Children at risk* (pp. 199–224). New York: Plenum Press.

Ammerman, R. T., Van Hasselt, V. B., Hersen, M., McGonigle, J. J., & Lubetsky, M. J. (1989). Abuse and neglect in psychiatrically hospitalized multihandicapped children. *Child Abuse & Neglect, 13*, 335–343.

Anthony, E. J., & Kohler, B. J. (1987). *The invulnerable child*. New York: Guilford Press.

Azar, S. T., Barnes, K. T., & Twentyman, C. T. (1988). Developmental outcomes in abused children: Consequences of parental abuse or a more general breakdown in caregiver behavior? *Behavior Therapist, 11*, 27–32.

Barnett, O. W., Miller-Perrin, C. L., & Perrin, R. D. (1997). *Family violence across the lifespan: An introduction*. Thousand Oaks, CA: Sage.

Bauer, W. D., & Twentyman, C. T. (1985). Abusing, neglectful, and comparison mothers' responses to child-related and non-child-related stressors. *Journal of Consulting and Clinical Psychology, 53*, 335–343.

Belsky, J. (1980). Child maltreatment. *American Psychologist, 35*, 320–335.

Borgen, F. H., & Barnett, D. C. (1987). Applying cluster analysis in counseling psychology research: Quantitative foundations of counseling psychology research [Special issue]. *Journal of Counseling Psychology, 34*, 456–468.

Bousha, D. M., & Twentyman, C. T. (1984). Mother–child interactional style in abuse, neglect, and control groups: Naturalistic observations in the home. *Journal of Abnormal Psychology, 93,* 106–114.

Brunnquell, D., Crichton, L., & Egeland, B. (1981). Maternal personality and attitude in disturbances of child rearing. *American Journal of Orthopsychiatry, 51,* 680–691.

Cicchetti, D., & Lynch, M. (1993). Toward an ecological/transactional model of community violence and child maltreatment. *Psychiatry, 56,* 96–118.

Cohler, B. J., Stott, F. M., & Musick, J. S. (1995). Adversity, vulnerability, and resilience: Cultural and developmental perspectives. In D. Cicchetti & D. Cohen (Eds.), *Developmental psychopathology: Vol. 1. Theory and methods* (pp. 753–800). New York: Wiley.

Elder, G. H. (1974). *Children of the Great Depression.* Chicago: University of Chicago Press.

Fantuzzo, J., & Boruch, R. (1997). Children exposed to family violence: Towards better and more useful knowing. In *Child abuse and neglect interventions strategic planning.* Washington, DC: U.S. Department of Justice, National Institute of Justice. Retrieved from the World Wide Web: http://www.doj.gov

Fantuzzo, J., DePaola, L. M., Lambert, L., Martino, T., Anderson, G., & Sutton, S. (1991). The effects of interparental violence on the psychological adjustment and competencies of young children. *Journal of Consulting and Clinical Psychology, 59,* 258–265.

Festinger, T. (1983). *No one ever asked us.* New York: Columbia University Press.

Folman, R. (1995). *Resilience and vulnerability among abused and neglected children in foster care.* Doctoral dissertation, University of Michigan, Ann Arbor.

Friedrich, W. N., & Boriskin, J. A. (1976). The role of the child in abuse: A review of the literature. *American Journal of Orthopsychiatry, 46,* 580–590.

Garmezy, N. (1983). Stressors of childhood. In N. Garmezy & M. Rutter (Eds.), *Stress, coping, and development* (pp. 43–84). New York: McGraw-Hill.

Garmezy, N. (1985). Stress-resistant children: The search for protective factors. *Journal of Child Psychology and Psychiatry Book Supplement, 4,* 213–233.

Garmezy, N. (1991). Resilience in children's adaptation to negative events and stressed environments. *Pediatric Annals, 20,* 459–466.

Garmezy, N., Masten, A. S., & Tellegen, A. (1984). The study of stress and competence in children: A building block for developmental psychopathology. *Child Development, 55,* 97–111.

Gelles, R. J., & Cornell, C. P. (1990). *Intimate violence in families.* Newbury Park, CA: Sage.

Graham-Bermann, S. A. (1998). The impact of woman abuse on children's social development. In G. W. Holden, R. Geffner, & E. N. Jouriles (Eds.), *Children exposed to marital violence: Theory, research, and applied issues* (pp. 21–54). Washington, DC: American Psychological Association.

Graham-Bermann, S. A., & Follett, C. A. (2000). *Fostering resilience in young children exposed to family violence: The Preschool Kids' Club*. Ann Arbor: University of Michigan, Department of Psychology.

Graham-Bermann, S. A., & Levendosky, A. A. (1998). Traumatic stress symptoms in children of battered women. *Journal of Interpersonal Violence, 14*, 111–128.

Graham-Bermann, S. A., Levendosky, A. A., Porterfield, K., & Okun, A. (2000). *Children exposed to family violence: An ecological model of the role of stress and social relationships on children's adjustment*. Manuscript under review, University of Michigan, Ann Arbor.

Hetherington, M. E., Bridges, M., & Insabella, G. (1998). What matters? What does not? Five perspectives on the association between marital transitions and child adjustment. *American Psychologist, 53*, 167–184.

Holden, G. W., Stein, J. D., Ritchie, K. L., Harris, S. D., & Jouriles, E. N. (1998). Parenting behaviors and beliefs of battered women. In G. W. Holden, R. Geffner, & E. N. Jouriles (Eds.), *Children exposed to marital violence: Theory, research, and applied issues* (pp. 289–334). Washington, DC: American Psychological Association.

Hughes, H. M. (1988). Psychological and behavioral correlates of family violence in child witnesses and victims. *American Journal of Orthopsychiatry, 58*, 77–90.

Hughes, H. M. (1997). Research concerning children of battered women: Clinical implications. In R. Geffner, S. B. Sorenson, & P. K. Lundberg-Love (Eds.), *Violence and sexual abuse at home: Current issues, interventions, and research in spousal battering and child maltreatment* (pp. 225–244). Binghamton, NY: Haworth.

Hughes, H. M., Etzel, J. C., & Luke, D. A. (2001). *Heterogeneity in psychological functioning among African-American children of battered women*. Paper submitted for presentation, St. Louis University, St. Louis, MO.

Hughes, H. M., & Graham-Bermann, S. A. (1998). Children of battered women: Impact of emotional abuse on development and adjustment. *Journal of Emotional Abuse, 1*, 23–50.

Hughes, H. M., & Luke, D. A. (1998). Heterogeneity in adjustment among children of battered women. In G. W. Holden, R. Geffner, & E. N. Jouriles (Eds.), *Children exposed to family violence: Theory, research, and applied issues* (pp. 185–221). Washington, DC: American Psychological Association.

Hughes, H. M., Luke, D. A., Cangiano, C., & Peterson, M. (1998, October). *Clinical implications of heterogeneity in adjustment among children of battered women*. Paper presented at the fourth annual Conference on Children Exposed to Family Violence. San Diego, CA: Family Violence and Sexual Abuse Institute.

Hughes, H. M., Parkinson, D. L., & Vargo, M. C. (1989). Witnessing and experiencing family violence: A double whammy? *Journal of Family Violence, 4*, 197–209.

Jaffe, P., Wolfe, D., & Wilson, S. (1990). *Children of battered women*. Newbury Park, CA: Sage.

Kolbo, J. R., Blakely, E. H., & Engelman, E. (1996). Children who witness domestic violence: A review of the empirical literature. *Journal of Interpersonal Violence*, *11*, 282–292.

Luthar, S. (1993). Annotation: Methodological and conceptual issues in research on childhood resilience. *Journal of Child Psychology and Psychiatry and Allied Disciplines*, *34*, 441–453.

Luthar, S., Doernberger, C., & Zigler, E. (1993). Resilience is not a unidimensional construct: Insights from a prospective study of inner-city adolescents. Milestones in the development of resilience [Special issue]. *Developmental Psychopathology*, *5*, 703–717.

Luthar, S., & Zigler, E. (1991). Vulnerability and competence: A review of research on resilience in childhood. *American Journal of Orthopsychiatry*, *61*, 6–22.

Margolin, G. (1998). Effects of domestic violence on children. In P. K. Trickett & C. J. Schellenbach (Eds.), *Violence against children in the family and in the community* (pp. 57–102). Washington, DC: American Psychological Association.

Mash, E. J., Johnston, C., & Kovitz, K. (1983). A comparison of the mother–child interactions of physically abused and non-abused children during play and task situations. *Journal of Clinical Child Psychology*, *12*, 337–346.

Masten, A. S., Best, K., & Garmezy, N. (1990). Resilience and development: Contributions from the study of children who overcome adversity. *Development and Psychopathology*, *2*, 425–444.

Masten, A. S., & Coatsworth, D. (1995). Competence, resilience and psychopathology. In D. Cicchetti & D. Cohen (Eds.), *Developmental psychopathology: Vol. 1. Theory and methods* (pp. 715–752). New York: Wiley.

Masten, A. S., & Coatsworth, D. (1998). The development of competence in favorable and unfavorable environments. *American Psychologist*, *53*, 205–220.

Masten, A. S., Miliotis, D. M., Graham-Bermann, S. A., & Neeman, J. (1993). Children in homeless families: Risks to mental health. *Journal of Consulting and Clinical Psychology*, *61*, 335–343.

Murphy, L. B., & Moriarty, A. (1976). *Vulnerability, coping and growth: From infancy to adolescence*. New Haven, CT: Yale University Press.

Newberger, C. M. (1980). The cognitive structure of parenthood: Design a descriptive measure. *New Directions in Child Development*, *7*, 45–67.

Newberger, C. M., & Cook, S. J. (1983). Parental awareness and child abuse: A cognitive–developmental analysis of urban and rural samples. *American Journal of Orthopsychiatry*, *53*, 512–524.

Paniagua, F. A. (1998). *Assessing and treating culturally diverse clients* (2nd ed.). Thousand Oaks, CA: Sage.

Pianta, R., Egeland, B., & Erickson, M. F. (1989). The antecedents of maltreatment: Results of the Mother–Child Interaction Research Project. In D. Cicchetti & V. Carlson (Eds.), *Child maltreatment: Theory and research on the causes and consequences of child abuse and neglect* (pp. 203–253). New York: Cambridge University Press.

Radke-Yarrow, M., & Sherman, T. L. (1990). Hard growing: Children who survive. In J. E. Rolf, A. S. Masten, D. Cicchetti, K. Neuchterlein, & S. Weintraub (Eds.), *Risk and protective factors in the development of psychopathology* (pp. 97–119). New York: Cambridge University Press.

Rapkin, B. D., & Luke, D. A. (1993). Cluster analysis in community research: Epistemology and practice. *American Journal of Community Psychology, 21*, 247–277.

Rosenberg, M. (1987). Children of battered women: The effects of witnessing violence on their social problem-solving abilities. *The Behavior Therapist, 4*, 85–89.

Rossman, B. B. R. (1998). Descartes's error and posttraumatic stress disorder: Cognition and emotion in children who are exposed to parental violence. In G. W. Holden, R. Geffner, & E. N. Jouriles (Eds.), *Children exposed to marital violence: Theory, research, and applied issues* (pp. 223–256). Washington, DC: American Psychological Association.

Rossman, B. B. R., Hughes, H. M., & Hanson, K. L. (1998). The victimization of school-age children. In B. B. R. Rossman & M. S. Rosenberg (Eds.), *Multiple victimization of children: Conceptual, developmental, research, and treatment issues* (pp. 87–106). New York: Haworth.

Rutter, M. (1979). Protective factors in children's responses to stress and disadvantage. In M. W. Kent & J. Rolf (Eds.), *Primary prevention of psychopathology: Vol. III. Social competence in children* (pp. 49–74). Hanover, MA: University Press of New England.

Rutter, M. (1985). Resilience in the face of adversity: Protective factors and resistance to psychiatric disorder. *British Journal of Psychiatry, 147*, 598–611.

Sameroff, A. J., & Seifer, R. (1990). Early contributions to developmental risk. In J. E. Rolf, A. S. Masten, D. Cicchetti, K. Neuchterlein, & S. Weintraub (Eds.), *Risk and protective factors in the development of psychopathology* (pp. 52–66). New York: Cambridge University Press.

Sameroff, A. J., Seifer, R., & Bartko, W. T. (1997). Environmental perspectives on adaptation during childhood and adolescence. In S. S. Luthar, J. A. Burack, D. Cicchetti, & R. J. Weisz (Eds.), *Developmental psychopathology: Perspectives on adjustment, risk, and disorder* (pp. 507–526). New York: Cambridge University Press.

Sternberg, K. J., Lamb, M. E., Greenbaum, C., Cicchetti, D., Dawud, S., Cortes, R., Krispin, O., & Lorey, F. (1993). Effects of domestic violence on children's behavior problems and depression. *Developmental Psychology, 29*, 44–52.

Straus, M. A. (1983). Ordinary violence, child abuse and wife beating: What do they have in common? In D. Finkelhor, R. J. Gelles, G. T. Hotaling, & M. A. Straus (Eds.), *The dark side of families: Current family violence research* (pp. 213–234). Beverly Hills, CA: Sage.

Strauss, A., & Corbin, J. (1990). *Basics of qualitative research: Grounded theory procedure and techniques.* London, England: Sage.

Trickett, P. K., & Kuczynski, L. (1986). Children's misbehaviors and parental discipline strategies in abusive and nonabusive families. *Developmental Psychology, 22,* 115–123.

U.S. Department of Health and Human Services. (1994). *Child Maltreatment 1992: Reports from the states to the National Center on Child Abuse and Neglect.* Washington, DC: U.S. Government Printing Office.

Werner, E. (1989). High-risk children in young adulthood: A longitudinal study from birth to 32 years. *American Journal of Orthopsychiatry, 59,* 72–81.

Werner, E. (1990). Protective factors and individual resilience. In S. Meisels & J. Shonkoff (Eds.), *Handbook of early childhood intervention* (pp. 97–116). New York: Cambridge University Press.

Werner, E., & Smith, R. (1992). *Overcoming the odds: High-risk children from birth to adulthood.* Ithaca, NY: Cornell University Press.

Wolfe, D. A. (1985). Child-abusive parents: An empirical review and analysis. *Psychological Bulletin, 97,* 462–482.

Wolfe, V. V., Gentile, C., & Wolfe, D. A. (1989). The impact of sexual abuse on children: A PTSD formulation. *Behavior Therapy, 20,* 215–228.

4

STUDYING THE CO-OCCURRENCE OF CHILD MALTREATMENT AND DOMESTIC VIOLENCE IN FAMILIES

JEFFREY L. EDLESON

Battered women fleeing violent partners often bring their children with them. Annual statistics from battered women's shelters reveal that the majority of residents in these shelters are children (Illinois Coalition Against Domestic Violence, 1996; Minnesota Department of Corrections, 1993; New Jersey Coalition for Battered Women, 1992). Reviews of historical case records also show repeatedly how trauma to children and to mothers are linked and how their well-being is interdependent (see Edleson, 1991; Gordon, 1988; and Pleck, 1987).

The growing realization that children are deeply affected by the violence committed against their mothers has raised new concerns for their welfare. Recent reviews of the research literature indicate that large numbers of children who are exposed to adult domestic violence exhibit negative developmental outcomes, such as behavioral, emotional, and cognitive problems, that are both short and long term (Edleson, 1999a; Holtzworth-Munroe, Smutzler, & Sandin, 1997; Margolin, 1998; Peled & Davis, 1995). These reviews also indicate that some children remain unaffected by exposure to violence and that intervening factors such as social support moderate negative outcomes.

Negative outcomes resulting from children's exposure to violence have generated additional concerns for children's physical safety. Two recent reviews show that in different settings and with different samples, the overlap between child maltreatment and woman battering is very great (Appel & Holden, 1998; Edleson, 1999b). The majority of more than 36 studies reviewed indicate that approximately 30–60% of children whose mothers are being abused are themselves likely to be abused.

DEVELOPMENTS IN POLICY AND PRACTICE

Policymakers and practitioners have reacted to the evident risks associated with children's exposure to woman battering in several significant ways. For example, in July 1997, Utah became the first state to enact a law that makes the commission of an adult domestic assault two or more times in the presence of a child a separate offense chargeable as a misdemeanor (Utah Criminal Code 76-5-109.1). California adopted a different approach by enhancing possible criminal sanctions for adult domestic assaults when children were present (California Penal Code 1170.7A). Similar legislation has been proposed in other states, such as Washington and Minnesota.

Beyond legislation, there are many other emerging initiatives aimed at addressing the co-occurrence of child maltreatment and woman battering. On a policy level, the National Council of Juvenile and Family Court Judges published a set of guidelines for juvenile courts, child protection agencies, and domestic violence programs to follow when working with families in which both child maltreatment and woman battering are occurring (National Council of Juvenile and Family Court Judges, 1999). This guidebook, with more than 60 recommendations for changes, aims to reshape current institutional responses to these families in a way that ensures the safety, stability, and well-being of all victims in a family.

Legislative and policy changes often occur after new models of practice have emerged. Several hundred programs for battered mothers and their children in the United States were recently identified by the National Council of Juvenile and Family Court Judges (1998). Twenty-nine of these programs were visited and documented in *Emerging Programs for Battered Mothers and Their Children*. These programs include statewide changes in child protection systems and family preservation programs, advocacy on behalf of battered mothers and their children, and specialized group programming for child witnesses in shelters and community-based programs.

RESEARCH TO INFORM POLICY AND PRACTICE

Existing research, policy, and practice on the co-occurrence of child maltreatment and woman battering raises a host of concerns that require new thinking in the design of future research studies. These include (a) improving the definitions of abuse, samples, data sources, and measures used in studies of the overlap; (b) determining the specific effects and interaction of multiple violence exposures; (c) deepening the understanding of the evolution and dynamics of co-occurring violence; and (d) evaluating the effects of emerging policies and interventions with these families.

Data on the Overlap

Existing studies of co-occurring child maltreatment and woman batter-ing have a host of methodological problems that require revision in future research. Several issues seem particularly important, including the definitions used in measuring abuse, the manner in which study samples are developed, the possible problems regarding the accuracy of data obtained from the informants, and the availability of adequate standardized measures.

Definitions of Abuse

A review of the studies reporting co-occurring violence in families (see Edleson, 1999b) reveals a spectrum of maltreatment definitions for both children and adults involved. The term *child maltreatment* is expansive and includes neglect and various forms of physical abuse, including sexual abuse. For example, the 1996 federal law that defines national intervention on this issue, the Child Abuse Prevention and Treatment Act, defines *child abuse and neglect* as

> 'any recent act or failure to act resulting in imminent risk of serious harm, death, serious physical or emotional harm, sexual abuse, or exploi-tation of a child (a person under the age of 18) by a parent or caretaker (including any employee of a residential facility or any staff person providing out-of-home care) who is responsible for the child's welfare.' Section 111, 42 U.S.C. 5106g).

The National Center for Child Abuse and Neglect (of the U.S. Department of Health and Human Services) and much of the field have divided child maltreatment into the following four categories: (a) physical abuse, (b) neglect, (c) sexual abuse, and (d) emotional abuse (psychological or verbal abuse or mental injury).

The studies reporting co-occurring violence in families often simply report the number of "abused" children; do not apparently use standardized definitions of maltreatment; and often do not even specify if the reported abuse was sexual, physical, emotional, or neglectful. For example, Stacey and Shupe (1983) reported children being "physically abused or neglected," and Dobash (1976–1977) referred to "violence" also directed at the child. In addition, several of the studies do not specify who was maltreating the child—whether it was the child's mother, father, both parents, or others.

The literature examining children's witnessing of adult domestic vio-lence also fails to differentiate and measure various forms of witnessing violence, such as seeing the violence, hearing it from another room, seeing police arresting a perpetrator, or seeing the injuries of a victim. As pointed out below, children with multiple exposures to violence are seldom distinguished in studies of child witnesses, thereby reducing the certainty by which one can conclude that child problems attributed to witnessing adult domestic violence do, in fact, result from such exposure.

The same problems exist in how adult-to-adult violence is defined in these studies. The most commonly used measure of adult domestic violence is the Conflict Tactics Scales (CTS; Straus, 1979) that gauges the occurrence of a specific set of behaviors over a set time. Although some studies do rely on the CTS or a close derivation of it, many published reports use terms such as *battering, spouse abuse,* or *adult domestic violence,* which do not offer precise understandings of the types of violence in which adults were engaged. For example, Silvern et al. (1995) referred to adults' retrospective reports of "parental abuse" and identify neither the gender of the victimized or perpetrating spouses nor the types of violence committed. In another study, Stanley and Goddard (1993) reported violence between adult caregivers.

Unfortunately, many existing studies are not specific regarding the type of child maltreatment, child witnessing, or adult domestic violence that occurred. Statistics on the overlap are often reported as an aside, and the imprecise nature of terms used most likely reflects the researchers' unfamiliarity with the way in which another field defines the terms. Future studies would greatly benefit from the use of widely accepted definitions and from improved reporting of precise findings. Such clarity would allow greater comparisons across studies and allow the field to develop a more accurate understanding of this problem.

A final issue concerns what is not included in some of these definitions. Although child maltreatment definitions include the results of such behavior, definitions and measures of adult domestic violence often do not include the effects of such events. For example, the original CTS was widely criticized for operationalizing adult domestic violence as a series of differing violent tactics without considering their outcomes (see Straus, 1990, for a discussion of these criticisms). For example, a slap or a shove was not considered severe domestic violence even if it resulted in a victim falling down stairs and being hospitalized. The newest version of the CTS, the CTS2 (Straus, Hamby, Boney-McCoy, & Sugarman, 1996), has been expanded to include physical injuries.

Study Samples

Studies of the co-occurrence of violence appear to rely on mostly clinical samples that are generated in one of two ways. One strategy is to identify evidence of woman battering in families in which known cases of child maltreatment exist. These studies most often examine archived case records of child abuse and look for information indicating that a child's mother was also being abused. For example, Hangen (1994) studied the

Massachusetts Department of Social Services' Child Protection case records for indications that an incident of adult domestic violence had occurred since the last case review. He examined computerized records for all active child protection cases in Massachusetts over a 7-month period and found that the average incidence of adult victimization as recorded on a case summary form by the social worker was 32.48% across all cases in state child protection offices. The statewide average overlap jumped to 48.20% when Hangen added into the computer analysis any cases in which the social worker also indicated a service goal of protecting the child from adult domestic violence. In another study, Stark and Flitcraft (1988) used suspected cases of child abuse and neglect at a major hospital to then search for indications of victimization in the mother's medical records. They found that 45% of these records showed some evidence of battering.

A second and more frequent strategy is to look for evidence of child maltreatment in the families in which violence against mothers is known to exist. The percentages of overlap reported in existing studies most often includes only battered women with children present in the home, not all battered women in a particular sample. Some of these studies draw their data from interviews of women residing in battered women's shelters; others advertised in the media to recruit families; and still others located battered women who were using other social services. For example, Bowker, Arbitell, and McFerron (1988) advertised in a national magazine, developed a national sample of 1,000 battered women—775 of which with children in the home—and found that 70% of the wife abusers were also reported to maltreat their children.

The approaches to sample development are numerous in the studies so far reported and probably account for much of the variation in results between studies, making it difficult to draw comparative conclusions. These samples also present several problems. Samples drawn from existing child protection or hospital case records likely represent only those most extreme cases of child maltreatment that are reported, investigated, and recorded by county or state child protection agencies or hospital personnel. Similarly, women seeking shelter are only one segment of the population of battered women and may represent a group of women that lack sufficient alternative safety resources and thus turn to a shelter for support.

The literature on problems associated with children's exposure to adult domestic violence suffers from the same drawbacks. Most children in the studies were current residents in battered women's shelters. Not only have shelter resident children probably witnessed a recent violent event, but they may also have been removed from the familiar surroundings of their homes, neighborhoods, and often schools. The number and types of problems observed among these children may be at their peak during the study period and not representative of children exposed to domestic violence.

Expanded attempts to capture information from more representative samples should be undertaken. Community-based samples that include families not yet involved with social and health services would improve the ability to draw stronger conclusions about the true prevalence of this overlap.

Sources of Information

Several issues arise when considering the sources of information used in studies of the co-occurrence. These issues revolve around the use of single sources of information, such as archival records, self-reported information, or retrospective recall of events and the limitations of each.

As stated earlier, studies relying on archival case data, such as those examining hospital or child protection records, depend on the motivation and ability of staff members both to accurately screen for child maltreatment and woman battering and to consistently document their findings in agency records. My experience in using existing county child protection records revealed many cases in which significant amounts of information were missing (Beeman, Hagemeister, & Edleson, in press). How missing information biased the outcomes of existing studies is unknown. It is likely, however, that incidents appearing in formal records represent only a fraction of all incidents.

Studies relying only on client self-reports present a different problem. It is known from other studies, for example, that men and women differ in their level of reporting violence (see Edleson & Brygger, 1986; and Szinovacz, 1983) and that children report different views than do their mothers or fathers on how witnessing violence affects them (see Sternberg & Dawud-Noursi, 1998). Who reports information and when are likely to affect the findings of a particular study. In addition, self-reports by battered women or children in a shelter or using another social service are likely to give a different picture of overlapping violence and maltreatment than are archival records such as child protection reports.

The use of self-reports given by adults recalling their childhood experiences presents even more questions about the accuracy of reports. Adult recollections of childhood experiences may be highly edited, yet retrospective reports are the source of information in some studies of co-occurring violence. For example, Rosenbaum and O'Leary (1981) asked adults in their study to recount their partners' childhood experiences. Women reported that 82% of their husbands who had witnessed one parent abuse another (no gender specified) were also physically abused as children.

Given the above information, it is clear that studies relying on only one source of information may distort the true level of overlap. One needs to consider carefully the source of information reported and likely reasons for under and overreporting of violent incidents. In some studies, mothers may be fearful of reporting child maltreatment, unknown to official sources. In other studies, county child protection agencies are unlikely to record all instances of child maltreatment because most workers do not screen for adult domestic violence. For example, Layzer, Goodson, and DeLange (1986) stated that only 20% of the battered women they interviewed were in contact with child protection agencies, yet these women reported rates of child maltreatment reaching nearly 70%.

A few studies use multiple sources including data collected from battered women, children, and archival sources. McGee, Wolfe, Yuen, Wilson, and Carnochan (1995) found that adolescents being served by a child protection agency reported less domestic violence than official sources indicated. In another study, Petchers (1995) found that 46% of the battered women interviewed reported that at least one of their children had been maltreated. Because some women reported that one but not all of their children had been maltreated, this totaled 34% of the children in the study. Interestingly, when Petchers examined county child protection records, she found that 62% of the children in her study had reports of child maltreatment. Mothers' reports and those of the county were consistent in only 41% of the cases. Mother evidently reported many incidents of child maltreatment that were not recorded in county files and vice versa (Petchers, 1995). Adult and child self-reports combined with information drawn from archival records may be the most comprehensive method of securing accurate information.

Measures

Another major problem in this domain of research is the overreliance on the Child Behavior Checklist (CBCL; Achenbach & Edelbrock, 1983) and adapted versions of the CTS. No measure currently exists for systematically gathering the types and frequencies of child exposure to adult domestic violence. Some researchers have adapted the CTS to be a report of children's witnessing of violent events, but this is inadequate for several reasons. First, such adaptations do not separate witnessing that is direct and visual from that which is indirect or auditory or which involves events in the aftermath of violence. Second, the use of an adapted CTS usually relies on an adult judge who may or may not be aware of the full exposure that a child has experienced. Finally, the frequent use of adapted CTS measures raises many questions about their psychometric properties.

The CBCL is by far the most frequently used measure in studies of children's exposure to domestic violence. This measure is a rough gauge of general functioning but was not developed to tap the unique effects of witnessing violence. Adjustment problems that may be uniquely related to exposure to adult domestic violence may have more to do with some of the following factors: the moderating effects of key present and future relationships; fear and anxiety that is situational, such as that related to a perpetrator's continued harassment or stalking of a child's mother; stress that occurs during visitation exchanges; isolation from social support networks caused by frequent moves; posttraumatic effects of witnessing violent events; and the short- and long-term impact on a child's social attachments.

Development of more sensitive measures of violence exposure is needed. So, too, is the development of measures that tap the specific difficulties that children are likely to experience as a result of witnessing adult domestic violence. A few promising measures relevant to this domain have been developed in recent years but are not widely used yet. Grych, Seid, and Fincham (1992) developed the Children's Perception of Interparental Conflict Scale; Martinez and Richters (1993) developed a Survey of Children's Exposure to Community Violence measure; Singer and Song (1995) used their Exposure to Violence Scales in several studies; Graham-Bermann (1996) reported the development of the Family Worries Scale; and McGee, Wolfe, and Wilson (1997) used a global rating measure, the Record of Maltreatment Experiences, in a recent study. The use of these and similar measures promise a more precise measurement of children's exposure to violence and its impact in future studies.

Co-Occurrence With Other Forms of Violence and Exposure

Any discussion of co-occurring violence and problems associated with children witnessing violence must acknowledge several areas of related research, including the research on (a) the co-occurrence of other childhood victimization, (b) witnessing discord in marital relationships, (c) witnessing community violence, and (d) witnessing violence conveyed over popular media. These other ways that children witness conflict and violence are closely related to witnessing domestic assaults. The results reported in these areas are often difficult to separate from exposure to woman battering, and it is therefore important to acknowledge the connection of these areas to the primary focus of this chapter.

Other Childhood Victimization

A significant problem in studies so far reported is that many researchers have failed to differentiate abused children from those who are not themselves abused but who witness domestic violence. Many studies appear to attribute child problems to the effects of witnessing violence, when they may in fact be more strongly associated with having been a direct victim of abuse. In an extreme example, Kolbo (1996) noted that all but 2 of the

60 child witnesses he studied were also targets of violence, but he still attributed reported problems to the effects of witnessing violence. As Silvern, Karyl, Waelde, et al. (1995) stated, "the relationship between reported partner and child abuse should warn that research could be flawed if it is assumed that shelter samples of children have been exposed solely to partner abuse" (p. 195)

Sorting out the unique effects of witnessing adult domestic violence also requires that other forms of family violence exposure be measured. Sibling-to-sibling, sibling-to-parent, and adult-to-elder violence all possibly co-occur in these families, and the understanding of their effects on children is minimal.

Relationship Discord

The violence that children witness in their homes is most often part of a larger context of marital or relationship discord. The research on children who are exposed to discord between adults at home is reported in a literature mostly separate from that on children and domestic violence. This body of research examines the emotional health and behavior of children who live in families characterized by marital dissatisfaction, conflict, and divorce. Some studies include but do not separate violent marital conflict from nonviolent forms. Much greater clarity is needed in the definition of "marital conflict" if the effects of violent and nonviolent conflict exposure are to be understood.

A range of child adjustment problems, similar to those reported in the violence exposure literature, were found to be associated with exposure to marital conflict. These included externalized problems such as conduct disorder, delinquency, antisocial behavior, and aggression, and internalized problems, such as depression, anxiety, and withdrawal (see Grych & Fincham, 1990).

Grych and Fincham's (1990) review of studies of the relationship between marital conflict and children's adjustment argues that marital conflict is multidimensional. They stated that conflict "may vary in frequency, intensity, content, and resolution and can be overt and covert" (p. 267). They also asserted that children's adjustment is multidimensional, with adaptiveness, emotional health, self-concept, and achievement all being important moderating factors of it. These same concerns may also be raised when considering children's adjustment in the aftermath of violence exposure.

Community Violence

Marital discord is not the only type of conflict that children may observe in their surroundings. Several studies suggest that some children witness significant violence in their communities. For example, Eth and Pynoos (1985) estimated that 10–20% of homicides in Los Angeles were witnessed by children. Jenkins, Bell, and their colleagues (Jenkins & Thompson, 1986; Bell & Jenkins, (1993) have found in studies of Southside Chicago that more than one-fourth of all children interviewed had witnessed either a shooting or a murder. In a more recent study, Jenkins and Bell (1994) found of a high-violence neighborhood that almost a half (47%) of the youths interviewed had witnessed a stabbing and almost two-thirds (60.9%) a shooting. Other studies in U.S. urban centers support the widespread witnessing of community violence among children and youths (see Fitzpatrick & Boldizar, 1993; Osofsky, Wewers, Hann, & Fick, 1993; Richters & Martinez, 1993; and Schubiner, Scott, & Tzelepis, 1993).

Again the effects of witnessing community violence are identified as similar to those in the domestic violence-witnessing literature: acting-out behavior (Eth & Pynoos, 1985), higher levels of stress (Fitzpatrick & Boldizar, 1993; Lorion & Saltzman, 1990; Osofsky et al., 1993), more depression (Freeman, Mokros, & Poznanski, 1993; Martinez & Richters, 1993), and belligerence (Green et al., 1991).

Violence in the Media

The final area of related research is also the most studied and discussed area: children's exposure to violence in the media. Perhaps the most comprehensive review of the effects viewing violent media has on children and adults is found in Paik and Comstock's (1994) analysis of 217 studies on individuals' observation of media violence. They found a consistent "positive and significant correlation between television violence and aggressive behavior" (p. 516). These associations remained strong across a variety of types of studies from experiments to surveys.

Multiple Victimizations and Exposures to Violence

It is clear from the above sections that study designs must enable researchers to differentiate the unique contributions of child exposure to adult domestic violence from those of child abuse and exposure to other forms of violence. As one studies the co-occurrence of child maltreatment and woman battering, this larger context of a child's life should be kept in mind. Children view multiple forms of conflict and violence, and all of these forms appear to affect the child's emotional health and behavioral development.

Several studies examining exposure to community violence show that exposure to domestic violence is frequently present and plays a significant role in predicting negative effects on children. For example, Osofsky et al. (1993) stated that their results "showed strong and significant relationships between reports of intrafamily violence and exposure to community violence" (p. 43). The prominence of intrafamily violence exposure is also evident in studies by Singer (Singer, Miller, Guo, Slovak, & Frierson, 1998; Song, Singer, & Anglin, 1998) and DuRant (DuRant, Cadenhead, Pendergrast, Slavens, & Linder, 1994; DuRant, Pendergrast, & Cadenhead, 1994) in which the combination of community and domestic exposure to violence predict negative results for children.

Evolution of Co-Occurring Violence

Most of the current research on this topic does not indicate how child maltreatment and woman battering evolve in a family or what effect their combination has on adult and child victims. A few studies hint at these dynamics.

Bowker et al.'s (1988) study sheds some light on these interactions. In addition to finding a high degree of overlap, Bowker et al. found that the severity of abuse to a woman is associated with the severity of abuse to children in the home. That is, the more severely a woman is battered the more severely her child is likely to be abused. Two other large studies reinforce this finding. Stacey and Shupe (1983) found in their study of 452 mothers residing in shelters for battered women that "men who battered women more severely were also likely to harm their children" (p. 65). Examining the frequency of beatings, Straus and Gelles (1990) found that the men who were reported to most frequently beat their wives were also the ones most likely to be reported abusing children in the home. Fifty percent of the fathers who abused their wives three or more times in a given 12-month reporting period also abused their children three or more times during that year (see p. 409). Interestingly, O'Keefe (1996) found that as the level of parent-to-child violence increased, the effects of witnessing violence on a child's adjustment decreased. As parent-to-child violence decreased, the effects of witnessing violence increased.

There are many possible iterations of how these two forms of violence may interact. These include situations in which the same perpetrator commits violence against both his partner and children, as seen in the studies above. They also, however, might include a child caught in the "cross fire" during an adult domestic assault, a child who intervenes to defend his or her mother, a child who is abused by a battered woman, or a child whose needs are neglected as a result of his or her mother's injuries and subsequent inability to parent. When mothers respond to their own battering with violence against children, it is called "maternal reciprocity" (Holden & Ritchie, 1991). Two decades ago, Hilberman and Munson (1977–1978) suggested this scenario in families, and more recently, Straus and Gelles (1990) reported that women who were beaten were at least twice as likely to abuse their children when compared with nonabused women.

These studies indicate a type of link between woman battering and subsequent abuse of the child by the mother. The issue of mothers' use of violence toward her spouse and her children is controversial and unclear. It is not currently known how such violence is used by women. Some people have argued that women are just as violent as men, but available data provide a different picture. The revised National Crime Victimization Survey and Federal Bureau of Investigation *Uniform Crime Reports* show that women are six times more likely to be victims of intimate violence than are men and that 28% of female homicides are at the hands of current or former intimate partners, as compared with 3% for men (see Bachman & Saltzman, 1995). More than a decade ago, Saunders (1986) found that a great deal of women's partner-directed violence was in self-defense. Some researchers have also argued that mothers may use violence toward their children to prevent more serious violence against the children by a male perpetrator. An in-depth understanding of how men's and women's use of violence differs and how these forms of violence are linked to the use of violence against children in the home remains unclear and in need of greater study.

Other family characteristics have been examined in association with the overlap between child maltreatment and woman battering. Bowker et al. (1988) found two family factors to be significant statistical predictors of children being maltreated in families in which known woman battering existed. First, they found that the more dominant a husband was in a family's decision making, the more likely a child was to be maltreated. Second, the more children in a family, the more likely there was to be child maltreatment in the home.

The gender and birth order of a child also appear to be factors in who is targeted for abuse. Male children are more at risk of being abused when adult domestic violence is present in the home. For example, Ross (1996) reported that female children were much less likely than their male siblings to be abused by the violent men (47% decrease) or by violent women (27% decrease) in the household. Prescott and Letko (1977) also found that the oldest male child was the most likely victim of child physical abuse when men who also batter their women partners turned on their children.

Bowker et al. (1988) examined only children who were biologically related to the abuser. Others have reported that the presence of children fathered by previous male partners put women at greater risk of victimization (Daly, Singh, & Wilson, 1993) and that the presence of a step-parent put children at greater risk of being maltreated (Wilson & Daly, 1987). Contrary to this last finding, however, is one by McCloskey, Figueredo, and Koss (1995), who did not find an association between the biological relationship of an adult male to the children in the home and their subsequent maltreatment.

Other aspects of the father–child relationship may also influence the degree to which a child is likely to be maltreated. For example, O'Keefe (1995) found that the poor quality of the father–child relationship predicted that the child would also be a victim of abuse by a spouse abuser. The risk of violence continues during separation and after divorce, raising concerns about safe custody visitation arrangements (see Saunders, 1994). In a Canadian study (Leighton, 1989), one quarter of the women reported threats against their lives during custody visitations.

Many questions regarding the dynamics of this overlap remain unanswered. So little is known about how these forms of violence develop and interact with each other over time. Is child maltreatment committed in an effort by the man to intimidate, control, or harm the mother? What percentage of the time do incidents of woman battering and child maltreatment occur in conjunction with or separate from each other? How does the woman's use of violence occur within this context? What other family factors play an influential role in the overlap between these two forms of violence? How do all of these dynamics differ within varied racial, ethnic, and cultural subgroups? What are the protective factors that exist for children and how do they use them?

My colleagues Sandra Beeman, Annelies Hagemeister, Lyungai Mbilinyi and I have embarked on a study that is providing further information on this topic. With support from the David and Lucile Packard Foundation, we conducted anonymous telephone interviews with battered women who had children present during the period that they were being battered. We completed 114 of these interviews. Our results indicated that a large proportion of the children in this study were exposed to their mothers' experience with violence but that only a quarter of the mothers reported that their children were physically involved in the events. In addition, children in this sample were reported less often exposed to violence and intervened less when their mothers' financial, social, and living situations at the time of the interview were more stable (Edleson, Mbilinyi, Beeman, & Hagemeister, 2001).

Evaluations of New Initiatives

New legislation, policies, and practices are developing rapidly in this area of study. There is a dire need to evaluate their effects on the safety, stability, and well-being of the intended beneficiaries. Research on the impact of policies is needed, as are evaluations of programmatic efforts. Universal screening of domestic violence is being widely promoted by professional organizations and some institutions, yet little is known about the impact of such protocols. What intended outcomes result from such screenings? Are women and children given new options and resources as a result? What are the unintended negative outcomes of, for example, a child disclosing to a nurse the presence of adult domestic violence in his or her home? What are the unintended negative outcomes of an adult victim doing the same?

New laws such as those found in Utah and California raise many concerns about their unintended consequences. First, laws making child exposure to adult domestic assaults a separate crime may unnecessarily involve child victims of violence in the criminal justice system for a second time. If the adult domestic assault case was adequately tried, is a second trial really necessary? Creating a separate charge or even enhancing criminal sanctions for the presence of children raise other questions as well. Is the crime against the woman being devalued by adding more severe sanctions when children are present? Will these laws—initially designed for use against perpetrators—be applied to nonabusive women who are charged with "failure to protect" their children?

Some state legislatures and child protection agencies have explicitly defined a child's witnessing of adult domestic violence as a form of child maltreatment. Generally, both battered women's advocates and child protection workers have resisted including a child's witnessing of domestic violence within the definition of child maltreatment. As pointed out at the beginning of this chapter, research shows that some children who witness violence exhibit few, if any, developmental problems and that associated problems are frequently moderated by a variety of factors (Edleson, 1999a). A careful assessment of the harm that results from witnessing violence and of protective factors existing in the child's environment may reveal that witnessing, at least in some cases, does not result in maltreatment of a child. What does this imply for practice definitions and guidelines around this issue?

Finally, many new programs for children exposed to adult domestic violence and for families where both child maltreatment and woman battering occur are being established or expanded. Very little is known about the intended and unintended outcomes of programs, which vary greatly from statewide coordination efforts to small-group programs offered by battered women's shelters or other agencies.

Small-group and individual counseling programs for child witnesses are the most discussed in the literature, and evaluations of them are reported in two chapters (Sandra Graham-Bermann and David Wolfe, Peter Jaffe, in this volume). Evaluations of larger, coordinated interventions that involve statewide changes in practice and policy have yet to be conducted. Massachusetts and Michigan have statewide initiatives under way in this area (see Finlater & Kelly, 1999; Whitney & Davis, 1999), and Miami–Dade County's Juvenile Court has a significant intervention program in this area (see Lecklitner, Malik, Aaron, & Lederman, 1999). All are attempting to evaluate the impact of their projects. In one preliminary evaluation of Massachusetts' project, Hangen (1994) found that cases handled by child protection offices with domestic violence specialists on staff were closed in approximately one-third less time, raising the possibility that addressing adult domestic violence concerns may accelerate the completion of case plans. A survey of the Massachusetts child protection services system also found high awareness among workers of domestic violence protocols and use of domestic violence specialists in consultations. The survey revealed that 62% of the supervisors had consulted with a domestic violence specialist five times or more (Heller, Gyurina, & Rosenbaum, 1997). These evaluations do not answer the critical question of whether their efforts improve the safety, stability, and well-being of child and adult victims in families served. Answers to these questions must wait for more comprehensive evaluations to be completed.

CONCLUSION

Growing attention to the co-occurrence of child maltreatment and woman battering has led to many new policy and practice initiatives in this domain. Unfortunately, the current understanding of the overlap, its interaction with other forms of violence exposure, its dynamics, and the effects of new responses to the problem are sorely inadequate. Support for more controlled and in-depth studies that examine the complex nature of children's exposure to violence and how it co-occurs with adult domestic violence is needed. Equally important is support for evaluations of emerging policies and practices aimed at ameliorating the effects of multiple violence exposures of children.

REFERENCES

Achenbach, T. M., & Edelbrock, C. (1983). *Manual for the Child Behavior Checklist and Revised Child Behavior Profile*. Burlington: University of Vermont, Department of Psychiatry.

Appel, A. E., & Holden, G. W. (1998). The co-occurrence of spouse and physical child abuse: A review and appraisal. *Journal of Family Psychology, 12,* 578–599.

Bachman, R., & Saltzman, L. E. (1995). *Violence against women: Estimates of the redesigned survey*. Washington, DC: U.S. Department of Justice, Office of Justice Programs.

Beeman, S. K., Hagemeister, A. K., & Edleson, J. L. (in press). Case characteristics that distinguish between child abuse and dual violence families: A secondary analysis of administrative data. *Journal of Interpersonal Violence*.

Bell, C. C., & Jenkins, E. J. (1993). Community violence and children on Chicago's Southside. *Psychiatry, 56*, 46–54.

Bowker, L. H., Arbitell, M., & McFerron, J. R. (1988). On the relationship between wife beating and child abuse. In K. Yllo & M. Bogard (Eds.), *Feminist perspectives on wife abuse* (pp. 158–174). Newbury Park, CA: Sage.

Child Abuse Prevention and Treatment Act, P.L. 104-235, Section 111, 42 U.S.C. 5106g (1996).

Daly, M., Singh, L. S., & Wilson, M. (1993). Children fathered by previous partners: A risk factor for violence against women. *Canadian Journal of Public Health, 84*, 209–210.

DuRant, R. H., Cadenhead, C., Pendergrast, R. A., Slavens, G., & Linder, C. W. (1994). Factors associated with the use of violence among urban and Black adolescents. *American Journal of Public Health, 84*, 612–617.

DuRant, R. H., Pendergrast, R. A., & Cadenhead, C. (1994). Exposure to violence and victimization and fighting behavior. *Journal of Adolescent Health, 15*, 311–318.

Edleson, J. L. (1991). Social workers' intervention in woman abuse: 1907 to 1945. *Social Service Review, 65*, 304–313.

Edleson, J. L. (1999a). Children's witnessing of adult domestic violence. *Journal of Interpersonal Violence, 14*, 839–870.

Edleson, J. L. (1999b). The overlap between child maltreatment and woman battering. *Violence Against Women, 5*, 134–154.

Edleson, J. L., & Brygger, M. P. (1986). Gender differences in reporting of battering incidents. *Family Relations, 35*, 377–382.

Edleson, J. L., Miblinyi, L., Beeman, S. K., & Hagemeister, A. K. (2001). *How children are involved in adult domestic violence: Results from a four city telephone survey*. Manuscript submitted for publication, University of Minnesota, Minneapolis.

Eth, S., & Pynoos, R. S. (1985). Developmental perspective on psychic trauma in childhood. In C. R. Figley (Ed.), *Trauma and its wake* (pp. 36–52). New York: Brunner/Mazel.

Finlater, J. E., & Kelly, S. (1999). Reframing child safety in Michigan: Building collaboration among domestic violence, family preservation and child protection services. *Child Maltreatment, 4*, 167–174.

Fitzpatrick, K. M., & Boldizar, J. P. (1993). The prevalence and consequences of exposure to violence among African-American youth. *Journal of the American Academy of Child and Adolescent Psychiatry, 32*, 424–430.

Freeman, L. N., Mokros, H., & Poznanski, E. O. (1993). Violent events reported by normal urban school-aged children: Characteristics and depression correlates. *Journal of the American Academy of Child and Adolescent Psychiatry, 32*, 419–423.

Gordon, L. (1988). *Heroes of their own lives: The politics and history of family violence— Boston 1880–1960*. New York: Viking Penguin.

Graham-Bermann, S. A. (1996). Family worries: Assessment of interpersonal anxiety in children from violent and nonviolent families. *Journal of Clinical Child Psychology, 25,* 280–287.

Green, B., Korol, M., Grace, M., Vary, M., Leonard, A., Gleser, G., & Smitson-Cohen, S. (1991). Children and disaster: Age, gender, and parental effects of PTSD symptoms. *Journal of the American Academy of Child and Adolescent Psychiatry, 30,* 945–951.

Grych, J. H., & Fincham, F. D. (1990). Marital conflict and children's adjustment: A cognitive–contextual framework. *Psychological Bulletin, 108,* 267–290.

Grych, J. H., Seid, M., & Fincham, F. D. (1992). Assessing marital conflict from the child's perspective: The Children's Perception of Interparental Conflict Scale. *Child Development, 63,* 558–572.

Hangen, E. (1994). *D.S.S. Interagency Domestic Violence Team Pilot Project: Program data evaluation.* Boston: Massachusetts Department of Social Services.

Heller, J., Gyurina, C. H., & Rosenbaum, M. (1997). *Survey of Department of Social Services social workers, supervisors and area program managers on the use of the domestic violence specialists, domestic violence protocols and understanding of domestic violence in DSS caseloads.* Boston: Massachusetts Department of Social Services.

Hilberman, E., & Munson, K. (1977–1978). Sixty battered women. *Victimology, 2,* 460–470.

Holden, G. W., & Ritchie, K. L. (1991). Linking extreme marital discord, child rearing, and child behavior problems: Evidence from battered women. *Child Development, 62,* 311–327.

Holtzworth-Munroe, A., Smutzler, N., & Sandin, B. (1997). A brief review of the research on husband violence: Part II. The psychological effects of husband violence on battered women and their children. *Aggression and Violent Behavior, 2,* 179–213.

Illinois Coalition Against Domestic Violence. (1996). *Annual report—FY 1995.* Springfield: Author.

Jenkins, E. J., & Bell, C. C. (1994). Violence exposure, psychological distress, and high risk behaviors among inner-city high school students. In S. Friedman (Ed.), *Anxiety disorders in African-Americans* (pp. 76–88). New York: Springer.

Jenkins, E. J., & Thompson, B. (1986). *Children talk about violence: Preliminary findings from a survey of Black elementary children.* Paper presented at the 19th Annual Convention of the Association of Black Psychologists, Oakland, CA.

Kolbo, J. R. (1996). Risk and resilience among children exposed to family violence. *Violence & Victims, 11,* 113–128.

Layzer, J., Goodson, B. D., & DeLange, C. (1986). Children in shelters. *Response, 9,* 2–5.

Lecklitner, G. L., Malik, N. M., Aaron, S. M., & Lederman, C. S. (1999). Promoting safety for abused children and battered mothers: Miami–Dade County's model Dependency Court Intervention Program. *Child Maltreatment, 4,* 175–182.

Leighton, B. (1989). *Spousal abuse in metropolitan Toronto: Research report on the response of the criminal justice system* (Report No. 1989–02). Ottawa, Ontario: Solicitor General of Canada.

Lorion, R. P., & Saltzman, W. (1990, November). *Children's exposure to community violence: Following a path from concern to research to action*. Paper presented at the National Conference on Community Violence and Children's Development, Bethesda, MD.

Margolin, G. (1998). Effects of witnessing violence on children. In P. K. Trickett & C. J. Schellenbach (Eds.), *Violence against children in the family and the community* (pp. 57–101). Washington, DC: American Psychological Association.

Martinez, P., & Richters, J. E. (1993). The NIMH Community Violence Project: II. Children's distress symptoms associated with violence exposure. *Psychiatry, 56*, 22–35.

McClosky, L. A., Figueredo, A. J., & Koss, M. P. (1995). The effects of systemic family violence on children's mental health. *Child Development, 66*, 1239–1261.

McGee, R. A., Wolfe, D. A., & Wilson, S. K. (1997). Multiple maltreatment experiences and adolescent behavior problems: Adolescents' perspectives. *Development & Psychopathology, 9*, 131–149.

McGee, R. A., Wolfe, D. A., Yuen, S. A., Wilson, S. K., & Carnochan, J. (1995). The measurement of maltreatment: A comparison of approaches. *Child Abuse & Neglect, 19*, 233–249.

Minnesota Department of Corrections. (1993). *Battered women's programs: Data summary for FY93*. St. Paul: Author.

National Council of Juvenile and Family Court Judges. (1998). *Emerging programs for battered mothers and their children*. Reno, NV: Author.

National Council of Juvenile and Family Court Judges. (1999). *Effective intervention in domestic violence and child maltreatment cases: Guidelines for policy and practice*. Reno, NV: Author.

New Jersey Coalition for Battered Women. (1992). *Annual report—1991*. Trenton: Author.

O'Keefe, M. (1995). Predictors of child abuse in maritally violent families. *Journal of Interpersonal Violence, 10*, 3–25.

O'Keefe, M. (1996). The differential effects of family violence on adolescent adjustment. *Child and Adolescent Social Work Journal, 13*, 51–68.

Osofsky, J. D., Wewers, S., Hann, D. M., & Fick, A. C. (1993). Chronic community violence: What is happening to our children? *Psychiatry, 56*, 36–45.

Paik, H., & Comstock, G. (1994). The effects of television violence on anti-social behavior: A meta-analysis. *Communication Research, 21*, 516–546.

Peled, E., & Davis, D. (1995). *Groupwork with children of battered women*. Thousand Oaks, CA: Sage.

Petchers, M. (1995, July). *Child maltreatment among children in battered mothers households*. Paper presented at the Fourth International Family Violence Research Conference, Durham, NH.

Pleck, E. H. (1987). *Domestic tyranny: The making of social policy against family violence from Colonial times to present*. New York: Oxford University Press.

Prescott, S., & Letko, C. (1977). Battered women: A social psychological perspective. In M. Roy (Ed.), *Battered women*. New York: Van Nostrand Reinhold.

Richters, J. E., & Martinez, P. (1993). The NIMH Community Violence Project: I. Children as victims of and witnesses to violence. *Psychiatry, 56*, 7–21.

Rosenbaum, A., & O'Leary, K. D. (1981). Children: The unintended victims of marital violence. *American Journal of Orthopsychiatry, 51*, 692–699.

Ross, S. M. (1996). Risk of physical abuse to children of spouse abusing parents. *Child Abuse & Neglect, 20*, 589–598.

Saunders, D. G. (1986). When battered women use violence: Husband-abuse or self-defense? *Violence and Victims, 1*, 47–60.

Saunders, D. G. (1994). Child custody decisions in families experiencing woman abuse. *Social Work, 39*, 51–59.

Schubiner, H., Scott, R., & Tzelepis, A. (1993). Exposure to violence among inner-city youth. *Journal of Adolescent Health, 14*, 214–219.

Silvern, L., Karyl, J., Waelde, L., Hodges, W. F., Starek, J., Heidt, E., & Min, K. (1995). Retrospective reports of parental partner abuse: Relationships to depression, trauma symptoms and self-esteem among college students. *Journal of Family Violence, 10*, 177–202.

Singer, M. I., Miller, D. B., Guo, S., Slovak, K., & Frierson, T. (1998). *The mental health consequences of children's exposure to violence*. Cleveland, OH: Case Western Reserve University, Mandel School of Applied Social Sciences, Cuyahoga County Community Mental Health Research Institute.

Singer, M. I., & Song, L. (1995). *Exposure to Violence Scales*. Cleveland, OH: Case Western Reserve Universeity, Mandel School of Applied Social Sciences.

Song, L., Singer, M., & Anglin, T. (1998). Violence exposure and emotional trauma as contributors to adolescents' violent behaviors. *Archives of Pediatric and Adolescent Medicine, 152*, 531–536.

Stacey, W., & Shupe, A. (1983). *The family secret: Domestic violence in America*. Boston: Beacon Press.

Stanley, J., & Goddard, C. (1993). The association between child abuse and other family violence. *Australian Social Work, 46*, 3–8.

Stark, E., & Flitcraft, A. H. (1988). Women and children at risk: A feminist perspective on child abuse. *International Journal of Health Services, 18*, 97–118.

Sternberg, K. J., & Dawud-Noursi, S. (1998). Effects of domestic violence on children's behavior problems: Multiple perspectives. In R. Tessier, & G. M. Tarbulsy (Eds.), *Child and family: Contexts for development* (French). Quebec City, Quebec, Canada: Les Presses de l'Université Laval.

Straus, M. A. (1979). Measuring intrafamilial conflict and violence: The Conflict Tactics (CT) Scales. *Journal of Marriage and the Family, 45,* 75–78.

Straus, M. A. (1990). The Conflict Tactics Scales and its critics: An evaluation and new data on validity and reliability. In M. A. Straus & R. J. Gelles (Eds.), *Physical violence in American families* (pp. 49–73). New Brunswick, NJ: Transaction.

Straus, M. A., & Gelles, R. J. (Eds.) (1990). *Physical violence in American families.* New Brunswick, NJ: Transaction.

Straus, M. A., Hamby, S. L., Boney-McCoy, S., & Sugarman, D. B. (1996). The revised Conflict Tactics Scales (CTS2). *Journal of Family Issues, 17,* 283–316.

Szinovacz, M. E. (1983). Using couple data as a methdological tool: The case of marital violence. *Journal of Marriage and the Family, 45,* 633–644.

Utah Criminal Code 76-5-109.1, Commission of domestic violence in the presence of a child. (1997).

Whitney, P., & Davis, L. (1999). Child abuse and domestic violence in Massachusetts: Can practice be integrated in a public child welfare setting? *Child Maltreatment, 4,* 158–166.

Wilson, M., & Daly, M. (1987). Risk of maltreatment of children living with stepparents. In R. J. Gelles & J. B. Lancaster (Eds.), *Child abuse and neglect: Biosocial dimensions* (pp. 215–232). New York: Aldine de Gruyter.

5

ETHICALLY SOUND RESEARCH ON CHILDREN'S EXPOSURE TO DOMESTIC VIOLENCE: A PROPOSAL

EINAT PELED

This chapter provides an analysis of the ethics of research on children's exposure to domestic violence. To do justice to this complex issue, the proposed analysis is grounded in knowledge developed on the ethical dimensions of research with children and on domestic violence, child abuse, and sensitive issues. Furthermore, the analysis considers ethical dimensions of quantitative and qualitative methodologies. Finally, the analysis attends to the standards and procedures for ensuring an ethically proper research design and implementation.

My goal is to advance a fair and caring treatment of participants in studies on children's exposure to domestic violence. Although many of the views I propose on ethical practice in this research domain are critical, my point of view is constructive. I believe that for too long we as researchers have been deeply influenced by a scientific paradigm that regards research participants as means to an end, essential raw material for the operation of the highly esteemed scientific machine with which we can achieve an understanding and control of our world. Following many critical and constructivist writers (e.g., Apter, 1996; Lather, 1991; Lincoln, 1995; Massat & Lundy, 1997; Reason, 1994), I suggest that we are ready now to try to integrate our expertise in developing valid and reliable knowledge with a perception and treatment of "our subjects" as partners to the scientific undertaking in which we are involved. My use of the term *partnership* in this context does not indicate shared responsibility of researchers and participants for research processes and outcomes but rather calls attention to the relational aspect of the social inquiry, as examined further below.

Both the theory and practice of research ethics are grounded in and shaped by values, attitudes, knowledge, and experiences held by the individual investigators, their professional milieu, and the social–cultural context within which the study is conducted (Kaplan, 1964; Kuhn, 1970; Lincoln & Guba, 1985). All these, separately and interactively, are in a state of constant change. Judgments regarding the ethical appropriateness of research procedures and designs are, thus, situational, temporal, and subjective, depending on a specific constellation of the above factors. Accordingly, the views expressed in this chapter regarding research ethics in the domain of children's exposure to domestic violence are heavily influenced by my particular standpoint, which, I believe, should be stated explicitly.

The lenses through which I examine the issue of research ethics are those of my gender, female; my profession, social worker; my occupation, full-time academic at a research university; the paradigm that dominates my scientific thinking, naturalism–constructivism with some grains of post-positivism; my ideological commitment, the advancement of all disempowered people in the world's societies, including women, children, and abuse victims; and my accumulating experience, studying children's exposure to domestic violence and other distressing life circumstances, using mainly qualitative methodology. This is the constellation within which I constructed the proposed set of assumptions regarding the nature of ethical research in the domain of children's exposure to violence and through which I examined research reports in this domain.

GUIDING PRINCIPLES

Six interrelated principles guide my ethical thinking on social research in general and research on children's exposure to violence in particular: ethical research (a) is an integral aspect of the research act and of each phase of the research process, (b) is a relational undertaking, (c) empowers participants of vulnerable and oppressed groups, (d) considers children as social actors in their own right, (e) benefits the individual participants, and (f) prevents harm to participants and involved others. These principles are explained below and used to examine the ethics of research on children's exposure to domestic violence, as reported in the literature.

Research Ethics Is an Integral Aspect of the Research Act and of Each Phase in the Research Process

Ethical standards should be viewed as fundamental quality criteria used to judge the rigor and merit of any social sciences study (Lincoln, 1995). Ethical considerations are not limited to the design phase but may evolve in any phase of the study, including the dissemination stage. Researchers may have to face and respond to damaging effects, such as a participant's distress caused by a seemingly harmless data-collection procedure or the published research report (e.g., Bussel, 1994; Chase, 1996) or unintended negative consequences for the studied population following the dissemination of the findings (Channels, 1993). A study in which appropriate ethical standards were not maintained cannot be a good study, even when other methodological quality criteria have been met satisfactorily.

Research Is a Relational Undertaking

The knower and the known can never be entirely separated (Lincoln & Guba, 1985). Thus, ethical standards and procedures should be developed and understood in the context of a relationship that takes place between the researchers and the researched (Lincoln, 1995). Research can be seen as a dialogue aiming to produce valid knowledge (Reason & Rowan, 1981). It is a meeting point and a shared experience of people (the investigators and the participants) who often differ in their social power, lifestyles, experiences, and understanding of and expectations from the research and its products (Sieber, 1992). Ethical research attends to these aspects of the research relationship when the welfare of the participant is considered.

Ethical Research Empowers Participants of Vulnerable and Oppressed Groups

Many of the participants in domestic violence studies, especially women and children, have experienced victimization, poverty, disempowerment, and oppression. In ethical research, participants' personal tragedies should not become just another research opportunity (L. Thompson, 1992). Instead, the research serves as an opportunity for the empowerment of the participants. *Empowerment* is defined here as a process of enabling people to master their environment and achieve self-determination through the acquisition of skills, knowledge, and emotional and material resources by which personally meaningful social roles are fulfilled (Simmons & Parson, 1983; Solomon, 1976). On the one hand, being a research participant may constitute such a meaningful social role through which a person contributes to the development of new knowledge and may even experience personal learning and growth. On the other hand, without an empowering perspective, there is always the threat of exploitation of vulnerable participants in the name of science (Demi & Warren, 1995; Massat & Lundy, 1997).

Empowerment as a dimension of research is impossible to achieve if participants are treated as "subjects." Instead, empowerment entails (a) providing potential participants with complete information on research goals, processes, and results, so they can make a truly informed choice regarding participation; (b) treating them respectfully throughout the research; (c) helping them find meaning in their research participation; and (d) allowing their voices to be heard during the research process and through the results (Massat & Lundy, 1997; Morrow & Richards, 1996; L. Thompson, 1992). Of course, these goals, and particularly the last one, can be more fully obtained through qualitative methods drawing on personal experiences and perceptions of the individual studied. However, as discussed in detail in the last section of this chapter, free choice, respect, and personal meaning can and should be incorporated as fundamental aspects of the research relationship in any study.

Ethical Research With Children Considers Children as Social Actors in Their Own Right

Children, especially younger ones, are generally acknowledged to be vulnerable research participants because of the inherent power differential between them and the adult research staff (Fine & Sandstrom, 1988; R. A. Thompson, 1992). Furthermore, many adults (including many researchers) usually hold fundamental biases against children, regarding them as (a) unfinished, in process, and not anywhere yet; and (b) incompetent, routinely wrong, in error, and not understanding (R. A. Thompson, 1992; Waksler, 1986). If we as researchers believe that the purpose of ethical research is to provide a positive, empowering, and respectful experience to all its participants, we should acknowledge childhood as a culture in its own right, within which children are proficient and competent (Mandell, 1988; Tammivaara & Enright, 1986). Accordingly, we should develop research strategies that enable a suspension of those adult biases that lead to a disrespectful attitude toward children and distort their authentic voice (Morrow & Richards, 1996; Waksler, 1986). Such strategies may involve data collection through open interviews, observations, preparation of art objects, photography, filming, and the like and a consideration of children's own perceptions and interpretations at the data analysis stage.

Ethical Research Benefits the Individual Participants

The perception of both risk and benefit is highly subjective. Thus, for example, the contribution of a study to a knowledge domain or to an amelioration of a social problem is not necessarily perceived as a research benefit by an individual research participant. Ethical research maximizes the direct benefits of research participation for participants. For example, researchers may provide participants with counseling services, money, or an opportunity to tell their story. Those who have experienced participation in research as beneficial (and were not harmed by it) will not feel exploited by the researcher (Massat & Lundy, 1997). Moreover, it can be claimed that because research findings are jointly produced by the researcher and the participants, particularly in qualitative studies, both should share the benefits that accrue from the research (Lincoln, 1995; L. Thompson, 1992).

Ethical Research Prevents Harm to Participants and Involved Others

Researchers should do their utmost to prevent the infliction of any damage or harm to participants as a consequence of their participation and to provide appropriate intervention in case such harm does occur, as a minimal ethical requirement. Furthermore, the researcher has a moral obligation to act on any information received during the study regarding risks to participants or involved others independent of the research procedures (Gondolf, in press). The more vulnerable the participants (e.g., children, abuse victims), the more efforts should be devoted to ensuring their well-being throughout the research process (Demi & Warren, 1995; Sieber, 1992). The researcher's commitment to ensuring the well-being of participants supersedes considerations regarding the quality of the data produced (Rosenbaum, 1988).

The six principles above provide a framework of expected ethical standards in research on children's exposure to domestic violence. With the help of this framework, one can examine the ethical practices in existing research and develop guidelines for the future implementation of ethically sound research in this domain.

AN EXAMINATION OF CURRENT ETHICS

Close to 100 studies on children's exposure to domestic violence have been published in professional journals and books since the mid-1970s (for recent reviews, see Edleson, 1999; Margolin, 1998). Although varied in sophistication and design, almost all of these studies use quantitative methodologies to learn about the negative impact of children's exposure to violence and the factors that mediate such impact. This section is focused on the ethical dimension of this body of research, as examined through the principles proposed above.

Research Ethics as an Integral Aspect of Research Methodology

Most, if not all, of the reviewed studies can be defined as "sensitive"; they focus on a private, stigmatic problem and commonly collect data from participants who belong to vulnerable groups (e.g., battered women and their children) and are situated in a vulnerable context (e.g., a shelter for battered women). As described below, such research raises multiple and complex ethical dilemmas requiring systematic and thoughtful handling. Still, scant, if any, reporting of ethical considerations and practices is the general rule in the literature. Only a few exceptional reports include a relatively detailed discussion of ethical issues (e.g., Ericksen & Henderson, 1992; Hughes, 1988; Jouriles et al., 1998; Laumakis, Margolin, & John, 1998; McCloskey, Figueredo, & Koss, 1995; Peled, 1998). As a general trend, ethical considerations are marginal to a detailed treatment of other methodological procedures aimed at guaranteeing the quality of the data produced.

Of course, it is always possible that satisfactory ethical standards were maintained during the research process but omitted from the final research report. However, as regarding all other aspects of research methodology, this is an unacceptable practice. Unfortunately, it appears that the professional community, composed of authors, reviewers of research reports, and journal editors, does not consider the ethical dimension to be a cardinal aspect of the quality and merit of empirical work in this domain.

Research as a Relational Undertaking and the Empowerment of Vulnerable Participants

With the use of the definition for empowering research provided above, participation in most of the studies reviewed seems to have provided participants with little, if any, sense of empowerment. In several research reports, participants were described and maybe treated as subjects. In accordance with traditional research conventions, participants entered a rigidly structured and usually brief relationship with the researchers, in which their role was confined to the provision of specific, fractured information on highly intimate and often painful aspects of their lives. Once the information was provided, the relationship ended.

Participants may have experienced their role in the construction of new understandings in this domain as empowering. However, for this to happen, they needed to understand what the research is about and how their individual contribution fits into the larger picture and then freely choose to share their lives with the strangers who collected the data. This would have entailed a fully and truly informed-consent process, which in the studies reviewed, seemed to be the exception rather than the rule (e.g., Hughes, 1988; Lehmann, 1997; Peled, 1998). A closure of such an empowering experience through the sharing of the final research results with the participants was reported only in the study by Ericksen and Henderson (1992).

Imagining possible reactions of participants to the research reports raises further concerns regarding the ability to provide an empowering experience without allowing participants' voices to be heard. For example, it is doubtful that battered women interviewed in a shelter would have supported the presentation of the abuse they have been experiencing as "interparental violence" (Fantuzzo, DePaola, Lambert, Martino, & Sutton, 1991; Jouriles et al., 1998; Rossman, 1998) or "marital conflict" (Jouriles, Norwood, McDonald, Vincent, & Mahoney, 1996; Rossman & Rosenberg, 1992). Similarly, child participants would not have been likely to feel empowered when understanding that their multidimensional experience of exposure to violence was reduced through the research process to labels describing resulting pathology.

Child Participants as Social Actors

Although most of the studies reviewed were aimed at developing an understanding of the children's adjustment following exposure to domestic violence, almost none of the studies were concerned with the children's own understandings of their lives. In many studies, children's experiences were assumed on the basis of their mothers' reports (e.g., Gleason, 1995; Holden & Ritchie, 1991; Smith, Berthelsen, & O'Connor, 1997; Wolfe, Jaffe, Wilson, & Zak, 1988). However, two studies in which researchers found significant differences in children's and parents' perceptions of domestic violence (Hughes, 1988; Sternberg et al., 1993) raise the question regarding the validity of such practice. Studies that include children as participants differed in the "child friendliness" of their data-collection techniques. These techniques ranged from open and informal interviews (e.g., Peled, 1998) to a gamelike procedure, such as the Family Relations Test (Sternberg et al., 1994), to structured but open questioning in response to recorded vignettes (e.g., Adamson & Thompson, 1998; Laumakis et al., 1998) to the common standardized pen-and-pencil measures (e.g., Hughes, Parkinson, & Vargo, 1989; Kolbo, 1996; O'Keefe, 1996). Overall, standardized measures were the rule, molding and quantifying the children's perspectives into an adult way of thinking. As a consequence with a few exceptions (Ericksen & Henderson, 1992; Graham-Bermann, 1996; Peled, 1998), children's voices are almost nonexistent in this body of empirical literature in which they are treated mostly as the subjects of investigation rather than as partners to it.

Research as Beneficial for Participants

Empowerment and the opportunity to "be heard," as discussed above, are two kinds of related benefits that may result from participation in research. The provision of other, more traditional benefits of research participation is reported in several studies. These benefits included monetary awards (e.g., Gleason, 1995; Graham-Bermann, 1996; Hughes et al., 1989; McCloskey et al., 1995; Spaccarelli, Sandler, & Roosa, 1994); feedback on participants' performance, given mostly to parents (e.g., Jouriles, Barling, & O'Leary, 1987; Wolfe et al., 1988); presents, given mostly to children (e.g., Sternberg et al., 1994); course credit, given to participating students (e.g., Blumenthal, Neeman, & Murphy, 1998); and a referral of both women and child participants to services, either on request or when identified as in need by the research team (Kilpatrick & Williams, 1998; McCloskey et al., 1995; Wolfe et al., 1988). Many researchers have omitted any discussion of the benefits of research for the participants, and almost none of them have reported the final study results to the participants.

Some aspects of the reported benefits raise ethical concerns. First, material benefits, such as money, presents, and course credits, may be used to tempt reluctant participants into participating, thus serving as a form of subtle coercion. It is often not clear whether benefits such as monetary awards were promised in the recruitment phase or were first discussed with participants only after data collection. Second, in some studies (e.g., Fantuzzo et al., 1991; McCloskey et al., 1995; Moore & Pepler, 1998), the benefits seemed to be disproportionately divided between parents and children. Kerig (1998), for example, gave her 8–10-year-old participants a certificate of completion and their mothers $40. Third, Ericksen and Henderson (1992) noted that by providing feedback on child performance to parents, the researchers may have breached the confidentiality agreement made with the child (e.g., Kilpatrick & Williams, 1998). Finally, in an appropriately funded service world, a referral to treatment should not be proposed as a research benefit but rather as a potential derivation of research participation, so as not to serve as another road leading to coerced participation.

Prevention of Harm for Participants and Involved Others

Most of the studies on children's exposure to domestic violence were based on data gathered from women who were being or had been abused by their intimate partners; in some, as mentioned above, the children themselves were also interviewed. Women and children were commonly approached through services for battered women and, especially in more recent studies, through general public avenues, such as newspapers and neighborhood stores. The personal situation of these participants and the timing and location of their participation rendered them vulnerable to potential harmful effects of the research process. Indeed, almost all the studies report one or more strategies used in the course of research in an effort to minimize harm and maximize protection for participants (e.g., maintaining informed consent, guaranteeing confidentiality). However, in only a few studies did researchers attend to the complex risks associated with research participation for abused women and their children. I next discuss these risks briefly. Following Gondolf (in press), I differentiate between risks for participants associated with research procedures and risks independent of the research procedures.

Risks Associated With Research Procedures

The potential for harming research participants exists throughout the research process, from sample recruitment to dissemination of findings.

Coerced participation. Research participation in all the studies reviewed was voluntary to the extent that participants seemed to have given their verbal or written consent to participation. However, methodological procedures in some of the studies may have limited participants' ability to make a truly informed free choice to undertake and then complete participation (see Bradley & Lindsay, 1987, for a similar critique of child abuse research).

First, many of the studies provide few or no details on the informed-consent procedures used (Gleason, 1995; Hennessy, Rabideau, Cicchetti, & Cummings, 1994; Rossman & Rosenberg, 1992; Stagg, Wills, & Howell, 1989; Sternberg et al., 1993; Wolfe et al., 1988) or report that consent was not fully informed (e.g., McCloskey et al., 1995). Such an omission is particularly troubling when the participants are in such a relatively disempowered or vulnerable position, as are children and battered women seeking shelter. Second, it is not clear whether women and children felt free to refuse participation or even fully understood the nature of participation in those occasions in which data collection was carried out as part of routine agency procedures (Jouriles et al., 1996; Kolbo, 1996), while in a battered women's shelter (e.g., Graham-Bermann, 1996), or as part of a children's summer camp activity (Hennessy et al., 1994). This may be especially true for child participants. Third, money awards of $20–$45 provided in some of the studies (e.g., Kerig, 1998; McCloskey et al., 1995) may have been an offer poor participants could not have refused, regardless of what they thought about the study itself. Furthermore, it is possible that such attractive awards caused parents to pressure their children to participate in the study. Finally, research questions in some studies seem to have been formed long after the data-collection phase, so participants could not have been aware of them when they initially consented to participate (e.g., Jouriles et al., 1998; Spaccarelli et al., 1994).

Distress stemming from data-collection procedures. A disturbing and most common risk for participants in the reviewed studies was emotional distress during and following the data-collection phase. In almost all the studies, battered women and, at times, exposed children, some in their first days of shelter residence, were asked to report highly painful and intimate information, including detailed descriptions of the violence they had experienced (e.g., Carlson, 1990; Forsstrom-Cohen & Rosenbaum, 1985; Kolbo, 1996; McCloskey et al., 1995; Rossman & Rosenberg, 1992; Smith et al., 1997; Wolfe et al., 1988). Two aspects of such reporting, the secret of violence and children's entanglements in conflicts between their parents, are a source of potential distress for child participants that some of the researchers may have not been aware of.

In many of the families where women are abused, the abuse or some of its aspects are kept secret, both inside and outside the family. The changing boundaries of secrecy are usually imposed on children by their parents and influence children's willingness and ability to discuss violence-related issues with people outside the family (Peled, 1998; Peled & Edleson, 1992). A girl who is asked to report about the violence she was exposed to may experience difficulty because she is not sure exactly what and how much she is allowed to tell. Such distress may intensify when the child has not received explicit, clear permission from both of her parents to disclose to the interviewer family matters that are routinely kept secret. Children may experience an additional and related distress if they perceive that the questions present themselves or their parents in a negative light (e.g., their father as cruel, themselves as helpless).

Although close attention was paid in few studies to an appropriate training of the interviewers (e.g., Jouriles et al., 1998; Levendosky & Graham-Bermann, 1998) and referral of participants to counseling was offered when deemed necessary (Jouriles et al., 1998; McCloskey et al., 1995; Peled, 1998; Wolfe et al., 1988), almost none of the studies report what steps were taken to ease participants' distress during and immediately after data collection. Paradoxically, the knowledge developed by researchers on the vulnerabilities of abuse victims, with the goal of improving the ability to support them, seems to not have been used by the same researchers to support these children in their role of research participants.

Research participation as a trigger for abuse. As recognized for a long time by counselors and advocates, abusive men may perceive any communication of a spouse or a child with people outside the family as a threat and react violently, especially when family matters are discussed (e.g., Davidson, 1978; Gondolf, in press; Sonkin, Martin & Walker, 1985). Most studies with battered women who were living at home (rather than in a shelter; e.g., Fantuzzo et al., 1991; Levendosky & Graham-Bermann, 1998; Smith et al., 1997), for whom this risk may have been relevant, did not report whether any steps were taken to avoid such threat.

Risks Independent of Research Procedures

When studying people who are likely to harm themselves, to be abused at the time of study, or to have been abused in the past, researchers face moral and legal duties to protect participants and report suspected abuse. Surprisingly, these issues are rarely discussed in the reviewed research reports.

Child abuse. Only a few of the studies (e.g., Carlson, 1990; Jouriles et al., 1998; Peled, 1998) mention that the researchers' duty to report previously unreported suspected child abuse was communicated to participants, and almost none of the studies report whether and how this duty was acted on (but see Carlson, 1990; McCloskey et al., 1995). At the same time, it is unlikely that no disclosure of child abuse occurred during the studies explicitly measuring domestic violence. Beyond the legal obligation to report, almost none of the studies describe a mechanism for providing professional support to children suspected of being abused.

Although the findings of many of the studies provide strong and clear evidence of the emotional abuse suffered by children's exposure to domestic violence, none of the studies discusses children's exposure as a reportable condition. Furthermore, there is almost no information on action taken by researchers to facilitate intervention with exposed children who were suggested by their mothers or by other informants to suffer from various negative effects of their exposure

Woman abuse. In most of the reviewed studies, researchers questioned women participants on the abuse they had been experiencing. Although many of these women were residing in a shelter at the time of the study, some were living in the community, possibly with their abuser (e.g., Graham-Bermann & Levendosky, 1998; Moore & Pepler, 1998; Rossman & Rosenberg, 1992; Smith et al., 1997). In most countries, states, and provinces, there is no legal obligation to report woman abuse. However, researchers do have a duty to protect victims from a foreseeable danger of severe injury and the moral obligation to help women who are abused and in danger to find immediate shelter and support (Appelbaum & Rosenbaum, 1989). Still, almost none of the reviewed studies mention whether any steps were taken to offer support and protection to the women who disclosed that they were being abused.

A PROPOSAL OF GUIDELINES FOR ETHICALLY SOUND RESEARCH

The guidelines for ethically sound research proposed in this section are inspired by the principles elaborated above, borrow from the general literature on research ethics, and incorporate examples of careful ethical conduct set by researchers in the domain of children's exposure to domestic violence. For reasons of practicality, the guidelines are organized according to a chronological order of the research project, from design to dissemination. Throughout this section, the term *participants* refers to both adults and children.

Design

Developing Ethical Protocol and Training Staff

- Potential ethical dilemmas are considered and, when possible, solved at the design phase.
- A sensitive assessment of research risk and benefits for child participants takes into consideration the influence of developmental changes on children's strengths and vulnerabilities (R. A. Thompson, 1992). For example, young children's understanding of authority renders them more vulnerable to coercive manipulations than older children, for whom authority relations are better balanced by an understanding of individual rights (R. A. Thompson, 1992).
- Risk management protocol are developed before the project is implemented (Bussel, 1994; Gondolf, in press; Massat & Lundy, 1997). The protocol includes cues for the detection of distress, imminent violence, suicidality, child abuse (including exposure to violence), and procedures for responding to such cues.
- Staff are extensively trained in the dynamics and dangers of domestic violence, including the experiences of exposed children (Gondolf, in press; Levendosky & Graham-Bermann, 1998).

Including Participants' Voice and Perspective

- An effort is made to use methods of data collection and analysis through which participants' voices can be heard (Gondolf, in press; Socolar, Runyan, & Amaya-Jackson, 1995). This requires researchers to consider participants' culture, language, communication styles, and relational position (Morrow & Richards, 1996; Sieber, 1993). Feminist, anthropological, and qualitative approaches can be relied on to achieve this end (Mauthner, 1997; Peled, 1998; Smith, 1994; L. Thompson, 1992).

Maximizing Benefits for Participants

- The question "What are the participants going to get out of the research?" is asked and answered during the design phase, taking into consideration the subjective perspective of future research participants on this matter.
- Ideally, both research procedures and research dissemination are planned so as to benefit participants directly. For example, participants may perceive telling their story as a form of taking action and would enjoy getting an understandable report of the research findings (Massat & Lundy, 1997; Morrow & Richards, 1996).

Recruitment of Participants

Establishing Partnership-Based Participation

- Participants are recruited as partners to the research project rather than as its subjects. This requires the researchers to hold and communicate a reciprocal view of the research relationship. The research contract should specify participants' contribution to the project, the benefits they are to gain from it, potential risks, and the extent of control they will have in the process and on the resulting data.

Providing Complete Information to Participants

- Participants are given understandable, accurate, and complete information about the project, including expected products and avenues of dissemination. Special efforts are made to communicate directly with children, using developmentally and culturally appropriate language.
- Participants are notified about circumstances requiring breach of confidentiality, that is, the researchers' obligation to act on

information about suspected child abuse, imminent danger, and suicidality (Bussell, 1994).

Securing Free Informed Consent

- Both child and adult participants should complete informed-consent procedures before the data-collection phase. Such procedures include the information detailed above, presented in a language and within a social context so as to facilitate open and clear communication with all the potential participants.
- Coercion to participate in research is avoided, including that which may result from attractive material awards, pressure put by social services agencies, and participants' deference to authority figures, such as children's deference to their parents (Demi & Warren, 1995; Mahon, Glendinning, Clarke, & Craig, 1996; Socolar et al., 1995).

Avoiding Harm as a Consequence of Consent

- A child should not participate in the study if a parent with which the child has an ongoing contact is known or suspected to oppose the child's research participation (Peled, 1998, 2000). A parent's opposition to the child's research participation may create tension, distress, and even risk of abuse for the child (Peled & Edleson, 1992).
- Abuse victims (both women and children) should not participate in the study if there are reasonable grounds to assume that participation will provoke the abuser to harass, threaten, or abuse the participant (Gondolf, in press).

Data Collection

Respecting Participants' Privacy

- Researchers need to protect the privacy of participants and avoid unnecessary intrusion into private space and information. Because the invasion of children's privacy is common in Western culture, increased efforts should be devoted to protecting children's privacy (Melton, 1992).

Maintaining Participant Choice and Control

- Participants are provided with maximal control over the setting of interview (e.g., time, place, sitting arrangements) and, when possible, over the contents (Massat & Lundy, 1997).

- Noncoercive interviewing (Gilgun, 1989) is used to protect vulnerable participants. The researcher avoids communicating to participants any open or subtle pressure to complete participation. Participants' ongoing choice to participate is facilitated by explicitly acknowledging difficulties they may be experiencing during the research and reminding them of their right to quit without any negative consequences (Demi & Warren, 1995; Peled, 1998).

Holding a Debriefing Session

- Any research in which participants are asked emotionally laden questions, that is, any study conducted in the domain of children's exposure, should include a debriefing session following data collection (Bussell, 1994; Gondolf, in press; Mahon et al., 1996). The purpose of the debriefing is to provide a closure to the participation experience, correct misconceptions and alleviate anxiety about research participation, provide reassurance about typical reactions to research procedures, and uncover and respond to distress that may have developed during data collection (Bussell, 1994).
- During the debriefing session, participants who request or seem to need additional support are provided with information about relevant, accessible, social services and about how to contact the researcher after the study in case they have further questions or concerns (Bussell, 1994; Gondolf, in press).

Protecting Participants From Abuse

- On disclosure or suspicion of either child abuse or woman abuse, the relevant research protocol is implemented (for a detailed example of such protocol, see Gondolf, in press). The following principles may be used in the construction of such a protocol: (a) Whether or not the researcher is legally mandated to report abuse (Liss, 1994), he or she has the moral duty to protect children from being abused and to offer support to abused adults; (b) exposure to domestic violence is a form of emotional abuse; (c) parents, including battered women, will not necessarily act on the best interest of their abused children, and the best interests of battered women and their children may conflict (Peled, 1997); (d) a victim has a right to be notified of any action taken to report the abuse or protect her or him from the abuse; and (e) dual relationships should be avoided; the researcher does not also act as a therapist or an advocate (Bussell, 1994; Gondolf, in press).

Providing Ongoing Staff Supervision and Support

- Research team members, who are also at risk for distress as a result of their exposure to painful information, are provided with ongoing training and support (Urquiza, Wyatt, & Goodlin-Jones, 1997).
- Periodic team meetings are held to review ongoing ethical dilemmas and supervise the implementation of the risk management protocol by individual team members (Bussell, 1994; Gondolf, in press).

Data Analysis Writing and Dissemination

Providing Detailed Descriptions of Ethical Procedures

- The evaluation of ethical standards is an integral part of any review processes of research design or research reports, including those carried out for the purposes of funding and publication. Research reports are only published if the reported performance of ethical procedures in the study was judged satisfactory.

Adhering to Agreement Made With Participants

- Data analysis and writing focus on the issues and questions presented to participants when recruited to the study. Any significant change of these understandings is regarded as a breach of contract, requiring participants' approval before it can be implemented.

Thinking About Participants as Readers

- The authors of the research report ask themselves "How would the participants feel about this report?" The inclusion of contents and wording assessed to be potentially harmful or disrespectful to participants is reconsidered.

Sharing Results With Participants

- Participants are provided with an opportunity to learn about the results of the research to which they have contributed. This could be done through a written report tailored to participants' developmental stage (if children) and language skills, a public presentation, or an audiovideo recording.

CONCLUSION

The principles that I have proposed in this chapter for proper ethical conduct in research on children's exposure to violence may seem ambitious, unrealistic, or even misguided. I acknowledge conflicts that are likely to exist between such ethical considerations and other aspects of the research endeavor, particularly financial constraints and an adherence to other methodological quality criteria. However, I would like to see these principles applied in every study in this domain.

The meanings of values and ethics are subject to negotiations and redefinitions (Denzin, 1970). What is ethical in one period, profession, or group may be unethical in another. Although my particular construction of the meaning of research ethics may not be applicable for all those who study children's exposure to domestic violence, I hope that it will facilitate a process of re-examination, negotiation, and redefinition of the ethical dimension of research in this domain.

REFERENCES

Adamson, J. L., & Thompson, R. A. (1998). Coping with interparental verbal conflict by children exposed to spouse abuse and children from nonviolent homes. *Journal of Family Violence, 13,* 213–232.

Appelbaum, P. S., & Rosenbaum, A. (1989). *Tarasoff* and the researcher: Does the duty to protect apply in the research setting? *American Psychologist, 44,* 885–894.

Apter, T. (1996). Expert witness: Who controls the psychologist's narrative. In R. Josselson (Ed.), *Ethics and process in the narrative study of lives* (pp. 22–44). Thousand Oaks, CA: Sage.

Blumenthal, D. R., Neeman, J., & Murphy, C. M., (1998). Lifetime exposure to interparental physical and verbal aggression and symptom expression in college students. *Violence and Victims, 13,* 175–195.

Bradley, E. J., & Lindsay, R. C. L. (1987). Methodological and ethical issues in child abuse research. *Journal of Family Violence, 2,* 239–255.

Bussell, D. A. (1994). Ethical issues in observational family research. *Family Process, 33,* 361–376.

Carlson, B. E. (1990). Adolescent observers of marital violence. *Journal of Family Violence, 5,* 285–299.

Channels, N. L. (1993). Anticipating media coverage: Methodological decisions in criminal justice research. In C. M. Renzetti & R. M. Lee (Eds.), *Researching sensitive topics* (pp. 267–280). Newbury Park, CA: Sage.

Chase, S. E. (1996). Personal vulnerability and interpretive authority in narrative research. In R. Josselson (Ed.), *Ethics and process in the narrative study of lives* (pp. 45–59). Thousand Oaks, CA: Sage.

Davidson, T. (1978). *Conjugal crime: Understanding and changing the wifebeating pattern.* New York: Hawthorn.

Demi, A. S., & Warren, N. A. (1995). Issues in conducting research with vulnerable families. *Western Journal of Nursing Research, 17,* 188–202.

Denzin, N. K. (1970). *The research act: A theoretical introduction to sociological methods.* Chicago: Aldine.

Edleson, J. L. (1999). Children's witnessing of adult domestic violence. *Journal of Interpersonal Violence, 14,* 839–870.

Ericksen, J. R., & Henderson, A. D. (1992). Witnessing family violence: The children's experience. *Journal of Advanced Nursing, 17,* 1200–1209.

Fantuzzo, J. W., DePaola, L. M., Lambert, L., Martino, G. A., & Sutton, S. (1991). Effects of interparental violence on the psychological adjustment and competencies of young children. *Journal of Counseling and Clinical Psychology, 59,* 258–265.

Forsstrom-Cohen, B., & Rosenbaum, A. (1985). The effects of parental marital violence on young adults: An exploratory investigation. *Journal of Marriage and the Family, 47,* 467–472.

Fine, G. A., & Sandstrom, K. L. (1988). *Knowing children: Participant observations with minors.* Newbury Park, CA: Sage.

Gilgun, J. F. (1989). Freedom of choice and research interviewing in child sexual abuse. In B. G. Compton & B. Gallaway (Eds.), *Social work processes* (4th ed., pp. 358–369). Homewood, IL: Dorsey Press.

Gleason, W. J. (1995). Children of battered women: Developmental delays and behavioral dysfunction. *Violence and Victims, 10,* 153–160.

Gondolf, E. W. (in press). Human subject issues in battered program evaluation. In S. Ward & D. Finkelhor (Eds.), *Program evaluation and family violence research.* Thousand Oaks, CA: Sage.

Graham-Bermann, S. A. (1996). Family worries: Assessment of interpersonal anxiety in children from violent and nonviolent families. *Journal of Clinical Child Psychology, 25,* 280–287.

Graham-Bermann, S. A., & Levendosky, A. A. (1998). Traumatic stress symptoms in children of battered women. *Journal of Interpersonal Violence, 13,* 111–128.

Hennessy, K. D., Rabideau, G. J., Cicchetti, D., & Cummings, E. M. (1994). Responses of physically abused and nonabused children to different forms of interadult anger. *Child Development, 65,* 815–828.

Holden, G. W., & Ritchie, K. L. (1991). Linking extreme marital discord, child rearing, and child behavior problems: Evidence from battered women. *Child Development, 62,* 311–327.

Hughes, H. M. (1988). Psychological and behavioral correlates of family violence in child witnesses and victims. *American Journal of Orthopsychiatry, 58,* 77–90.

Hughes, H. M., Parkinson, D., & Vargo, M. (1989). Witnessing spouse abuse and experiencing physical abuse: A "double whammy"? *Journal of Family Violence, 4,* 197–209.

Jouriles, E. N., Barling, J., & O'Leary, D. K. (1987). Predicting child behavior problems in maritally violent families. *Journal of Abnormal Child Psychology, 15,* 165–173.

Jouriles, E. N., McDonald, R., Norwood, W. D., Shinn Ware, H., Collazos Spiller, L., & Swank, P. R. (1998). Knives, guns and interparental violence: Relations with child behavior problems. *Journal of Family Psychology, 12,* 178–194.

Jouriles, E. N., Norwood, W. D., McDonald, R., Vincent, J. P., & Mahony, A. (1996). Physical violence and other forms of marital aggression: Links with children's behavior problems. *Journal of Family Psychology, 10,* 223–234.

Kaplan, A. (1964). *The conduct of inquiry: Methodology for behavioral sciences.* San Francisco, CA: Chandler.

Kerig, P. (1998). Gender and appraisals as mediators of adjustment in children exposed to interparental violence. *Journal of Family Violence, 13,* 345–363.

Kilpatrik, K. L., & Williams, L. M. (1998). Potential mediators of post-traumatic stress disorder in child witnesses to domestic violence. *Child Abuse and Neglect, 22,* 319–330.

Kolbo, J. R. (1996). Risk and resilience among children exposed to family violence. *Violence and Victims, 11,* 113–128.

Kuhn, T. S. (1970). *The structure of scientific revolutions* (2nd ed.). Chicago: University of Chicago Press.

Lather, P. (1991). *Getting smart: Feminist research and pedagogy with/in the postmodern.* New York: Routledge.

Laumakis, M. A., Margolin, G., & John, R. S. (1998). The emotional, cognitive and coping responses of preadolescent children to different dimensions of marital conflict. In G. W. Holden, R. Geffner, & E. N. Jouriles (Eds.), *Children exposed to marital violence: Theory, research, and applied issues* (pp. 257–288). Washington, DC: American Psychological Association.

Lehmann, P. (1997). The development of posttraumatic stress disorder (PTSD) in a sample of child witnesses to mother assault. *Journal of Family Violence, 12,* 241–257.

Levendosky, A. A., & Graham-Bermann, S. A. (1998). The moderating effects of parenting stress on children's adjustment in woman-abusing families. *Journal of Interpersonal Violence, 13,* 383–397.

Lincoln, Y. S. (1995). Emerging criteria for quality in qualitative and interpretive research. *Qualitative Inquiry, 1,* 275–289.

Lincoln, Y. S., & Guba, E. G. (1985). *Naturalistic inquiry.* Newbury Park, CA: Sage.

Liss, M. B. (1994). Child abuse: Is there a mandate for researchers to report? *Ethics and Behavior, 4,* 133–146.

Mahon, A., Glendinning, C., Clarke, K., & Craig, G. (1996). Researching children: Methods and ethics. *Children and Society, 10,* 145–154.

Mandell, N. (1988). The least-adult role in studying children. *Journal of Contemporary Ethnography, 16,* 433–467.

Margolin, G. (1998). Effects of domestic violence on children. In P. K. Trickett & C. J. Schellenbach (Eds.), *Violence against children in the family and the community* (pp. 57–102). Washington, DC: American Psychological Association.

Massat, C. P., & Lundy, M. (1997). Empowering research participants. *Affilia, 12,* 33–56.

Mauthner, M. (1997). Methodological aspects of collecting data from children: Lessons from three research projects. *Children and Society, 11,* 16–28.

McCloskey, L. A., Figueredo, A. J., & Koss, M. (1995). The effects of systemic family violence on children's mental health. *Child Development, 66,* 1239–1261.

Melton, G. B. (1992). Respecting boundaries: Minors, privacy and behavioral research. In B. Stanley & J. E. Sieber (Eds.), *Social research with children and adolescents* (pp. 65–87). Newbury Park, CA: Sage.

Moore, T. E., & Pepler, D. J. (1998). Correlates of adjustment in children at risk. In G. W. Holden, R. Geffner, & E. N. Jouriles (Eds.), *Children exposed to marital violence: Theory, research, and applied issues* (pp. 157–184). Washington, DC: American Psychological Association.

Morrow, V., & Richards, M. (1996). The ethics of social research with children. *Children and Society, 10,* 90–105.

O'Keefe, M. (1996). The differential effects of family violence on adolescent adjustment. *Child and Adolescent Social Work Journal, 13,* 51–68.

Peled, E. (1997). The battered women's movement response to children of battered women: A critical analysis. *Violence Against Women, 3,* 424–446.

Peled, E. (1998). The experience of living with violence for preadolescent children of battered women. *Youth and Society, 29,* 395–430.

Peled, E. (2000). The parenting of men who abuse women: Issues and dilemmas. *British Journal of Social Work, 30,* 25–36.

Peled, E., & Edleson, J. L. (1992). Multiple perspectives on groupwork with children of battered women. *Violence and Victims, 7,* 327–346.

Reason, P. (Ed.). (1994). *Participation in human inquiry.* Thousand Oaks, CA: Sage.

Reason, P., & Rowan, J. (Eds.). (1981). *Human inquiry: A sourcebook of new paradigm research.* Chichester, England: Wiley.

Rosenbaum, A. (1988). Methodological issues in marital violence research. *Journal of Family Violence, 3,* 91–104.

Rossman, B. B. R. (1998). Descartes's error and posttraumatic stress disorder: Cognition and emotion in children who are exposed to parental violence. In G. W. Holden, R. Geffner, & E. N. Jouriles (Eds.), *Children exposed to marital violence: Theory, research, and applied issues* (pp. 223–256). Washington, DC: American Psychological Association.

Rossman, B. B. R., & Rosenberg, M. (1992). Family stress and functioning in children: The moderating effects of children's beliefs about their control over parental conflict. *Journal of Child Psychology and Psychiatry, 33,* 699–715.

Sieber, J. E. (1993). The ethics and politics of sensitive research. In C. M. Renzetti & R. M. Lee (Eds.), *Researching sensitive topics* (pp. 14–26). Newbury Park, CA: Sage.

Simmons, C. H., & Parson, R. G. (1983). Empowerment for role alternatives in adolescents. *Adolescence, 18,* 193–200.

Smith, J., Berthelsen, D., & O'Connor, I. (1997). Child adjustment in high conflict families. *Child: Care, Health and Development, 23,* 113–133.

Smith, M. D. (1994). Enhancing the quality of survey data on violence against women: A feminist approach. *Gender & Society, 8,* 109–127.

Socolar, R. R. S., Runyan, D. K., & Amaya-Jackson, L. (1995). Methodological and ethical issues related to studying child maltreatment. *Journal of Family Issues, 16,* 565–586.

Solomon, B. B. (1976). *Black empowerment: Social work in oppressed communities.* New York: Columbia University Press.

Sonkin, D. J., Martin, D., & Walker, L. E. A. (1985). *The male batterer: A treatment approach.* New York: Springer.

Spaccarelli, S., Sandler, I., & Roosa, M. (1994). History of spouse violence against mother: Correlated risks and unique effects in child mental health. *Journal of Family Violence, 9,* 79–96.

Stagg, V., Wills, G. D., & Howell, M. (1989). Psychopathology in early childhood witnesses of family violence. *Topics in Early Childhood Special Education, 9,* 73–87.

Sternberg, K. J., Lamb, M. E., Greenbaum, C., Cicchetti, D., Dawud, S., Cortes, R. M., Krispin, O., & Lorey, F. (1993). Effects of domestic violence of children's behavior problems and depression. *Developmental Psychology, 29,* 44–52.

Sternberg, K. J., Lamb, M. E., Greenbaum, C., Dawud, S., Cortes, R. M., & Lorey, F. (1994). Effects of domestic violence on children's perceptions of their perpetrating and nonperpetrating parents. *International Journal of Behavioral Development, 17,* 779–795.

Tammivaara, J., & Enright, S. D. (1986). On eliciting information: Dialogue with child informants. *Anthropology and Education Quarterly, 17,* 218–238.

Thompson, L. (1992). Feminist methodology for family studies. *Journal of Marriage and the Family, 54,* 3–18.

Thompson, R. A. (1992). Developmental changes in research risk and benefit: A changing calculus of concerns. In B. Stanley & J. E. Sieber (Eds.), *Social research with children and adolescents* (pp. 31–64). Newbury Park, CA: Sage.

Urquiza, A. J., Wyatt, G. E., & Goodlin-Jones, B. L. (1997). Clinical interviewing with trauma victims. *Journal of Interpersonal Violence, 12,* 759–772.

Waksler, F. C. (1986). Studying children: Phenomenological insights. *Human Studies, 9,* 71–82.

Wolfe, D. A., Jaffe, P., Wilson, S. K., & Zak, L. (1988). A multivariate investigation of children's adjustment to family violence. In G. T. Hotaling, D. Finkelhor, J. T. Kilpatrick, & M. A. Straus (Eds.), *Family abuse and its consequences: New directions in research* (pp. 228–241). Newbury Park, CA: Sage.

II

PROVIDING CONTEXT:
THE ROLE OF FAMILIES
AND SOCIAL SUPPORT

6

OVERCOMING MOTHER BLAMING? FUTURE DIRECTIONS FOR RESEARCH ON MOTHERING AND DOMESTIC VIOLENCE

LORRAINE RADFORD AND MARIANNE HESTER

Despite almost 30 years of research into and activism against violence against women, little has been written about mothering in the context of abuse, whether from the viewpoint of women's experiences, of children's experiences, or on the basis of reviews of social policy and academic discourse. In this chapter, we aim to begin filling this gap in the research literature. We write as feminist sociologists rather than as psychologists and start from the premise that the social, historical, cultural, and political contexts in which thinking about violence, the family, and mothering is positioned has a profound influence on policy responses to women and children surviving abuse.

Policy, practice, and ideologies dominant in the United Kingdom and the United States differ in several respects (Dobash & Dobash, 1992). We start this chapter by charting recent changes in policy and programs in the United Kingdom, in particular. We next review trends in the research literature and look at how the growth of research on children and domestic violence has influenced thinking about mothering. We argue that important questions about what might be effective social support for women as mothers and children living through domestic violence have not been adequately considered within the research. In the final sections of the chapter, we outline three areas in which further research on social support for abused women as mothers would be particularly worthwhile: (a) research that explores women's coping and caring strategies when mothering in the context of domestic violence; (b) research that looks at the effectiveness of social support, taking into account the cultural context in which social support is received and how race, culture, poverty, and wealth may influence women's and children's experiences and needs; and (c) research that explores how work with violent men and efforts to change their behavior affects women's parenting and their relationships with children.

CURRENT POLICY AND PROGRAM ISSUES

Policy developments in recent years have compounded the problems faced by women who mother in the context of domestic violence. This section considers developments in policy and practice, mostly in the United Kingdom, and the women as mothers who have been constructed as the major problem for children within family law and social work practice. A particular concern is the way that debates about "family crisis" and "lost" or "absent" fathers have influenced courts' and practitioners' responses to mothers living through domestic violence.

Crime Control, Child Protection, and Family Law

Since the mid-1970s in the United Kingdom, the United States, and many other countries, there has been increasing recognition of domestic violence as a widespread and serious crime. In the United Kingdom, the criminalization of domestic violence was, by the late 1980s, beginning to have an impact, especially on police intervention and practices (Hester & Radford, 1996a; Radford, 2000). It has been reflected in positive initiatives such as the domestic violence units set up in police stations across the nation, which have brought a more proactive approach and have improved support, access to services, and the monitoring and recording of domestic violence incidents reported to the police (Hoyle, 1998).

Problems remain, however, with the police response to domestic violence in the United Kingdom. Changes in police practices have not been uniform, the rates of arrest are low over most of the country, and only a small proportion of cases reported to the police are prosecuted (Lees, 1997; Plotnikoff & Woolfson, 1999). Moreover, for Black women, the police are frequently seen to be an inappropriate agency to approach, and police intervention can be a negative and unhelpful experience (Mama, 1996). In response to these problems in the United States and the United Kingdom, there has been a shift in emphasis away from solely policing toward community and multiagency interventions to combat crime (Hague, Malos, & Deer, 1996).

Feminists have mostly supported the crime control agenda as part of a project to ensure that violent men are accountable for their crimes. The trends cannot, however, be separated from the broader social and political changes that have brought an increasing emphasis on law-and-order issues

(Stanko, 1997). Moreover, efforts to ensure that violent men are accountable for their crimes have been frustrated by contradictory trends in family law and child protection policy. In England, practice changes following the introduction of the Children Act 1989 (Oldham, 1997) have been significant. The act sets out local authorities' responsibilities toward children in need and children requiring protection from abuse or neglect (public law) as well as parents' responsibilities toward their children during separation and divorce (private law).

Introduced in an era of declining welfare spending and reduced local authority involvement in service provision, the Children Act of 1989 was followed by a privatization of responsibilities in social work and family law to protect children from abuse. Child abuse issues have been moving out of the courts, and attempts have been made to reduce court and social services interventions by working in partnership with parents. Concurrently, parental arrangements for the care of children during separation and divorce have developed in a laissez faire and mediated direction. Until very recently, risk of domestic violence and its impact on parenting was not even identified as a factor requiring consideration (Radford et al., 1997). Generally, policies relating to children have ignored and undermined the safety of mothers.

Mother blaming is an entrenched part of social services intervention (O'Hagan & Dillenburger, 1995). Agencies such as the courts, social services, and the National Society for the Prevention of Cruelty to Children, which implement the law and work with child protection issues, have been slow to recognize domestic violence as a child welfare issue. Violence committed by male perpetrators is frequently ignored because of the tendency of social services to work predominantly with mothers, whether they were responsible for any risk or neglect to the children or not (Farmer & Owen, 1998; Hester, Pearson, & Harwin, 2000). In an overview of social work responses to domestic violence in the United Kingdom, Mullender (1996) identified the direction that social work practice has taken during the past couple of decades:

- In the 1980s, the expectation that women should stay with violent men "for the sake of the children" was particularly prevalent and led to social workers encouraging reconciliations.
- During the 1990s, women were expected to protect their children by leaving their partners.

Moving from the expectation that a family should stay together no matter what toward the recognition that women and children may be better off leaving has clearly been a positive step forward in social work practice. However, many women experienced the 1990s approach as punitive (Hester et al., 2000). Social workers in the United Kingdom tend to be uncomfortable working with domestic violence and often have no local policies or guidelines on domestic violence to which they can refer. Only 55% of social services departments have developed domestic violence policy guidelines (Humphreys et al., 2000). Because social workers work predominantly with women, responsibility for protecting the children lies with their mothers. Therefore, professionals have tended to respond to domestic violence by threatening to remove the children to "care," seeing this as the push women need to leave a violent partner. Women who do not leave, who leave and return, or who are viewed as being no longer able to parent effectively because of abuse run the risk of having their children removed (Hester et al., 2000). These may appear to be sensible courses of action for child protection agencies, but they are counterproductive because the primary abuser, the violent man, is ignored.

Legislation has strengthened the ability of social workers countrywide to remove a domestic violence perpetrator from the home rather than requiring a woman to leave with her children. A male perpetrator can be removed if he is suspected of abusing the child, if the mother consents to his removal, and if an interim care or emergency child protection order has been issued (Family Law Act 1996, S52; Oldham, 1997). This gives social workers an opportunity to offer abused mothers better social support and perform informative evaluations. Overall, however, social work practice has yet to turn around women's fears that their children will be lost to care if they disclose their domestic violence to social services (Hester, 2000b; Hester et al., 2000).

These difficulties are made even more complex where public law (child protection) and private law (parental arrangements for children on divorce or separation) intersect. Reviewing social work decisions in the 1990s, Humphreys (1997) concluded that social services expected abused women to be actively, indeed "aggressively," protecting children. Yet in relation to divorce and separation, the message to mothers has been very different. The thinking that families need fathers dominated the courts throughout the 1990s, and the most important issue became preserving children's ties with absent fathers. Fathers have increasingly been placed in the victim role in sociolegal discourses and are seen as having been squeezed out of parenting and viewed as redundant by mothers (Radford et al., 1997).

In divorce and separation proceedings, mothers fearing domestic violence or child abuse have received harsh treatment. Mothers fearful of contact visits being set up between children and violent ex-partners have been labeled "implacably hostile" by the courts and deemed to be a threat to the welfare of their children. Some women in this position have been imprisoned and many more obliged to agree to unsafe contact visits, following a threat that failure to comply would lead to their imprisonment. A recent study of 130 parents who separated from violent partners found that 39% of those involved with the courts were threatened with imprisonment if they did not comply with a contact order, and 92% were abused again when the contact was set up. Seventy-six percent of the children were reported to have been emotionally or physically abused, or both, by the violent parent during contact visits (Radford, Sayer, & AMICA, 1999). Mothers have been stuck in a Catch-22 situation: They are expected to protect their children by keeping the ex-partner away but are unable to do so because they are pushed by the law into agreeing to an unsafe contact (Hester & Radford, 1996b; Radford et al., 1999).

In contrast, in Australia, New Zealand, and the United States, concerns about domestic violence after separation and the impact on children have had a greater influence on policy responses and the availability of services. One striking difference between the United States and United Kingdom response to domestic violence is the much greater emphasis in the former on risk assessment within family law and professional practice. Criminologists and sociologists have linked risk assessment to the individualization of responsibilities to manage crime and welfare (Beck, 1992; Stanko, 1997). Both the United Kingdom and the United States have hosted this move to focus increasingly on risk in everyday life, but domestic violence has not played such a central part in developments in the United Kingdom. Although rebuttable presumptions against violent parents getting custody or unsupervised access to a child exist in the United States and New Zealand family law, in England there has been a great reluctance to introduce similar statutory amendments for fear of undermining the child's "right" to parental contact (Children Act Sub-Committee, 2000).

Contact Services and Parenting Programs

Different approaches to safety and risk are also reflected in recent program developments that have affected abused mothers living in the United Kingdom and the United States. Two are potentially significant: the development of child contact services and the development of parenting programs. In the United Kingdom, there is limited provision of professionally supervised visitation or contact services for children. In recent years, however, there has been an increase in the availability of centers offering "supported" contact (i.e., not directly supervised but overseen by volunteers). Domestic violence has been a low priority within the supported-contact center movement. Centers have largely adopted the "father deprivation" stance and have tended to have more concerns with the preservation of contact and persuading mothers to comply than with issues of safety. Thus, women's resistance to contact, whether based on the fear of violence to themselves or to their children or not, has become the major concern within contact centers. Centers and the courts expect mothers involved in supported contact to rapidly overcome their fears of abuse and, in the interests of their children, to move as fast as possible toward informal, unsupervised contact arrangements (Radford et al., 1999). In contrast, in Australia, New Zealand, and the United States, the need for supervised contact services to protect children and mothers at risk of postseparation abuse has been recognized.

The safe-contact center movement internationally promises to lift the burden of fear and mother blaming from women currently harassed by violent fathers pursuing contact orders through the courts. The future is likely to bring an increase in safe-contact services. Yet little research has been done on the work that these services claim to do to safeguard the rights and welfare of children (see Chetwin, Knaggs, Te Wairere, & Young, 1999, for an exception). Little is known about the outcome of contact orders made and supported by these new services, nor how they affect women's subsequent parenting and relationships with children. Evaluation studies are needed to consider how contact affects children and mothers over time and to establish whether children who have lived with domestic violence want and ultimately benefit from having contact with their father who has been violent.

Family courts in England are advised to consider a violent father's motive in applying for contact and his capacity to change his behavior (Children Act Sub-Committee, 2000), yet they do not have the power to mandate his attendance in a perpetrator or parenting program. Also in contrast to the situation in the United States, parenting projects that look specifically at domestic violence issues are a rarity in the United Kingdom. The establishment of perpetrator and parenting programs in the United Kingdom is relatively recent and linked more to concerns about youth and juvenile crime than about domestic violence (Sclater & Piper, 2000).

Refuges (shelters) in the United Kingdom generally show less interest in therapeutic interventions than in the United States, for example, and focus their energies more on gaining practical and material support for women and children by campaigning for welfare reforms and housing provisions (Dobash & Dobash, 1992). Perhaps more than in the United States, refuges in the United Kingdom have been unsure of the value of perpetrator programs. Self-help, self-determination, and empowerment work for women and children were pioneered by refuges and form the foundation of much of their approach, although their lack of funding means that development of focused programs to support mothers has been difficult. Most women's refuges provide "outreach," services (i.e., care for support for women after leaving the refuge). The majority of refuges have specified children's workers or voluntary support staff (Humphreys et al., 2000).

Other programs and services to support children living with domestic violence are limited in the United Kingdom, although there have been several regionally based innovations in the voluntary sector, social services, and multiagency projects (Humphreys et al., 2000). There has been a modest

increase in the availability of re-education programs, mostly run by a probation service or the voluntary sector (Mullender, 1996), but only a handful
of these currently work with violent men on fathering issues (N. Blacklock,
men's program coordinator, Violence Prevention Program, Hammersmith
and Fulham Domestic Violence Intervention Project, personal communication, March 2000). A recent survey found that 7 out of 26 perpetrator
programs had no child protection policies (Humphreys et al., 2000). Few
evaluation studies of these programs exist (Burton, Regan, & Kelly, 1998;
Dobash, Dobash, Cavanagh, & Ellis, 1996), so their success rates, in terms of
changing behavior and stopping domestic violence, are difficult to determine.
Little is known about how the existence or absence of these programs affects
children and women who mother in the context of abuse.

This necessarily brief review of the impact of policy and program
developments highlighted how concerns about crisis in the family and absent
fathers have had detrimental effects on abused women as mothers. Our
discussion in the next section shows that concerns in recent policy about
the "failed mothering" of abused women and their children's father deprivation are not validated by findings from the academic research.

RESEARCH ON MOTHERING AND DOMESTIC VIOLENCE

There is a large amount of domestic violence research now in existence,
but many of the findings on domestic violence and children are limited
because results are drawn from studies based on "convenience" samples of
women living in refuges or shelters, who are only a small proportion of the
one in four women who report suffering abuse during their lives (Mirlees-
Black, 1999; Radford, Richardson, & Davies, 1998). Therefore, little is
known about how domestic violence affects the broader population of women
and children who do not need to, do not feel it is appropriate to, or cannot
because of lack of access contact a refuge or shelter program.

This emphasis has had a noticeable influence on the therapeutic and
problem-oriented focus of much of the research. There is a shortage of work
looking specifically at mothering and even less that examines the different
experiences women have of mothering within particular social contexts.
Much of the research emphasizes the harm that domestic violence causes
by looking at its impact on the physical and mental health of mothers and
children. Some studies draw links between maternity and the onset of abuse
(Mezey & Bewley, 1997) or examine how the harm caused by domestic
violence might interfere with a mother's capacity to provide care for her
children (Walker, 1984). Studies also consider whether women who are
abused are as a consequence poorer mothers or are suffering from parental
stress (Holden, Stein, Ritchie, Harris, & Jouriles, 1998). The overlap

between woman abuse and child abuse has been a particular concern in the 1990s (Hester & Pearson, 1998). We briefly outline some of the findings from these studies before presenting our views on the limitations of the research.

Domestic Violence and Women's Health

There is no doubt that domestic violence worldwide has a significant impact on the health and welfare of women (World Health Organization, 1997). Links among domestic violence, pregnancy, and childbirth have been well explored and have challenged the idea that domestic violence and the welfare of children are separate issues (Radford et al., 1998). Domestic violence often begins with a pregnancy or shortly after the birth of the child (Mezey & Bewley, 1997). Up to 60% of women in refuges have reported having suffered abuse during pregnancy (Radford et al., 1998), and hospital screening studies show up to 17% of pregnant women currently being abused (Campbell, Oliver, & Bullock, 1998). The risks of moderate and severe domestic violence are greater for women battered during pregnancy (Campbell, Soeken, McFarlane, & Parker, 1998; Mezey & Bewley, 1997), and women who are abused in pregnancy seem to be at greater risk of homicide (Campbell, Soeken, et al., 1998). Miscarriage and low-birthweight babies are more common (Bullock & McFarlane, 1989; Curry & Harvey, 1998). Women who are battered are four times more likely to have miscarriages than are women who are not abused (Schornstein, 1997). Poor diet and restricted access to antenatal care also has some impact, as yet not fully explored, on the health of mothers and their children (McWilliams & McKiernan, 1993).

Various reasons have been offered to explain this association between pregnancy and abuse. Sexual jealousy of the unborn child, an immature personality unable to cope with competition for the woman's emotion or time, fear of the responsibilities the child will bring, desire to cause an abortion, and anger that the pregnancy will make the woman "less attractive" are some of the varied explanations (Schornstein, 1997). The gender of the unborn child—whether the child is a girl—may also be a relevant issue (Radford & Hester, in press), although for some women, violence during pregnancy is just "business as usual" (Campbell, Oliver, et al., 1998). There is also a growing body of research that suggests that direct and intentional links may exist between some men's abuse of a partner and the sexual abuse of children (Gordon, 1989; Hester & Pearson, 1998; Radford & Hester, in press). However, beyond this work on maternity and other anecdotal studies of women living in refuges and shelters (Binney, Harkell, & Nixon, 1988), little is known about how and why abuse may be linked to mothering. Relatively little consideration has been given to the public health consequences of domestic violence, particularly during pregnancy. Clearly, there is a need for further research.

Research in the United Kingdom into the health care costs and consequences of domestic violence is in its infancy, and no studies are available that show the extent to which women suffer permanent or temporary disability as a result of abuse (Radford et al., 1998). In our own recent analysis of the experiences of mothering through domestic violence of 65 women, we found that 7% suffered permanently disabling violence that affected their capacity to parent and 37% of the women suffered violence that temporarily disabled them and left them temporarily unable to provide physical care (Radford & Hester, in press).

The associated mental health and social care costs of domestic violence have also been researched over many years in North America by Stark and Flitcraft (1996). Looking at hospital emergency room and antenatal care records, Stark and Flitcraft found that women who were abused by their partners were 15 times more likely than were nonabused women to overuse alcohol, 9 times more likely to abuse drugs, 3 times more likely to be diagnosed as depressed or psychotic, and 5 times more likely to attempt suicide. They also found that one in seven battered women were institutionalized in psychiatric hospitals or received psychiatric referrals. Depression, alcohol, or drug abuse rates rose after the first episode of violence had occurred and may have been a consequence of this. Specialist programs and refuge services for women who have health problems, whether these result are from abuse or not, are in short supply, especially in the United Kingdom. Services and programs need to be more available to women and children with health problems and disabilities.

The Impact of Domestic Violence on Mothering

There has been much discussion on the extent to which women living with domestic violence suffer adverse effects on their parenting. The extent to which women victimized by violent men and the legal system have the ability or responsibility to protect children has been a topic of considerable controversy, leading to divided thinking within feminism (e.g., Johnson, 1991; O'Hagan & Dillenburger, 1995). One trend emphasizes the victim status of abused women and the constraints on them (Walker, 1984). The other trend, although acknowledging the impact of abuse, rebels against a perceived "victimism" in the literature by emphasizing women's agency and abilities to exercise "choice" (e.g., Johnson, 1991). Walker's (1984) work on the mental health impact of domestic violence has been quoted worldwide. Her work has also been used in courts to explain battered women's failure to leave violent men and to protect their children. Walker argued that sustained domestic violence can result in a state of learned helplessness, such that a mixture of depression, low self-esteem, and hopelessness about the possibility of escape lead victims to believe that there is no way out of the relationship and that no one cares. The idea discussed at the start of this chapter—that women who suffer domestic violence are likely to be poor mothers because of the abuse—also exists in the literature, and some researchers have criticized Walker's work for promoting this thinking (Dobash & Dobash, 1992).

Perhaps unsurprisingly, women do sometimes report higher levels of stress when parenting in the context of abuse. In England, a survey of mothers attending NCH Action for Children's Family Centers found that several had lost confidence in their mothering skills, were emotionally drained and distant, felt that they had little to give their children, and at times took out their frustrations on their children. These feelings were compounded by the difficult behavior of children at a time when they, too, would be trying to come to terms with the violence they had experienced or witnessed (Abrahams, 1994). In a study of women in shelters in the United States, Holden and Ritchie (1991) found that mothers might be inconsistent in their parenting because of the abusive, controlling, and isolating behavior of their partner. The husband's abuse prevented the wife from maintaining standards of care or led them to perceive child care as more stressful. Significant improvements have been found in parenting relationships 6 months after separation if the source of stress on mothers— the partner's violence—is stemmed (Holden et al., 1998).

It has also been argued that mothers who experience domestic violence are more ready to use physical punishment than are women who are not abused, although recent research suggests that few differences can be found between the parenting and discipline styles of battered and nonbattered women. Battered women are just as likely or unlikely to abuse and neglect children as are nonbattered women (Holden et al., 1998). Feminist researchers have, perhaps justifiably, taken a defensive stance and challenged the assumption that abused mothers will themselves bully children (Kelly, 1991). Yet are different issues raised for child protection work with the (minority of) mothers who do abuse and neglect? Little guidance can be found in the research findings for professionals working with mothers who do abuse or neglect their children in the context of domestic violence (although see Hester et al., 2000, chap. 8).

Research findings on the harm and injuries women suffer from violent partners suggest that domestic violence is likely to have an impact, temporary or lasting, on a mother's capacity to provide physical and emotional care for children. However, there are dangers for programs and for researchers that focus solely on harm or on deficiencies in mothering. Research, based on the experiences of mothers and children, shows that after separation, many women who have lived through domestic violence enjoy parenting and are very emotionally supportive toward their children. Distinctions need to be drawn between the difficulties of parenting while living with an abuser and the possible difficulties after separation. Parenting after separation may be stressful less because the mother is unable to cope but more because the children are showing signs of distress or difficult behavior as a result of having lived with and witnessed the abuse (Sullivan, Nguyen, Allen, Bybee, & Juras, 1999).

The efforts that women living with violent partners may make to resist the violence and continue parenting on a daily basis are not adequately considered in the research literature. Many women make great efforts to maintain an appearance of "normality" and to shield their children from the effects of the abuse (Radford & Hester, in press). A more constructive future research agenda would build on women's efforts and experiences to consider ways of working with them in meeting the needs of children.

The polarization of mothers into "abusive" and "nonabusive" may also be profoundly unhelpful to practitioners and survivors because it encourages the belief that if the husband as the perpetrator of the abuse is removed, the mother and children will be safe and secure and no longer in need of support. Resources and support are then removed much more quickly (Hooper & Humphreys, 1998), so that women coping with contact problems, frequent changes in residence, poverty, and perhaps the disturbed behavior of their children are left to muddle through. Although not all women will be in the position of needing or wanting support, services should be flexible enough to respond to those that do in an appropriate and empowering way.

Different Identities and Experiences of Mothering

We assumed that the experience and activity of mothering is fundamentally tied to the gender entrapment and survival processes associated with abuse (Radford & Hester, in press; also see Richie, 1995). Recent research into gender entrapment takes a less individualistic approach to understanding mothering through abuse by considering the varied social and cultural contexts in which women and children live their lives. The gender entrapment literature emphasizes the differential yet cross-cutting effects that family, life history, race, culture, community, and poverty have on women's identities and commitment to relationships (Richie, 1995). The meanings individuals ascribe to their personal histories and experiences are mediated through socially constructed representations of reality. Concepts of "good-enough mothering" (Chodorow, 1989) vary cross-culturally and historically. Historically, in Western industrial societies women have negotiated rights to protection from violence and support from agencies on the basis of their special qualities as mothers (Gordon, 1989).

Women's identities as mothers exert powerful influences on their decisions to stay or leave abusive men or to seek help from relevant agencies (Radford & Hester, in press). Children can influence a woman's decision to stay or leave and, depending on the social policy context, might limit or increase her opportunities to find practical solutions (Pahl, 1985). We argued that current policy in the United Kingdom and United States has demonized single parenting, and father deprivation is increasingly being constructed as harmful to children (Radford & Hester, in press). For some mothers, the need to "fit" their experiences into a prescribed framework of "ideal" mothering and family life may mean they respond to the stress and harm resulting from domestic violence by trying harder to make the relationship work (Crogman & Miell, 1998). Ironically, the harder women, especially impoverished and Black women, try to conform to socially prescribed ideals of family life, the more likely they will be judged deviant and fail in the job of parenting (Richie, 1995). Further research needs to explore this complex relationship among social and cultural context, identity, mothering, and abuse. Research is also needed to explore how women, together with their children, are able to resist negative stereotypes and construct more positive identities for themselves as survivors of abuse.

MOVING BEYOND MOTHER BLAMING: AN AGENDA FOR MORE CONSTRUCTIVE RESEARCH

The direction of future research will undoubtedly be influenced by the current political climate and specific governmental agendas on family, social welfare, and law-and-order issues. Further comparative research and collaboration is needed among researchers, providers, and practitioners. It is time to move beyond the mother-blaming stalemate by shifting the research agenda on to new trajectories. We consider the following three lines of enquiry: (a) research that explores mothers' experiences as copers and survivors; (b) outcome-oriented research that looks especially at the question, What is effective support? and takes into consideration the varied social and cultural contexts in which mothering takes place; and (c) research that explores how work with violent men and efforts to change their behavior affects women's parenting and relationships with children.

Mothers as Copers and Survivors

There is generally a growing consensus in the literature that providing support for and ensuring the safety of mothers is an effective way to improve the welfare of their children (Hester et al., 2000). However, very little research centers on what mothers themselves want or have found most influential in the survival process and in caring for their children (this topic is considered in Radford & Hester, in press). Much of the research literature is based on the assumption that mothers need and indeed should seek outside help, preferably from public agencies. Women who do not go for help, for whatever reasons, have been ignored. This oversight raises questions about service accessibility and social exclusion as well as questions about the possible availability of informal networks of support that some women may draw on. Research suggests that informal sources of support are often women's first port of call (Dominy & Radford, 1996), but this fact has generated little interest in the literature. Researchers could do much to develop this area of work by working more effectively in partnership with the women and children who do and do not use such services.

The research on mothering mostly documents the harm and negative impact of abuse on women's behavior or capacity to parent and protect children. Some of this work has fuelled negative stereotypes about battered women and deficient mothering. The practical steps that women take to compensate their children for living with domestic violence has had little attention in the literature. Acknowledging, documenting, and building on women's efforts to protect their children and compensate for the abuse could have far-reaching implications for social services and other agencies offering community support.

Similarly, the part children play throughout their lives in supporting mothers has not seen enough attention. Little more than anecdotal information is known about how children and young people experience mothering in the context of domestic violence. Research is especially needed that looks at how children and young people view and reassess their relationships with their mother over time. Future researchers should explore the extent to which abuse and neglect by the father or the mother and witnessing domestic violence influence children's and young people's assessment of mothering.

Black feminist researchers have challenged the dominance of White perspectives on violence and the family that either subsumes Black women's experiences within universalizing concepts or constructs White women's experiences as the norm while Black women become the "other." There is a need to look critically at the experience and activity of mothering in different cultural and historical contexts, particularly in contexts other than the White, heterosexual nuclear family. How is the identity and experience of mothering through domestic violence affected by such variables as childhood experiences of abuse, race, culture, disability, sexuality, and financial security or insecurity? Researchers of gender entrapment (Richie, 1995) and of coping and survival (Hoff, 1990; Kirkwood, 1993) have started to examine the complex relationship among victimization, survival, and identity. However, very little is known about the impact that theories, culturally prevalent beliefs, and public education campaigns about domestic violence have on women's own expressions of their experiences and identities as mothers. Further research needs to explore how women and children resist negative stereotypes of abuse and construct for themselves positive identities as survivors. Little is known about the role that social workers, medics, clinicians, and therapists play in this negotiation of identity.

Effective, Culturally Appropriate Support

We argued here and elsewhere (Hester & Radford, 1996b) that the social and institutional context in which mothering takes place inevitably influences family well-being. The question of effectiveness is similarly influenced by the context. Feminist researchers of gender and citizenship in different welfare state regimes have started to document the social and legal constructions of state–family obligations and the impact that these constructions have on power relationships within the family (Lewis, 1993; Sevenhuijsen, 1998). There is a need to further develop the research on a state's responses to violence and abuse by drawing on this cross-national work on gender and citizenship. Effective support is likely to be different in varying national and cultural contexts. For instance, a treatment program for violent men in the United States might be regarded as a progressive antiviolence initiative. In Russia, however, it might be viewed as a human rights abuse. The need to explore the differing social and political contexts of violence has become more pressing in response to the globalization of discourses on human rights and the management of violence (Hester, 2000a).

There clearly is a dearth of research on what works in social work and child protection practice. Evaluation research is needed that focuses on outcome, particularly in relation to new policy measures and legal changes outlined earlier in this chapter. The interagency and community-based focus of contemporary responses present good opportunities for collaborative, outcome-focused research. There is a need to assess recent changes in professional practice. One feature of the trend in interagency work with social services in the United Kingdom has been an outbreak of "protocol fever," the rapid proliferation of professional training programs and of the introduction of practice guidelines and protocols. Some attempts have been made to evaluate these (Dominy & Radford, 1996; Shepard & Pence, 1999), but further research is needed on how child protection and social work agencies have applied awareness of domestic violence to everyday practice. How does an understanding of the links between domestic violence and child protection or child welfare affect the actual practice of social workers and family center workers? How are social workers' statutory powers in the United Kingdom to exclude abusers working in practice?

The research on effective social work and child protection practice so far focuses predominantly on two areas: (a) the identification and incorporation of domestic violence into everyday practice (Hester & Pearson, 1998) and (b) retrospective surveys of mothers' (unhappy) experiences of involvement with these agencies (Maynard, 1985). Little understanding exists of how recent work on risk assessment and supportive work with mothers has affected the decisions that courts and social workers make. The literature on risk assessment in North America is arguably more advanced than that in the United Kingdom; this emphasizes the importance of assessing lethality, despite the evidence from child protection research that suggests that it is difficult to get this right (Reder, Duncan, & Gray, 1993). Critics have argued that it is no accident that the emphasis on risk has arisen at the same time that resources available for social services have been cut (Parton, 1996). Research is needed that contextualizes risk by asking whether child protection agencies are making decisions more on the basis of concern about risk or on the rationing of resources.

Of relevance is work in the area of safety planning. At the practitioner level, particularly within refuges and shelters or victim advocacy services, safety planning has been developed within an empowerment model of working as a way to acknowledge and build on the protection and survival strategies that mothers and children develop. Within the multiagency and community intervention context, the practice of safety planning has started to spread, especially to the work of health care professionals and practitioners supporting women and children in the family court arena. The further development of safety planning promises a more empowering, culturally appropriate partnership approach to social services work with mothers as it focuses positively on women's experiences and efforts to tackle the constraints and barriers they face in the wider social context. As the professionalization of domestic violence work accelerates, however, safety planning could also lead to a marginalization of individual women's experiences by encouraging the further development of expert discourses on how mothers cope with and survive abuse. Evaluation studies are needed that look at the effectiveness of safety planning as an empowering method of working with mothers.

The feminist literature has been rightly critical of the apparent readiness of social workers and child protectors to blame abused mothers for "failure to protect" (Mullender, 1996), but there is still a need for work on appropriate interventions with mothers who neglect or abuse their children. There is especially a need for research that informs policy and practice in professions working to repair relationships between abused mothers and children with whom they have lost contact. Little is known about disrupted mothering in which women leave their children in residence with violent ex-partners nor about the type of social support given to the children living in this situation. The bulk of research interest on post-separation contact looks predominantly at fathers as the visiting parent (Burgess & Ruxton, 1996; Simpson, McCarthy, & Walker, 1994). This is likely to present challenges because the literature indicates that re-establishing contact between children and mother in the context of domestic violence is the most difficult relationship to support (Masson, Harrison, & Pavlovic, 1997). Questions could be asked about the gender aspects of parenting and contact for children. For instance, is contact with a father viewed differently than contact with a mother following a separation because of abuse?

Women living with domestic violence may experience ambivalent feelings toward children, especially if a child has been conceived through rape or implicated by the father in the abuse. Fathers may try to disrupt the emotional relationships between mother and children, especially between mothers and sons by, for instance, imposing limits on displays of affection or emotion (Radford & Hester, in press). There is a need for more research to explore this ambivalence toward children.

Challenging the Violence of Men

Current thinking about the necessity for a child to have a father has been generally detrimental to the well-being and safety of women and children surviving abuse (Radford et al., 1999). Research is needed that evaluates the new powers of courts to take domestic violence into account when making custody or visitation and contact orders and that assesses, over time, the advantages and disadvantages of either stopping contact or making orders for indirect contact instead. The concept of "safety," particularly the "psychological safety" of children and mothers, needs to be explored. Some studies show that a cessation in contact between the children and the abusive father has a positive impact on mothering and on the welfare of the children (Mertin, 1995). Qualitative research into these positive effects is needed to inform policy and decision making in family law. More attention might also be given to the quality of the relationship a violent man is able to offer his children. Further research is needed into what fathering means and what it involves for men, whether abusive or non-abusive.

Reliable research and evaluation studies are needed of work with violent men as fathers, whether in social work, probation practice, or perpetrator and parenting programs. Like perpetrator projects, parenting programs present an opportunity to challenge the abusive behavior of violent men. In recognition of this potential, courts in the United States, Australia, and New Zealand have been given powers to mandate parenting program attendance for a violent parent when custody or access issues are being considered. Little research has been done into the effectiveness of these programs in improving the safety of women and children and in sustaining relationships that have value for the children. What ideologies of fathering and family life inform practice within these groups? What is the curriculum? What methods are used to challenge abuse? How is success perceived and measured? These questions could also be usefully addressed by visitation and contact services. Research is needed that explores how attendance at these groups affects women as mothers and their relationships with their children over time.

CONCLUSION

The ideas in this chapter do not exhaust the many issues raised for future research and practice. Our primary intention has been to highlight some of the key concerns and challenges for domestic violence policy at the beginning of the 21st century. One important theme has been our desire to encourage a shift away from the mother-blaming focus of much of the recent work to look more constructively at developing empowering and effective social support for mothers and children surviving abuse. We have stressed the need to consider the varied social contexts in which both violence and mothering are constructed. Therefore, future research studies need to broaden the focus on convenience samples to include the many more mothers and children who never approach shelters and public services.

A second major concern has been the need to challenge dangerous aspects of the contemporary reconstitution of fatherhood, especially the notion that children always necessarily need to have their father in their life. Antiviolence researchers and activists can challenge the notions of child welfare that have underpinned these debates. Research designed to better inform the debates on mothering, the new fatherhood, and the needs of children surviving domestic violence is urgently needed.

REFERENCES

Abrahams, C. (1994). *The hidden victims: Children and domestic violence*. London: NCH Action for Children.

Beck, U. (1992). *Risk society*. London: Sage.

Binney, V., Harkell, G., & Nixon, J. (1988). *Leaving violent men*. Bristol, England: Women's Aid Federation.

Bullock, L., & McFarlane, J. (1989). The birth weight/battering connection. *American Journal of Nursing, 89*, 1153–1155.

Burgess, A., & Ruxton, S. (1996). *Men and their children: Proposals for public policy*. London: Institute for Public Policy Research.

Burton, S., Regan, L., & Kelly, L. (1998). *Supporting women and challenging men: Lessons from the Domestic Violence Intervention Project*. Bristol, England: Policy Press.

Campbell, J., Oliver, C., & Bullock, L. (1998). The dynamics of battering during pregnancy: Women's explanations of why. In J. Campbell (Ed.), *Empowering survivors of abuse: Health care for battered women and their children* (pp. 81–89). Thousand Oaks, CA: Sage.

Campbell, J., Soeken, K., McFarlane, J., & Parker, B. (1998). Risk factors for femicide among pregnant and non-pregnant battered women. In J. Campbell (Ed.), *Empowering survivors of abuse: Health care for battered women and their children* (pp. 90–97). Thousand Oaks, CA: Sage.

Chetwin, A., Knaggs, T., Te Wairere, A., & Young, P. (1999). *The domestic violence legislation and child access in New Zealand*. Wellington, New Zealand: Ministry of Justice.

Children Act Sub-Committee. (2000). *Report to the Lord Chancellor on the question of parental contact in cases where there is domestic violence*. London: Lord Chancellor's Department.

Chodorow, N. (1989). *Feminism and psychoanalytic theory*. Cambridge, England: Polity.

Crogman, R., & Miell, D. (1998). Making sense of family conflict: Influences on account. In R. Klein (Ed.), *Multi-disciplinary perspectives on family violence* (pp. 41–57). London: Routledge.

Curry, M., & Harvey, S. (1998). Stress related to domestic violence during pregnancy and infant birth weight. In J. Campbell (Ed.), *Empowering survivors of abuse: Health care for battered women and their children* (pp. 98–108). Thousand Oaks, CA: Sage.

Dobash, R., & Dobash, R. (1992). *Women, violence and social change*. London: Routledge.

Dobash, R., Dobash, R., Cavanagh, K., & Ellis, R. (1996). *Research evaluation of programmes for violent men*. Edinburgh, Scotland: Her Majesty's Stationery Office.

Dominy, N., & Radford, L. (1996). *Domestic violence in Surrey*. Kingston, Surrey, England: Surrey County Council, Social Services.

Farmer, E., & Owen, M. (1998). Gender and the child protection focus. *British Journal of Social Work, 28*, 545–564.

Gordon, L. (1989). *Heroes of their own lives: The politics and history of family violence*. London: Virago.

Hague, G., Malos, E., & Deer, W. (1996). *Multi-agency work and domestic violence*. Bristol, England: Policy Press.

Hester, M. (2000a). Domestic violence in China. In J. Radford, L. Harne, & M. Friedman (Eds.), *Women, violence and strategies for action* (pp. 149–166). Buckingham, England: Open University Press.

Hester, M. (2000b). *Women in abusive relationships: Group work and agency support.* Barkingside, England: Barnardos.

Hester, M., & Pearson, C. (1998). *From periphery to centre: Domestic violence in work with abused children.* Bristol, England: Policy Press.

Hester, M., Pearson, C., & Harwin, N. (2000). *Making an impact: Children and domestic violence—A reader.* London: Jessica Kingsley.

Hester, M., & Radford, L. (1996a). Contradictions and compromises: The impact of the Children Act 1989 on women and children's safety. In M. Hester, L. Kelly, & J. Radford (Eds.), *Women, violence and male power* (pp. 81–98). Buckingham, England: Open University Press.

Hester, M., & Radford, L. (1996b). *Domestic violence and child contact arrangements in England and Denmark.* Bristol, England: Policy Press.

Hoff, L. (1990). *Battered women as survivors.* London: Routledge.

Holden, G., & Ritchie, K. (1991). Linking extreme marital discord, child rearing and child behaviour problems: Evidence from battered women. *Child Development, 62,* 311–332.

Holden, G. W., Stein, J. D., Ritchie, K. L., Harris, S. D., & Jouriles, E. N. (1998). Parenting behaviors and beliefs of battered women. In G. W. Holden, R. Geffner, & E. N. Jouriles (Eds.), *Children exposed to marital violence: Theory, research, and applied issues* (pp. 289–334). Washington, DC: American Psychological Association.

Hooper, C., & Humphreys, C. (1998). Women whose children have been sexually abused: Reflections on a debate. *British Journal of Social Work, 28,* 565–580.

Hoyle, C. (1998). *Negotiating domestic violence.* Clarendon, England: Oxford University Press.

Humphreys, C. (1997). Child sexual abuse allegations in the context of divorce: Issues for mothers. *British Journal of Social Work, 27,* 529–544.

Humphreys, C., Hester, M., Hague, G., Mullender, A., Abrahams, H., & Lowe, P. (2000). *From good intentions to good practice: Mapping services working with families where there is domestic violence.* Bristol, England: Policy Press.

Johnson, J. (1991). *What Lisa knew: The truth and lies about the Steinberg case.* London: Bloomsbury.

Kelly, L. (1991). Unspeakable acts: Women who abuse. *Trouble & Strife, 21,* 13–20.

Kirkwood, C. (1993). *Leaving abusive partners.* Thousand Oaks, CA: Sage.

Lees, S. (1997). *Ruling passions: Sexual violence, reputation and the law.* Buckingham, England: Open University Press.

Lewis, J. (1993). *Women and social policies in Europe.* Aldershot, England: Elgar.

Mama, A. (1996). *The hidden struggle: Violence to women and the voluntary and statutory agencies' response.* London: London Race and Housing Group. (Original work published 1989)

Masson, J., Harrison, C., & Pavlovic, A. (1997). *Working with children and "lost" parents: Putting partnership into practice.* York, England: Joseph Rowntree Foundation.

Maynard, M. (1985). The response of social workers to domestic violence. In J. Pahl (Ed.), *Private violence and public policy* (pp. 125–140). London: Routledge.

McWilliams, M., & McKiernan, J. (1993). *Bringing it out into the open: Domestic violence in Northern Ireland.* Belfast, Ireland: Her Majesty's Stationery Office.

Mertin, P. (1995). A follow up study of children from domestic violence. *Australian Journal of Family Law, 9,* 76–85.

Mezey, G., & Bewley, S. (1997). Domestic violence in pregnancy. *British Medical Journal, 104,* 523–528.

Mirlees-Black, C. (1999). *Domestic violence: Findings from a new British crime survey self-completion questionnaire* (Home Office Research Study 191). London: Home Office.

Mullender, A. (1996). *Rethinking domestic violence.* London: Routledge.

O'Hagan, K., & Dillenburger, K. (1995). *The abuse of women in child care work.* Milton Keynes, England: Open University Press.

Oldham, M. (1997). *Blackstone's statues on family law 1997–1998* (6th ed.). London: Blackstone Press.

Pahl, J. (Ed.). (1985). *Private violence and public policy.* London: Routledge.

Parton, N. (1996). Social work, risk and the "blaming system." In N. Parton, (Ed.). *Social theory, social change and social work* (pp. 4–18). London: Routledge.

Plotnikoff, J., & Woolfson, R. (1999). *Policing domestic violence: Effective organisational structures.* London: Home Office.

Radford, L. (2000). Domestic violence. In M. May, R. Page & E. Brunsden (Eds.), *Understanding social problems* (pp. 70–83). Oxford, England: Blackwell.

Radford, L., & Hester, M. (in press). *Mothering through domestic violence.* Thousand Oaks, CA: Sage.

Radford, L., Hester, M., Humphries, J., & Woodfield, K. (1997). For the sake of the children: The law, domestic violence and child contact in England. *Women's Studies International Forum, 20,* 471–482.

Radford, L., Richardson, J., & Davies, L. (1998). *Domestic violence: A health care issue.* London: British Medical Association.

Radford, L., Sayer, S., & AMICA. (1999). *Unreasonable fears?* Bristol, England: Women's Aid Federation.

Reder, P., Duncan, S., & Gray, M. (1993). *Beyond blame: Child abuse tragedies revisited.* London: Routledge.

Richie, B. (1995). *Compelled to crime: The gender entrapment of Black battered women.* London: Routledge.

Schornstein, S. (1997). *Domestic violence and health care.* Thousand Oaks, CA: Sage.

Sclater, S., & Piper, C. (2000). Re-moralising the family? Family policy, family law and youth justice. *Child and Family Law Quarterly, 12,* 135–151.

Sevenhuijsen, S. (1998). *Citizenship and the ethics of care*. London: Routledge.

Shepard, M., & Pence, E. (1999). *Coordinating community responses to domestic violence: Lessons from Duluth and beyond*. London: Sage.

Simpson, B., McCarthy, P., & Walker, J. (1994). *Being there: Fathers after divorce*. Newcastle Upon Tyne, England: University of Newcastle, Relate Centre for Family Studies.

Stanko, E. (1997). Safety talk: Conceptualising women's risk assessment as a "technology of the soul." *Theoretical Criminology, 1*, 479–499.

Stark, E., & Flitcraft, A. (1996). *Women at risk: Domestic violence and women's health*. Thousand Oaks, CA: Sage.

Sullivan, C., Nguyen, H., Allen, N., Bybee, D., & Juras, J. (1999, October). *Beyond searching for deficits: Evidence that battered women are nurturing mothers*. Paper presented at the International Conference on Children Exposed to Family Violence, San Diego, CA.

Walker, L. (1984). *The battered woman syndrome*. New York: Springer.

World Health Organization. (1997). *Violence against women: A priority health issue*. Geneva, Switzerland: Author.

7

FATHERHOOD AND DOMESTIC VIOLENCE: EXPLORING THE ROLE OF MEN WHO BATTER IN THE LIVES OF THEIR CHILDREN

OLIVER J. WILLIAMS, JACQUELYN L. BOGGESS,
AND JANET CARTER

In cases in which men and women are in dispute about their relationships, additional complications develop when children are involved. What is in the best interest of children when parents break up? In divorce, what characteristics make a good mother or father? What roles should parents and, particularly for this discussion, fathers play in the lives of their children in the context of a marital dispute: breadwinner, adult male role model, coequal parent, or all of these? The answers to such questions are complex and cause much debate. These questions become even more complicated when the father in question has been abusive to the mother of his children. Partner abuse raises several concerns about women's and children's safety for advocates of battered women. Although it is clear that not all men who get divorced are abusive, each year estranged partners kill or injure their wives or girlfriends through domestic violence disputes (Bachman & Saltzman, 1995; Jaffe & Geffner, 1998). Many of these men are also fathers. Advocates in the field of domestic violence are concerned with the continuous pattern of abusive behavior by men who batter. These men abuse women and expose children to physical and emotional abuse during the course of an intimate relationship and in its aftermath (Doyne et al., 1999; Saunders, 1994; Sheeran & Hampton, 1999).

In contrast, there are advocates who are concerned about the rights of fathers. These advocates primarily want to provide emotional support to fathers and to assist them in taking responsibility for their offspring. They encourage fathers to spend time with their children and to address their financial and emotional needs. Keeping fathers involved in the lives of their children is an important contribution of this field. Many fathers face challenges in raising their children or remove themselves from the lives of their children during relationship conflicts and divorce. This disconnection between fathers and children has been referred to as an epidemic (Doherty, Kouneski, & Erickson, 1996).

Advocates in this field and supporters of father involvement call for a critical analysis and removal of barriers to fathers' access and opportunities to engage and parent their children. They say that contemporary attitudes and laws involving fathers discriminate against their access to their children and capacity to parent (Doherty et al., 1996). Poor fathers have concerns about child support enforcement and the lack of economic resources, which are barriers to their access. Responsible-fatherhood groups believe that today's society de-emphasizes the importance of fatherhood and marriage and that a disregard for morals has contributed to this crisis faced by children and families. Middle-class and resource-rich divorcing fathers are often concerned with judicial codes that set limits on their access and involvement with their former partners and their children. Some advocates in this field encourage these fathers to gain joint or sole custody of their offspring. Fathers' rights advocates promote challenging any perceived barriers that they think prevent fathers from acquiring access to their children and set limits on them. Domestic violence is viewed by some in this field as another rationale to deny fathers access and to set limits.

Currently, the domestic violence movement and the fatherhood movement influence each other regarding laws, national policy, access of fathers, and the safety and protection of battered women and children. For the advocates in these movements to continue to address their important work of creating healthy, safe, protected, nurturing, and secure environments for parents (married, unmarried, separated, divorced, male or female) and children, differences in the perspectives held by the movements must be reconciled. In general, distrust and skepticism exist among practitioners and advocates of each of these two areas concerning the philosophy and motivation of the other. Although caution should be a consideration in assessing the intention, mission, and philosophy of those doing the work, it is also clear that there is room for collaboration and common ground.

The primary goal of this chapter is to increase the reader's understanding of the concerns and challenges of the two fields. A second goal is to point out the research questions that must be addressed to respond to the issues faced by battered women and children exposed to violence by men who batter who are also fathers. First, we discuss why father involvement is considered an important concern. We provide an overview of the various elements that make up the fatherhood field. We examine the issues that make fathers' rights efforts a concern for domestic violence advocates. Finally, we identify research questions associated with safety for battered women and access to children by fathers who are also batterers. Although there are many types of fathers, father figures, and role models that we could discuss, for the purpose of this chapter we focus primarily on issues associated with nonresidential and noncustodial biological fathers who batter.

FATHERHOOD AS AN EMERGING MOVEMENT

In general, fatherhood as an emerging movement is unknown to many researchers, practitioners, and advocates in domestic violence, with the exception of perhaps fathers' rights advocates and groups. For those who work in domestic violence to develop an appreciation of the various advocates of this movement, it is important to examine the different groups working to improve father and child relationships and their concerns and points of view.

In recent years, the issue of fatherhood has developed increasing attention in the nation's thinking. Many fatherhood advocates are sounding the alarm concerning children being raised in households without fathers. They say that there is a crisis in the United States caused by the economic, physical, and emotional disconnection between fathers and their children (Blankenhorn, 1995; Popenow, 1996; Whitehead, 1993). In 1994, Vice President Al Gore held a national summit in Nashville, TN, on the role of fathers in the lives of their children. Groups, organizations, members of the academic community, government agencies, and legislators have organized to address responsible fatherhood and the concerns of nonresident parents.

More children than ever before are living in a home in which their father is not in residence. The reason for this trend includes the high rates of divorce: 50% of all marriages in the United States end in divorce (Cherlin, 1992). Also out-of-wedlock birth rates are at an all-time high. One-third of all births in the United States are to single women, and the numbers have risen steadily over the past 40 years (Garfinkel, McLanahan, Meyer, & Seltzer, 1998). There is an unprecedented increase in the number of female-headed households, which has contributed to the feminization of poverty (Doherty et al., 1996).

There is a declining presence of noncustodial fathers; 90% of children in single-parent families reside with their mothers. In the 2 years following a divorce, half of a group of fathers lost contact with their children (Doherty et al., 1996). Very few fathers engage and remain in the lives of their children because fathers often retreat in the face of marital conflict. In addition, for those fathers who want to remain involved with their children, many report that ex-partners and U.S. laws and policies are biased against them (Doherty et al., 1996).

Fathers who do not live with their children full time are, by definition, "nonresident parents." Many fathers are also, by means of a legal custody determination, "noncustodial parents." This second situation is the result of a court ruling that the child's mother (or other person or institution) shall have custody of the child. Generally, the fatherhood movement emerged to address the needs of fathers who neither live with nor have custody of their children but who want to be involved and supportive in their children's lives.

Over the years, U.S. society has tended to enforce a family division of labor in which mothers have been responsible for the care and nurturing of children and fathers have been the wage earners. Traditionally, married men have been able to interact with their children as the mothers have cared for the children. In today's society, many women have taken on a role of emotional and financial supporter of their children. Given statistics about divorce and out-of-wedlock births and that women typically have custody of their children, father's rights advocates are now faced with the question of how to support and encourage serious parenting and positive contributions from men who do not live with their children (Garfinkel et al., 1998).

THE FATHERHOOD MOVEMENT

The general term *movement* implies a cohesive effort by groups with similar makeup and a common goal. The fatherhood movement is more accurately characterized as a confluence of activity by various fathers' groups, men's groups, individual fathers, and other kinds of organizations and government agencies with overlapping but significantly different agendas, objectives, and methods. The call for father involvement comes from many quarters: advocates for poor families, men's and fatherhood groups, government agencies, and individual men who feel alienated from their families.

In the past 5 years, the federal government has been instrumental in continuing the discussion about fathers and their contribution to their children's lives. In 1995, President Clinton requested that each agency of the federal government review its programs and policies with the purpose of strengthening the role of fathers in families.

What follows is our description of the various elements that make up the fatherhood field. Some in the field may disagree with these labels because there are overlapping terms and shared philosophies. Our intention is to provide a general overview of the major ideas that represent these elements of the fatherhood field.

Father Involvement Programs

Father involvement projects and organizations encouraged by the federal government are designed to help fathers find employment and reorder their lives, so that they will be able to meet the financial, emotional, and physical responsibilities of raising their children. Some poor fathers believe that they have been crowded out of their parenting opportunities and responsibilities by the social welfare and child support systems (Johnson, Levine, & Doolittle, 1998); the call for a discussion about fathers also comes from these men and their advocates. A national discussion about fatherhood is especially urgent. Noncustodial fatherhood, whether the man is married or not married, has a unique and deleterious impact on poor men, women, and their children. The concern of these fathers and children is a more basic one of sustenance and maintenance than it is for families in higher socioeconomic groups.

Families experiencing poverty and social isolation often require government assistance. Over time and with an increased public disenchantment with welfare, there has been a move from many quarters to bring fathers back into their families so that they can provide financial assistance, thus relieving the burden on the government. Some agents (including some responsible-fatherhood programs) would have fathers reclaim what they perceive to be a position of responsibility, which has been taken over by the government through the provision of welfare.

To describe people who conduct or participate in father involvement program activities as members of a cohesive fatherhood group would be inaccurate. Instead, father involvement activities are more often centered in fatherhood programs sponsored by nonprofit, community-based organizations in low-income, high-unemployment communities. Low-income fathers who participate in these programs are engaged in employment, training, and peer group support programs and, when needed, substance abuse treatment. But in general, these men do not become members of a fatherhood group or organization. The fatherhood organizations provide services to help respond to the special needs of this segment of men. Although such programs have been targeted for men and fathers, some of them also provide similar services for female parents when requested.

Supporters of father involvement often encourage positive outcomes for all family members: fathers, children, and mothers. But they are primarily focused on helping fathers become more involved in their children's lives through a range of positive ways, including financial and emotional support. These fatherhood programs are not necessarily promoting marriage or a gender-based division of labor. They are, however, concerned about the social welfare and social policy issues facing poor families, specifically unmarried fathers and their children in families who receive welfare.

On the one hand, father involvement advocates encourage paternity establishment and child support contributions by fathers. On the other hand, they are concerned that welfare and child support systems exacerbate barriers to father involvement among low-income families. For example, many couples who have children together do not get married but continue to live together in a family situation. They may be unmarried parents in a safe and healthy parenting relationship (whether they are in a romantic relationship or not). They pool their emotional and modest financial resources to take care of their children and themselves. But the father may be legally designated as a noncustodial parent even though he does physically reside with the child and the child's mother. These fathers are not nonresident fathers, but they are, by law, noncustodial parents. Often parents faced with this reality conclude that the best thing for their children is for the mother to deny knowledge of the father's whereabouts and for him to provide support directly to her as he is able, either in kind or financially. He goes "underground" to avoid the system. Although he may actually be available, nurturing, and supportive to his children, child support and welfare systems operate to his detriment (and perhaps to the detriment of his children and their mother) as if he is physically absent from his children's life.

This distinction is important in analyzing how the current child support system works. A resident, noncustodial father still must pay child support (send money outside the family home) to a central child support office location. There are many valid reasons for requiring a central location payment, but if the mother in this situation is receiving welfare, the money is used to repay the government for cash assistance; if she does not receive welfare, the money eventually comes back to her. If both parents are very poor and have little income, the precarious security of the household can be devastated by the mandatory payment of a large portion of the total household income.

For many low-income parents, whether the father is a resident of the household and on good terms with the mother or not, the child support enforcement system can hurt rather than help the children and their fathers (and mothers). The system sets an initial payment amount on the basis of current circumstances, which cannot be changed quickly or efficiently when there is a change in financial circumstances for either party.

The basis of father involvement programs is the belief that most fathers want to be responsible, involved, and supportive of their children to the best of their ability, but that bureaucratic, societal, and family barriers prevent involvement. Many father involvement advocates would agree with Ed Pitt and Jim Levine (Levine & Pitt, 1995), who outlined a strategy for community-based organizations and others interested in promoting father involvement:

- Prevent men from having children before they are ready for the financial and emotional responsibilities of fatherhood.
- Prepare men for the legal, financial, and emotional responsibilities of fatherhood.
- Establish paternity at childbirth, so that every father and child has, at a minimum, a legal connection.
- Involve men who are fathers, whether married or not, in a emotional connection to and financial support of their children.
- Support fathers in the variety of their roles and in their connection with their children, regardless of their legal and financial status (married, unmarried, employed, and unemployed). (p. 6)

In a 1995 research and evaluation project, the U.S. Department of Health and Human Services researchers visited and interviewed practitioners who worked at five community-based organizations that ran fatherhood programs. In the introduction to the resulting report, one common theme emerged: "To be effective and responsible fathers, men needed first to develop the capacity to take care of themselves" (U.S. Department of Health and Human Services, 1997a, 1997b). Concerns voiced by fathers' rights groups, such as fathers' access to and visitation of their children, divorce mediation, and child custody, are important issues for father involvement programs. However, unlike the two groups discussed below, the inclination of those who support father involvement is to respect a mother's life choices and to acknowledge the impact of a father's situation and his actions on both mother and child. Some fatherhood involvement programs are reluctant to address domestic violence directly in their programming because of fear that it will reduce the number of men who seek help from such programs. In contrast, other programs have developed relationships with battered-women's programs and batterers' treatment programs to attend to issues associated with domestic violence.

Responsible-Fatherhood Groups

The word *responsible* signals the basic moral tenor of these organizations. The call is for men to assume their moral responsibility as fathers and husbands. Fathers in these groups can be men from any socioeconomic level. Researchers, analysts, and scholars in this field have collaborated and developed national organizations to send their message. Two of the most visible responsible-fatherhood organizations are the Institute for American Values (IAV) and the National Fatherhood Initiative (NFI). Representatives of these groups suggest that one of the most devastating outcomes of divorce is the loss of the father from a child's home. According to David Blankenhorn

(1995), director of IAV and author of *Fatherless America*, "if he vacates the house his children live in—particularly if his nonresidency is voluntary, something that he and former wife have chosen—he vacates the only headquarters available to him for effective fatherhood" (p. 157).

Responsible-fatherhood organizations contend that the absence of fathers in families and the inadequacy of parenting in female-headed households have led to dysfunctional families and a dysfunctional society. According to Travis Ballard, president of the National Congress for Fathers and Families (NCFC),

> more than any other single factor, the absence of biological fathers is the leading cause of many of our nation's problems. Crime, drug problems, teen violence, inner-city strife, and juvenile delinquency are cited among the results of fatherless homes. The compelling implication of these findings is clear: one parent is simply not enough. (Ballard, 1995)

NFI is a "social movement" created to "restore responsible fatherhood as a national priority" (National Fatherhood Initiative, 1998–1999, p. 2). According to NFI's analysis of sociological and demographic statistics,

- Eighty percent of suicidal youth come from single-parent homes.
- Fatherless children are twice as likely to drop out of school.
- Seventy percent of juveniles in state reform institutions grew up in single-parent or no-parent situations.
- Sixty percent of America's rapists grew up in homes without fathers.
- Seventy-two percent of adolescent murderers grew up without fathers.
- Eighty percent of adolescents in psychiatric hospitals come from broken homes.

Organizations with this kind of "family values" stand (which would include Promise Keepers and other religion-based organizations) use their moral and religious beliefs to support a gender-based family structure and division of labor that encourages marriage between parents.

Fathers' Rights Groups

Since the early 1960s, divorced, middle-class fathers have made concerted efforts to demand their "rights" (Vaux, 1997). Many of them feel pushed out of their children's lives by the court system and their children's mother. Fathers' rights organizations are composed mostly of men who are divorced from their children's mothers. Some of the common experiences and frustrations of these noncustodial fathers have led them to organize to discuss common issues and to challenge what they perceive as an unfair or uninformed system. They often exchange information with each other and those outside their organizations by way of the Internet.

The perception of an especially angry contingent of this group is that women and the court system have conspired together against fathers. This category actually represents a collection of membership groups because fathers' rights groups are usually founded and administered by individual leaders. Many fathers' rights groups are drawn to various high-profile divorce lawyers who write how-to books and provide seminars to explain and educate noncustodial fathers about matrimonial law (Baskerville, 1998). Finally, there are a few larger, more influential, and well-known fathers' rights organizations toward which smaller groups gravitate. These small organizations tend to constitute the constituency and consumers of the information provided by larger, more visible organizations. Collectively these groups are working toward a common goal of preserving (or restoring) what they view as fathers' rights. These are the stereotypical fathers' rights groups. When people outside the movement think about this issue, it is usually with the characteristics of these organizations in mind. Part of the reason these men and these groups are so vocal and visible is that they are more likely to have the resources to be heard by the system.

Individually, these divorced fathers tend to have the resources and the inclination to battle in court for custody of their children. Collectively, that inclination and resources allow them to lobby legislators and policymakers as a special-interest group. In that capacity, fathers' rights groups lobby state legislatures to change matrimonial and child support laws, including a state-mandated presumption of joint physical and legal custody (or "shared parenting").

The men in the fathers' rights groups distinguish themselves from men in the father involvement programs and in the responsible-fatherhood organizations by taking little responsibility for ending their marriages, conflict-ridden relationships with their wives or girlfriends, or separation from their children. In fact, some pointedly disagree with the implication from responsible-fatherhood organizations that some fathers have shirked their responsibility to their families. Steven Baskerville, a political science lecturer at Howard University, appreciated the fatherhood publicity generated by David Popenow and David Blankenhorn (two leaders in the responsible-fatherhood arena) but wished that they would focus more on the fact that father absence is not always voluntary (Baskerville, 1998).

Baskerville (1998) cited father's rights advocate Sanford Braver, who showed "that it is overwhelmingly wives who initiate divorce and courts that routinely throw fathers out of their families without any grounds whatever." Baskerville said, "with the exception of convicted criminals, no group in our society has fewer rights than fathers. Not just divorced fathers, not never-married fathers: fathers." Divorced fathers have voiced many reasons for feeling resentment toward their former spouses and alienation from their children. Some of the early fathers' rights organizations sprouted from grassroots efforts of one or more fathers, who believed that the family court system, the child support system, and U.S. law's divorce policy were unfair to men and biased in favor of women.

FATHERHOOD FACTIONS AND DOMESTIC VIOLENCE PERSPECTIVES

In general, fatherhood groups view violence between intimate partners as a result of conflict and negative interactions between men and women. To some, the natural result of such conflict is violence. There are distinctions among the groups concerning their willingness to acknowledge and respond to male violence.

Father Involvement Advocates

Most father involvement supporters strongly and sincerely denounce individual acts of violence. However, their inclination is to explain violence as a result of and a reaction to a man's own feeling of powerlessness and inefficacy as an individual. They tend to expend the bulk of resources and concentration to address a father's social and personal problems. They say that the most effective way to improve a man's family life and to stop the violence is to help him change his life and get rid of those feelings of powerlessness. Get him a job and a good reputation in the community; then the violence will stop.

Responsible-Fatherhood Groups

This faction of the fatherhood movement acknowledges that domestic violence happens but suggests that blame should be placed on society and on its move away from traditional family values. It is propagandized that because of men's biological makeup, they are naturally aggressive and uncivilized (Blankenhorn, 1995) and that women and children pacify and tame them. However, they say that when the family breaks down, when society allows men to dissociate themselves from families, or when men are no longer expected to be accountable for the welfare of their family, they revert to a more savage (violent) state.

Blankenhorn (1995) contended that some research suggests that there is significantly less violence between married couples as compared with unmarried couples and that marriage reduces the chance that a man will be violent. He said that "the institutional inhibitor of male violence is married fatherhood" (p. 36). He added that

> the plot line running through all of these crimes is the growing incoherence of paternity and the steady weakening of marriage as an institution that brings order and meaning to men's lives. As marriage weakens, more and more men become isolated and estranged from their children and from the mothers of their children. One result, in turn, is the spread of male violence. (p. 38)

The Children's Rights Council (1999) seeks means of strengthening families during marriage. If divorce occurs, they work for custody reform, "substituting conciliation and mediation for the adversarial process" (p. 2). An article for the organization's newsletter, "Locating Missing and Hidden Children," states that "local officials are used to thinking only in terms of finding parents who owe financial child support, so some of them aren't ready yet to find children being hidden by the custodial parent" (p. 12). The article goes on to sketch the scenario of a man who claimed that the custodial mother was hiding his children from him. Sometimes, mothers resort to hiding children from their father and from the courts when the father has exhibited sexual or other violent behavior toward the child. The article, however, does not affirmatively acknowledge that sexual abuse or partner abuse actually occurred and that women's and children's safety was a sufficient rationale for actions associated with protection.

Some policies that support responsible fatherhood do not take domestic violence into account. This is especially evident in discussions about women and families who receive welfare benefits. In a written statement to the White House, Travis Ballard (1995) of the NCFC made a policy recommendation strongly supporting the cooperation requirement of the welfare law. This requires women who are not married to the father of their children to provide the father's name and identifying information for use in paternity establishment and collection of child support.

Ballard made this recommendation without reference to domestic violence. He further suggested that "prior to issuance of any government aid, the party applying for the subsidy produce an affidavit from the other parent and themselves indicating that no other child care is available from the father, other relatives, or grandparents." Finally, he suggested that

> when there is a genuine need for the subsidy, applicable policies should be reformulated to ensure that the father remains in the home after the birth of children and require both parties to actively participate in their children's raising and care. This might include marriage and taxpayer savings.

But clearly in situations in which a man has been continuously violent and dangerous to his partner and children, this kind of exchange is not advised.

Wade Horn (1995) of the NFI recommended that

the welfare system should be restructured. Either the system require mothers to identify the fathers of their children prior to receiving benefits or to give preference in enrollment to families where the presence of the father in the home can be documented.

In 1997, Horn (Horn & Bush, 1997) stated that

strategies for promoting fatherhood and marriage are, to a very large extent, in conflict with those that seek to help single mothers achieve self-sufficiency through work. Indeed, a welfare system that helps single mothers become employed, but ignores the need to promote fatherhood and marriage, may serve only to enable unmarried women to rear children without the presence of the father.

Even when there is some lip service paid to the issue of domestic violence, there is no real respect for the contention that public policy should be made with this important issue in mind. Wade Horn (1995) said, "I think the institution of divorce must be restigmatized." Proponents of this viewpoint hold that although no one wants to go back to a period in human history where women (or men) could be physically or sexually abused by their spouses and not have any escape from that abuse, divorce should be made "less easy to obtain." However, if this is done so, how can the women who are victims of the abuse be protected?

Members of this group continue to say that they acknowledge that there is domestic violence and that abused women should be protected. In fact, they admit that some of their policy suggestions would create an environment that would put abused women at more risk and that those women and their children should be protected. However, they never address how to do both things at once.

Fathers' Rights Groups

Fathers in these groups tend to be angry at the child's mother and at the system. Many of these groups deny that domestic violence is prevalent enough to warrant a concerted effort to deal with it. In fact, some fathers' rights groups contend that men are the victims of domestic violence at least as often as are women. These groups often imply that charges of violence perpetrated by men against women are fabricated or exaggerated to intimidate men and strip them of their rights as fathers.

According to men's rights advocate Walter Vaux (1997), whose article appears on the web site of the National Coalition of Free Men (NCFM), "until the current trend of sequestering fathers is reversed, the nation will be crippled with dysfunctional children, weakened households, and abused men." He also implied that society should be concerned about the innate and unavoidable violence from women. Vaux referred to men's rights advocate Paul Herzog, who "explains, on the dangerous practices arising with a single parent, that two parents provide checks. In the father's absence, the mother loses this protection, and the mother's aggressive and libidinous inclinations center on the child," and to men's rights advocate Raymond Hughes, who referenced a Children's Rights Council survey of state child protective service agencies, which found that mothers abuse children at a rate almost double that of men. In a guest editorial at the Internet site of the NCFM, Hughes generally ridiculed and attempted to discredit advocates for victims of domestic violence. He suggested that statistics about domestic violence in his state, New Hampshire, were exaggerated and in some cases fabricated. He accused advocates of "shameless skewing of the numbers" to secure federal grant money.

CONCERNS OF DOMESTIC VIOLENCE ADVOCATES

Do the attitudes, beliefs, intentions, and policies promoted by fatherhood advocates erode the capacity of domestic violence advocates to keep women safe? Through the information cited above, a general impression is that fatherhood advocates question the realities and challenges of battered women. They do not trust domestic violence advocates and believe that they are overstating their concerns.

Fatherhood advocates believe that feminist and battered-women's advocates label all men as batterers. They also believe that these advocates view women as innocent despite their behaviors in relationships. A prevailing view is that many battered women falsely allege partner abuse as a way to gain advantage in a marital dispute in court and child custody cases. Although researchers have found that battered women rarely falsely allege domestic violence (Everson & Boot, 1989; Faller, Olafson, & Corwin, 1993; Geffner, 1997; Jaffe & Geffner, 1998; Pagelow, 1997; Thoennes & Tjaden, 1990), many practitioners and fathering advocates recite cases in which men have been falsely accused.

Another belief of fatherhood advocates is that domestic violence is a natural result of conflict between two individuals and that women are equal contributors to the violence. The fact is that women are significantly less likely to be perpetrators of partner abuse than are men (Doyne et al., 1999; Saunders, 1988; Stets & Straus, 1990). Relatively few women are the primary aggressors of physical abuse; this fact must be placed in context and not be used as a ploy to minimize and discredit the issues associated with violence against women (Jaffe & Geffner, 1998). Mutual violence occurs in domestic violence cases as well. Often in such cases, battered women are protecting themselves from their abuser in self-defense, but this type of violence gets reported as mutual (Doyne et al., 1999; Gelles & Straus, 1988). The prevailing view among domestic violence prevention advocates is that violence is behavior that batterers choose as a method to resolve conflict or control their partners (Gondolf, 1985; Williams, 1999). As a result, battered-women's advocates are concerned with the continuous patterns of violent and abusive behavior of those men who batter women, some of whom are fathers. Until recently, few attempts have been made to confront men with such abusive behaviors and hold them accountable for their actions.

To this point, fatherhood groups have not clearly identified nonviolent and nonabusive behavior toward a female partner as among the characteristics of positive fathering. Nor, in general, do these advocates address abusive behavior among fathers who abuse either their wife or their children. This lack of attention about domestic violence reduces a family's capacity to be safe and secure. It also gives the impression that regardless of the consequence to the family, a father must be present at any cost. Battered-women's advocates believe that it is equally important to expect healthy behavior from fathers, whether they are residential or not. The quality of the fathering relationship is as important as having a father present. To promote the safety and well-being of battered women and children, fatherhood advocates must acknowledge battered women's unique experiences with men who batter. What is the reality of battered women and children exposed to domestic violence? The remainder of this section explores that question.

Creating Safe, Stable Environments for Battered Women

Many fatherhood advocates are uninformed or misinformed about the status of battered women and children. It is as important for these advocates to be aware of the issues and concerns of battered women to critically examine how to respond to the behavior of fathers who batter. Thirty percent of all women are victims of a form of abuse in an adult relationship during their lifetime (Doyne et al., 1999; Jaffe & Geffner, 1998); 10% of those victims receive the most severe abuse. Often the victimization of battered women begins during pregnancy; 16% of women are physically or sexually abused during pregnancy (Campbell, 1994; Saunders, 1994). Battered women are at risk for continued abuse when they leave the relationship, become separated, or get divorced (Doyne et al., 1999; McMahon & Pence, 1993; Saunders, 1994).

Children are not immune to the effects of their mother's abuse. Children are at an increased risk for abuse in a home where their mother is being abused (Jaffe, Wolfe, & Wilson, 1990; Saunders, 1994). Many adolescents are injured when they attempt to protect their mother from their father's violence (Williams, 1993). Battered women are six times more likely than are nonbattered women to have children reported for child abuse (Saunders, 1994). A truism in the field is that to protect the child, one must also protect the mother.

Men who batter abuse women physically, emotionally, and spiritually. They use a range of tactics to intimidate and harass their partners. What follows is an edited letter from a battered woman whose abuser used the court and other systems against her. She wanted the opportunity to have her experiences reported. In place of the batterer's name, we have substituted "my abuser." The comments that she shares express the basic concerns for many battered women and their advocates in the United States.

> I appreciate the opportunity to express my thoughts and feelings about the harassment and stalking I was subjected to by my abuser. Although I would very much like to protect my privacy, I think it is important that law enforcement officials and professionals involved in domestic violence know my abuser. My abuser will be going to prison. He won't get life—he will get out. Sadly, I believe he will certainly stalk and harass me again once he gets out of prison, or he may send someone else after me.
>
> . . . During my brief marriage to my abuser, I was subjected to consistent emotional and verbal abuse. He stated he wanted a divorce, but he refused to leave my home. (I had purchased the home years before our marriage and had always paid all the bills.) He always said if he left, he would take my son with him. I felt terribly trapped and frightened because I felt he would certainly take my son and possibly leave the county. I know that if I forced him out of my home, he would come after me with a vengeance, which he certainly did. I knew I would never be rid of him, and, sadly, I won't. My abuser thrives on conflict and lives for revenge. In order to have proper perspective, I would like you to know some of the things he did prior to being convicted of violating a protection order and later stalking: established false medical and police reports accusing me of hitting him with a broom; accused me of being an alcoholic, drug user, and child abuser. All of these accusations are ridiculous and totally untrue. However, I was required to take a drug and alcoholic evaluation and submit to periodic drug and alcohol testing as well as parenting evaluation. [I] tried to have my son put in foster care since my abuser insisted I was likely to kill my boy. I am a good and loving mother and have never abused my child. . . . One of his many allegations of abuse created an extensive conflict at my child's pediatrician's office that involved the police. He later sued the practice, and I was forced to find another doctor for my son. . . . He refused to turn my son over after a visitation, again alleging abuse. I was told and had to obtain a special court order to get my boy

back from this man. He got a friend of his to file a lien against my house, claiming he was owed for work that was never done. [He] broke into my house when he knew I was out of town and stole a photocopier, family pictures, and unplugged my refrigerator. This was done in the few hours before my house sitters arrived. A neighbor saw him take the photocopier out of the house but refused to get involved because he was afraid of my abuser. [He] poured dirty paint thinner into the gas tank of my car, causing extensive damage to the car, and certainly putting my son and me into potential danger. [He] slashed a tire on my car. [He] came to my house at night and used a scanner to intercept my portable telephone; then he called the same person. The friend then reported me to the police for making harassing phone calls, which of course I didn't make. . . . [He] established a Web page about our divorce and me. He posted outrageous and humiliating lies about me, which thousands of people saw, along with my picture. Among the many lies were accusations of drug and alcohol abuse, child abuse, spousal abuse, mental instability, and suicidal inclinations. The Web page was also extremely abusive to my attorney and the judges and commissioners involved with our divorce case. The above are just a fraction of the incidents I had to endure at the hands of my abuser, even though I had obtained a protection order against him. He engaged in a consistent and relentless campaign of harassment and intimidation against friends, family, and me. I have lived in constant fear of my abuser for the past three to four years. . . . For the past two years, I have had either my elderly mother or aunt living with me at all times. They have had to act as witnesses to my every action and to support me against the unfounded accusations and my abuser's various lawsuits. This has been a tremendous hardship for them, as they live in another state. The most insidious thing about this whole situation shows my abuser's ability to manipulate the legal system as a method of harassment and abuse. By acting pro se in our divorce, he filed numerous frivolous motions to generate extensive legal fees to financially destroy me.

. . . I paid a staggering amount of money for what should have been a simple divorce, with virtually no property issues. I absolutely dread the day when my abuser will be released from prison, as he will be able to continue his campaign of abuse against me with no restraints. I live in fear of him. Since he has supervised visitation rights to my son, it will be impossible for me to get away from him. As long as my abuser has access to my son, he has access to me. Even if he doesn't kill me or hire someone else to kill me, I will be subjected to endless legal abuse, lawsuit after lawsuit, and unknown incidents of property damage and terrorism. This is something I cannot afford, either financially or emotionally. I have frequently felt that my abuser's rights to "free speech" outrank my son's and my rights to privacy and safety.

. . . Unless you have experienced this type of abuse, it's virtually impossible to imagine what terror it can bring. I hope that my sharing with you will encourage you to strongly enforce what laws currently exist and to work for tougher laws and stiffer sentencing for criminals who participate in this kind of frightening abuse.

This woman was not effectively protected or supported by the justice system. The acts of the abuser described by this woman are not unfamiliar to battered women and their advocates. Battered women look to the community, the court, and human services professionals for protection and support. They also expect community members and helping professionals to understand what they are going through. Too often this does not happen. This experience is not an isolated one. For example, in 1998 many people read in the *Seattle Times* or saw the television program *America's Most Wanted* about the case of Carlton Edwards, who killed his wife Melanie and their daughter—and then himself—at a court-ordered supervised visitation site. The visitation and murder happened even though Melanie had a protection order against Carlton. She had stated on many occasions that he had threatened to kill her. However, Carlton had legally ordered visitation.

Recently, the authors interviewed two battered women who had similar experiences with the system and with their abuser to those described above. For example, a 38-year-old woman from the East Coast spoke of the terror she felt because her ex-husband would eventually get out of jail one day and locate her and their child. On several occasions, he threatened to kill her and her family; given his history this was not an idle threat. She was fearful that the court may encourage her to maintain a relationship with her ex-husband, if he chooses to reconnect with their child. Despite obtaining a protection order during her divorce, she received no protection or support through the court system associated with their domestic violence and divorce dispute. Her order of protection did not keep her or her daughter safe from his threats. The criminal justice system convicted and incarcerated her abuser on weapons charges when the police found guns and explosives in his car. He was not incarcerated or held accountable for partner violence.

A 50-year-old woman from the West Coast recalled her ordeal as she left an abusive husband 25 years ago. She left in the middle of the night with her four boys, all younger than age 10. She remembers how her abuser seemed to manipulate the court system. Although she got custody of the kids, he would not cooperate or take on his financial responsibility, despite having the means to do so. She recalls that she and her boys went homeless for a time because he would not pay child support. He vowed never to help her or his children unless she came back. She did not and today boasts about raising her four boys who are all college graduates.

In all of the cases above, the criminal justice system was not able to address the concerns and danger related to partner abuse. If the court systems are not sensitive enough to address these examples, what should battered women expect in their situation? Abuse reduces battered women's capacity to maintain safe and stable lives for themselves and their children. What is the system's capacity to effectively determine when abuse occurs, who the victims truly are, and how to protect them? According to the literature, minimal attention has been given to domestic violence in divorce and custody disputes. Few courts and related human services systems have the capacity to accurately assess how battered women are affected by partner violence (Doyne et al., 1999; Jaffe & Geffner, 1998). Judges, social workers, psychologists, and attorneys often do not have the training to understand and assess domestic violence. Thirty-five states have laws by which domestic violence can be used as a consideration in divorce and child custody cases, yet other states do not consider it at all (Doyne et al., 1999; Sheeran & Hampton, 1999).

Also although visitation centers and services are becoming important pieces in a coordinated response to domestic violence, a number of key considerations remain. Visitation centers are no guarantee of safety and protection for battered women and children. They do little to improve the ability of a batterer to parent in a responsible, nonviolent way (Sheeran & Hampton, 1999).

To exacerbate the current state of affairs, there is an aggressive effort by some fathers' rights advocates to minimize the importance of domestic violence as it relates to women and children. These advocates have been reported to encourage the tactic of blaming battered women for child abuse and neglect, as noted above. Through child custody cases, many battered women are also labeled with *malicious mother syndrome* or *alienated parent syndrome*, terms that have been used to describe women who choose not to cooperate in working with the father of their children. Typically, this labeling and assessment of battered women occurs during the process of divorce. In certain cases, labeling is used as an attempt to discredit battered women and their ability to parent (Faller & Devoe, 1994; Jaffe & Geffner, 1998; Saunders, 1994).

Such labeling may also be a ploy to shift the attention from an abusive husband's behavior (McMahon & Pence, 1993). In cases in which a woman is a victim and is reluctant to cooperate with a man who has eroded her safety and stability, it is important to consider abuse as an influence on her choices, decisions, and capacity to provide security for herself and her children.

In child abuse and neglect cases as well as in intimate partner violence, abuse must be addressed regardless of the gender of the perpetrator. But the appropriate systems must be able to definitively determine who the victim is. The important fact is that the systems are not presently sensitive enough to evaluate the circumstances and unique concerns associated with male violence, as noted above.

Battered women and their advocates are being challenged for addressing safety and protection issues. These concerns are especially apparent in the area of orders of protection, custody, and visitation. The unwillingness to acknowledge domestic violence and the adversarial approaches of the fathers' rights contingent of the fatherhood movement make it difficult to sort out which fathers are not a threat to mothers and children and which are. If the goal of fathers' rights groups is the best interest of the children, addressing partner violence should be a common goal of the two fields. But even when children are not involved, women have the right to safe and secure lives. We follow this with brief, edited reminiscences of battered women and adult children of men who batter, concerning the impact of the father's violence.

Assessing the Impact of Men Who Batter on Children

Heidi, a 35-year-old battered woman, described her 5-year-old son coming up to her after an episode during which she was severely beaten by her husband. Her son said, "mommy, if you just did what daddy told you, he would not have to beat you."

The same woman reported how, after she was divorced for a year, her ex-husband threatened her and came over to her house to shoot her because of his feelings of jealousy brought on by her new relationship with another man. Their daughter intervened and was shot, along with the new boyfriend. The woman asked the daughter, "Why did you intervene to protect mommy when you knew daddy had a gun?" Her daughter replied, "the last time daddy beat you, I did not help you. I promised that if it ever happened again I would help you."

Recalling Adult Children's Memories of Their Abusive Fathers

George, a 52-year-old son of a man who battered, stated, "I did not want to have a relationship with my father. My younger brothers and sisters did. They may have been too young to remember everything I did." "When I was age 16, I had to defend my mother from the abuse of my dad." "My experience with my father completely shapes the way I relate to my children and wife. Nonviolence is a part of my behaviors." His father recently died, but George commented, "I do not grieve for his death . . . I remember what he put me and my mother through."

Liz, age 35 and the daughter of a man who batters, recalled being a child and witnessing her 12-year-old brother attempt to defend his mother against their father with a baseball bat and then ordering their father out of the house. Tom, a 35-year-old son of a man who batters, described how when he was a child, his mother took him and his two siblings away in the middle of the night to escape their abusive father. He also stated how his father "continues his abuse with his second wife. He has never admitted to my other siblings and me what we saw when we were young. . . . He has not come clean. I have been concerned for my half brother, who is the product of this second marriage."

These reminiscences reinforce the point that the quality of fatherhood is as significant as the presence of a father. Instead of living by a credo that promotes fatherhood at any cost, one should encourage healthy behaviors regardless of the gender of the parent.

RESEARCH QUESTIONS

The answers to research questions concerning the role of men who batter in the lives of their children are complex and may result in approaches and solutions that differ from the conventional wisdom of both the fatherhood and domestic violence practice philosophies. Given what has been presented above, researchers must fully examine the important intersections of fatherhood, women's safety, and ending men's violence. Because little research is available about these intersections, there are more questions than answers. This section is less about methodology in conducting research and more about what investigative questions will increase insight into this issue. In this section, we discuss the critical research questions that help fatherhood and domestic violence advocates understand how to promote women and children's safety. At the same time, we also consider questions that help us to determine when it is (or is not) appropriate to involve fathers who have battered their intimate partner, children, or both. The harm done to women and children by a man who batters is a point of record. We recommend safety and security first, even as we explore these critical questions.

Predicting Which Men Will Continue to Threaten Battered Women and Their Children

Many researchers in the field of domestic violence have studied men who batter. One unifying characteristic of men who batter is their need to control (Gondolf, 1985; Williams, 1990). They tend to deny and minimize their abusive behavior. They have few skills in resolving conflict in nonabusive and nonviolent ways; as a result, they escalate their use of conflict resolution tactics until they become violent and abusive (Williams, 1990). Men who batter are carriers of abuse from relationship to relationship (Doyne et al., 1999; Dutton, 1996). If a man abuses his partner, he is more likely to abuse his children; 50% of men who abuse their partners also abuse their children (Campbell, 1994; Saunders, 1994). Court mandates, jail time, educational efforts, and treatment programs have been used to confront men who batter to reshape their abusive behaviors. Even with these efforts, ending violence against women continues to be a challenge. Men who batter tend to control and intimidate their victims.

Given what has been described above, violence is often ignored in assessing parents' behaviors in custody disputes (Doyne et al., 1999). Fathers who batter are more likely to sue for custody of their children and to get it (Jaffe & Geffner, 1998; McMahon & Pence, 1993; Saunders, 1994). It is difficult to determine the intention of batterers who also want joint or sole custody of their children. Typologies have been developed by Saunders (1992), Gondolf (1998), and Holtzworth-Munroe and Stuart (1994) that attempt to help researchers understand the types of batterers and the men who have the greater or lesser potential for change. The results from these studies tend to vary and are inconclusive. Still, the critical question is, What are the characteristics of men who are the least likely to change and continue to be a threat to their partner and children? Given this type of abuser, what is the most appropriate response to keep women and children safe through legal and community responses?

Educating Court Systems and Human Services Professionals

McMahon and Pence (1993) reported that when courts have to choose between battered women's safety and fathers' access to their children, typically fathers' access wins. Given what has been discussed in previous sections, the capacity and the will of court administrators and human services professionals to respond to the needs of battered women is of primary concern. There are several critical questions concerning evaluating the legal systems' capacity to keep battered women safe.

In cases in which violence has occurred and the court chooses to give fathers custody or access to their children, has the court also received evidence that demonstrates that the man has changed? What has the court done to determine whether an abusive father is still a threat? What safeguards exist to protect the women and children and hold him accountable for his behavior? What can the court system do to improve its capacity to assess and hold men who batter accountable for their abuse, particularly when there is a threat of deadly force?

Considering Socioeconomic Status and Race

Another consideration associated with the intersection of fatherhood and domestic violence is the role that race and socioeconomic status play in defining the tactics typically used by fathers to resolve divorce or custody disputes with their partner. Above we discussed how resource-rich men use the court and other systems to address marital disputes. Certain men harass battered women through the courts as the women attempt to achieve safety and stability. Yet poor people, particularly in communities of color, are often less likely to use these systems to arbitrate disputes because of a lack of resources and of trust of formal systems.

Is there a differential use of the court systems to resolve marital or relationship disputes based on race and socioeconomic status? If poor women, married or unmarried, do not use the courts, how do they achieve safety and protection and resolve disputes with men who batter, particularly with regard to access to their children? What role do level of abuse, culture, race, and socioeconomic status have on battered women's feeling about their safety? Do race and socioeconomic status influence choices for allowing children access to their fathers? What fears and concerns do battered women from these groups have about father and child involvement in custody and visitation matters? When the court system is used, what are the attitudes of battered women and men who batter concerning mediation versus litigation as a way to resolve marital disputes and visitation for fathers?

Resolving Visitation

Generally, for families in which there has been no abuse, the question of visitation comes down to the parents' ability to work together respectfully and honestly to arrange schedules and provide for smooth transitions. For families with high parental conflict or a history of abuse, however, resolution of visitation issues is difficult. Visitation is an important issue in this discussion because it (a) allows for the routine interaction between fathers and children that is necessary for meaningful involvement and (b) in situations in which there has been abuse, it can be dangerous for women and children. It is necessary to examine child access (visitation) in at least three situations: (a) the father has been violent before, and the mother believes that she may be in current danger of abuse from him; (b) the father has been violent in the past, but the mother believes there is little likelihood that she is in danger; and (c) there has been no history of abuse, and the mother has no safety concerns.

What are the characteristics of drop-off and pick-up visitation centers that allow mothers and fathers to transfer their children without interacting with each other? More research is necessary to understand how or whether battered women can safely use these centers. What kind of expertise is necessary on the part of the administrators and directors of these facilities? What kind of visitation support services will provide the best outcomes? What are the effects and emphasis of the fathers' rights groups who are requesting and receiving government grants to administer visitation centers?

How do their emphasis and outcomes differ from those of other visitation models?

Working With Men Who Battered But Have Changed

It should be acknowledged that some men who batter do change (Gondolf, 1987, 1998). Little has been written about these men in the literature on domestic violence. Yet batterer treatment programs often identify men who have significantly altered their behavior. Some of these men have become peer counselors in batterer treatment programs. It is important to understand why and how this process occurs for them. The fact that they end their violence can have an important impact on their future partner relationship and on their relationship with their children. An important research question is whether men who change increase their child's emotional well-being and unlearn social learning messages about violence. Practitioners and men who have been in treatment report that this does happen.

Levesque, Gelles, and Velicer (in press) reported that men who attend treatment and want to change view treatment as having a positive impact on their families and children. Sullivan, Juras, Nguyen, and Allen (1999) noted that biological fathers who are batterers have a differential impact on their children as compared with other fatherhood models, in particular stepfathers.

Stith, Rosen, and McCollum (1999) reported on a family therapy project that worked with batterers who had greater potentials to end their abuse within their family. The project centered on the needs of the children. A total of 245 men were screened who went through batterers' treatment. Only 38 men were appropriate for family or couples therapy. This research indicates that in some cases, battered women are willing to collaborate with the father on the needs of the child if there is evidence that he has changed and if her and her children's safety are assured. Fathers who have been abusive can either help or inhibit their child's development. It is important to determine the ways that batterers who change can contribute to the lives of their children.

Understanding Battered Women's Choices

All battered women want safety and security for themselves and their children. The potential terror from continual torture causes many women to find ways to escape their abuser. Because of the extent and nature of the abuse, commonsense would dictate that many battered women and children sever any contact with the perpetrator. As noted above, many women are reluctant to re-establish a relationship with their tormentor but are forced into sharing or giving over custody to the abusive father by the courts (Jaffe & Geffner, 1998; McMahon & Pence, 1993).

Yet not all women who are battered suffer the most severe forms of abuse. Some battered women who have been less severely victimized may want their children to have a relationship with the father provided that a standard of safety from physical and emotional abuse is met. What is known about women and children who either maintain or re-establish parental connections with a man who abuses because battered woman or her children choose it? Are there examples of formerly battered women who are continuing with a dual or coparenting relationship with a partner who has been abusive after their romantic relationship is over? How do divorced or never-married parents work it out? How can one be informed about these cases? What is the impact of these relationships on the children?

Interviewing Adult Children of Abuse

What is the impact of exposure to violence on children? Although we know that children are affected, much of the literature comes from children with current and proximal exposures to violence. The perspectives of adult children who were exposed to violence against their mothers offer important insight into the effects of exposure to violence over time. These adults have had an opportunity to reflect on their experiences and how the exposure to violence has influenced them and their relationships with parents, partners in their own marriage, and their children. Researchers can learn what those respondents wanted from their mother, father, or both. They can also report on what was or what could have been helpful for them in these situations. Such insights may influence interventions with children. This information can also be used in developing parenting and fatherhood models, interventions, and educational components for men in father involvement programs and for batterers' treatment programs associated with the impact of their behaviors on children.

EFFECTIVENESS OF GROUP WORK INTERVENTIONS

In fatherhood programs, it is important to provide programming focused on prevention of domestic violence and interventions if it occurs. It is also important to identify the best response for the battered woman, father, and children in father involvement programs once domestic violence has been detected.

However, some fatherhood involvement programs are reluctant to even bring up the subject of domestic violence because they fear it will discourage the men's participation in these programs. Still, they address other issues that facilitate healthy male parenting behaviors, such as the nonuse and abuse of drugs, job readiness, child support enforcement, and, in some cases, altering criminal behaviors and activities. Researchers in the future should compare which problem behaviors these men are reluctant to discuss and identify the best methods to address these difficult topics among this population.

Groups have been cited as an important approach in working with fathers and with men who batter. In the field of fatherhood, researchers have reported that peer support groups are particularly helpful to the men in father involvement programs in which practitioners lead these support groups, set an agenda for the meetings, or encourage spontaneous conversation (Doherty et al., 1996). The support group structure is one way to encourage fathers to address issues of importance to them, despite the subject. Group treatment is typically used to re-educate and counsel men who batter (Williams, 1999). The group acts to decrease a batterer's sense of isolation and belief in his exceptionality. It improves his interpersonal skills, offers mutual aid, identifies and develops expertise in critical areas, maximizes confrontation of denial and inappropriate behavior, develops a norm for personal and social change, and maximizes rewards for change (Bennette & Williams, 1999). Groups encourage these men to discuss issues in other areas of their life that result in their violence toward women (Williams, 1999).

Researchers should explore the efficacy of this method in addressing the intersection of domestic violence and fatherhood. Can research inform investigators about the use of groups to facilitate the exploration of these issues in both fatherhood programs and batterers' treatment programs? Can it identify the common codes of healthy behavior to be advanced in relationships in fatherhood and batterers' groups? Regarding batterers' treatment, researchers should examine the extent to which fathering themes influence effective parenting and the reduction of violence among men who batter. Researchers should examine within a fatherhood group the influence of introducing information about domestic violence on reducing violence in intimate partner relationships.

Some fatherhood advocates note that regardless of marital status or romantic association, fathers should maintain a strong positive relationship with the mother of their children. Given that the mother tends to have custody of the children, a positive relationship with the mother often results in an enhanced access to the children and more a positive relationship with them (McLoyd, 1990). Researchers have reported on the importance of strong and positive parent relationships but do not explain how to achieve it. One question regarding fathers who have a history of abuse and whose partner wants to maintain a coparenting relationship is, How do these men develop a cooperative, supporting relationship with the mother? This is an important question for both domestic violence prevention and fatherhood advocates.

CONCLUSION

As mentioned earlier, to accomplish the important goals of these two fields, collaboration is essential. Obviously, collaboration between advocates for battered women and the advocates of the fathers' rights faction of the fatherhood movement is impossible. However, because many individuals, interest groups, advocates, and government agencies consider themselves discussants and stakeholders in the outcome of this public discussion of nonresident and noncustodial father involvement, it is crucial that the voices of mothers and children and their advocates be heard. The research element of this work is of critical importance. Research helps to construct collaborations and shape the common concerns of the stakeholders and partners in each field.

As this collaboration is defined and conducted, the common goal of domestic violence prevention advocate groups and advocates for father involvement must be safe, healthy environments and positive family connections for children and their parents. To decide how these two advocate groups with different agendas can work together, these stakeholders must talk and exchange ideas and information at meetings, conferences, and collaborative projects. It is likely that there will be a substantial amount of disagreement between domestic violence prevention advocates and father involvement supporters about many issues, not the least of which are custody, mediation, and visitation. However, it seems that the best chance for finding common ground is contact between these two groups.

Domestic violence advocates and father involvement supporters must create an alliance through these conversations and information exchanges. This alliance can inform social welfare policy and, more importantly, can provide more comprehensive services for families in need. This task is daunting, and the difficult issues that will frame and fuel the ongoing discussion must be addressed. Below are three recommendations.

First, if we are to encourage men to become active parents, we must acknowledge that men perpetrate domestic violence against women at higher rates and more frequently than vice versa. The unacceptably high numbers of women who experience domestic violence in the United States are well documented. Moreover and more specifically, if we are to construct a public policy agenda that will support and encourage father involvement in low-income families with never-married parents, we must be mindful of the incidence of domestic violence among women who receive welfare. Research shows that and social services practitioners can attest to the number of women on welfare who are or have been victims of domestic violence. These numbers are significantly higher than for the general population (Raphael, 2001).

Second, we must remain collectively mindful that our honest and vigilant concern about violence is not an implication and is not perceived to be an implication that all men (or all poor men, all men of color) are prone to this kind of violence. One of the concerns of fathers' groups is that the insertion of the issue of domestic violence in a discussion about father involvement is an implication that all fathers are or will be violent. Great numbers of fathers have never committed violent or abusive acts against anyone in their families and would never consider such an offense; some fathers who have been violent may never be again. Still, in large part because we cannot be sure who will commit a violent act against a woman or child, we must continue to pay serious attention to the possibility of violence in the context of father involvement. This vigilance is not, however, an indictment of all men and fathers.

Third, researchers in the fatherhood field suggest that fathering cannot be isolated from mothering and mothers' expectations. Mothers often mediate fathers' access to their children. The extent to which fathers are successful in negotiating this issue is often determined by the quality of their relationship with their children's mother. This now widely researched phenomenon has significant ramifications for those seeking to improve family functioning. Relationship problems between mothers and fathers typically have disastrous effects on father–child relationships. Significant here is that the relationship between partners is viewed as an important component for healthy coparenting regardless of whether the couple is together.

How violence or abuse affects the potential for a collaborative relationship is not available in the literature on fatherhood. Healthy nonabusive behavior by men who have battered is a goal in the field of domestic violence. Domestic violence advocates know the destructive consequence of violence on battered women, on children exposed to domestic violence, and on many men who batter. Intuitively, one could agree that nonabusive relationships increase the potential for healthy relationships between partners and between parents and children. This has been the message of the domestic violence field. Perhaps this message will become a common belief held by father involvement advocates as well in the near future. The two fields can construct what it means to have a good relationship with the mother and what is in the best interest of children. They might also agree that nonabusive behavior toward one's partner is among the characteristics of good parenting. Finally, advocates can construct how to involve fathers who have been abusive but who are no longer a threat in the lives of their children, without risk to the mothers or the children.

REFERENCES

Bachman, R., & Saltzman, L. E. (1995, August). *Violence against women: Estimates from the redesigned survey.* Washington, DC: U.S. Department of Justice, Bureau of Justice Statistics.

Ballard, T. (1995, November 27). *Meeting on Supporting the Role of Fathers in Families,* the White House (statement of Travis Ballard, president of the National Congress for Fathers and Children). Retrieved on June 25, 1999, from the World Wide Web: http://www.acfc.org/study/ballard.htm

Baskerville, S. (1998). Sins of the fathers: Review of divorced dads: Shattering the myths by Sanford Braver. *Fathering Magazine* [On-line serial]. Retrieved on May 27, 1999, from the World Wide Web: http://www.fathermag.com/news/3786-DDads.shtml

Bennette, L., & Williams, O. J. (1999). Men who batter. In R. Hampton (Ed.), *Family violence prevention and treatment* (2nd ed., pp. 227–260). Newbury Park, CA: Sage.

Blankenhorn, D. (1995). *Fatherless America: Confronting our most urgent social problem.* New York: Beacon Press.

Campbell, J. C. (1994, February). Child abuse and wife abuse: The connections. *Maryland Medical Journal,* pp. 349–350.

Cherlin, A. (1992). *Marriage, divorce, remarriage.* Cambridge, MA: Harvard University Press.

Children's Rights Council. (1999, winter). Locating missing and hidden children. *Speak Out for Children* [Newsletter], p. 2.

Doherty, W. J., Kouneski, E. F., & Erickson, M. F. (1996). *Responsible fathering: An overview and conceptual framework* (Report HHS-100-93-0012, pp. 1–55). Washington, DC: U.S. Department of Health and Human Services, Administration for Children and Families and the Office of the Assistant Secretary for Planning and Evaluation.

Doyne, D. E., Browermaster, J. D., Meloy, J. R., Dutton, D., Jaffe, P., Temiko, S., & Monies, P. (1999). Custody disputes involving domestic violence: Making children's needs a priority. *Juvenile and Family Court Journal, 50*(2), 1–12.

Dutton, D. (1996). Antecedents of borderline personality disorder organization in wife assaulters. *Family Violence, 11,* 26–54.

Everson, M. D., & Boot, B. (1989). False allegations of sexual abuse by children and adolescents. *American Academy of Child and Adolescent Psychiatry, 28,* 230–268.

Faller, K. C., & Devoe, E. (1994). Allegations of sexual abuse in divorce. *Journal of Child Sexual Abuse, 4*(4), 1–25.

Faller, K. C., Olafson, E., & Corwin, D. (1993). Research on false allegations of sexual abuse in divorce. *APSAC Advisor, 6*(3), 1, 7–10.

Garfinkel, I., McLanahan, S., Meyer, D. R., & Seltzer, J. A. (1998). *Fathers under fire: The revolution in child support enforcement.* New York: Russell Sage Foundation.

Geffner, R. (1997). Family violence: Current issues, interventions, and research. *Journal of Aggression, Maltreatment, & Trauma, 1*, 1–25.

Gelles, R. J., & Straus, M. A. (1988). *Intimate violence.* New York: Simon & Schuster.

Gondolf, E. (1985). *Men who batter: An integrated approach for stopping wife abuse.* Holmes Beach, FL: Learning.

Gondolf, E. (1987). Changing men who batter: A developmental model for integrated intervention. *Journal of Family Violence, 2*, 335–349.

Gondolf, E. (1998). How some men stop their abuse: An exploratory program evaluation. In G. T. Hotaling & D. Finkelhor (Eds.), *Coping with family violence: Research and policy perspectives* (pp. 53–87). Newbury Park, CA: Sage.

Holtzworth-Munroe, A., & Stuart, G. L. (1994). Typologies of male batterers: Three subtypes and differences between them. *Psychological Bulletin, 116*, 476–497.

Horn, W. (1995). Achieving full fathering: A conversation on the new furor over fathering. [Introduction and panel discussion moderated by H. Cordes]. *Utne Reader* [Online serial version], retrieved on May 20, 1999, from the World Wide Web: http://www.utnereader.com/lens/lparenting/conversation.html

Horn, W., & Bush, A. (1997, March). *Fathers, marriages, and welfare reform* [Report]. Retrieved on August 6, 1999, from the World Wide Web: http://www.hudson.org/wpc/articles/father.htm

Jaffe, P. G., & Geffner, R. (1998). Child custody disputes and domestic violence: Critical issues for mental health, social service, and legal professionals. In G. W. Holden, R. Geffner, & E. N. Jouriles (Eds.), *Children exposed to marital violence: Theory, research, and applied issues* (pp. 371–408). Washington, DC: American Psychological Association.

Jaffe, P. G., Wolfe, D., & Wilson, S. (1990). *Children of battered women.* Newbury Park, CA: Sage.

Johnson, E., Levine, A., & Doolittle, F. C. (1998). *Father's fair share: Helping poor men manage child support and fatherhood.* New York: Russell Sage Foundation.

Levesque, D. A., Gelles, R. J., & Velicer, W. F. (in press). Development and validation of a stages measure for men in batterer treatment. *Cognitive Therapy Research.*

Levine, J. A., & Pitt, E. W. (1995). *New expectations: Community strategies for responsible fatherhood.* New York: Families and Work Institute.

McLoyd, V. C. (1990). The impact of economic hardship on Black families and children: Psychological distress, parenting, and socioemotional development. *Child Development, 61*, 311–346.

McMahon, M., & Pence, E. (1993). Doing more harm than good? Some cautions on visitation centers. In E. Peled, P. G. Jaffe, & J. L. Edleson (Eds.), *Ending the cycle of violence: Community responses to children of battered women* (pp. 186–206). Newbury Park, CA: Sage.

National Fatherhood Initiative. (1998–1999, winter). Statement of purpose. *Fatherhood Today, 3*(3), 2.

Pagelow, M. D. (1997). Battered women: A historical research review and some common myths. In R. Geffner, S. Sorrenson, & P. K. Lundberg-Love (Eds.), *Violence and sexual abuse at home: Current issues, interventions, and research in spousal battering and child maltreatment* (pp. 26–48). Binghamton, NY: Haworth Press.

Popenow, D. (1996). *Life without father*. New York: Pressler Press.

Saunders, D. G. (1988). Other truths about domestic violence: A reply to McNeely and Robinson-Simpson. *Social Work, 33,* 179–183.

Saunders, D. G. (1992). A typology of men who batter: Three types derived from cluster analysis. *American Journal of Orthopsychiatry, 62,* 264–275.

Saunders, D. G. (1994). Custody decisions in families experiencing woman abuse. *Social Work, 39,* 51–59.

Sheeran, M., & Hampton, S. (1999). Supervised visitation in cases of domestic violence. *Juvenile and Family Court Journal, 50*(2), 13–26.

Stets, J. E., & Straus, M. A. (1990). Gender differences in reporting marital violence and its medical psychological consequences. In M. A. Straus & R. J. Gelles (Eds.), *Physical violence in American families: Risk factors and adaptations to violence in 8,145 families*. New Brunswick, NJ: Transaction.

Stith, S., Rosen, K. H., & McCollum, E. E. (1999). Domestic violence focused couples treatment. In *The Sixth Annual International Conference on Family Violence* (pp. 1–32). Durham: University of New Hampshire, Family Violence Research Laboratory.

Sullivan, C. M., Juras, J. D., Nguyen, H., & Allen, N. (1999). *How children's relationship to their mother's abuser affects their adjustment.* Unpublished manuscript, National Center for Injury Prevention and Control of the Centers for Disease Control and Prevention, Washington, DC.

Thoennes, N., & Tjaden, P. (1990). The extent, nature, and validity of sexual abuse allegations in custody/visitation disputes. *Child Abuse & Neglect, 14,* 151–163.

U.S. Department of Health and Human Services, Office of the Assistant Secretary for Planning and Evaluation. (1997a, August 6). *An evaluability assessment of responsible fatherhood programs: Final report* [Directed by B. S. Barnow of Johns Hopkins University and D. C. Stapleton of the Lewin Group, with the assistance of G. Livermore, J. Johnson, and J. Trutko]. Washington, DC: U.S. Government Printing Office. Retrieved on September 10, 1999, from the World Wide Web: http://www.aspe.hhs.gov

U.S. Department of Health and Human Services. (1997b). *Nurturing fatherhood: Improving data and research on male fertility, family formation and fatherhood.* Washington, DC: U.S. Government Printing Office. Retrieved on September 10, 1999, from the World Wide Web: http://www.fatherhood.hhs.gov/fi-eval.htm

Vaux, W. G. (1997). *Are fathers really necessary?* Retrieved on February 12, 2001, from the World Wide Web: http://www.ncfm.org

Whitehead, B. D. (1993, April). Dan Quayle was right. *Atlantic Monthly Digital Edition* [Online serial], retrieved on February 12, 2001, from the World Wide Web: http://www.theatlantic.com/politics/family/danquayl.htm

Williams, O. J. (1990). Spouse abuse: Social learning, attribution and intervention. *Journal of Health and Social Policy, 1*(2), 91–109.

Williams, O. J. (1993). Developing an African American perspective to reduce spouse abuse: Considerations for community action. *Black Caucus: Journal of the National Association of Black Social Workers, 1*(2), 1–8.

Williams, O. J. (1999). African American men who batter: Treatment considerations and community response. In R. Staples (Ed.), *The Black families: Essays and studies* (6th ed., pp. 265–280). New York: Wadsworth.

8

DOMESTIC VIOLENCE AND HIGH-CONFLICT DIVORCE: DEVELOPING A NEW GENERATION OF RESEARCH FOR CHILDREN

PETER G. JAFFE, SAMANTHA E. POISSON,
AND ALISON CUNNINGHAM

> Family laws as well as court policies are often justified by research findings from the broad population and are insufficiently backed by studies of the special sub-group of the divorcing population to which they are most frequently applied, that is, to families of high-conflict divorce. High-conflict divorce is characterized by all of the following: intractable legal disputes, ongoing conflict over parenting practices, hostility, physical threats, and intermittent violence. (Johnston, 1994, p. 172)

This quotation, from Janet Johnston's (1994) literature review of child adjustment in the context of high-conflict divorces, is an appeal for a new generation of research in an area that has sparked passionate public debates and posed complex, far-reaching, and disquieting questions for the legal system. An obvious starting point is to bridge two discrete bodies of literature: one focused on the impact of divorce on children and one focused on the effects of being exposed to adult domestic violence. Although the development of social and legal policy on divorce has been influenced by empirical evidence, much of that research does not consider the full spectrum of factors that affect child adjustment postseparation, especially those present in high-conflict divorces. Uniting these bodies of research would allow policymakers, legislators, the courts, and professionals working with families to consider the myriad factors that influence children's postdivorce

We gratefully acknowledge the support of the Atkinson Charitable Foundation.

adjustment, including exposure to violence, poverty, protracted legal conflicts, and custody and visitation arrangements that place children and their mothers at risk for continued abuse.

Divorce is a reality for millions of children across North America. Almost 1 million Americans were divorced in 1998, representing a rate of 3.6 per 1,000 people (National Center for Health Statistics, 1999) and probably affecting more than 1 million children each year. In Canada, the rate is lower (2.3 divorces per 1,000 population), but one third of all divorces involved custody orders for children (Statistics Canada, 2000), a figure that does not include the cases where parents made informal agreements without court involvement. Moreover, children are experiencing divorce at higher rates and earlier in their lives than in previous years (Statistics Canada, 1996). Given the changes in family composition, remarriage, and a growing tendency to live common law rather than marry, these divorce statistics grossly underestimate the number of children who are affected by family breakups.

NEGOTIATING POSTDIVORCE RELATIONSHIPS WITH ABUSIVE FATHERS

Within the divorce literature, it is axiomatic that children benefit from a positive and ongoing relationship with both parents after the separation. Communication and cooperation between parents provide an ideal circumstance for children postdivorce. Concepts such as *joint custody* and *shared parenting plans* reflect this ideal by underscoring the importance of both parents' active participation in the lives of their children after a marriage ends. Joint custody, both legal and physical, is a reality for many children after divorce. However, in other cases, children are essentially abandoned by one parent, in general their father, after divorce. The results of one follow-up study suggested that visitation was not occurring in 35% of cases 30 months following a custody and access assessment, even when the assessors recommended regular and frequent contact with the father (Radovanovic, Bartha, Magnatta, & Hood, 1994).

Whether it is because most parents can devise a workable child care arrangement or because the absence of one parent obviates that need, the majority of families (probably 80%; Johnston, 1994) do not become embroiled in legal battles over the children. However, 20% of couples do approach the justice system through lawyers (or increasingly are unrepresented) looking for a form of conflict resolution, such as mediation, arbitration, assessment, or custody trial. For this subgroup of highly conflicted families, the literature of children witnessing violence may be most relevant because it is in these cases, characterized by ongoing acrimony, litigation, and conflict over the custody and visitation arrangements for the children, that a history of domestic violence is likely.

However, there is great interjurisdictional variation in legislation that recognizes the implications of domestic violence in child custody decision making. In Canada, the federal Divorce Act (1985) is silent on the issue, and most provincial statutes do not specify domestic violence as an issue to be considered; however, judicial precedence increasingly recognizes the negative impact of exposure to violence on children (Bala et al., 1998). In the United States, the National Council of Juvenile and Family Court Judges (1994) developed the Model Code on domestic violence in the child custody area that clearly delineates several important principles. First, there is the presumption that it is detrimental to the child to be placed in sole custody, joint legal custody, or joint physical custody with the perpetrator of family violence. Second, visitation orders can be tempered with such conditions as supervised transfers, supervised access, and treatment orders for the batterers. Finally, there is a presumption against mediation in cases with domestic violence.

Most states have used parts of the Model Code to include domestic violence as one relevant factor in the determination of a child's best interest. However, most domestic violence advocates would probably describe a significant gap between theory and practice when it comes to recognizing domestic violence as a pertinent factor in custody determinations and affording due consideration to maternal and child safety (Jaffe & Geffner, 1998). Key among the problems is the length of time to resolve disputes. Sinclair (1999) conducted focus groups with 52 women who were victims of domestic violence and engaged in custody and access proceedings. The average length of time to resolve the dispute was 3.5 years, with some women spending in excess of 6.5 years trying to resolve the dispute. In 74% of the cases, the women were awarded sole custody with access (unsupervised) by their ex-partners. In 20% of the cases, the abusive ex-partners were awarded joint custody. For 6% of the cases, supervised access to the abusive ex-partner was awarded. Given that 88% of the women reported that their children had been present during the abuse and that 79% of the women reported that their children were directly abused by their partner, the current discrepancy between theory and practice is disconcerting. A well-publicized example occurred when the California Court of Appeal overturned the trial court decision awarding O. J. Simpson custody of his two children, ruling in essence that due consideration had not been given to the probability he had murdered their mother (*Simpson v. Brown*, 1998).

As legislators' awareness of domestic violence grows, the fathers' rights movement is garnering considerable media attention by defining the true problem as the willful lodging of false abuse allegations by malicious mothers to block paternal access to children. In their view, legal remedies should be available to punish these mothers and restore the parental rights of falsely accused men. Their efforts, in what can fairly be described as a backlash, can generate sensational headlines, such as this front-page story in a national newspaper in Canada: "Flawed Claims of Child Abuse Rampant: Study" (Galashan, 1999). The article declares that 30% of allegations of child abuse in custody battles are unprovable or false and quotes an Ontario judge as saying, "if the allegations of abuse are determined to have been unfounded, then the raising of these allegations by the accuser parent are in themselves the ultimate abuse by that parent against the child" (p. A1). The actual study suggests that the majority of abuse allegations are true and that a minority cannot be validated on a balance of probabilities because of the nature of child abuse victims and the unique circumstances of this violence (Bala & Schuman, 1999).

CHILDREN'S EXPOSURE TO ADULT DOMESTIC VIOLENCE

The reality is that many children are affected by witnessing violence between their parents, usually male-to-female violence. Although estimates on the incidence of violence in homes vary, depending on the definitions and research methodology used, one of the more comprehensive recent studies suggests that approximately 29% of all women experience a form of violence in an adult relationship during their lives (Johnson & Sacco, 1995). For 10% of battered women, the abuse is so severe that they worry about their personal safety and lives (Canadian Panel on Violence Against Women, 1993; Rodgers, 1994). In Canada, between 1978 and 1997, one-third of all homicides involved victims and offenders who were related by marriage, common law, or kinship (Fitzgerald, 1999). Moreover, risk for severe or lethal assault is elevated in the period after separation.

Children exposed to adult domestic violence can also be victims of direct abuse themselves. In a Canadian study, Jaffe and Austin (1995) found that domestic violence was an issue in 75% of custody assessment cases at a children's mental health center. Wife assault alone was reported in 30% of the cases, and wife assault in combination with child abuse was reported in 32% of the cases. In a recent American study (Ross, 1996), marital violence was found to be a statistically significant predictor of physical child abuse. The greater the frequency of violence against a spouse, the greater the probability of child physical abuse by the aggressor. The likelihood of child physical abuse rose to "near certainty" when more than 50 acts of violence perpetrated by the husband against his wife had occurred within the relationship.

Battering men frequently do not end their domination over their families once separation has occurred. Abusers may use threats to seek custody as a means of perpetuating control over their former partner. Lengthy and costly litigation, fear of abduction, harassment, intimidation and violence during transfers, and the real possibility of losing custody are issues that may plague battered women during a time in which they anticipated being free from abuse. Research also suggests that the power and control issues that underlie domestic violence may be exacerbated during child custody disputes waged by batterers. Batterers are twice as likely to apply for custody and equally likely to convince the court to award them custody as are nonviolent fathers (Bowermaster & Johnson, 1998; Zorza, 1995).

SETTING POLICY IN THE CHILDREN'S
BEST INTERESTS

How should legislators and policymakers answer the following questions: What are the best parenting arrangements for children after their parents separate? What can the justice system and community services do to help children when separating parents cannot agree on a parenting plan?

Most reform efforts are aimed at promoting shared parenting or joint custody arrangements, perhaps facilitated by a skilled mediator who can help parents stay focused on the best interests of their children. Because the best-interests doctrine has an uneasy alliance with the essentially adversarial concept of custody, in which one parent "wins" and the other "loses," a proposed direction in Canada is to abandon the win–lose paradigm in favor of an approach that presumes the ongoing involvement of both parents. The Special Joint Committee on Child Custody and Access (1998) recommended dropping the terms *child custody* and *access* (visitation) and replacing them with *shared parenting plans*, on the basis of the assumption that children's adjustment difficulties can be minimized through the maintenance of regular and meaningful contact with both parents.

Such approaches seem sensible in reference to the growing literature on divorce and children but may be ill conceived when applied to high-conflict families in which there is a history of domestic violence. Most nonwarring parents can make child-centered arrangements without being legally mandated to do so. But the children in high conflict–violent families stand to lose the most with these simplistic solutions derived from an idealistic belief that it is always beneficial to children to have equal contact with both parents postseparation. The prevalence of these inappropriate assumptions, whether applied by the courts or by lawmakers, can be traced to the state of the research in the field, which supports the involvement of both parents while not recognizing the role of domestic violence in separating families.

RESEARCH ON VIOLENCE
AND CONFLICT

Research on the impact of abuse and exposure to domestic violence on children emerged as an independent area of study and tends not to be referenced by those who study divorce. This literature discusses the negative impact of exposure to violence on children, effects of which can include internalizing symptoms (anxiety, depression, low self-esteem, withdrawn behaviors), externalizing problems (aggression, impulsivity, antisocial behavior, poor peer relationships), and poor academic performance and truancy (e.g., Holden, Geffner, & Jouriles, 1998; Holden & Ritchie, 1991; Jaffe & Austin, 1995; Jouriles & Norwood, 1995). It is the synthesis of these two research fields that will ultimately assist the families in high-conflict divorces. Policies and practices that more accurately reflect the spectrum of families going through divorce will materialize only when reformers are able to draw on a body of research that takes into account the complex interplay of factors that affect children.

In the general divorce literature, emphasis has been placed on the role parental separation plays in child adjustment. Among the areas examined, researchers have studied the structure of postseparation contact with parents, age and gender of children at time of separation, custodial parent's psychological adjustment, parenting skills, financial circumstances, parental loss, coping strategies, and interparental conflict. Although this last category hints at the existence of domestic violence, its meaning in the divorce literature fails to be defined.

Therefore, *interpersonal conflict* became a catchall term into which anything from normal parental discord at time of separation to extreme and persistent violence was lumped. More recently, there has been a recognition that the magnitude of adjustment difficulties previously attributed to the divorce itself was misplaced. Kelly (1998) summarized the current research on children's adjustment after separation and concluded that "the deleterious effects of divorce per se have been overstated, with insufficient attention paid in the clinical and research literature to the damaging effects of highly troubled marriages on children's adjustment" (p. 259). Other researchers have reached similar conclusions, recognizing that the dimensions associated with conflict (e.g., the presence of domestic violence) account for a greater proportion of adjustment difficulties than the divorce per se (Gano-Phillips & Fincham, 1995). It may be that failure to clearly define and examine interpersonal conflict between separating parents has led to the spurious finding that divorce on its own had long-lasting and serious repercussions for children.

Whereas the divorce literature has ignored domestic violence until recently, the child-witness-to-violence researchers have not developed enough to move much beyond simplistic cause-and-effect thinking based on correlations between exposure and an array of short- and long-term adjustment difficulties. Gender, developmental stage at onset of exposure to domestic violence, and relationship to abuser are all correlated with degree of maladjustment evidenced by children. However, researchers thus far have not isolated a pattern of problems associated with these factors. In fact, studies on differential gender responses to exposure to marital violence are contradictory: some finding that boys are more affected than girls (e.g., Wolfe, Jaffe, Wilson, & Zak, 1985), others suggesting the opposite (e.g., Spaccarelli, Sandler, & Roosa, 1994), and others finding no gender differences at all (e.g., O'Keefe, 1994).

Although the literature demonstrates a general trend of emotional and behavioral problems related to this exposure, there is variability in findings that suggest that 25%–75% of children in any given sample have difficulties that are in the clinically significant range (Holden et al., 1998). In other words, some children exposed to domestic violence appear relatively resilient to problems and have no symptoms in the clinical range, as measured by instruments such as the Achenbach Child Behavior Checklist (see Peled, Jaffe, & Edleson, 1995). These types of inconsistent findings suggest that determination of child adjustment is neither straightforward nor simple. Such variables as the severity of violence witnessed, adjustment of mothers (as principal caretaker), and disruptions in children's lives such as frequent moves and separations (Wolfe et al., 1985) may contribute to how a particular child is affected by exposure to parental violence. One of the obvious factors may be the nature of the separation, including exposure to postseparation violence, legal conflicts, and the type of custody arrangements.

THE NEXT GENERATION OF RESEARCH

The first generation of research on children exposed to family violence sought to find correlations between exposure and negative effects. This research was important in creating awareness about the deleterious effects of witnessing—as opposed to experiencing—abuse. The next generation of research will have the following characteristics.

First, the next generation of research will draw on heretofore discrete knowledge bases to synthesize the findings and expand the predictive power of explanatory models. Attempts to understand the effects of divorce on children will be greatly aided by what researchers have learned about the effects of violence on children and vice versa.

Second, future researchers will attempt to increase the representativeness of samples of children under study, a deficiency in both fields. In the divorce area, the field is dominated by the work of Wallerstein, which is based on 130 average-income California children and parents who were monitored for 25 years (Wallerstein & Lewis, 1998). The child-witness-to-violence area is dominated by studies of children in shelters for abused women, samples which are biased toward poverty and families in crisis (Peled et al., 1995) in part because a minority of abused women contact a shelter or even call the police to report the assault (Rodgers, 1994). Furthermore, a majority of studies are limited to White, mother-custody families, and the sample sizes are generally small.

Third, researchers will move beyond dichotomous and categorical operational definitions of abuse to classification schemes that reflect the complexity of the phenomenon. Instead of comparing exposed and nonexposed children, for example, researchers will develop measures that incorporate the various dimensions of abuse, including intensity, duration, frequency, and type. As a field, clarity and consistency with respect to operational definitions and how they are being measured must be a priority. Inconsistent definitions for terms such as *interpersonal conflict* lead to each researcher exploring a range of variables yet labeling them with the same name.

Fourth, researchers will follow children prospectively and longitudinally to highlight the impact of divorce and exposure to violence across developmental stages and the long-lasting effects during adulthood. There are many outstanding questions related to the intergenerational transmission of violence, key among them being why some children carry forward violent patterns and others do not.

The fifth and related characteristic is that researchers will explore the interplay between risk and protective factors. Through the study of resiliency, one can learn much about how to design intervention programs that maximize existing strengths and foster them where they do not exist.

Sixth, researchers will consider a fuller spectrum of outcome variables using multiple data sources. At present, when data collecting, researchers rely heavily on maternal reports of child adjustment. Particularly in cases of domestic violence, garnering fathers' participation may not be easy, advisable, or appropriate. However, the absence of paternal participation may have adverse consequences for the validity of any generalizations: (a) Fathers' perceptions of child functioning may be more accurate than the mothers' in some cases. (b) Relying on assessments by and of mothers can leave the erroneous impression that observed problems are related to mothers' parenting skills, psychological adjustment, and relational capacity rather than fathers' violence, psychological adjustment, and substance dependency.

Seventh, researchers will use sophisticated multivariate statistical techniques, such as structural equation modeling, to incorporate the many variables that interact with each other to determine and mediate children's adjustment after the trauma of violence and in the aftermath of separation. Researchers who can examine the causal relations, rather than the correlative association, between variables—probably the third generation of research—will ultimately be possible.

To this end, a conceptual model for child adjustment after exposure to violence and parental separation is proposed (see Figure 8.1). This model is best viewed as a conceptual framework rather than a predictive research model. It highlights the multitude of factors that may be determinates of adjustment for any one child who has been exposed to violence and whose family is no longer intact. The purpose of the figure is to illustrate the multiplicity and complexity of the variables that may interact to affect childhood adjustment for children who have been exposed to marital violence and suffered the trauma of family breakup. There are no causal pathway arrows between columns because the sequelae vary depending on the presence or absence of a host of variables.

Variables located in the upper half of the model are positive–protective factors, which theoretically contribute to adjustment. Variables located in the lower half of the model are negative-risk–vulnerability factors, which are hypothesized to impair childhood adjustment. The first column addresses the exposure to varying levels of violence and the associated risk and protective factors for children. The severity, frequency, and duration of the violence the children were exposed to need to be measured as well as the overlapping forms of direct abuse such as physical and sexual. The extent of sibling abuse is seen as another important factor from the research in this area.

Risk and protective factors are included as major variables that help determine children's adjustment. Risk factors include poverty, parental drug or alcohol abuse, parental mental disorder, repeated disruptions from homes and schools, and special needs, such as learning disabilities. Protective factors include children's temperament, intelligence, special talents, support systems, and a positive relationship with a principal caretaker.

The next column in the figure represents the factors associated with the final separation. A major factor is the level of litigation over child custody and access decisions. As a source of further stress, there may be parallel criminal hearings related to assault charges and, in some circumstances, child protection hearings if there are child abuse allegations. During this phase, access to services is an essential protective factor. These services

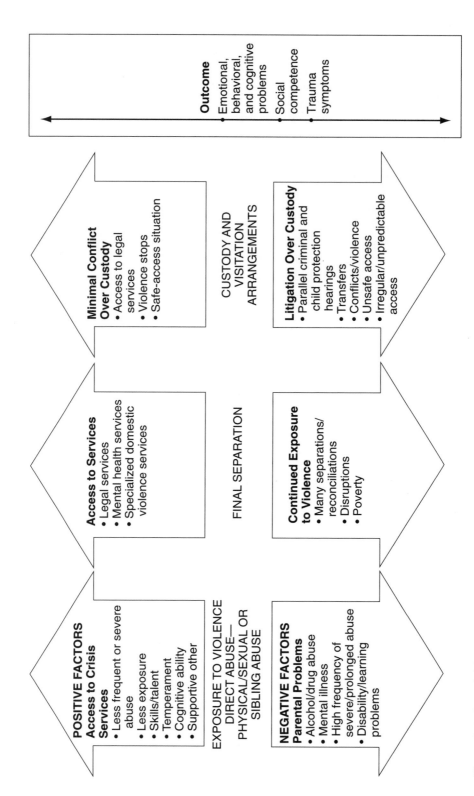

Figure 8.1. A model for predicting children's adjustment after exposure to violence and parental separation.

may include legal advice and mental health or supportive counseling. An important issue may be access to specialized domestic violence services, such as intervention programs for child witnesses, treatment groups for batterers, and advocacy services for abused women.

The third column represents the aftermath of the separation and the extent to which there is ongoing exposure to violence. Some researchers have found that as many as 25% of batterers who have visiting rights to children use this time as an opportunity to assault or threaten their ex-partners (Nova Scotia Law Reform Commission, 1995). Another critical factor is the custody and access arrangements and the extent of a safety plan or supervision for contact with a violent father. Also the children's relationship with each parent and their perceptions of that parent must be considered.

The final column is the outcome, the range of children's adjustment focusing on emotional and behavioral problems; social competence (e.g., friends, activities, school achievement); unhealthy coping mechanisms; and suicidal or homicidal ideations, gestures, and actions. As part of the model, specific trauma symptoms should also be examined as a potential outcome variable.

To examine how all the factors in Figure 8.1 interact to determine child adjustment requires appropriate measurement tools, large and representative samples, and multivariate analysis. Disentangling the multitude of interacting, moderating, and mediating factors, both risk and protective, will be challenging yet necessary for better understanding the issues affecting a child's adjustment after exposure to violence and the separation of his or her parents.

In our view, this research direction is an important one to guide courts and community agencies to better serve abused women and their children after separation. This research would help focus the divorce literature on this subgroup of high-conflict cases with special needs, typically the ones appearing before judges across North America. As well, the child-witness-to-violence researchers could begin to explore the ongoing nature of violence that occurs after separation. The key to future programs and policies aimed at ameliorating the negative effects for children is to develop a fuller understanding of the interplay of risk and protective factors that may combine to determine the level of adjustment difficulties.

CONCLUSION

Legislation, policy, and resources related to divorcing couples need to address the issue of exposure to domestic violence in custody disputes. More resources need to be devoted to public education campaigns for the general population to understand the detrimental impact of children's exposure to domestic violence. Professionals working in the area, such as lawyers, judges, doctors, educators, and mental health professionals, also need to improve their training, so that early-warning signs of domestic violence can be detected. Screening for domestic violence must be an integral component of all agencies that may have contact with battered spouses and their children. Specialized treatment and intervention programs for children exposed to marital violence need to be developed, funded, implemented, and evaluated. More legislative changes are necessary to ensure presumptions against custody for batterers and to include witnessing violence as a factor to consider postseparation (Doyne et al., 1999).

The most critical issue is that the research must inform legislation. Judges and service providers must rely on the most appropriate research to address the real problems rather than on a mindlessly idealized notion of shared parenting for high-conflict divorcing families.

REFERENCES

Bala, N. M. C., Bertrand, L. D., Paetsch, J. J., Knoppers, B. M., Hornick, J. P., Noel, J.-F., Boudrea, L., & Miklas, S. W. (1998). *Spousal violence in custody and access disputes: Recommendations for reform.* Ottawa, Ontario: Status of Women Canada.

Bala, N., & Schuman, J. (1999, June). *Allegations of sexual abuse when parents have separated.* Paper presented at education programs of the Ontario Office of the Children's Lawyer, Toronto, Ontario, Canada.

Bowermaster, J., & Johnson, D. (1998, October). *The role of domestic violence in family court child custody determinations: An interdisciplinary investigation.* Presented at the Fourth International Conference on Children Exposed to Family Violence, San Diego, CA.

Canadian Panel on Violence Against Women. (1993). *Changing the landscape: Ending violence, achieving equality.* Ottawa, Ontario: Minister of Supply and Services Canada.

Divorce Act. (1985). *Revised statutes of Canada*, c. 3 (2nd suppl.).

Doyne, S., Bowermaster, J., Meloy, J. R., Dutton, D., Jaffe, P., Temko, S., & Mones, P. (1999). Custody disputes involving domestic violence: Making children's needs a priority. *Juvenile and Family Court Journal, 50*(2), 1–12.

Fitzgerald, R. (1999). *Family violence in Canada: A statistical profile, 1999.* Ottawa, Ontario: Statistics Canada, Minister of Industry.

Galashan, S. (1999, May 27). Flawed claims of child abuse rampant: Study. *National Post*, p. A1.

Gano-Phillips, S., & Fincham, F. D. (1995). Family conflict, divorce, and children's adjustment. In M. A. Fitzpatrick & A. L. Vangelisti (Eds.), *Explaining family interactions* (pp. 206–231). Thousand Oaks, CA: Sage.

Holden, G. W., Geffner, R., & Jouriles, E. N. (1998). *Children exposed to marital violence: Theory, research, and applied issues.* Washington, DC: American Psychological Association.

Holden, G. W., & Ritchie, K. L. (1991). Linking extreme marital discord, child rearing, and child behavior problems: Evidence from battered women. *Child Development, 62,* 311–327.

Jaffe, P., & Austin, G. (1995, July). *The impact of witnessing violence on children in custody and visitation disputes.* Paper presented at the Fourth International Family Violence Research Conference, Durham, NH.

Jaffe, P. G., & Geffner, R. (1998). Child custody disputes and domestic violence: Critical issues for mental health, social service, and legal professionals. In G. W. Holden, R. Geffner, & E. N. Jouriles (Eds.), *Children exposed to marital violence: Theory, research, and applied issues* (pp. 371–408). Washington, DC: American Psychological Association.

Johnson, H., & Sacco, V. F. (1995). Researching violence against women: Statistics Canada's national survey. *Canadian Journal of Criminology, 37,* 281–304.

Johnston, J. R. (1994). High-conflict divorce. *Future of Children, 4,* 165–182.

Jouriles, E. N., & Norwood, W. D. (1995). Physical aggression toward boys and girls in families characterized by the battering of women. *Journal of Family Psychology, 9,* 69–78.

Kelly, J. B. (1998). Marital conflict, divorce and children's adjustment. *Child & Adolescent Psychiatric Clinics of North America, 7,* 259–271.

National Center for Health Statistics. (1999). Births, marriages, divorces and deaths: Provisional data for 1998. *National Vital Statistics Report, 47*(21).

National Council of Juvenile and Family Court Judges. (1994). *Family violence: A model state code.* Reno, NV: Author.

Nova Scotia Law Reform Commission. (1995). *Ending domestic violence in Nova Scotia.* Halifax, Nova Scotia, Canada: Author.

O'Keefe, M. (1994). Adjustment of children from maritally violent homes. *Families in Society, 75,* 403–415.

Peled, E., Jaffe, P. G., & Edleson, J. L. (1995). *Ending the cycle of violence: Community responses to children of battered women.* Thousand Oaks, CA: Sage.

Radovanovic, H., Bartha, C., Magnatta, M., & Hood, E. (1994). A follow-up of families disputing child custody/access: Assessment, settlement, and family relationship outcomes. *Behavioral Sciences & the Law, 12,* 427–435.

Rodgers, K. (1994). Wife assault: The findings of a national survey. *Canadian Center for Justice Statistics: Juristat, 14,* 1–22.

Ross, S. M. (1996). Risk of physical abuse to children of spouse abusing parents. *Child Abuse & Neglect, 20,* 589–598.

Simpson v. Brown, 67 Cal. App. 4th 914, 79 Cal. Rptr. 2nd 289 (1998).

Sinclair, D. (1999). *In the center of the storm: 52 women speak out.* Oshawa, Ontario, Canada: Steering Committee for Custody and Access Issues Affecting Woman Abuse Survivors and Their Children.

Spaccarelli, S., Sandler, I. N., & Roosa, M. (1994). History of spouse violence against mothers: Correlated risks and unique effects in child mental health. *Journal of Family Violence, 9,* 79–98.

Special Joint Committee on Child Custody and Access. (1998). *For the sake of the children: Report of the Special Joint Committee on Child Custody and Access.* Ottawa, Ontario: Senate, Parliament of Canada.

Statistics Canada. (1996). *National longitudinal survey of children and youth.* Ottawa, Ontario, Canada: Minister of Industry.

Statistics Canada. (2000, September 28). Divorces, 1998. *The Daily,* pp. 6–8.

Wallerstein, J. S., & Lewis, J. (1998). The long-term impact of divorce on children: A first report from a 25-year study. *Family & Conciliation Courts Review, 36,* 368–383.

Wolfe, D. A., Jaffe, P., Wilson, S. K., & Zak, L. (1985). Children of battered women: The relation of child behavior to family violence and maternal stress. *Journal of Consulting and Clinical Psychology, 53,* 657–665.

Zorza, J. (1995). How abused women can use the law to protect their children. In E. Peled, P. Jaffe, & J. Edleson (Eds.), *Ending the cycle of violence: Community responses to children of battered women* (pp. 147–169). Thousand Oaks, CA: Sage.

9

RESEARCHING CHILDREN'S EXPERIENCE OF INTERPARENTAL VIOLENCE: TOWARD A MULTIDIMENSIONAL CONCEPTUALIZATION

ZVI EISIKOVITS AND ZEEV WINSTOK

There is growing evidence that many children are affected by interparental violence (e.g., Edleson, 1999; Rosenberg & Mercy, 1991; Straus, 1991) and that such exposure carries severe physical, cognitive, behavioral, and emotional consequences. Research interest in the plight of these children is growing but is still limited in scope (e.g., Holden, 1998).

Two sets of terminologies seem relevant for understanding the evolution of scientific and clinical discourse on the phenomenon: One is related to the labels or names used to identify these children, which changed from *forgotten, ignored,* and *unintended victims* to *witnesses* and, more recently, to *being exposed to* and *experiencing interparental violence.* The difference between these terms is significant: The former set implies a passive and present orientation from the part of the child, whereas the latter set, used in this chapter, implies an active and a more futuristic orientation. The other set of terminologies identifies violence against women in a manner that clarifies the ways in which children are part of it. For example, the term *intimate violence* disregards the presence of children, which is in contrast to *interparental violence,* taking their presence into account.

The terminology is further complicated by the potential use of terms that blur men's role as initiators of the violence. For instance, interparental violence may be understood as stressing the reciprocity and mutuality of parental input in the violence. Because we use this term, we must state that our purpose is to emphasize the presence of children rather than to veil the responsibility of the perpetrator. It should be reiterated that in this chapter, we are concerned with children who experience interparental violence, not with children who are directly abused by their parents.

Most research on intimate violence focuses on the circular linkage of violence and intimate relationships. Another body of research examines the circular relationship between various ways of parenting and children's constructions of reality. There have been few if any attempts to examine these two sets of relationships in an integrated fashion to understand how children who live in a violence-ridden environment construct their reality, consisting of intimate relationships, violence, and parenting (Eisikovits, Winstok, & Enosh, 1998).

Earlier studies of children of battered women focused on the negative impact of violence on children (e.g., Hughes & Barad, 1983; Jaffe, Wolfe, & Wilson, 1990). Underlying this approach was the belief that children are affected by but do not affect interparental violence and that the negative consequences of violent events on children are so powerful and overwhelming that they make effects related to parenting or to interpersonal relationships between the parents insignificant. These studies were either atheoretical or used a fairly narrow theoretical focus.

Recently, theoretical formulations using a more integrative approach have been suggested. For instance, Grych and Fincham (1990) proposed a conceptualization of the cognitive–contextual processing of marital conflict by children. Their model is composed of marital conflict variables, contextual variables, primary and secondary cognitive processes, coping behavior, and affect. However, the model was not specifically designed for understanding children's experience of interparental violence.

Similarly, Cummings (1998) suggested a conceptualization of children's adjustment to interparental conflict in terms of "emotional security," as articulated by emotion regulation, internal representation of family relations, and regulation of exposure to family affect. Graham-Berman (1998) proposed an expanded conceptual model based on factors influencing the adjustment of children exposed to domestic violence, including maternal stress and mental health, positive and negative social networks, and child adjustment. These conceptualizations broaden the understanding of the interrelationships among variables in the family ecology and conflict or violence as well as the ways in which children's construction of meaning is affected by their cognitive and emotional reactions to the conflicts.

However, these conceptualizations work within specific theoretical traditions, such as social learning, trauma, or attachment theory, so they have limited heuristic value for housing or generating alternative conceptualizations. For this, a integrative conceptual framework is needed, which may not necessarily provide new and unresearched components but may serve to foster the integration of a variety of theoretical and empirical interests. The categories of the conceptual framework are kept as broad as possible, and specific content areas are included that illustrate rather than define to allow for future inclusion of specific content areas relevant to a specific theoretical orientation. The development of such conceptualization seems timely, considering that the field is at crossroads "with new methodological and theoretical directions required for significant advances to occur" (Cummings, 1998, p. 84). This state of affairs calls for the development of a flexible formulation that allows communication between and across empirical endeavors stemming from diverse theoretical orientations and enhances the cumulative and systematic nature of the emerging body of knowledge.

Generally, a set of theoretical assumptions seems to be commonly agreed on by most researchers in the field and should serve as the basis for any unifying conceptualization: (a) Children are not passive receptacles of the effects of interparental violence but influence and are influenced by such events; (b) parental expectations both frame the boundaries and provide the scripts for the content of children's construction of interparental violence; (c) the impact of parental expectations and behaviors are mediated by extrafamilial influences, such as availability of support, significant others, peers, and various organizations in which children and youths participate; and (d) children's reality is constructed through negotiation processes, including perceiving, explaining the causes of, and giving meaning to events in general and violent events in particular.

Building on this set of assumptions, we attempt to suggest a multidimensional conceptualization that may serve as a road map for researching children's experience in a violence-ridden family context. More specifically, it helps to develop and report on research in this field while critically using what was done, to develop and report on the evolution and change of concepts over time, and to identify what is missing. As such, it enables efficient communication across research projects by creating joint parameters and a common language, thus enabling the development of a cumulative body of knowledge. The test of such conceptual frameworks is whether they make sense (in the naturalistic tradition) and whether they hold heuristic power without specific commitment to one theoretical tradition.

To this end, we explore first the dimensions along which children's construction of reality can be studied and then the boundaries and content of parental expectations acting on the child and the ways in which these constructions are affected by parental expectations. Finally, we expand our formulation to include extrafamily influences as they mediate children's construction of reality and parental expectations.

What is unique about interparental relationships in which conflicts escalate to violence? In such relationships, the ontological basis of the couple as a collective entity is gradually eroded: The "we-ness" is gone and is replaced by a mutually antagonistic perception of the parties, who live in a state of varying degrees of hostility toward each other. Through violence, such partners come to define each other as enemies (Gergen, 1994). The child living alongside such parents learns about himself or herself and his or her environment through hostility rather than harmony, through conflict rather than intimacy, and he or she develops a rigid worldview. Within such a perception, people are divided into winners and losers, perpetrators and victims, predators and predated. Intimacy and closeness are redefined as dangerous. The child's resources in such contexts are mobilized to construct his or her life to be as tolerable and livable as possible.

CHILDREN'S CONSTRUCTIONS OF INTERPARENTAL VIOLENCE

What is the process by which a child constructs and negotiates his or her reality as livable in a violence-ridden environment in the setting of the overall family discourse? Although here we focus on the violent event as the topic under scrutiny, we should emphasize that such negotiation is ongoing and may take place around other significant life events as well. For the purpose of the present analysis, the family discourse can be divided into three interrelated components: (a) recollection (i.e., what happened), (b) causality (i.e., why it happened), and (c) meaning (i.e., what it means). Thus, we are focusing on the multiple ways in which violent events are assimilated in the family unit.

The process described below is spiral and continuous. Renegotiating occurs at every stage, as soon as one or more participants become dissatisfied with the temporary agreements reached or some outside interference disturbs the temporary homeostasis among the partners.

Recollection: Negotiating What Happened

The first stage begins after violence has occurred. The family members attempt to negotiate within the boundaries of the event to determine what happened, who did what to whom, and so forth. The purpose of this negotiation is to arrive at an agreed-on scenario of the violent event. At this stage, partners may exaggerate, dramatize, minimize, or show indifference to the event. The child who experiences the actual occurrence and the negotiation process is learning how the collective memory is negotiated and constructed as well as how he or she can live with the gap between what was witnessed and what is to be remembered. At times, the child is a passive observer of the above processes; at other times, the child is forced into participating, either as a witness who is expected to bear testimony or as a judge who is expected to validate one or another version of the parties' stories. The child's position may disappoint one or both parent, which may be experienced as a loss of love because it is seen as letting them down. The child copes with this by considering what to admit and what to deny about the event in question and, subsequently, with whom to side. Reality perception and constructed meanings interact and mutually influence each other dynamically until an understanding is reached between the two.

Causality: Negotiating Why It Happened

The second stage is concerned with negotiating causality: Why did it happen? Causality is pursued by the use of categories of "folk psychology" (Bruner, 1990) available to the young person, which help to order the events and make them comprehensible. At this stage, the negotiation moves beyond the descriptive boundaries of the event. The causes attributed to it can range from accounts related to the perpetrator's mental and emotional state (e.g., "My dad came home upset from work") to mystical beliefs (e.g., "He is a Taurus, so he is explosive"). Such causal explanations include a mixture of cognitive and emotional attitudes. At this stage, the participants in the overall family context either feel satisfied with the explanation and agree on it or adjust the explanation to the event or the event to the explanation. Throughout, the child learns how to attribute causality and to adjust events and causes to each other. He or she further learns to assign responsibility for specific causes to specific objects. One possibility is that the child becomes the object of responsibility for the event; another is that one or other parent is made responsible or neither is perceived as responsible.

Moralization: Negotiating What It Means

In the third stage, the child draws the moral implications of what took place. For instance, he or she may judge the violent event as well deserved or undeserved or may perceive violence as a legitimate or illegitimate means toward achieving a specific goal. This moves the child's understanding of the event beyond its boundaries and places it in the overall value and attitudinal context of the family culture as a whole. In this way, the moral lessons the child learns from the event affect and are affected by the normative structure of the family context.

Dimensions of the Process

The process underlying the previously described stages can be conceptualized along two dimensions. One refers to the degree of specificity from low to high levels of generalization and is important because it helps determine the extent to which a specific violent event will be generalized into a person's overall existence. The other dimension is the continuum of high to low emotionality, which goes together with low to high cognitive orientation throughout the construction of the event. This dimension is important in ascertaining the immediacy and urgency of the event and the extent to which a person is distanced from it and hence able to judge his or her actions as opposed to reacting emotionally and with a high degree of spontaneity. Throughout the process of reality construction, attitudes are played out and shaped.

PARENTAL EXPECTATIONS ACTING ON THE CHILD

Two broad types of expectations are active in most parenting activities. We term the first set *framing expectations* and the second *scripting expectations*. The first treats the range of possibilities suggested to the child for constructing his or her reality. These expectations fulfill mainly a boundary function, expressing the limits within which the child is expected to experience his or her world. By providing the child with such frames, the parent largely determines what the child should experience in the world and how he or she should think and feel. Within this set of expectations, the child is perceived as a reflective witness of the world, which acts on him or her. The second set of expectations is essentially the opposite. It provides a content for the frame and categorizes it in terms of activity scripts. In other words, the function of this set prescribes the ways that the child should act on the world, within the boundaries of how the world experiences him or her.

Every type of expectation may range from demand for unconditional compliance (frame, e.g., "You're all I have," or script, e.g., "Don't behave like your father") to rejection (frame, e.g., "You aren't my son any more," or script, e.g., "Your behavior disgusts me"), with indifference in the middle (e.g., "I don't care what you feel or do—just leave me alone"). We termed this continuum from total acceptance to total rejection the *acceptance continuum*, and it operates on both the framing and the scripting expectations. Each parent presents the child with both types of expectations. At times, the expectations exercised by a specific parent may be coherent (e.g., script and frame expectations of unconditional identification) or contradictory (e.g., frame expectation of identification and script expectations of rejection). This is complex because there can be symmetrical or complementary relationships between one or both sets of expectations in the two parents (two sets of two types each). Table 9.1 is an illustration of the personal and interparental types of interactions between frames and scripts. These two sets of expectations seem to encompass the range of possible influences of parental expectations on the child. From the analysis of these four types of interactions, we can derive 25 distinct types of parent–child interactions

TABLE 9.1
Personal and Interparental Interaction Types Between Frames and Scripts

Type of within-person interaction	Personal (father or mother)	
	Frame	Script
Coherent	+	+
Coherent	−	−
Contradictory	+	−
Contradictory	−	+
Type of between-person interaction	Interparental (frame or script)	
	Father	Mother
Symmetrical	+	+
Symmetrical	−	−
Complementary	+	−
Complementary	−	+

characteristic of children's experience of interparental relationships. Figure 9.1 maps these possibilities and the interactions among them.

Figure 9.1 elaborates the relative location of each parent on the acceptance continua for framing (on the left side) and scripting (on the right side). They are identical. Each one consists of an acceptance continuum for the father and the mother. Several discernible positions are marked on each set of axes (A to E). For instance, if the father says, "We men need to stick together," and the mother says, "Don't turn to me, you've got a father," their expectation can be represented as A on the frame because the father is accepting and the mother is rejecting (complementary type).

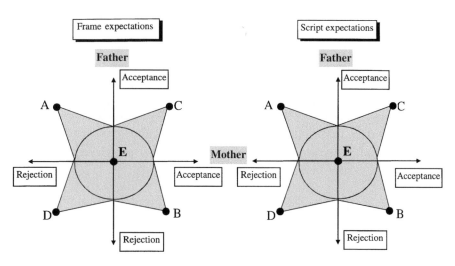

Figure 9.1. Parental expectations toward a child.

Similarly, we can identify the location of parental expectations on the set of axes related to scripts. The attitudinal location of the parents as a couple on both the framing and the scripting sets of axes represents the type of interparental expectation used with the child. Observe that the lines drawn to connect the possible types on the two axes result in a star shape, which represents the entire range of possible locations. Such a shape was chosen to symbolize our hypothesis that when one side chooses an extreme expectation, the other side is also forced to choose an extreme one; when one side chooses a softer position, the other does not necessarily choose an extreme one.

CHILD'S REALITY CONSTRUCTION AS SHAPED BY PARENTAL EXPECTATIONS

Now we discuss the child's construction of reality in relation to parental expectations. Figure 9.2 presents parental expectations (on the left side) in relation to the child's construction of reality (on the right side). The child's reality construction can be conceptualized along four parallel continua. We call the first the awareness continuum, the second the competence continuum, the third the self-perception continuum, and the fourth the worldview continuum. The location of a specific child along these continua is affected by the framing and scripting expectations of his or her parents toward him or her. The continua seem to encompass the child's experience in the world because being aware and actualizing this awareness through competence define a child's perception of self and of the world.

Awareness

Awareness refers to the extent to which the child is willing to recognize and relate to what is happening in his or her life in general and around the violence between his or her parents in particular. Awareness can be conceptualized in terms of a continuum ranging from denial and lack of awareness at one end (e.g., "My parents play and don't argue") to exaggerated or dramatized awareness at the other (e.g., "My father flattens my mother every day"), with varying levels of blurred awareness in between (e.g., "I'm not sure what's going on between my parents").

Competence

Competence addresses the child's sense of mastery in terms of his or her acting on the world. It is the result of his or her sense of control over

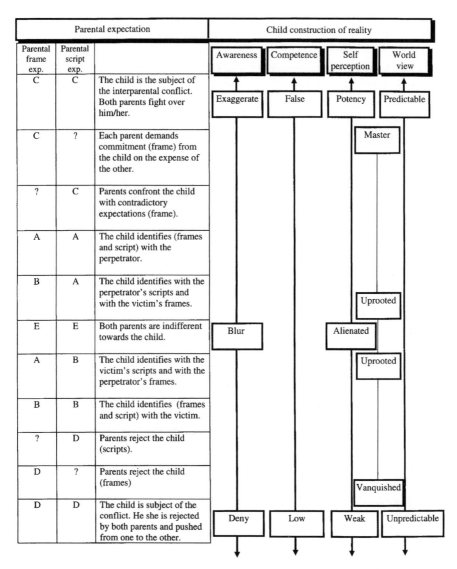

Figure 9.2. The interaction between parental expectation and a child's construction of reality.

a certain stock of knowledge and skills that enable him or her to cope with the environment. These may include physical strength, school performance, negotiation, and other interpersonal skills. Competence can be conceptualized in terms of a continuum that ranges from low (e.g., "I am helpless") to high (e.g., "I can do anything I want"), including in extreme cases a sense of false competence (e.g., "I am the master of the universe").

Self-Perception

Self-perception encompasses the relationship between a child's self-evaluation and what the child believes about others' evaluation of him or her. This continuum can range from a sense of potency and a feeling that others depend on him or her to a sense of weakness and dependence on others. In between are those who are ambivalent and alienated.

Worldview

Worldview reflects the child's overall perception of the world as predictable or unpredictable. The child's worldview can move along a continuum of predictability from high to low.

Child Profiles: The Master, the Uprooted, and the Vanquished

The constructs resulting from these continua as influenced by parental expectations can be arranged in three distinct profiles of children: the master, the vanquished, and the uprooted. The master child is part of the interparental conflict. The parents are fighting over him or her. On the acceptance dimension, the parents are accepting the child both in terms of frames (e.g., "The child is mine") and scripts (e.g., "He'll do as I tell him"). The child's reality construction is characterized by extreme awareness arising from his or her centrality both in the conflict and in the parents' wishes to have him or her on their respective side. Such awareness and centrality creates in the child a sense of unrealistic power, control over his or her own and the parents' lives, and an illusion of pseudocompetence and a self-perception of a strong and central figure, with others depending on him or her. The world seems to be clear and predictable as the child comes to believe that he or she can shape his or her and the parents' world.

We now examine how such parental expectations combined with a child's construction of reality are processed in the case of a violent event in terms of what happened, why it happened, and what it means. Following violence, when parents negotiate what happened, the child's role is central. He or she not only is a witness or an active participant but may be called to testify to the injustice done to one of the parents by the other. The parents are unlikely to allow the child to remain neutral. The child cannot escape awareness of the power position in which he or she is trapped. In terms of causality, the child is quick to realize that he or she is the cause of the violence. As both the cause and the judge of the event, the child's sense of competence and self-perception become unrealistically high. An omnipotent worldview is the obvious consequence of such construction. The universe created and judged by the child can be readily predicted.

The uprooted child is not part of the interparental conflict, and the parents are fighting over issues unrelated to him or her. He or she is neither rejected nor accepted, and the parents are indifferent to the child. Because no normative frames or scripts are provided to the child (lack of expectations), he or she is uprooted. The child is unsure about what he or she knows and does not know, and his or her awareness is blurred. In such a state of awareness, the child has little if any opportunity to experiment with his or her competence and assess it. The child perceives himself or herself as a stranger in the family. This experience is carried over to his or her overall worldview. The child does not know what is to be predicted, so his or her strangerlike expectation is reinforced. When negotiation occurs in the family following the violence, the child is aware that something happened but has no ability to figure out what happened. Was it a fight or perhaps a game? Accordingly, no causality can be attributed to the event As in the case of the master child, the vanquished child is at center stage of the conflict. However, in contrast to that profile, here the child is rejected by both parents by being rejected from one to the other (reject–reject). The awareness of being emotionally and physically rejected to a degree that entails violence is difficult to bear, so the child is likely to limit his or her awareness to a minimum. Limited awareness is associated with limited competence. The child's self-perception reflects dependence and searches for an anchor. The experience resulting from unpredictability is one of a "leaf blowing in the wind," which leads to a chaotic worldview. Whereas in the previous profiles, the child is either actively participating (master) or is passively present (uprooted), here the sense of rejection is likely to encourage the child to extract himself or herself from the negotiation altogether.

For each profile, we can hypothesize about the existence of a set of typical emotions. For the master, overt anger can be expected; for the vanquished, covert and more introvert emotions, such as fear, anxiety, and helplessness, are more likely. The in-between profile of the uprooted is likely to be characterized by mixed emotions, such as anger, fear, and alienation.

So far we have described three distinct profiles that are essentially pure or theoretical because they imply a total overlap between both the frames and the scripts inherent in parents' normative expectations. In other words, all four sets of expectations have been applied identically. In the profile of master child, the mother and the father accepted the child by means of both the frames and the scripts provided; in the vanquished child profile, they both rejected the child; and in the uprooted child profile, they were indifferent to the child. But reality is far more complex because parental expectations are seldom coherent for one of the parents (in terms of frames and scripts) and between parents (in terms of interparental frames and scripts). Furthermore, expectations vary over time and context.

Consider a father who said, "I don't need you to love me, but look at me and learn. Behave like a man." The mother said, "I love you and need you, and I really need you to be strong . . . with me." Here, the father uses a reject frame and an accept script. The mother, however, uses an accept frame and a reject script. Under those conditions, the child is likely to behave aggressively and be rewarded by heightened levels of control. His or her worldview is likely to be governed by the law of the jungle: eat or be eaten. The child may feel sorry for the victimized mother for her suffering and feel angry toward the brutality of the father. At the same time, he or she may feel contempt for the victimized mother for her weakness and look up to the father for his force and authority.

EXTRAFAMILY INFLUENCES

So far we have developed our conceptualization within the boundaries of the parent–child relationship with no broader social context. Although this set of relationships is central in the construction of children's experiences, the process does not take place in isolation. Significant others (people and organizations) may serve as mediating factors between parental expectations and children's constructions of their experience of interparental violence. As such, they may either reinforce (e.g., a child who is rejected at home may also be rejected at school) or contradict (e.g., a child who is rejected at home may be well accepted by peers or teachers) parental expectations. Figure 9.3 is a graphic representation of the extent of correspondence between parental expectations and the child's construction of reality. The existence of such correspondence is an indicator of how much others, outside the family system, affect the children's constructs. If we find a high degree of correspondence between parental expectations and children's constructions, we can safely assume that outside expectations are either correspondent with parental expectations or their influence on the child's constructions is marginal. Conversely, a low degree of correspondence indicates that outside influences are significant.

The two horizontal, parallel lines represent the parental expectations and the child's constructions, respectively. On these lines, there is a normative range of expectations and constructions. This normative range encompasses what is considered acceptable within a given cultural and developmental context. Four possible degrees of correspondence have been identified, as represented by the cross-lines in Figure 9.3. Crossline 1 illustrates a situation of total correspondence between expectations and constructions, which is outside of the normative range (e.g., parental accept–accept expectations, both parents are accepting the child in their own direction, and the child's construction of reality about himself or herself is one of an

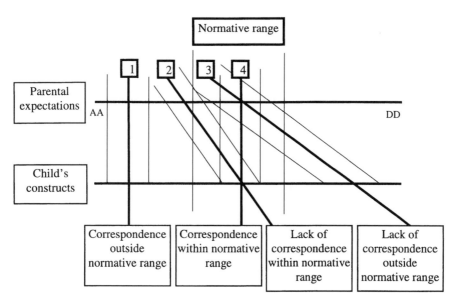

Figure 9.3. Correspondence between parental expectations and a child's construction of reality.

all-capable master). Under such conditions, outside expectations are either correspondent with parental expectations, or their influence on the child's constructions is marginal.

Crossline 2 illustrates a lack of correspondence between parental expectations that are outside of the normative range, and normative constructions by the child (e.g., parental accept–accept expectations, normative reality construction by the child). Under such conditions, outside expectations are not correspondent with parental expectations, and they influence child construction toward the normative range, in spite of parental expectations. Crossline 3 is the inverse of crossline 2; namely, the lack of correspondence is between normative parental expectations and nonnormative child's constructions of reality (e.g., parental normative expectations, child's reality construction of himself as vanquished). Crossline 4 is identical to crossline 1 but within the normative range of expectations and constructs.

OPERATIONALIZING THE CONCEPTUAL FRAMEWORK

The suggested framework should be viewed as a "skeleton in search of flesh." The specific content areas brought into the suggested structure throughout the chapter are illustrative rather than comprehensive. To illustrate the usefulness of this structure, we must study first the ways in which parents' and significant others' expectations are presented to the child;

second, the ways in which the child perceives these expectations; and third, the child's construction of reality. It should be emphasized that all the elements are culturally and developmentally bound.

To study the ways in which parental and significant other's expectations are presented to the child, we must ask the informant a set of prescriptive questions about how he or she would want the child to perceive (feel, think about) a specific topic (including the informer, the partner, and significant others). The questions need to discriminate between the commonalities and the differences in the various topics and to provide the causes and meanings attributed by the informant in question. This can be accomplished by assembling a list of cognitive and emotional representations, each scaled in order of importance. For example, one set of questions would address frame expectations, including "To what extent is it important for you that your son loves you?" "To what extent is it important for you that your son respects you?" The same questions need to be asked in relation to the mother and significant others to identify commonalities and differences. We proceed by asking the opposite questions: e.g., "To what extent do you care that your son doesn't?" The causes and meanings of each option must also be explored.

Another set of questions addresses script expectations, such as "How do you perceive your child?" (using the same set of cognitive and emotional representations). Here, we ask questions about the child's behavior as operationalized by his or her parents' cognitive and emotional representations: e.g., "To what extent do you perceive your son as intelligent?" Next we would ask the father about the meaning and causality of each option.

To study the ways in which the child perceives the parents' and significant others' expectations, we must ask questions about the child's perception of parental expectations for purposes of validation. Along these lines, we need to ask the same questions as those asked of the parents but address to them to the child (using the same list of cognitive and emotional representations). By exploring causality and meaning of parental expectations in the child's perception, we can examine the child's construction of reality in terms of his or her awareness (e.g., "To what extent do you know that . . .?"), competency (e.g., "To what extent are you capable of . . .?"), self-perception (e.g., "To what extent do you see yourself as . . .?") and worldview ("To what extent do you believe that . . . will occur at home, in your neighborhood, or at school?").

The above three content areas must be examined in the context of everyday family life and specifically in the context of violent events. The items in the questions should be formulated both in terms of expectations (indirect questions, e.g., "Is it okay to use force with a child to educate him?") and behaviors (direct questions, e.g., "How often do you use force with your child for educational purposes?").

Many issues remain to be addressed during the empirical validation of the model. For instance, as shown in Figure 9.3, the child may be faced with parental expectations outside the normative range, which may direct the child to similar constructions, yet he or she may arrive at a normative construct because of outside influences that lead to resiliency. Similarly, we can expect that for the younger the child, the more influential parental expectations are going to be at the expense of outside influences on his or her reality construction. We can also hypothesize that female children, who are more relationship oriented, are likely to be more influenced in their reality construction by both parental and significant other's expectations than are male children.

CONCLUSION

In this chapter, we attempted to provide a multidimensional dynamic structure that can be used to map the components of children's construction of interparental violence. This structure can be considered a unifying framework for researching various aspects of child experience using different theoretical perspectives and methodologies. Such a framework allows for the development of a coherent and cumulative body of knowledge in this domain. The framework is holistic and based on information from multiple sources, thus reflecting multiple perspectives. The framework is also based on the principle that one never seeks an informant's evaluation of another's experience but only his or her own. The suggested conceptualization is based on studying attitudes and behaviors, and it enables the exploration of the extent of correspondence between the two. It further allows validation across situations (violent and nonviolent) for the same informant and as a comparison of divergent versions of informants on the same issues. Finally, we believe that such formulation has mapping, descriptive, and predictive potential if it is properly supported by empirical evidence.

REFERENCES

Bruner, J. (1990). *Acts of meaning*. Cambridge, MA: Harvard University Press.

Cummings, E. M. (1998). Children exposed to marital conflict and violence: Conceptual and theoretical directions. In G. W. Holden, R. Geffner, & E. N. Jouriles (Eds.), *Children exposed to marital violence: Theory, research, and applied issues* (pp. 55–93). Washington, DC: American Psychological Association.

Edleson, J. L. (1999). Children's witnessing of adult domestic violence. *Journal of Interpersonal Violence, 14*, 839–870.

Eisikovits, Z., Winstok, Z., & Enosh, G. (1998). Children's experience of interparental violence: A heuristic model. *Children and Youth Services Review, 20,* 547–568.

Gergen, K. J. (1994). *Realities and relationships.* Cambridge, MA: Harvard University Press.

Graham-Bermann, S. A. (1998). The impact of woman abuse on children's social development: Research and theoretical perspectives. In G. W. Holden, R. Geffner, & E. N. Jouriles (Eds.), *Children exposed to marital violence: Theory, research, and applied issues* (pp. 21–54). Washington, DC: American Psychological Association.

Grych, J. H., & Fincham, F. D. (1990). Marital conflict and children's adjustment: A cognitive–contextual framework. *Psychological Bulletin, 108,* 267–290.

Holden, G. W. (1998). Introduction: The development of research into another consequence of family violence. In G. W. Holden, R. Geffner, & E. N. Jouriles (Eds.), *Children exposed to marital violence: Theory, research, and applied issues* (pp. 1–18). Washington, DC: American Psychological Association.

Holden, G. W., Geffner, R., & Jouriles, E. N. (1998). *Children exposed to marital violence: Theory, research, and applied issues.* Washington, DC: American Psychological Association.

Hughes, H. M., & Barad, S. J. (1983). Psychological functioning of children in a battered women's shelter: A preliminary investigation. *American Journal of Orthopsychiatry, 53,* 525–531.

Jaffe, P., Wolfe, D. A., & Wilson, S. (1990). *Children of battered women.* Newbury Park, CA: Sage.

Rosenberg, M. L., & Mercy, J. A. (1991). Assaultive violence. In M. L. Rosenberg & M. A. Fenley (Eds.), *Violence in America* (pp. 14–20). New York: Oxford University Press.

Straus, M. A. (1991, September). *Children as witnesses to marital violence: A risk factor for life-long problems among a nationally representative sample of American men and women.* Paper presented at the Ross Round Table on Children and Violence, Washington, DC.

10

CRITICAL ISSUES IN RESEARCH ON SOCIAL NETWORKS AND SOCIAL SUPPORTS OF CHILDREN EXPOSED TO DOMESTIC VIOLENCE

SANDRA K. BEEMAN

There is growing recognition that children are negatively affected by exposure to adult domestic violence. Most studies focus on the emotional and behavioral consequences associated with being exposed to intimate violence. In these studies, researchers have found that child witnesses of adult domestic violence are more likely than children from nonviolent households to experience behavioral, emotional, and cognitive problems (see reviews in Edleson, 1999; and Holden, 1998). In addition, in retrospective research with adults who witnessed abuse as children, Silvern et al. (1995) found evidence for long-term effects of witnessing violence, such as adult depression, low self-esteem, and adult use of violent behavior. As recognition of these negative effects has grown, so has a search for factors that may lessen the short- and long-term effects on children of exposure to adult domestic violence.

Recent child development research identifies resiliency factors that may reduce or buffer against the negative influence of a variety of negative childhood experiences, including poverty, neglect, poor parenting, and family conflict (Masten, Best, & Garmezy, 1990; Rutter, 1987). Much of this research examines characteristics of the child, such as the specific coping strategies used by children when confronted with a negative life event (e.g., Laumakis, Margolin, & John, 1998; Peled, 1993). More recently, however, attention has been paid to the environmental or social factors that are characteristic of resilient children. One environmental factor that has been increasingly identified as a critical protective factor is the child's relationships with others, in other words, social support (Cicchetti & Rizley, 1981; Werner & Smith, 1992).

In the past, researchers of the influence of social support on children have focused primarily on the processes by which parental networks or parents' social support positively influenced the child (e.g., Cochran & Brassard, 1979; Coletta, 1981; Crittenden, 1985). Recently, however, researchers have begun to examine children's own social networks and the support that they receive through them (Belle, 1989a; Cochran, Larner, Riley, Gunnarsson, & Henderson, 1990). A better understanding of the structure and function of children's social relationships and how these relationships may lessen the immediate impact of children's exposure to adult domestic violence and contribute to their long-term health and well-being is important to the development of effective programs and policies for children. Although models for understanding the influence of social support on children are still in their early stages of development, much can be learned from examining research on adults' social support. Over the past 25 years, research on the social support of adults has developed into a sophisticated field of study with well-developed conceptual models, reliable multidimensional research instruments, and multimethod approaches to measurement. This chapter reviews research on the protective functioning of social support for children, describes conceptual and methodological developments in the study of social support that can improve the understanding of the role of social support for children, and makes recommendations for a research agenda that will inform the development of effective program and policy for children exposed to adult domestic violence.

SOCIAL SUPPORT AND SOCIAL NETWORKS: TWO DISTINCT CONCEPTS

Ecological theories of human development recognize the critical role played by the social environment in healthy development and adaptation (Brofenbrenner, 1979). Over the past 25 years, the concepts of *social network* and *social support* have emerged as important operationalizations of the interpersonal aspects of the environment that are critical to health and well-being. In adults, social support has been linked to better physical and mental health, adaptation to stress, recovery from illness, and adequate parenting (e.g., Barrera, 1986; Cohen & Wills, 1985; Gottlieb, 1981). More recently, researchers have begun to examine the supportive resources of children, including a focus on the protective functioning of social support (e.g., Belle, 1989a). In addition, an extensive practice literature has developed on building and enhancing social networks and linking informal and formal supports (Cochran, 1988; Gottlieb, 1981; Lovell & Richey, 1991; Miller & Whittaker, 1988; Thompson, 1995; Whittaker & Tracy, 1991). It has been argued, however, that the understanding of social support and its relationship to well-being and development has been hampered by a lack of conceptual clarity (e.g., Barrera, 1986; Wellman, 1981).

The concepts of social support and social networks are often used interchangeably, but it is important to distinguish between them. *Social networks* are the broad collection of social ties of an individual: "the cast of characters in an individual's social world" (Belle, 1989c, p. 1). For children, this may include parents, siblings, friends, peers, neighbors, teachers, and other adults in the community. Social networks include not only supportive ties but also negative or stressful ties and ties of mixed valence (Wellman, 1981). Studies of social networks focus on the structural characteristics of the network—characteristics of the network as a whole, such as size, homogeneity, geographical dispersion, and density—and on interactional characteristics—characteristics of individual ties within the network, such as type of relationship, content of interaction, and frequency of contact. Over the years, the concept of social network has evolved from its early metaphorical usage into a well-developed analytical approach to studying the system of interpersonal relationships of individuals (Mitchell, 1969; Wellman, 1981).

Social support, however, refers specifically to the supportive resources that are available through social networks. Social support has been conceptualized in many ways but most often includes material and physical assistance, informational support, and emotional support. Perhaps one of the most useful conceptualizations of social support has been developed by Barrera (1986), who distinguished among social embeddedness, enacted support, and perceived support. Social embeddedness refers to the connections that individuals have to significant others in their social environments (often measured through the use of network analysis). Enacted support is the actions that others perform when they render assistance. Perceived support is the appraisal of being reliably connected to others or the perception that one is loved, valued, and able to count on others if the need arises. Some have argued that it is this perception of being supported that is the most critical aspect of social support (e.g., Cobb, 1976). The importance of the distinction among these three aspects of social support is strengthened by research that indicates only a weak relationship among them (Barrera, 1986).

Recognizing that the concepts of social support and social network are linked is useful both conceptually and methodologically. For example, focusing on the social network—the larger collection of social ties—provides a structure within which to search for the resource of social support (perceived and enacted). It also allows for the identification of both positive or supportive relationships and negative or stressful relationships. Recognizing that the concepts of social support and social network are not the same, however, is critical. It cautions, for example, against assuming that increasing the size of an individual's network or encouraging an individual to spend more time with those they already know will necessarily help them (Thompson, 1995). The distinction between the concepts, in other words, has important practical implications. Social support interventions may target the number of potential supports (social embeddedness), amount of help received (enacted support), or quality of relationships or interactions (perceived social support). An understanding of how social support functions is also important in making recommendations for practice and policy implications.

THE FUNCTIONING OF SOCIAL SUPPORT

In general, there are two broad views of how social support functions to enhance well-being: (a) a situational-specific view in which social support is tied to coping with a particular stressful event and (b) a developmental approach in which social support is seen as a contributor to personality and social development (Pierce, Sarason, Sarason, Joseph, & Henderson, 1996.) Both views are important in approaching the study of social support of children exposed to adult domestic violence: the situational view in terms of understanding the role of social support in responding to particular incidents of adult domestic violence, the developmental view in terms of understanding the role of social support in protecting against the long-term effects of adult domestic violence.

Within the situational view, it has been suggested that social support helps children under stress through a preventive path and a moderating or buffering path (Barrera, 1986; Cohen & Wills, 1985; Sandler, Miller, Short, & Wolchick, 1989; Vaux, 1988). As stress prevention, social support surrounds the child with people who provide emotional and instrumental assistance that contributes to healthy functioning and may even prevent the occurrence of a stressful event. For example, after a divorce, an existing supportive network may prevent stress caused by the family's financial troubles by providing financial support (Sandler et al., 1989). When stress occurs, however, social support can also be enlisted as a stress buffer, reducing its toll on physical and mental well-being. Here, social support plays a role in the child's effective coping with a stressful event through the receipt of emotional, instrumental, and material assistance.

Within the developmental view, social support is seen as protecting children from negative outcomes or contributing to the remediation of developmental consequences of exposure to adverse life circumstances, such as adult domestic violence (Cicchetti & Rizley, 1981; Thompson, 1995) Research on resilience in children often takes this view of social support (Masten et al., 1990; Rutter, 1987). There is a growing group of researchers who study the relationships between social networks and child development;

many of them identify with an ecological orientation to development (e.g., Cochran et al., 1990). In the past, developmental psychologists who studied the effects of social support on children most often examined the social networks of mothers because these might affect maternal morale or child-rearing competence and thus indirectly affect the child. More recently, however, their attention has focused on the effects of children's own social relationships on their development. Although most commonly examining the child's relationship with his or her mother, more recent research includes relationships with fathers, siblings, friends, and other adults (e.g., Belle, 1989c; Dunn & Kendrick, 1982; Parke, 1981).

Other researchers, working from the perspective of attachment theory, have emphasized the primacy of perceived support in healthy development (e.g., Bretherton, Walsh, & Lependorf, 1996). As stated by Bowlby (1979),

> evidence is accumulating that human beings of all ages are happiest and able to deploy their talents to best advantage when they are confi-dent that, standing behind them, there are one or more trusted persons who will come to their aid should difficulties arise. The person so trusted, also known as an attachment figure (Bowlby, 1969), can be considered as providing his or her companion with a secure base from which to operate. (p. 103)

Applying these two views of the functioning of social support—the situational and the developmental—to children exposed to family violence suggests that children need not only assistance to recover developmentally from the effects of exposure but also the emotional affirmation, counseling, advice, companionship, and instrumental aid that social support can offer them in response to a crisis event (cf. Thompson, 1995). Yet few researchers of children exposed to adult domestic violence have examined the role of social support.

RESEARCH ON CHILDREN'S SOCIAL NETWORKS AND SOCIAL SUPPORT

There is a small but growing body of research that examines children's social support based on both the situational specific view and the develop-mental view. Researchers conducting studies on the supportive relationships of children have found parents to be a very important source of social support for children (e.g., Belle & Longfellow's study, as cited in Belle, 1989c). For example, children with positive relationships with their mother have been found to have high academic achievement and personality adjust-ment; and positive father–child relationships are associated with high self-esteem and satisfactory peer relations (Parke, 1981). A good relationship with at least one parent has been identified as a protective factor that buffers children from the potentially adverse effects of marital discord, parental mental illness, and social disadvantage (Rutter, 1987).

Although adults appear to be the major providers of support to children—particularly to young children—there is also empirical evidence that siblings and other children can provide stress-buffering support to children (Belle, 1989c). Sandler (1980), for example, found that children with older siblings were protected from the negative impact of stressful life events. Cauce (1986) found that positive support from friends of African American adolescents in low-income families was positively related to school competence. Taken as a whole, this research indicates that two potential sources of resilience for children exposed to severe stress are family support and extrafamilial support from peers and other adults (e.g., Cowen & Work, 1988; Sandler et al., 1989).

Although the practice literature emphasizes the importance of the availability of supports outside the home to children exposed to adult domestic violence (Wilson, Cameron, Jaffe, & Wolfe, 1989), little research focuses specifically on the social relationships of children exposed to family violence. Some researchers have examined the child's relationships with his or her battered mother or battering father, primarily exploring how their relationships changed as a result of the violence (e.g., Peled, 1998). Only a few researchers have looked beyond the parental relationship to relationships with other adults or with peers.

Blanchard, Molloy, and Brown (1992), in their study of 18 children living in violent homes, examined the way in which social support may function in response to crisis events. They asked children where they went for help during a crisis and immediately after a violent incident at home. They found that although some children mentioned their mothers as a source of support, many recognized that their mothers were "too stressed" to help them. According to the children, the best support for them was a strong caring adult within easy distance of home or school to whom the child could talk openly and safely about the violence at home. For some, it was a neighbor, for others a relative, a teacher, or a adult domestic violence worker. From the children's point of view, the most valuable support at the time of crisis was a capable, sympathetic adult to take control of the situation for them, stop the violence, and ensure their and their mother's safety. These children recognized that "most people" would not respond to their requests for help because they did not understand or want to know about adult domestic violence. In the longer term, the children in their study indicated a need for support after the violence and even after the violent father was no longer living with them. Blanchard, Molloy, and Brown suggested that children need help to understand that the violence is not their responsibility and that their father could have behaved without violence.

Recognizing that the social relationships of children exposed to adult domestic violence may provide both protection and harm, Graham-Bermann, Levendosky, Porterfield, and Okun (1998) examined the characteristics of the social networks of 60 children residing in battered women's shelters and 61 nonsheltered children from the same communities. Using the Networks of Relationships Inventories (Furman & Buhrmester, 1985), the researchers asked each child to assess the qualities of relationships for up to 10 network members. Negative relationships included those rated as "conflictual" and "controlling"; positive relationships included those assessed as "nurturing" and "helping." They found that the weight of negative relationships in the child's network added direct risk to the child's problems in adjustment, whereas the presence of positive social support did not contribute to the child's adjustment. Furthermore, they found that the sheer number of social supports identified by the child, as part of his or her network, was not related to outcomes for children in either group. Although these studies begin to explore the social support and social networks of children exposed to adult domestic violence, there is an obvious need for additional research in this area.

RECOMMENDATIONS FOR RESEARCH

Researchers are just beginning to examine the complex relationship between exposure to adult domestic violence and children's social relationships with family, teachers, friends, and others in their interpersonal social networks. How might children's relationships with parents, siblings, extended family, friends, neighbors, and other adults function to prevent adverse outcomes for children exposed to adult domestic violence? How are these relationships affected by their experience with adult domestic violence? What do researchers need to know about how these relationships function situationally and developmentally to design effective programs and policies for children? This section discusses important conceptual and methodological principles taken from the literature on adults' social support that can inform research on social support for children exposed to family violence.

Social Support Is a Multidimensional Concept

Barrera's (1986) conceptualization of social support as including social embeddedness, enacted support, and perceived support has important implications for studying children's social support. How do these different dimensions function, and which is most important in the lives of children? Specifically, in studying children exposed to family violence, which of these three aspects is most important in mediating the negative effects of children's exposure: the availability of supportive others; the actual things people do in response to crisis events (e.g., providing children with a place to stay temporarily, listening, or linking them with formal supports); or the child knowing that a competent, caring adult will be there for him or her when needed?

Social Relationships Are Two Way

Research on adults emphasizes that individuals are, in any relationship, both sources and recipients of social support. In fact, research on adults illustrates that the reciprocal nature of social relationships is an important factor in enhancing well-being. For example, in a study comparing mothers involved in the child welfare system with those considered by key community contacts to be "successful" parents, reciprocity and perception of "fairness" in social relationships were important distinguishing factors between the two groups of mothers (Beeman, 1997).

Furthermore, the giving and receiving of social support is only a part of the complex nature of relationships with others. Children, like adults, are not simply recipients of social support but interact with others. Does reciprocity play a significant role in the social relationships of children? Do peers and siblings, in particular, recognize the ebb and flow of receiving and giving help to children? For children exposed to adult domestic violence, how does the experience affect a child's ability to engage in a reciprocal relationship? For children whose mothers are the victims of adult domestic violence, what is the complex nature of the give-and-take between the mother and the child? Particularly in the case of older children, is the mother also relying on the child for support? For example, Peled (1998) in her research on children who witnessed adult domestic violence and Wallerstein and Kelly (1980) in their research on children of divorced parents found that mothers sometimes sought emotional support from their children.

Social Networks Are Fluid

Research on social support and social networks often takes a static approach, treating networks as if they were fixed in shape and content (Cochran et al., 1990). Yet the "membership" of networks comes and goes, and the content of relationships evolves over time. The membership of children's networks and the content of their relationships with others is likely to change as children move through developmental stages, begin school, and increase their involvement with peer groups. In addition, major life events often result in changes in social networks. This notion of the fluidity of social networks is especially important in research on children exposed to adult domestic violence. What happens to a child's existing network if a mother and her children move from their neighborhood to escape the batterer, leaving behind friends and adult neighbors? What about the changes in the child's relationship with his or her father's side of the family when his use of violence is exposed? Researchers of the social networks of children of divorced parents have found changes in the structure of the network because of the divorce, for example, losing access to one side of the extended family. In the case of children's exposure to adult domestic violence, the study of social support and social networks must look not only at their role in responding to the violence but also at how the violence affects the structure and nature of those relationships.

Social Relationships Are Positive, Negative, Mixed, and Contextual

As stated earlier, focusing only on social support ignores the presence of negative or stressful relationships within the social network. Graham-Bermann et al. (1998) found that negative relationships had an adverse influence on a child's adjustment and that positive relationships had no effect. Researchers of adults' social networks have found that relationships are rarely always positive or always negative but rather may change over time or be positive in some situations and negative in others (e.g., Beeman, 1997). A careful examination of children's entire networks will allow researchers to sort out the importance of these different types of relationships and to examine the circumstances under which particular social relationships have positive or negative influences. For example, do social network members respond differently to incidents of adult domestic violence than to other crisis events in children's lives? In particular, the application of social network analysis to research on children provides a useful analytical tool to the study of social relationships.

The Relationship Between Social Support and Well-Being Is Mutual

It has been suggested that the relationship between social support and well-being is mutual (Specht, 1986). In other words, whereas social support may enhance well-being and healthy functioning, healthy functioning most likely contributes to higher levels of social interaction and social support. Past research emphasized the role of social skills in maintaining relationships and accessing social support (Burleson & Kunkel, 1996). This research suggested that it is necessary for individuals to possess the social skills that enable them to negotiate supportive transactions. What social skills are needed by children at different developmental levels to access support? More specifically, what social skills do children who witness adult domestic violence need? How does the experience of living with family violence interfere with a child's development of appropriate social skills?

Social Networks Define and Communicate Social Norms

Social networks and social relationships are a source not only of support but also of role-modeling and social norms. For example, research on child maltreatment suggests that social networks are a source of positive role models for parenting (Belsky, 1984; Garbarino & Gilliam, 1980). What is the influence of adult role models within a child's social network on the eventual development of the child's own parenting skills? In the case of children exposed to adult domestic violence, what is the potential of a child's social network for providing alternative models of adult relationships? What contribution can positive role models within children's interpersonal networks make to preventing children's own use of violence?

Cultural, Gender, and Developmental Differences Exist in Social Support

Research within the United States shows systematic differences in the structure and functioning of social networks by race, ethnicity, and class (e.g., Cross, 1990). For example, the importance of kin relations is emphasized within many communities of color (Delgado & Humm-Delgado, 1982; Stack, 1974). Research also shows gender differences in children's social networks and supports (Belle, 1989b; Fiering & Lewis, 1989). Differences were also found according to the child's age or developmental level (Berndt, 1989; Bryant, 1989; Furman & Buhrmester, 1992). Cultural, gender, and age differences must all be considered when examining children's social support. How do different cultural traditions for help seeking and help giving influence children's receipt of social support? Do social support and social networks function differently for girls than for boys? How do social support needs differ for young children, who often spend their day in a primarily home-centered environment, than for older children, who spend their day in a primarily school-centered environment? How do social support needs of adolescents differ from those of younger children? For children exposed to adult domestic violence, how does the gender aspect of adult domestic violence influence the help-seeking behaviors of boys and girls who witness it? How do age, developmental level, and gender influence help seeking and social support among children exposed to violence?

Multiple Methods and Measures Are Important

Research on the social support of adults emphasizes the importance of multiple approaches to measurement and data collection. A variety of standardized instruments for measuring social support now exists, including many designed specifically to measure children's social support (Wolchik, Beals, & Sandler, 1989). Although these measures allow for the reliable measurement of social support, they are often limited in terms of gathering information on the complex and fluid qualities of relationships, and few measure perceived social support. It has been suggested that qualitative data collection and analysis are useful in capturing perceived social support and that fine-grained case studies capture the details of the functioning of social networks (Cochran, 1990; Cochran & Brassard, 1979; Mitchell, 1969). It has also been suggested that longitudinal studies allow for the careful study of developmental changes over time and capture the fluidity of social networks.

Finally, a crucial methodological issue is the choice of an informant concerning a child's social network. Many measures of social support rely on maternal report. Yet in one study, Zelkowitz (1989) found that children and mothers have distinct perspectives on children's networks. In the case of children exposed to adult domestic violence, are mothers the best source of valid information about the child's use of social support? Sternberg, Lamb, and Dawud-Noursi (1998) emphasized the importance of using multiple informants when collecting data about history of violence and its effects on children. This same recommendation applies to the collection of data on social networks and social support.

RECOMMENDATIONS FOR PRACTICE AND POLICY

There is not yet a body of empirical research on the social support and social networks of children exposed to adult domestic violence that can guide the development of practice and policy for these children. However, our knowledge about the functioning of social support for adults and children suggests the following:

- Interventions to increase social support to children exposed to adult domestic violence must target not only the children who will be the recipients of social support but also the adults and other children who will provide it. For example, teachers, school social workers, medical personnel, and other providers must be trained to recognize exposure to adult domestic violence and to respond to children nonjudgmentally. Increasing the larger community's awareness will better prepare neighbors and peers to respond supportively to children. In addition, interventions that provide positive adult role models may play an important preventive role.

- The distinction between social support concepts suggests that interventions must focus not only on increasing the availability of supportive others who are knowledgeable about adult domestic violence and increasing the provision of support to children but also on enhancing children's skills at accessing and obtaining support.
- The coordination of formal and informal supports is important to an overall intervention strategy. Informal supports often act as a link to existing formal supports. In addition, existing settings designed for children and parents can be enhanced to better support network building. For example, day care, schools, and community centers could contribute to the natural network-building of children and parents who attend them.
- The interventions to enhance the support of children must be coordinated with the interventions to enhance the support of their mothers.

Social support and social networks hold great potential for protecting children against the long-term effects of exposure to adult domestic violence. Children exposed to family violence need not only the emotional support, advice, companionship, and instrumental aid that social support can offer them in response to specific incidents of violence but also the long-term support to recover developmentally from the effects of exposure (Thompson, 1995). Research that contributes to the understanding of the complex relationship between exposure to adult domestic violence and children's social relationships will enhance the ability to prevent and remediate the negative effects of their exposure to violence.

REFERENCES

Barrera, M. (1986). Distinctions between social support concepts, measures, and models. *American Journal of Community Psychology, 14*, 413–435.

Beeman, S. (1997). Reconceptualizing social support and its relationship to child neglect. *Social Service Review, 71*, 421–440.

Belle, D. (Ed.). (1989a). *Children's social networks and social supports*. New York: Wiley.

Belle, D. (1989b). Gender differences in children's social networks and supports. In D. Belle (Ed.), *Children's social networks and social supports* (pp. 173–190). New York: Wiley.

Belle, D. (1989c). Introduction: Studying children's social networks and social supports. In D. Belle (Ed.), *Children's social networks and social supports* (pp. 1–14). New York: Wiley.

Belsky, J. (1984). The determinants of parenting: A process model. *Child Development, 55,* 83–96.

Berndt, T. (1989). Obtaining support from friends during childhood and adolescence. In D. Belle (Ed.), *Children's social networks and social supports* (pp. 308–321). New York: Wiley.

Blanchard, A., Molloy, F., & Brown, L. (1992). *Western Australian children living with domestic violence: A study of the children's experiences and service provision.* Perth, Western Australia: Curtin University School of Social Work.

Bowlby, J. (1979). *The making and breaking of affectional bonds.* London: Tavistock.

Bretherton, I., Walsh, R., & Lependorf, M. (1996). Social support in postdivorce families: An attachment perspective. In G. Pierce, B. Sarason, & I. Sarason (Eds.), *Handbook of social support and the family* (pp. 345–374). New York: Plenum Press.

Brofenbrenner, U. (1979). *The experimental ecology of human development: Experiments by nature and design.* Cambridge, MA: Harvard University Press.

Bryant, B. (1989). The need for support in relation to the need for autonomy. In D. Belle (Ed.), *Children's social networks and social supports* (pp. 332–352). New York: Wiley.

Burleson, B., & Kunkel, A. (1996). Emotional support skills in childhood. In G. Pierce, B. Sarason, & I. Sarason (Eds.), *Handbook of social support and the family* (pp. 105–140). New York: Plenum Press.

Cauce, A. (1986). Social networks and social competence: Exploring the effects of early adolescent friendship. *American Journal of Community Psychology, 14,* 607–628.

Cicchetti, D., & Rizley, R. (1981). Developmental perspectives on the etiology, intergenerational transmission, and sequelae of child maltreatment. *New Directions for Child Development, 11,* 31–55.

Cobb, S. (1976). Social support as a moderator of life stress. *Psychosomatic Medicine, 38,* 300–314.

Cochran, M. (1988). Parental empowerment in family matters: Lessons learned from a research program. In D. Powell (Ed.), *Parent education as early childhood intervention: Emerging directions in theory, research and practice* (pp. 23–50). Norwood, NJ: Ablex.

Cochran, M. (1990). Personal networks in the ecology of human development. In M. Cochran, M. Larner, D. Riley, L. Gunnarsson, & C. Henderson (Eds.), *Extending families: The social networks of parents and their children* (pp. 3–33). Cambridge, England: Cambridge University Press.

Cochran, M., & Brassard, J. (1979). Child development and personal social networks. *Child Development, 50,* 609–616.

Cochran, M., Larner, M., Riley, D., Gunnarsson, L., & Henderson, C. (1990). *Extending families: The social networks of parents and their children*. Cambridge, England: Cambridge University Press.

Cohen, S., & Wills, T. (1985). Stress, social support, and the buffering hypothesis. *Psychological Bulletin, 98*, 310–357.

Coletta, N. (1981). Social support and the risk of maternal rejection by adolescent mothers. *Journal of Psychology, 109*, 191–197.

Cowen, E., & Work, W. (1988). Resilient children, psychological wellness, and primary prevention. *American Journal of Community Psychology, 16*, 591–607.

Crittenden, P. (1985). Social networks, quality of child rearing, and child development. *Child Development, 56*, 1299–1313.

Cross, W. E. (1990). Race and ethnicity: Effects on social networks. In M. Cochran, M. Larner, D. Riley, L. Gunnarsson, & C. R. Henderson (Eds.), *Extending families: The social networks of parents and their children* (pp. 67–85). Cambridge, England: Cambridge University Press.

Delgado, M., & Humm-Delgado, D. (1982). Natural support systems: Source of strength in Hispanic communities. *Social Work, 27*, 83–87.

Dunn, J., & Kendrick, C. (1982). *Siblings: Love, envy, and understanding*. Cambridge, MA: Harvard University Press.

Edleson, J. L. (1999). Children's witnessing of adult domestic violence. *Journal of Interpersonal Violence, 14*, 839–870.

Fiering, C., & Lewis, M. (1989). The social networks of girls and boys from early through middle childhood. In D. Belle (Ed.), *Children's social networks and social supports* (pp. 119–150). New York: Wiley.

Furman, W., & Buhrmester, D. (1985). Children's perceptions of the personal relationships in their social networks. *Developmental Psychology, 21*, 1016–1024.

Furman, W., & Buhrmester, D. (1992). Age and sex differences in perceptions of networks of personal relationships. *Child Development, 63*, 103–115.

Garbarino, J., & Gilliam, G. (1980). *Understanding abusive families*. Lexington, MA: Lexington Books.

Gottlieb, B. (1981). Social networks and social support in community mental health. In B. Gottlieb (Ed.), *Social networks and social support* (pp. 11–42). Beverly Hills: Sage.

Graham-Bermann, S., Levendosky, A., Porterfield, K., & Okun, A. (1998). *The impact of woman abuse on children: The role of social relationships and emotional context*. Manuscript submitted for publication, University of Michigan, Ann Arbor.

Holden, G. W. (1998). Introduction: The development of research into another consequence of family violence. In G. W. Holden, R. Geffner, & E. N. Jouriles (Eds.), *Children exposed to marital violence: Theory, research, and applied issues* (pp. 1–18). Washington, DC: American Psychological Association.

Laumakis, M. A., Margolin, G., & John, R. S. (1998). The emotional, cognitive, and coping responses of preadolescent children to different dimensions of marital conflict. In G. W. Holden, R. Geffner, & E. N. Jouriles (Eds.), *Children exposed to marital violence: Theory, research, and applied issues* (pp. 257–288). Washington, DC: American Psychological Association.

Lovell, M., & Richey, C. (1991). Implementing agency-based social support skill training. *Families in Society, 72,* 563–572.

Masten, A., Best, K., & Garmezy, N. (1990). Resilience and development: Contributions from the study of children who overcome adversity. *Development and Psychopathology, 2,* 425–444.

Miller, J., & Whittaker, J. (1988). Social services and social support: Blended programs for families at risk of child maltreatment. *Child Welfare, 67,* 161–174.

Mitchell, J. C. (1969). The concept and use of social networks. In J. C. Mitchell (Ed.), *Social networks in urban situations* (pp. 1–50). Manchester, England: University of Manchester Press.

Parke, R. (1981). *Fathers.* Cambridge, MA: Harvard University Press.

Peled, E. (1993). *The experience of living with violence for preadolescent witnesses of woman abuse.* Unpublished doctoral dissertation, University of Minnesota, Minneapolis.

Peled, E. (1998). The experience of living with violence for preadolescent children of battered women. *Youth & Society, 29,* 395–430.

Pierce, G., Sarason, B., Sarason, I., Joseph, H., & Henderson, C. (1996). Conceptualizing and assessing social support in the context of the family. In G. Pierce, B. Sarason, & I. Sarason (Eds.), *Handbook of social support and the family* (pp. 3–24). New York: Plenum Press.

Rutter, M. (1987). Psychosocial resilience and protective mechanisms. *American Journal of Orthopsychiatry, 57,* 316–331.

Sandler, I. (1980). Social support resources, stress, and maladjustment of poor children. *American Journal of Community Psychology, 8,* 41–52.

Sandler, I., Miller, P., Short, J., & Wolchick, S. (1989). Social support as a protective factor for children in stress. In D. Belle (Ed.), *Children's social networks and social supports* (pp. 277–307). New York: Wiley.

Silvern, L., Karyl, J., Waelde, L., Hodges, W., Starek, J., Heidt, E., & Min, K. (1995). Retrospective reports of parental partner abuse: Relationships to depression, trauma symptoms and self-esteem among college students. *Journal of Family Violence, 10,* 177–202.

Specht, H. (1986). Social support, social networks, social exchange, and social work practice. *Social Service Review, 61,* 19–31.

Stack, C. (1974). *All our kin: Strategies for survival in a Black community.* New York: Harper.

Sternberg, K. J., Lamb, M. E., & Dawud-Noursi, S. (1998). Using multiple informants to understand domestic violence and its effects. In G. W. Holden, R. Geffner, & E. N. Jouriles (Eds.), *Children exposed to marital violence: Theory, research, and applied issues* (pp. 121–156). Washington, DC: American Psychological Association.

Thompson, R. (1995). *Preventing child maltreatment through social support: A critical analysis.* Thousand Oaks, CA: Sage.

Vaux, A. (1988). *Social support: Theory, research and intervention.* New York: Praeger.

Wallerstein, J., & Kelly, J. (1980). *Surviving the breakup: How children and parents cope with divorce.* New York: Basic Books.

Wellman, B. (1981). Applying social network analysis to the study of support. In B. Gottlieb (Ed.), *Social networks and social support* (pp. 171–200). Beverly Hills: Sage.

Werner, E., & Smith, R. (1992). *Overcoming the odds: High-risk children from birth to adulthood.* Ithaca, NY: Cornell University Press.

Whittaker, J., & Tracy, E. (1991). Social network intervention in intensive family-based preventive services. *Prevention in Human Services, 9,* 175–192.

Wilson, S., Cameron, S., Jaffe, P., & Wolfe, D. (1989). Children exposed to wife abuse: An intervention model. *Social Casework, 70,* 180–184.

Wolchik, S., Beals, J., & Sandler, I. (1989). Mapping children's support networks: Conceptual and methodological issues. In D. Belle (Ed.), *Children's social networks and social supports* (pp. 191–220). New York: Wiley.

Zelkowitz, P. (1989). Parents and children as informants concerning children's social networks. In D. Belle (Ed.), *Children's social networks and social supports* (pp. 221–240). New York: Wiley.

III

PREVENTIVE INTERVENTION INITIATIVES AND EVALUATIONS

11

DESIGNING INTERVENTION EVALUATIONS FOR CHILDREN EXPOSED TO DOMESTIC VIOLENCE: APPLICATIONS OF RESEARCH AND THEORY

SANDRA A. GRAHAM-BERMANN

Research on the efficacy of direct intervention programs for children exposed to adult domestic violence and woman abuse is in its infancy. Unfortunately, this early state of development means that most of these programs have a "one size fits all" approach, few programs are targeted for a specific population, and few offer screening criteria or procedures. Nonetheless, all of the intervention programs described below are intended to reduce risks and to enhance protective factors in the aftermath of a child's exposure to violence. Their central challenge is to identify probable hazards or negative outcomes and design appropriate interventions to prevent or to treat them using established treatment outcome criteria.

These programs' relative success (or lack thereof) in meeting this challenge is evaluated in the following review. Thus, the first section of this chapter focuses on describing existing programs and the extent to which they satisfy evaluation criteria. The second section is dedicated to the kinds of issues that targeted intervention programs should and sometimes do seek to address, such as aggression, depression, anxiety, and problems in children's social relationships. These areas are highlighted by applying existing theory and available research to each topic. Finally, suggestions are offered for future work in designing interventions, creating screening procedures, and evaluating treatment (outcome studies). It is hoped that this review will show the need for children's programs that are well evaluated and clearly defined and for research studies that distinctly identify the clinical needs of children exposed to family violence.

As noted, the intervention programs described here have all been subjected to at least rudimentary scrutiny by evaluation (see Table 11.1). The programs are diverse; they range from those offered for young children, to those offered in shelters, to those provided in the community, to those having a broad set of goals (e.g., reducing the negative impact of violence), to those specifically targeting a single outcome (e.g., reducing aggression, improving parenting). Several innovative and varied approaches to prevention and treatment are practiced, including the use of mentors and group therapy for children, treatment of siblings together (and children and mothers in various combinations), and groups for empowering mothers, not to mention the use of home-based advocates and parenting interventions for battered women. However, most of these evaluations, thus far, rely on preliminary analyses—analyses that inevitably reflect the types of problems usually associated with the initial efforts.

SPECIFICITY OF DIRECT INTERVENTION PROGRAMS

In 1983, Gordon described three kinds of prevention programs, classifying them as universal, selective, and indicated. Whereas universal programs serve to prevent the occurrence of violence and are offered to all children, programs specifically designed for children after the violence has already taken place would be, by definition, either selective or indicated interventions (all programs listed in Table 11.1 are either selective or indicated interventions). Selective programs are those targeted at children deemed at above-average risk for developing social, emotional, or behavioral problems following exposure to violence in the home. For example, more than half of the children who witness the physical abuse of their mothers are expected to have difficulties as a result of observing such an event. Indicated programs are those designed for children from violent families who are shown to be in the category of highest risk for developing problems (e.g., children who already have problems with aggression and who have witnessed severe violence; children who have multiple exposures to traumatic violence).

Thus, this system relies on the interventionist's ability to assess risk and then to titrate or adjust the treatment to a given child's level of risk. However, the task of identifying which children are most at risk is not straightforward. Studies of the effects of exposure to family violence on children reveal that children can display several different responses and can present with a range of clinical symptoms. For sheltered children, approximately 26% of children appear to be adapting well at the time of evaluation, 36% have problems but are coping with them, and approximately 38% present with symptoms that indicate adjustment problems in the clinical

TABLE 11.1
Selective and Indicated Intervention Programs for Children of Batterers

Program and study	Sample and criteria	Evaluation design	Theoretical base	Assessment	Follow-up	Results
Treatment Groups for Children (Hughes, 1982; Hughes & Barad, 1983)	Mothers, children in DV shelters > 10 days, 3.5–11.5 years, N = 12	Pre-, postgroup evaluation for children and mothers, no comparison	Social–cognitive intergenerational transmission	Child anxiety, attitudes re: family violence, coping	No	No change in coping skill or attitude, did reduce anxiety
Wilson et al. (1989), Marshall et al. (1995)	Children 5–15 years and moms not in crisis, optional parenting group, N = 31 pairs	Pre-, postgroup evaluations for mothers and children, semistructured interviews, no comparison	Social cognition, social learning	Knowledge of DV, emotion expression, coping skills, conflict resolution skills	No	Mother and child's positive evaluation of groups, > knowledge, attitudes, skills, and intentions
Evaluation of Jaffe et al. program (Wagar & Rodway, 1995)	8–13-year-olds, witnessed DV but mother had no DV in last three months	Pre-, postgroup measures randomly assigned, two groups, N = 38	Same as above	Same as above	No	Changed attitudes to violence, coping and anger, not safety skills
Sibling Groups Treatment (Frey-Angel, 1989)	3–7-year-olds, sibling pairs, exposed to DV	Case examples, no comparison	Intergenerational and social learning theory	Coping skills, alternatives to violence	No	Qualitative, behavior change seen
Group Work With Child Witnesses to Domestic Violence (Peled & Davis, 1995)	4–12-year-olds, witness to DV, community violence, N = 30	Pre-, postgroup evaluations, child, caretakers group leaders, no comparison	Social cognition, social relations	> knowledge, changed attitudes about women and violence, coping skills	No	Change attitude > tell about violence, > DV knowledge, > emotion discussion

(continued)

TABLE 11.1

Selective and Indicated Intervention Programs for Children of Batterers *(Continued)*

Program and study	Sample and criteria	Evaluation design	Theoretical base	Assessment	Follow-up	Results
The Story Book Club (Tutty & Wagar, 1994; Cox, 1995)	4–7-year-olds, witnessed DV, $N = 13$	Pre-, postgroup evaluations by leaders or researcher, no comparison	Intergenerational transmission theory	Child anxiety, self-concept	No	< Anxiety, > self-esteem in abused child
Group Treatment for Children (Ragg et al., 1998)	6–17-year-olds, no parent group, $N = 143$	Pre-, posttest evaluations, a dropout group comparison	Social learning, social cognitive theory	Coercive control, delinquency, aggression	No	Boys less aggression, girls < anxiety, < depression
Parent Program (Van Horn, Johnson, & Lieberman, 1998)	Mothers and 0–4-year-olds in the home, $N = 9$	Pre-, posttest evaluations, no comparison	Psychoanalytic theory	Maternal psychopathology, parenting	No	Reduced PTSD, improved parenting
Family Follow-Up Pilot Study (Sullivan & Davidson, 1998)	Mothers and children 7–11 years, leaving shelter; $N = 85$	Pre-, post-, 8 months 16-week mentor program, 10-week child groups, random assignment	Community advocacy, feminist theory	Child adjustment, abuse, competence, mom social support, depression, esteem, quality of life, resources	Yes, 8 months	Child trend at follow-up, mom > mental health; < child abuse
Youth Relationships Project (Wolfe et al., 1997, ongoing)	14–16-year-olds, abused and family violence, teens, volunteer, $N = 58$	Pre-, post, 2-year follow-up, 18-week intervention group, comparison group, random assignment	Social learning, feminist theory, community advocacy	Peer relations, trauma, dating violence, conflict resolution	Yes, 2 years	> Social skill, < coercive acts, < conflict in relationships

(continued)

Intervention	Sample	Design	Theory	Measures	Random assignment	Follow-up	Results
Home-Based Parenting Intervention (Jouriles et al., 1998, preliminary)	Mothers postshelter and children 4–9 with identified behavior problems, N = 34	Pre-, post-, 8-month follow-up on parenting and mentor for child, random assignment, comparison group	Social learning theory	Child: conduct problems; Mom: parenting skill, mental health, social support	Yes	8 months	< Child aggression, > mother's parenting, < distress
The Kids' Club Evaluation study (Graham-Bermann, 1992, 2000, preliminary)	Children 6–12 years and mothers, exposed to severe domestic violence within the last year, N = 181	Pre-, during, post-, and follow-up for three groups compared: child only, child and mom, delayed treatment group, 10 weeks, random assignment	Social cognition, relationships theory, trauma theory, feminist theory for moms' empowerment groups	Child: social behavior in groups and school, adjustment, knowledge of DV, gender stereotyping, Moms: parenting, support, adjustment, empowerment	Yes	8 months	Child, child and mom > no treatment in child social behavior, mental health, and attitudes; Only child and mom > child
Rossman (1999, preliminary)	5–14-year-olds and moms, DV shelter and community, N = 29	Pre-, during, post-group and in-home evaluations, no comparison	Social cognition, social learning theory	Child: self-esteem emotion regulation, conflict with peers, information search	No		Less peer conflict, > emotion regulation, moms > support, > discussion DV

Note. DV = domestic violence.

range (Hughes & Luke, 1998). Other studies reveal that 50% of the children of batterers show behavioral and emotional difficulties (Margolin, 1998). Of those with clinical-level problems, some appear to be depressed, others aggressive, others anxious, and still others have mixed features (Graham-Bermann, Gruber, & Hughes, 2001). Furthermore, the trajectory of symptom expression has not yet been established. Some children may have symptoms that abate over time (e.g., adjustment reactions), whereas others may have delayed reactions (e.g., develop symptoms at a later date—the so called "sleeper effects"). All of these issues are revisited in the review of programs that follows.

PREVENTION PROGRAM EVALUATION CRITERIA

Although many shelters and communities have already initiated intervention programs for children exposed to adult domestic violence, there are still only a handful of studies aimed at documenting the potential, efficacy, and limitations of such programs. Contrast this state of affairs with a more historically mature field of intervention research: intervention with substance-abusing families (Stanton & Shadish, 1997). For their meta-analysis, Stanton and Shadish were able not only to select from literally hundreds of studies published over the course of the past 20 plus years or more but also distill those 15 "state-of-the-art" studies in which there was both random assignment to treatment conditions and the use of comparison groups. These 15 studies were subjected to a meta-analysis; the rest were excluded because of their inadequacies. As much as I would like to perform a similar meta-analysis for the intervention studies of children exposed to domestic violence, I am hardly positioned to attempt such here. Scarcely 3 or 4 of the 12 studies or so of interventions with children of battered women would even qualify for analysis if the Stanton and Shadish inclusion criteria were used.

Yet there is much to learn from their meta-analytic study about where the treatment research on children exposed to domestic violence stands (and, by extension, where it needs to go in the future). Building on the work of Gurman and Kniskern (1978), Stanton and Shadish (1997) elaborated a design quality rating system consisting of 15 criteria for evaluating treatment outcome research studies. Included among those criteria are the degree of contamination of the major independent variables, adequacy of follow-up assessment, cost-effectiveness considerations, and accounting for attrition, to name a few. In the sections that follow, I attempt to use these standards and criteria for judging the research on treatment outcomes for children exposed to family violence.

Program Inclusion Criteria

To compare programs, one needs to stipulate several intervention program evaluation criteria. For each program, inclusion criteria are the intended age and gender of children in the program (and hence, in the evaluation) and the definition of the extent of their exposure to domestic violence. Here, the sample population, ages, gender (same or mixed), and any rationale for inclusion of the population based on theoretical and research findings should be described.

Sample Population

All of the programs listed in Table 11.1 are offered for both boys and girls together. Only one program is designed for sibling pairs, whereas most programs opt to separate siblings into different groups to maximize their opportunity to participate freely in program activities. Programs span the developmental range from those for mothers and toddlers to those for teenagers. The treatment modalities described here are attuned to the developmental needs of the child. For example, programs for preschoolers rely primarily on story-telling techniques and puppet play in their methods (Tutty & Wagar, 1994). Programs for older children use more participatory methods, ranging from children creating their own plays and songs to teenagers working together to design a project to address an aspect of violence in their community (Wolfe et al., 1996). Programs with a large age range of children generally assign children to age-similar groups (Graham-Bermann, 1998a; Rossman, 1999; Wilson, Cameron, Jaffe, & Wolfe, 1989).

Sample Size

The reality of research in this area is that small samples of convenience have been the norm, although in some cases adequate funding has allowed for larger sample sizes with more precise sample delineation and more sophisticated sample selection procedures (Graham-Bermann, 2000; Jouriles et al., 1998). Studies with as few as 12 or 13 participants (Cox, 1995; Hughes & Barad, 1983) are used to illustrate initial program success, whereas other preliminary outcome evaluations use samples as large as 30 or 40 participants (Jouriles et al., 1998; Peled & Edleson, 1995; Rossman, 1998). Sample sizes of 11 to 40 children are simply insufficient for the task of testing models of risk and protection or of demonstrating robust effect sizes. Although promising programs can be identified with even rudimentary results, clearly more participants are needed to demonstrate the power of these interventions. Only a few intervention evaluation studies have robust sample sizes, ranging from 80 participants to almost 200 and include at least one group for comparison (Graham-Bermann, 1998b; Ragg, Sultana, & Miller, 1998; Sullivan & Davidson, 1998).

Sampling Methods

Unbiased sample selection is always most desirable, although this procedure also poses problems because a large pool of participants is required from which to draw representatives (Ammerman, 1998). Moreover, obtaining a representative group of participants for a given intervention may be difficult because the essential demographic parameters of the base population of children of battered women is unknown at this time (Fantuzzo, Boruch, Beriama, Atkins, & Marcus, 1997).

In earlier intervention studies, every child in need of treatment was included (often on the belief that it is clinically unethical to deny them services). This is particularly true of programs offered in shelters (e.g., Hughes, 1982). Still, battered women in shelters constitute a convenient sample; they also may be the safest population to treat because there is no immediate risk of retaliation for their therapeutic involvement. However, although sheltered women are readily available for participation in intervention studies, they may not stay long enough to implement the full or entire protocol of an intervention program. Battered women and children in the community are sometimes more difficult to locate, especially given the social isolation characteristic of abuser households. Wolfe et al. (1997) relied on adolescents in schools who volunteer their participation and, for the evaluation study, were assigned to either the intervention or the comparison group.

A number of programs rely on populations of women and children leaving the shelter. The women are selected as to whether they planned to remain in the area (and thus be available to participate) and whether they wished to participate in a year-long (or longer) program (Jouriles et al., 1998; Sullivan & Davidson, 1998). Given that only a small percentage of battered women are estimated to seek shelter following abuse, the generalizeability of the results of these programs may or may not extend to other populations (the majority) of battered women. Conversely, programs that advertise widely across communities for women who have been battered within the past year and who wished to participate in intervention for themselves or for their children include women who currently may be abused or still may be living with their batterer (Graham-Bermann, 1998b; Ragg et al., 1998). These programs may not serve the unique or specific needs of battered women in shelters.

Defining Children's Exposure to Violence

Some children have been exposed to family violence all their lives, whereas others have witnessed only one violent event. The reality of domestic violence study is that many children of battered women experience chronic traumatic stress. The shelter stay may not mark the end of their exposure to family violence because the mother may go back to the abuser before leaving for good or may select another batterer as her next partner. Furthermore, separation with the mother is no guarantee that the children of abused women will not have contact with the batterer through visitation and custody arrangements. Thus, it is essential that outcome evaluations carefully document the intended, targeted population of children.

As an example, the Kids Club program was designed for children exposed to recent, severe violence in the family (Graham-Bermann, 1992). The recency variable was operationalized as violence to the mother within the past year. The severity variable relied on items from the Conflict Tactics Scale (Straus, 1979) in combination with severity of injuries to estimate the level of violence exposure. Other intervention evaluation studies include women who have experienced only mild violence or who have been psychologically (but not necessarily physically) abused in defining the population (Rossman, 1999).

Most program evaluations define the child's exposure to violence as witnessing woman abuse and do not specify the extent to which the child also has been physically, sexually, or emotionally abused by either parent or a sibling. Yet it is known from studies of "double whammy" families that many children of batterers are at high risk for being physically abused themselves (Hughes & Graham-Bermann, 1999; Hughes, Parkinson, & Vargo, 1989) and that boys are at high risk for being abused by fathers who also abuse their mothers (Jouriles & Norwood, 1995). Edleson (chap. 4, this volume) addresses this topic in greater detail. Thus, it is difficult to compare results of evaluation studies because of the large differences in sampling procedures, definitions, and inclusion criteria.

Program Design Criteria

Program design criteria to consider in outcome research studies include mechanisms for providing evidence that change is the result of the program itself and ways of assessing or documenting the extent and the longevity of that change. Similarly, the use of comparison groups, pre- and postintervention assessments, long-term follow-up, longitudinal designs, and the issue of dosages all influence the degree of confidence that one may place in the reported results. Some studies have essential confounds—that is, design elements that produce misleading results. Such confounds may be the use of inappropriate comparison groups, the nonindependence of participants, or the nonindependence of people selected to do the evaluations from those selected to provide the clinical intervention. For studies with shelter populations, without comparing outcomes for similar, sheltered children in comparison groups, it is not possible to identify which improvements are caused by the direct intervention and which are associated with removal from the violence. A range of comparison groups is possible and include those in shelters who do not receive treatment, who receive different amounts of the same treatment, or who receive different types of services.

Still, without comparison groups, the effects or changes caused by the intervention cannot be determined. For example, Van Horn, Johnson, and Lieberman (1998) reported on a year-long intervention to reduce "malparenting" in battered women of very young children. Nine families agreed to enter this psychoanalytically informed, home-based intervention program for parenting of at-risk infants and preschoolers. To date, the preliminary sample has no comparison group against which to gauge the efficacy of these efforts.

Even when appropriate comparison groups are used, many outcome studies do not randomly assign participants to treatment conditions. In one case, dropout participants who did not differ significantly on major dependent variables at the beginning of the study were used as a comparison group (Ragg et al., 1998). However, the dropouts received at least some intervention and thus were not entirely independent of the treatment group. It should be noted that in other treatment evaluation studies (Stanton & Shadish, 1997), dropout participants are considered treatment failures and not appropriate for use as a comparison group.

The question of attrition becomes salient in determining who is included in assays of program success. Some studies have been successful in getting children to attend each session of the intervention (Sullivan & Davidson, 1998, reported 100% attendance) and in keeping families in the study after the intervention to the final follow-up evaluation (95% in Sullivan's evaluation and 94% in Graham-Bermann's). Yet in other studies, attrition rates were high and seriously hamper evaluation. For example, in the Tutty and Wagar (1994) preliminary study, attrition rates were reported at more than half, with many children having irregular attendance. It appears that only a few parents entered the concurrent support group in several other studies (cf. Hughes, 1982; Wilson et al., 1989). These examples raise questions about the dosage (the amount of intervention received) and how much and what components of an intervention are associated with change or the lack of change.

Although most of the studies described in Table 11.1 do not follow children past the end of the program, several include follow-up assessments in their design. The Sullivan and Davidson (1998) program evaluation, the Graham-Bermann (1998b) evaluation, and the Jouriles et al. (1998) outcome study all follow the women and children for 8 months postintervention. The Youth Relationships Project evaluation was designed to follow the teenagers for 2 years after program participation, with the initial outcome evaluation based on follow-up data collected at four time points over 6 months postintervention (Werkele & Wolfe, 1998).

Assessment Criteria

Assessment criteria include how the key variables directly associated with the program's goals are measured. Here, reports of the reliability and validity of measures, how children and parents were interviewed and by whom, and reports of who is asked about change all should lend assurance that the research constructs are accurately assessed. Still, some of the research described here has not used reliable, valid, standardized instruments.

Beyond asking whether a particular program is effective, one can assess in what areas it is most effective, in what areas it is least effective, and what about the program itself makes it effective. Although the existing studies have many drawbacks, they have been instructive in identifying at least some of these aspects of intervention success. A few programs reduce children's anxiety (e.g., Graham-Bermann, 1998b; Hughes, 1982; Hughes & Barad, 1983); others reduce their aggression (e.g., Graham-Bermann, 1998b; Jaffe, Wilson, & Wolfe, 1986; Ragg et al., 1998); and still others improve children's social skills or enhance the children's regulation of their emotion expression, or both (Jaffe et al., 1986; Rossman, 1998; Wolfe et al., 1997). Most studies report that children have gained knowledge about family violence and ways of coping with their experiences (Graham-Bermann, 1998b; Peled & Edleson, 1995). Still other programs target mothers, seeking to promote their parenting skills. These programs enhance parents' knowledge about the effects of violence on children, their coping capacities, and parenting efficacy (Graham-Bermann & Levendosky, 1994; Jouriles et al., 1998; Sullivan & Davidson, 1998).

New measures and new approaches to assessing adaptation have emerged from this body of work. When Hughes first evaluated a group intervention for children and mothers in shelters, she developed measures of the children's coping ability and their opinions about family violence (Hughes, 1982; Hughes & Barad, 1983). Wilson, Cameron, Jaffe, and Wolfe also conducted a group program for children in crisis, who were living in shelters for battered women, and successfully assessed a change in their attitudes toward violence (Jaffe, Wilson, & Wolfe, 1988; Wilson, Cameron, Jaffe, & Wolfe, 1989). Other intervention researchers have developed measures of children's fears and worries (Graham-Bermann, 1996), information-searching skills (Rossman, 1998), and family stereotypes (Graham-Bermann & Brescoll, 2000). A videotaped problem-solving exercise was created for the Youth Relationships Project and coded for dyadic interaction qualities, including conflict resolution (Werkele & Wolfe, 1998).

Data Analytic Strategies

Criteria for data analyses encompass the reporting of change over time from baseline, assessing effect sizes, and accurate accounting for missing data (e.g., sample attrition, incomplete data). For intervention program evaluation, it is useful to include a theoretical rationale for selecting the unit of analysis, whether it be the group, the dyad, or the individual that is assessed. Most of the programs identified here use the individual as the unit of analysis.

Regardless of the analytic units chosen (whether analyses of change are for the individual or the whole treatment group), adequate analyses require the assessment of baseline functioning and covarying, postintervention functioning. Comparative assessment of treatment efficacy relies on whole-group differences (either within smaller segments of a group or across groups) at Time 1, group change over time, and group-level follow-up. Ideally, the interactional analyses of variables at several ecological levels are used to shed light on the ways in which children are affected by domestic violence and on the various pathways leading to desired change (National Research Council, Institute of Medicine, 1998).

However, as already noted, because the field of intervention studies for children exposed to family violence is just beginning, most of these evaluations thus far rely on preliminary analyses—analyses that inevitably reflect the types of problems usually associated with initial efforts. Still, analyses by Sullivan (Sullivan & Davidson, 1998), Ragg et al. (1998), Graham-Bermann (1998b), and Jouriles (Jouriles et al., 1998) use the covariance method. Evaluation studies of the Wolfe, Sullivan, Graham-Bermann, and Jouriles programs include a third wave of evaluation a few months following the termination of the child's participation in the intervention program. To date, the most sophisticated analytic design is reported by Werkele and Wolfe (1998) who used hierarchical modeling in accounting for contributions to change and the rates of change over time by the child's intervention status.

Theoretical Explanations That Define Program Goals and Explain Results

Few intervention evaluation studies explicitly incorporate existing theory and research in their design. That is, most do not suggest a theory of change on which expectations are based and with which to frame results. In fact, for the most part, there has been a curious disconnection between what is known in the research literature and what is planned in interventions for children. By explicitly stating theoretical assumptions, theory-driven interventions can be created first and then tested with measures appropriate for detecting the kinds of changes that are hypothesized to occur. However, the forces that affect children exposed to family violence exist on many levels and have interactive effects on the child. Therefore, more than one theory may be needed to explain the many ways children are affected by family violence.

Several research outcome studies and the theoretical positions to support the research evidence are reviewed next, with an eye toward appreciating the theoretical underpinnings of existing programs and exploring the potential for creating new, indicated intervention strategies.

APPLYING RESEARCH AND THEORY TO INTERVENTIONS FOR CHILDREN EXPOSED TO FAMILY VIOLENCE

The emerging data from cluster analytic studies suggest that children have different responses when exposed to family violence (Graham-Bermann et al., 2001; Hughes & Luke, 1998). These major categories of response appear to be aggression, depression, anxiety (inclusive of traumatic stress responses), those who seem to be managing, and those who are coping well enough. Thus, the common one size fits all solution may not be the best approach to intervention for all such children in the future. The research, theory, and interventions in each of three areas—aggression, internalizing problems, and children's problems in social relationships—are considered in turn. For each area, the research findings are presented first, followed by a discussion of possible theoretical explanations for those findings, and concluded with an application of theory and research to interventions.

Aggression

Research Findings

Children of batterers consistently have been found to have difficulties in the areas of aggression and conduct disorder (Jaffe, Wolfe, & Wilson, 1990; Jouriles et al., 1998). It is less clear whether the expression of physical aggression is more characteristic of boys than of girls. Some researchers have shown higher rates of externalizing behaviors for boys (as measured by the Child Behavior Checklist; Achenbach, 1991; see Jouriles & Norwood, 1995), but others have reported no gender difference (see O'Keefe, 1994).

Still, physical violence in children's social relationships has been linked to violence between the parents in several studies. For example, adolescent dating violence has been associated with interparental violence for adolescents (Smith & Williams, 1992; Wolfe, Wekerle, Reitzel-Jaffe, & Gough, 1995). In another study, a history of abuse in sibling relationships was associated with woman abuse in the family (Graham-Bermann, Cutler, Litzenberger, & Schwartz, 1994). Observational studies comparing the social behavior of younger children raised in families with domestic violence with that of children in similar but nonviolent families also reveal clear differences in interpersonal behavior. Siblings (and their parents) in violent families were found to behave aggressively and to socialize one another to behave aggressively (Patterson, Reid, & Dishion, 1992). Even children ages 3–5 years raised in violent families showed more physical aggression and had higher rates of verbal aggression in interpersonal play than did their nonexposed peers (Graham-Bermann & Levendosky, 1998a).

Longitudinal data are needed to show both the stability of aggression across time for children in families with this form of violence and differences in the trajectories of the expression of aggression for boys and girls. There is short-term, longitudinal evidence that conduct disorder found in some children of battered women remains long after mothers leave the shelter (Wolfe, Zak, Wilson, & Jaffe, 1986). It also should be noted that children with early identified conduct disorder are most at risk for developing delinquency and possible criminal behavior as adults (Moffitt, 1993).

Theoretical Explanations for Findings

Social learning theory explanations have been invoked to explain how aggressive, observed, reinforced, and modeled behavior between parents is subsequently learned and then applied or re-enacted in similar situations (Bandura, 1977; Patterson, 1982). One variant of social learning theory is the intergenerational transmission of violence theory, which is offered as an explanation for why abuse may be found in more than one generation within a family (Straus, Gelles, & Steinmetz, 1980). Rates of intergenerational violence vary depending on the source of the report. Essentially, retrospective studies of the childhood experiences of abusive men show that approximately 60% reported having been abused in childhood (Herrenkohl, Herrenkohl, & Toedter, 1983; Rosenbaum & O'Leary, 1981), whereas prospective studies show rates between 18–40% (Egeland, Jacobvitz, & Sroufe, 1988; Hunter & Kihlstrom, 1979). These figures imply that abuse during childhood is not a prerequisite for partner abuse and that most children raised in abusive families do not develop into abusers as adults (Kaufman & Zigler, 1989). The question becomes one of discovering which experiences contribute to the legacy of violence. Perhaps it is those children with multiple violence experiences occurring in several areas of their lives and those with the fewest coping and protective resources who fit this intergenerational pattern.

Factors underlying aggressive behavior still need to be fully identified and addressed. Phrased otherwise, aggressiveness may be symptomatic of other processes, related, perhaps, to depleted or tarnished self-esteem, anxiety, and traumatic stress. Interestingly, in the study of children's fears and worries (Graham-Bermann, 1996), high levels of fear were associated with aggressive behavior by the child. These findings incline one to believe that children may, in part, lash out pre-emptively because they are afraid. In this view, aggression may, at least initially, be motivated by anxiety (see Berkowitz, 1978, for an exploration of the role of anxiety as an underlying mechanism in aggressive behavior).

Similarly, psychodynamic theorists have described children's identification with the aggressor as a defensive and compensatory mechanism— one that prompts the child to take on the characteristics of the violent perpetrator to maximize their safety and sense of empowerment and hence, to reduce their anxiety (Hartman & Burgess, 1989). This explanation of the aggressive behavior seen in some children of battered women also allows for the understanding of why some children make the seemingly irrational choice of aligning themselves with the abuser. The secondary gain of winning the batterer's attention and approval may work to keep this identification in place.

Another explanation of aggressive behavior found in young children of battered women relies on the psychoanalytic theory of drives, in which the internal conflicts of the mother are thought to be projected onto the child in the form of inappropriate expectations for and misinterpretations of the child's assertive behaviors. Lieberman and Van Horn (1998) argued that malparenting by the mother contributes to the problem of aggression in the child; that is, mothers who are battered women are thought to project and to transfer their anger and resentment at being abused onto their child in a number of steps. This process begins by the battered mother misinterpreting the child's needs and complaints as hostile and demanding. The mother may respond with aggression and anger toward the child, who internalizes these relationship schemas and, as a consequence, develops a negative and hostile relationship with others, including the mother.

In sharp contrast to presenting battered women as deficient parents, Sullivan et al. (1998) showed battered women to be no better or worse in their parenting when compared with similarly disadvantaged women who have not been abused. Using qualitative interview data with hundreds of battered women, these mothers are portrayed as highly concerned for the welfare of their children, putting children first, and sometimes succeeding in leaving unsafe situations on behalf of the welfare of their child.

To summarize, these theories are offered as additional ways to reframe the victimized child's aggressive behavior. Yet regardless of their conceptual differences, each perspective is prompted by the empirical data that some children exposed to domestic violence are themselves more likely to behave aggressively than their nonexposed peers. These data make it important for any intervention program to target, in some fashion, the hyperaggressive sequelae to witnessed violence.

Intervention Approaches to Reducing Aggression

Many theorists have asserted that aggression is learned and, therefore, can be unlearned (Huesmann, Eron, Loefkowitz, & Walder, 1984; Patterson, 1982). Most of the group intervention programs shown in Table 11.1 attempt to address problems of aggression by several means. First, they seek to provide children with alternative models primarily through group leaders. Group leaders take the time to help children work out their verbal or physical disputes. Any given session provides many opportunities for practicing and modeling nonaggressive problem solving. All of the children in group interventions can listen and learn first hand from illustrations about how to talk things through, how to take turns, ways of being polite to others, using apology, and through rehearsing other ways of solving similar problems in the future. Sanctions against physical altercations usually are made explicit, and rewards for positive behaviors and interactions are given throughout the course of programs in which group leaders have received training in behavior modification principles (cf. Graham-Bermann, 1992).

Most of these programs also teach children new conflict resolution strategies that cover a range of social problem situations (including peer aggression, sibling aggression, interparental aggression, and dating violence) and then give additional information with special concern for who is and who is not to blame for the violence. The behaviors of children who blame themselves for the violence in their families include trying to be perfect, to appease the abuser, and to protect the mother (Jaffe & Geffner, 1998).

One of the strengths of the Kids' Club (and other programs) is its emphasis on putting the blame completely on the perpetrators of violence and in reducing the shame associated with violence (Graham-Bermann, 1992). It is intended that all of the children in this program learn that it is never the child's fault when parents fight. The essential elements of material covered in previous sessions are reviewed each week, both to serve as a reminder and to reinforce concepts already learned.

Using a social learning paradigm, Jouriles et al. (1998) developed an intervention that relies on direct work with the mother and is aimed at reducing aggressive behavior in her child. Both the child and the mother engage in a series of sessions. These sessions are spent documenting aggressive behaviors exploring what strategies have previously been tried in her efforts to ameliorate the child's aggression, and then enlisting the mother and child in enacting new behaviorally based solutions to this problem. Modeling nonaggressive behavior, rewarding and reinforcing nonaggressive solutions, and implementing consistent and appropriate parental responses to aggression are all parts of the treatment program. By selecting a targeted group of children who have documented problems with aggressive behaviors, this program is designed expressly for use with this above-average-risk population.

Other Programs That Focus on Parenting

Parenting components are integral to several of the programs described here. The Sullivan et al. program (1998) focuses on advocating for the mother and providing instrumental help by solving the problems, thereby reducing her frustration. The 16-week in-home advocate is used by the mothers for help in finding jobs, arranging adequate transportation, obtaining information about educational opportunities, and assisting in interaction with the school system.

Similarly, the Graham-Bermann and Levendosky (1994) Mothers Empowerment Group Program was designed to give mothers the knowledge, confidence, and support to try new approaches in facing challenges in life, inclusive of challenges in parenting their children. This program is offered in conjunction with the Kids' Club intervention to facilitate the child's adjustment. While mothers share important information in the areas of children's development and their strategies for obtaining resources, the intervention program builds parenting competence, provides a safe place to discuss parenting fears and worries, and builds self-esteem for the mother in a supportive group environment. Thus, this mothers' 10-week intervention seeks to improve parenting skills and enhance the social and emotional adjustment of the women (and, by extension, their children).

In the Van Horn et al. (1998) parenting intervention program, weekly home visits by a therapist are designed to help the mother to identify her own hostility and psychopathology and to learn to interpret her child's aggression independently of that of the abuser. In this way, the mother is educated to identify, express, and appreciate her own contributions and anger and to take responsibility for these. In the process, it is hoped that mothers will find new ways to manage their dilemmas instead of directing their pent-up anger and frustration at their children.

Internalizing Problems

Research Findings

Using standardized indices of individual psychopathology, researchers have found that heightened levels of internalizing problems, such as depression and anxiety, characterize 33–75% of the children of batterers (Hughes & Luke, 1998; Margolin, 1998). In an attempt to go beyond identifying psychopathology and to provide a context for understanding the kinds of anxieties associated with high levels of family violence, Graham-Bermann

(1996) conducted a study to measure children's fears and worries specific to family violence. Two groups were compared: the children of severely battered women and similar children from families without severe violence. Children in the violence group were significantly more likely than were the comparison children to be afraid of and worried about the important people in their lives. Specifically, they were worried that their fathers would cause harm to others or get in trouble. They also worried that their mothers and their siblings were vulnerable to harm or to becoming upset.

Typically, traumatic stress symptoms are present for most children following violence exposure (Graham-Bermann & Levendosky, 1998b; Lehmann, 1997; Rossman, 1998; Wolfe, Gentile, & Wolfe, 1989). Diagnostically, these symptoms are characterized as adjustment reactions and, for most children, abate within a few months' time. However, some do not, and by definition, specific combinations of lingering traumatic stress symptoms (those that do not reduce within 3 months) are classifiable as posttraumatic stress disorder (PTSD, American Psychiatric Association, 1994). Symptoms associated with PTSD include intrusive thoughts and unwanted remembering of aspects of the traumatic events, avoidance of people or places associated with those events, and hyperarousal or physiological arousal when reminded of or remembering the traumas. Rates of diagnosable PTSD vary by the sample population—those in shelters and clinical samples evidence approximately 60%, whereas those in community groups have lower levels (13%; Graham-Bermann & Levendosky, 1998b; Rossman, 1998). Hence, children whose mothers seek out intervention programs are likely to have symptoms of traumatic stress. It is important to consider these symptoms in designing interventions because trauma symptoms have been found to interfere with children's cognitive processing and cognitive performance (Rossman, 1998).

Theoretical Explanations for Findings

Several theories have been advanced to explain the ways that children express symptoms of anxiety and depression following exposure to violence. Children are thought to be traumatized by violence, conditioned to express fear in the face of violence, and vulnerable to the negative effects of other forms of stress. In general, fear and anxiety are hypothesized to occur when the child is newly unable to accurately and effectively appraise and respond to events and feels unprotected, highly vulnerable, and endangered (Terr, 1983).

Trauma theory explanations link the core symptoms of posttraumatic stress (including the hypervigilance, physiological arousal or both, unwanted intrusions of traumatic material, and emotional numbing or dissociation from the intense feelings associated with having witnessed a traumatic event) to subsequent problems in adjustment for the child following exposure to violence (van der Kolk, 1996). These children may experience intrusive reminders, are detached from feelings, are hyperaroused, and exhibit fear and agitation—behaviors consistent with anxiety disorder.

Other researchers have described the ways that violence exposure leaves children with heightened sensitivity to other forms of stress in their lives, such as child abuse (Hennessy, Rabideau, Cicchetti, & Cummings, 1994) or threats from parents (Laumakis, Margolin, & John, 1998). Children's negative assessments of their level of emotional security following violent conflict in the home have been associated with anxiety and depression (Cummings & Davies, 1996). Here, the meaning of events to the child mediates the level of a child's response, inclusive of anxious reactions. Yet it is the combination of stressful and ameliorating features in the environment that presages a child's reaction to events and the outcome of anxiety. For example, children with difficult temperaments may be at higher risk for becoming sensitized to violence, whereas children with easier dispositions perhaps may be less alarmed in response to the same events.

Children exposed to family violence feel exposed to both the reminders of the assaults and worry about renewed fighting (Graham-Bermann, 1996, 1998a). In most violent families, threats to do harm are more common than actual physical assaults (Graham-Bermann, 1998a). Social learning theory suggests that for a child, threats to do harm associated with impending physical assault may elicit a child's anxiety. With repeated threats, punctuated by occasional violence, suggestions of impending violence can cue the fear response. Rossman (1999) contended that children can even become classically conditioned to express fear in the face of family violence. Chronic exposure to violence with a lack of efficacious coping by the child may lead to symptoms of withdrawal and depression.

Intervention Approaches for Internalizing Problems

These traumatized and anxious children require safety planning and the naming and identification of the problem—"breaking the secret" of family violence (Saunders & Azar, 1989). Groups designed to provide a trusting and confidential atmosphere and those that create the opportunity for children to share their experiences of family violence may be necessary. The Peled and Edleson (1995) program focuses on helping children to define domestic violence as unacceptable and to recognize that it is not their fault and they are not alone in their experience. Children learn to protect themselves with concrete plans of action in the event of additional family violence. Sessions such as these can be uncomfortable and, at times, difficult for children.

It is for these reasons that the first session of the Kids' Club is arranged so that confidentiality is ensured (or at least discussed) and children can feel safe and in control of their immediate environment (Graham-Bermann, 1992). Each group member helps to create the rules for the group, including rules stating that it is acceptable to "pass" or not speak. Sessions that focus on identifying feelings in general and feelings specific to family violence also help the children to realize that they are not alone, it is acceptable to discuss violence, and others feel the same about fighting in the family.

Although perhaps less severe than PTSD symptoms, the children's burden of concern for the welfare and behavior of their loved ones, associated with their exposure to family violence, deserves serious attention. To this end, a session of the Kids' Club was designed to explicitly name the worries and fears children have in association with family violence. These are often reported through the medium of drawing—drawings that sometimes illustrate death, injury, divorce, and sadness of family members. Children who can name and share their anxieties learn that they are not alone in their experience and thus may begin to consider alternative responses to events. The atmosphere of safety and trust develops over time in each group. In addition, all activities rely on displacement, so that children are not asked to directly relate experiences specific to their lives. The sessions are designed to build on each other in providing the safe context for addressing and working through issues related to violence.

Social Relationships

Research Findings

The successful development and maintenance of social relationships can be affected by the presence of domestic violence in several ways. First, violence in the family can limit the number and the range of the child's contacts with friends and other relatives outside the family (Graham-Bermann, 1998a). Second, the quality of support provided by significant figures may be compromised by the violence. Third, children exposed to physical violence in their families may have learned and adopted harmful social schemas or paradigms of social behavior—those images of the roles of men and women, fathers and mothers, in interaction with others.

In some studies, children's immediate relationships with peers and friends were reported as constrained by poor empathic ability and insensitivity in interpersonal situations (Hinchey & Gravelek, 1982; Rosenberg, 1987). Low self-ratings of social competence were found in other studies of children from violent homes (Wolfe et al., 1986). The strength of children's social relationships also explained differences in their adjustment in two studies of the children in homeless shelters and shelters for battered women. Specifically, the availability of key supports and the feeling of efficacy in relationships were associated with positive emotional adjustment for children in these highly distressed families. Nonetheless, when the levels of distress and violence were high, even supportive relationships did not seem to moderate the negative effects of family environment on children's adjustment (Graham-Bermann, Banyard, Coupet, Egler, & Mattis, 1996; Graham-Bermann, Levendosky, Porterfield, & Okun, 1998).

From studies of child abuse and child sexual abuse and some studies of domestic abuse, it would appear that young children are more likely to witness violence when it occurs at home than are older children (Fantuzzo, Boruch, Beriama, Atkins, & Marcus, 1997). The studies of the preschool-age and school-age children's friendships show that many children of battered women have difficulties interacting socially with peers and friends and seek out attention and cling to the teacher (Graham-Bermann & Levendosky, 1998a). For the younger children, the presence of emotional abuse in the home and the mother's mental health were the greatest predictors of the child's social and emotional adjustment outside of the home.

McGee, Wolfe, and Wilson (1997) studied the associations among a history of child maltreatment, insecure attachment style, and coercive behavior in dating relationships for high school boys and girls. They found that the combination of abuse in the family of origin and difficulties in early attachment greatly increased the risk of dating violence perpetration and victimization for male adolescents. Teenage girls with this family profile were found to be at risk for becoming victims of abuse but not for perpetrating abuse in dating relationships.

Children's social relationships can be affected by family violence in more subtle ways as well. Graham-Bermann and Brescoll (2000) studied the extent of children's stereotyped beliefs about power and violence in the family. Children who endorsed items indicating the acceptability of violence as a solution to problems and the idea that men should have power and privilege in the family had the highest rates of several kinds of family violence. That is, significant positive associations were found among physical violence and emotional abuse experienced by the mother and family role stereotyping in the child. These social role scripts were potentially powerful insofar as they may shape children's expectations, values, and behaviors when they are transferred from one social situation (the family) to another (children's relationships outside the family).

Theoretical Explanations for Findings

Several theories have been offered to account for the ways in which children's exposure to violence affects their social relationships with peers and friends. These include relationship theories of attachment, object relations, social–cognitive schemas, and a feminist theory of the values endorsed by the culture at large. Essentially, children's earliest relationships with parents influence the development of trust and security (Bowlby, 1988; Janoff-Bulman, 1992). Children also develop paradigms, or internal working models, of these relationships—a kind of template for other relationships in the child's life. In addition to forming images of particular individuals, children develop sets of expectations associated with gender and family roles. In one study, the presence of hostile internal working models was associated with adjustment problems in the child (Davies & Cummings, 1998).

Similarly, theories of social cognition explain the ways in which children create scripts for problem solving or other behaviors (e.g., a script concerning the conditions under which violence is necessary and justified) and for the expression of intense emotions. Cognitive–behavioral therapies focus on reframing the child's understanding by adding new information and changing existing cognitive scripts (Kendall, 1985). Some of the educational aspects of the intervention programs described here use the principles of cognitive theory in assisting the development of new ways of thinking about families, of understanding the unacceptability of violence, and of solving interpersonal problems.

Feminist theory emphasizes the ecological press of sexism and violence in the culture that reinforces negative messages about women, which the child may receive at home (French, 1992; Herman, 1992; Koss et al., 1994). Children are thought to develop distorted images of the roles of men and women when they are repeatedly exposed to messages reinforcing the acceptability of violence against women in several spheres of their environment (e.g., in the family, community, school, and media; Graham-Bermann & Brescoll, 2000). Symbolic interactionist frames (Mead, 1934) also suggest that people come to rely on those shared meanings that have been communicated to the society at large. Hence, the prominent role of the media in dispensing violence on television and, to a lesser extent, through video games, may be understood as decisive insofar as they are experienced by many children.

Intervention Approaches for Enhancing Social Relationships

Several group intervention programs have sessions devoted to addressing issues surrounding children's expectations for themselves as boys, girls, dating partners, and family members (Graham-Bermann, 1992; Werkele & Wolfe, in press; Wolfe et al., 1997). In the Wolfe program, the goal of one session was to identify stereotypes of gendered behavior and sexism and to help the teenage participants understand and expand their range of expectations for male and female behavior. In the Graham-Bermann program, using group discussion and relying on skits, drawings, puppet play or all three, children explored what they think most men are like; what most fathers are like; and what men do at work and when not at work, in their leisure time, and in social roles. Similarly, female sex roles, work roles, family roles, and recreational and social roles are discussed. It is expected that through these processes and by relying on the strong therapeutic alliance formed with group leaders, children and teenagers will share their images of gendered roles and exchange information about other possibilities.

There are strengths and drawbacks to being a member of any family, but there is little opportunity for most children to think about and share information about family relationships. In several group programs, exercises help children to explore their expectations of themselves as family members. Children are asked to draw a picture of what their own family will be like when they grow up and to make up a story about what is represented in the picture (Rossman, 1999). Because these can be difficult and troubling tasks, they can be presented later in the program once relationships with the group leaders and trust in other group members have been established (Graham-Bermann, 1992). It is hoped that children can share their images and expectations for themselves in the future and develop positive images of a potential future family. With the help of empathic group leaders who have formed a working alliance with the group, new concepts can be considered and possibly incorporated into the child's repertoire of interpersonal relationships.

WHAT IS NEEDED IN DESIGNING MORE EFFECTIVE INTERVENTIONS

The programs described here represent the state of the art in intervention with children of batterers. Although a number of suggestions have been made throughout this chapter, other evaluation and policy issues can be identified and added. Furthermore, the following topics should lead the research agenda in the next few years.

- To plan the most effective interventions, researchers need to know more about modal experiences and the range of experiences and overlaps of different kinds of abuse in children's lives. Basic research studies on the co-occurrence of violence and abuse in the family, community, and media would be informative. Research that develops profiles of risk related to violence in children's lives would be valuable for intervention efforts targeted to groups of children having similar profiles, violence experiences, and exposures.

- Samples in intervention studies of children exposed to domestic violence need to go beyond families living in shelters or departing from shelters. Given that most battered women (and, by extension, their children) do not seek refuge in shelters, additional programs must be designed to address the needs of this broader range of women and children. Additionally, although programs designed for sheltered populations may be unique or population specific, they may not show similar results (i.e., may not travel readily) when used with other children in community and clinical settings. Thus, evaluation studies that compare the same program with different populations of children exposed to family violence are needed.
- Comparative studies and systematically controlled studies comparing different types of treatments also are needed. Most of the programs described here test one kind of intervention rather than comparing different treatment modalities. In the future, studies designed to test differences in ways of implementing common program goals should be undertaken. For example, studies of the efficacy of changing children's attitudes about the acceptability of violence could compare didactic methods (using lessons, reading material) with experiential methods (group exercises, putting on a play) in determining the best ways of accomplishing goals for particular age groups.
- Outcome studies of interventions designed for children with different symptoms (e.g., withdrawn children vs. the aggressive children) are also needed. Some indicated programs already exist. Yet most of the program outcome evaluations reviewed here focus on identifying changes after the intervention has taken place rather than on identifying the symptom parameters of children receiving treatment and determining whether the intervention is effective for particular groups. Similarly, knowledge of who is not helped by the intervention should be reported.
- Although it is important to know whether and for whom the treatment is effective, it is also important to consider under what conditions particular interventions work best. By systematically studying elements of the programs themselves (e.g., therapist characteristics, setting effects, techniques), in addition to the children who participate in the programs, researchers can identify features of interventions that are especially effective.
- Researchers need to extend the follow-up period in studies to track who improves, who gets worse, and who stays the same. Only when they have discovered this, can they identify addi-

tional factors associated with these changes and answer questions such as, What contributes to risk in intervention studies? and, What are the protective features specific to this population?

- Not coincidentally, in most cases the large sample sizes of studies that can answer these questions require support over many years and substantial funding. Funding initiatives should be promoted that provide enough support to assess longitudinal outcomes associated with preventive intervention efforts for children exposed to family violence.

- There has been little commitment on the part of health insurance companies and health maintenance organizations to underwrite or reimburse for preventive intervention services for children exposed to family or other kinds of violence. However, by paying attention to children's needs early on, when they are first exposed to deleterious circumstances, rather than waiting for symptoms and disorders to develop, the health industry could not only save money but also could save considerable damage to the social, educational, and emotional lives of these children (and their future families).

- Finally, researchers need to adopt minimum standards and criteria (e.g., those suggested in this chapter) for assessing the efficacy of interventions for children who experience family violence. Funding agencies, grant reviewers, journal editors, and others should expect, encourage, and insist on the reporting of research that is well designed, well operationalized and assessed, appropriately analyzed, and carefully documented.

REFERENCES

Achenbach, T. M. (1991). *Manual for the Child Behavior Checklist: 4-18 and 1991 profile*. Burlington: University of Vermont, Department of Psychiatry.

American Psychiatric Association. (1994). *Diagnostic and statistical manual of mental disorders* (4th ed). Washington, DC: Author.

Ammerman, R. T. (1998). Methodological issues in child maltreatment research. In J. R. Lutzker (Ed.), *Handbook of child abuse research and treatment* (pp. 117–132). New York: Plenum Press.

Bandura, A. (1977). *Social learning theory*. Englewood Cliffs, NJ: Prentice Hall.

Berkowitz, L. (1978). External determinants of impulsive aggression. In W. W. Hartup & J. DeWits (Eds.), *Origins of aggression* (pp. 143–162). The Hague, The Netherlands: Mouton.

Bowlby, J. (1988). *A secure base*. New York: Basic Books.

Cox, G. M. (1995). *Changes in self-esteem and anxiety in children in a group program for witnesses of wife assault.* Unpublished master's thesis, University of Calgary, School of Social Work, Calgary, Alberta, Canada.

Cummings, E. M., & Davies, P. T. (1996). Emotional security as a regulatory process in normal development and the development of psychopathology. *Development and Psychopathology, 8,* 123–119.

Davies, P. T., & Cummings, E. M. (1998). Exploring children's emotional security as a mediator of the link between marital relations and child adjustment. *Child Development, 69,* 124–139.

Egeland, B., Jacobvitz, D., & Sroufe, L. A. (1988). Breaking the cycle of abuse. *Child Development, 59,* 1080–1088.

Fantuzzo, J. W., Boruch, R., Beriama, A., Atkins, M., & Marcus, S. (1997). Domestic violence and children: Prevalence and risk in five major cities. *Journal of the American Academy of Child and Adolescent Psychiatry, 36,* 116–122.

French, M. (1992). *The war against women.* New York: Summit Books.

Frey-Angel, J. (1989). Treating children in violent families: A sibling group approach. *Social Work With Groups, 12,* 95–107.

Gordon, R. (1983). An operational classification of disease prevention. *Public Health Reports, 98,* 107–109.

Graham-Bermann, S. A. (1992). *The Kids' Club: A preventive intervention program for children of battered women.* Unpublished manuscript. University of Michigan, Department of Psychology, Ann Arbor.

Graham-Bermann, S. A. (1996). Family worries: The assessment of interpersonal anxiety in children from violent and nonviolent families. *Journal of Clinical Child Psychology, 25,* 280–287.

Graham-Bermann, S. A. (1998a). The impact of woman abuse on children's social development. In G. W. Holden, R. Geffner, & E. N. Jouriles (Eds.), *Children exposed to marital violence: Theory, research, and applied issues* (pp. 21–54). Washington, DC: American Psychological Association.

Graham-Bermann, S. A. (1998b). *Preliminary findings from the Intervention in Domestic Violence Project. Final report* (Funded by the National Center for Injury Prevention and Control, Centers for Disease Control and Prevention, R49/CCR409-510499). Ann Arbor: University of Michigan.

Graham-Bermann, S. A. (2000). Evaluating interventions for children exposed to family violence. *Journal of Aggression, Maltreatment & Trauma, 4*(1), 191–216.

Graham-Bermann, S. A., Banyard, V., Coupet, S., Egler, L., & Mattis, J. (1996). The interpersonal relationships and adjustment of children in homeless and economically distressed families. *Journal of Clinical Child Psychology, 25,* 250–261.

Graham-Bermann, S. A., & Brescoll, V. (2000). Gender, power, and violence: Assessing the family stereotypes of the children of batterers. *Journal of Family Psychology, 14,* 600–612.

Graham-Bermann, S. A., Cutler, S. E., Litzenberger, B. W., & Schwartz, W. E. (1994). Perceived sibling violence and emotional adjustment during childhood and adolescence. *Journal of Family Psychology, 8*, 85–97.

Graham-Bermann, S. A., Gruber, G., & Hughes, H. M. (2001). *Resilient outcomes and factors discriminating among resiliency and distress in children of batterers.* Manuscript under review, University of Michigan, Department of Psychology, Ann Arbor.

Graham-Bermann, S. A., & Levendosky, A. A. (1994). *Empowering battered women as mothers.* Unpublished manuscript, University of Michigan, Department of Psychology, Ann Arbor.

Graham-Bermann, S. A., & Levendosky, A. A. (1998a). The social functioning of preschool-age children whose mothers are emotionally and physically abused. *Journal of Emotional Abuse, 1*, 59–84.

Graham-Bermann, S. A., & Levendosky, A. A. (1998b). Traumatic stress symptoms in children of battered women. *Journal of Interpersonal Violence, 14*, 111–128.

Graham-Bermann, S. A., Levendosky, A. A., Porterfield, K., & Okun, A. (1998). *The impact of women abuse on children: The role of social relationships and emotional context.* Manuscript under review, Department of Psychology, University of Michigan, Ann Arbor.

Gurman, A. S., & Kniskern, D. P. (1978). Research on marital and family therapy: Progress, perspective and prospect. In S. L. Garfield & A. E. Bergen (Eds.), *Handbook of psychotherapy and behavior change: An empirical analysis* (2nd ed., pp. 817–901). New York: Wiley.

Hartman, C. R., & Burgess, A. W. (1989). Sexual abuse of children: Causes and consequences. In D. Cicchetti & V. Carlson (Eds.), *Child maltreatment: Theory and research on the causes and consequences of child abuse and neglect* (pp. 95–128). New York: Cambridge University Press.

Hennessy, K. D., Rabideau, G. J., Cicchetti, D., & Cummings, E. M. (1994). Responses of physically abused and nonabused children to different forms of interadult anger. *Child Development, 65*, 815–828.

Herman, J. L. (1992). *Trauma and recovery: The aftermath of violence from domestic abuse to political terror.* New York: Basic Books.

Herrenkohl, E. C., Herrenkohl, R. C., & Toedter, L. J. (1983). Perspectives on the intergenerational transmission of abuse. In D. Finkelhor, R. J. Gelles, G. T. Hotalling, & M. A. Straus (Eds.), *The dark side of families: Current family violence research* (pp. 305–316). Beverly Hills, CA: Sage.

Hinchey, F. S., & Gravelek, J. R. (1982). Empathic responding in children of battered mothers. *Child Abuse & Neglect, 6*, 395–401.

Huesmann, L. R., Eron, L. D., Loefkowitz, M. M., & Walder, L. O. (1984). Stability of aggression over time and generations. *Developmental Psychology, 20*, 1120–1134.

Hughes, H. (1982). Brief interventions with children in a battered women's shelter: A model preventive program. *Family Relations, 31*, 495–502.

Hughes, H., & Barad, S. (1983). Psychological functioning of children in a battered women's shelter: A preliminary investigation. *American Journal of Orthopsychiatry, 53*, 525–531.

Hughes, H. M., & Graham-Bermann, S. A. (1999). Children of battered women: Impact of emotional abuse on development and adjustment. *Journal of Emotional Abuse, 1*, 23–50.

Hughes, H. M., & Luke, D. A. (1998). Heterogeneity in adjustment among children of battered women. In G. W. Holden, R. Geffner, & E. N. Jouriles (Eds.), *Children exposed to marital violence: Theory, research, and applied issues* (pp. 185–221). Washington, DC: American Psychological Association.

Hughes, H. M., Parkinson, X., & Vargo, M. C. (1989). Witnessing and experiencing family violence: A double whammy? *Journal of Family Violence, 4*, 197–209.

Hunter, R. S., & Kihlstrom, N. (1979). Breaking the cycle of abusive families. *American Journal of Orthopsychiatry, 136*, 1320–1322.

Jaffe, P. G., & Geffner, R. (1998). Child custody disputes and domestic violence: Critical issues for mental health, social service, and legal professionals. In G. W. Holden, R. Geffner, & E. N. Jouriles (Eds.), *Children exposed to marital violence: Theory, research, and applied issues* (pp. 371–408). Washington, DC: American Psychological Association.

Jaffe, P. G., Wilson, S. K., & Wolfe, D. A. (1986). Promoting changes in attitudes and understanding of conflict resolution among child witnesses of family violence. *Canadian Journal of Behavioural Sciences, 18*, 356–366.

Jaffe, P., Wilson, S., & Wolfe, D. (1988). Specific assessment and intervention strategies for children exposed to wife battering: Preliminary empirical investigations. *Canadian Journal of Community Mental Health, 7*, 157–163.

Jaffe, P. G., Wolfe, D. A., & Wilson, S. K. (1990). *Children of battered women.* Newbury Park, CA: Sage.

Janoff-Bulman, R. (1992). *Shattered assumption: Towards a new psychology of trauma.* New York: Free Press.

Jouriles, E. N., McDonald, R., Stephens, N., Norwood, W., Spiller, L. C., & Ware, H. S. (1998). Breaking the cycle of violence: Helping families departing from battered women's shelters. In G. W. Holden, R. Geffner, & E. N. Jouriles (Eds.), *Children exposed to marital violence: Theory, research, and applied issues* (pp. 337–369). Washington, DC: American Psychological Association.

Jouriles, E. N., & Norwood, W. D. (1995). Physical aggression toward boys and girls in families characterized by the battering of women. *Journal of Family Psychology, 9*, 69–78.

Kaufman, J., & Zigler, E. (1989). The intergenerational transmission of child abuse. In D. Cicchetti & B. Carlson (Eds.), *Child maltreatment: Theory and research on the causes and consequences of child abuse and neglect* (pp. 129–150). New York: Cambridge University Press.

Kendall, P. C. (1985). Toward a cognitive–behavioral model of child psychopathology and a critique of related interventions. *Journal of Abnormal Child Psychology, 13*, 357–372.

Koss, M. P., Goodman, L. A., Browne, A., Fitzgerald, L. F., Keita, G. P., & Russo, N. F. (1994). *No safe haven: Male violence against women at home, at work, and in the community.* Washington, DC: American Psychological Association.

Laumakis, M. A., Margolin, G., & John, R. S. (1998). The emotional, cognitive, and coping responses of preadolescent children to different dimensions of marital conflict. In G. W. Holden, R. Geffner, & E. N. Jouriles (Eds.), *Children exposed to marital violence: Theory, research, and applied issues* (pp. 257–288). Washington, DC: American Psychological Association.

Lehmann, P. (1997). The development of posttraumatic stress disorder (PTSD) in a sample of child witnesses to mother assault. *Journal of Family Violence, 12,* 241–257.

Lieberman, A. F., & Van Horn, P. (1998). Attachment, trauma, and domestic violence: Implications for custody. *Child and Adolescent Psychiatric Clinics of North America, 7,* 423–443.

Margolin, G. (1998). Effects of domestic violence on children. In P. K. Trickett & C. Shellenbach (Eds.), *Violence against children in the family and the communty* (pp. 57–102). Washington, DC: American Psychological Association.

Marshall, L., Miller, N., Miller-Hewitt, S., Sudermann, M., & Watson, L. (1995). *Evaluation of groups for children who have witnessed violence.* London, Ontario, Canada: Centre for Research on Violence Against Women and Children.

McGee, R. A., Wolfe, D. A., & Wilson, S. K. (1997). Multiple maltreatment experiences and adolescent behavior problems: Adolescents' perspectives. *Development & Psychopathology, 9,* 131–149.

Mead, G. H. (1934). *Mind, self, & society.* Chicago: University of Chicago Press.

Moffitt, T. E. (1993). Adolescence-limited and life-course-persistent antisocial behavior: A developmental taxonomy. *Psychological Review, 100,* 674–701.

National Research Council, Institute of Medicine. (1998). *Violence in families: Assessing prevention and treatment programs.* Washington, DC: National Academy of Sciences.

O'Keefe, M. (1994). Linking marital violence, mother–child/father–child aggression, and child behavior problems. *Journal of Family Violence, 9,* 63–78.

Patterson, G. R. (1982). *A social learning theory approach to family intervention: III. Coercive family processes.* Eugene, OR: Castalia.

Patterson, G. R., Reid, J. B., & Dishion, T. J. (1992). *Antisocial boys.* Eugene, OR: Castilia.

Peled, E., & Davis, D. (1995). *Groupwork with children of battered women.* Thousand Oaks, CA: Sage.

Peled, E., & Edleson, J. L. (1995). Process and outcome in small groups for children of battered women. In E. Peled, P. G. Jaffe, & J. L. Edleson (Eds.), *Ending the cycle of violence: Community responses to children of battered women* (pp. 77–96). Newbury Park, CA: Sage.

Ragg, D. M., Sultana, M., & Miller, D. (1998, July). *Decreasing aggression in child witnesses of domestic violence*. Presentation at Program Evaluation and Family Violence Research Conference, University of New Hampshire, Durham.

Rosenbaum, A., & O'Leary, K. D. (1981). Children: The unintended victims of marital violence. *American Journal of Orthopsychiatry, 51*, 692–699.

Rosenberg, M. (1987). New directions in research on the psychological maltreatment of children. *American Psychologist, 42*, 166–171.

Rossman, B. B. R. (1998). Descartes' error and posttraumatic stress disorder: Cognition and emotion in children who are exposed to parental violence. In G. W. Holden, R. Geffner, & E. N. Jouriles (Eds.), *Children exposed to marital violence: Theory, research, and applied issues* (pp. 223–256). Washington, DC: American Psychological Association.

Rossman, B. B. R. (1999). *Frost Foundation final report*. Unpublished manuscript, University of Denver, Denver, CO.

Saunders, D. G., & Azar, S. T. (1989). Treatment programs for family violence. In L. Ohlin & M. Tonry (Eds.), *Family violence* (pp. 481–546). Chicago: University of Chicago Press.

Smith, J. P., & Williams, J. G. (1992). From abusive household to dating violence. *Journal of Family Violence, 7*, 153–156.

Stanton, M. D., & Shadish, W. R. (1997). Outcome, attrition, and family–couples treatment for drug abusers: A meta-analysis and review of controlled, comparative studies. *Psychological Bulletin, 122*, 170–191.

Straus, M. A. (1979). Measuring intrafamily conflict and violence: The Conflict Tactics (CT) Scales. *Journal of Marriage and the Family, 41*, 75–88.

Straus, M. A., & Gelles, R. J. (Eds.). (1990). *Physical violence in American families*. New Brunswick, NJ: Transaction.

Straus, M. A., Gelles, R., & Steinmetz, S. (1980). *Behind closed doors: Violence in the American family*. Garden City, NY: Anchor.

Sullivan, C., Allen N., Nguyen, H., Gauthier, L., Shpungin, E., Bybee, D., & Baker, C. (1998). *Beyond blaming mom: Evidence for viewing mothers as nurturing parents of children exposed to domestic violence*. Manuscript under review, Michigan State University, East Lansing.

Sullivan, C., & Davidson, W. (1998). *Preliminary findings from the Family Follow-up Study* (Funded by the National Center for Injury Prevention and Control, Centers for Disease Control and Prevention R49/CCR510531). Lansing: Michigan State University.

Terr, L. C. (1983). Chowchilla revisited: The effects of psychic trauma four years after a school bus kidnapping. *American Journal of Psychiatry, 140*, 1543–1550.

Tutty, L. M., & Wagar, J. (1994). The evolution of a group for young children who have witnessed family violence. *Social Work With Groups, 17*, 89–104.

van der Kolk, B. A. (1996). The body keeps score: Approaches to the psychobiology of posttraumatic stress disorder. In B. A. van der Kolk, A. C. McFarlane, &

L. Weisaeth (Eds.), *Traumatic stress: The effects of overwhelming experience on mind, body, and society* (pp. 214–241). New York: Guilford Press.

Van Horn, P., Johnson, V., & Lieberman, A. F. (1998, July). *Assessing the effectiveness of an intervention model: Can parent–child psychotherapy ameliorate the effects of witnessing violence?* Presentation at Program Evaluation and Family Violence Research: An International Conference, the Family Research Laboratory, University of New Hampshire, Durham.

Wagar, J. M., & Rodway, M. R. (1995). An evaluation of a group treatment approach for children who have witnessed wife abuse. *Journal of Family Violence, 10,* 295–306.

Werkele, C., & Wolfe, D. A. (1998). Windows for preventing child and partner abuse: Early childhood and adolescence. In P. K. Trickett & C. J. Schellenbach (Eds.), *Violence against children in the family and the community* (pp. 339–370). Washington, DC: American Psychological Association.

Werkele, C., & Wolfe, D. A. (in press). Dating violence in mid-adolescence: Theory, significance, and emerging prevention initiatives. *Clinical Psychology Review.*

Wilson, S., Cameron, S., Jaffe, P., & Wolfe, D. (1989). Children exposed to wife abuse: An intervention model. *Social Casework, 70,* 180–184.

Wolfe, D. A., Wekerle, C., Gough, R., Reitzel-Jaffe, D., Grasley, C., Pittman, A., & Stumpf, J. (1996). *Youth relationships manual: A group approach with adolescents for the prevention of woman abuse and the promotion of healthy relationships.* Thousand Oaks, CA: Sage.

Wolfe, D. A., Wekerle, C., Reitzel-Jaffe, D., & Gough, R. (1995). Strategies to address violence in the lives of high-risk youth. In E. Peled, P. G. Jaffe, & J. L. Edleson (Eds.), *Ending the cycle of violence: Community response to children of battered women* (pp. 255–274). Newbury Park, CA: Sage.

Wolfe, D. A., Wekerle, C., & Scott, K. (1997). *Alternatives to violence: Empowering youth to develop healthy relationships.* Newbury Park, CA: Sage.

Wolfe, D. A., Zak, L., Wilson, S., & Jaffe, P. (1986). Child witnesses to violence between parents: Critical issues in behavioral and social adjustment. *Journal of Abnormal Child Psychology, 14,* 95–104.

Wolfe, V. V., Gentile, C., & Wolfe, D. A. (1989). The impact of sexual abuse on children: A PTSD formulation. *Behavior Therapy, 20,* 215–228.

12

EVALUATING COORDINATED COMMUNITY RESPONSES FOR ABUSED WOMEN AND THEIR CHILDREN

CRIS M. SULLIVAN AND NICOLE E. ALLEN

Since the Violence Against Women Act was enacted as Title IV of the Violent Crime Control and Law Enforcement Act of 1994 (P. L. 103-322), more and more communities have increased coordination and cooperation among police, prosecutors, victims' advocates, the judiciary, and other community institutions in responding to intimate violence against women. Some communities have also begun developing strategies for addressing the co-occurrence of domestic violence and child abuse, but these are often hindered by tensions and conflicts between child welfare workers and domestic violence advocates (Schechter & Edleson, 1995). Domestic violence advocates generally focus on the needs of the battered woman, whereas child welfare agencies are mandated to focus on the best interest of the child. These interests sometimes conflict or are perceived by one or both agencies as conflicting. More and more, however, communities are recognizing the importance of addressing the complex issues that arise when domestic violence and child abuse co-occur in the same home. This chapter briefly reviews the current emphasis on coordinating the community response to domestic violence and provides a multilevel framework for the evaluation of such efforts.

CREATING A SYSTEMS-BASED RESPONSE TO PROTECT BATTERED WOMEN AND THEIR CHILDREN

Creating a systems-based response to intimate male violence against women is complex (e.g., Clark, Burt, Schulte, & Maguire, 1996), especially when children are exposed to the abuse either as witnesses or victims. Often in human services delivery, multiple services agencies are needed to effectively serve those in need (Quinn & Cumblad, 1994; Williams, 1995). With regard to intimate violence against women and their children, there is the additional complexity of needing to involve not only multiple social services organizations but also a range of other systems (Clark et al., 1996; Hart, 1995), including health care, criminal justice, and educational systems as well as the government, religious organizations, and businesses. Some of these parties may have negative perceptions of each other or may have historically felt at odds with each other (e.g., child welfare workers, domestic violence advocates). However, each plays a critical role in formulating what is commonly termed a coordinated community response (CCR) to violence against women and their children.

COORDINATED COMMUNITY RESPONSE

A CCR involves community-wide efforts to bring together all relevant stakeholders to respond to domestic violence comprehensively and ultimately to end that violence. To date, little research has been conducted to evaluate the efficacy of CCRs, but early anecdotal evidence and evaluations of CCR components suggest that where these efforts exist, greater strides are being made (Clark et al., 1996; Edleson, 1991; Gamache, Edleson, & Schock, 1988; Shepard & Pence, 1999; Steinman, 1991).

Given the complexities of responding to domestic violence when children are also exposed to the abuse, it is vital to build a comprehensive understanding of how the component systems of a CCR work together. Human services are often fragmented and inefficient (e.g., Dill & Rochefort, 1989), and significant barriers prevent service organizations from cooperating (e.g., Wehlage & White, 1995). Furthermore, the history of collaboration in the human services system suggests that coordination efforts do not always result in intended outcomes (e.g., Bickman, 1996). It is reasonable to suspect that many of the issues that have emerged in collaborative efforts in other areas of human services will emerge in collaborative efforts specific to intervening in cases where mothers and their children are being abused in the same home. It is also important to recognize that barriers and facilitators to collaboration may exist that are specific to the context of domestic violence against women and children. In other words, collaborative efforts in one domain, such as early intervention with teenage mothers, may manifest differently than those in another domain, in this case, intervening in domestic violence.

One of the vehicles commonly used in the process of creating a CCR to violence against women is a coordinating council (Clark et al., 1996;

Hart, 1995). The goal of these councils is to enhance a CCR by reducing fragmentation and facilitating a shared vision among community members. These councils typically consist of representatives from all service systems and organizations that are deemed central to intervening in cases in which women are being abused, including but not limited to representatives from domestic violence programs, the police department, the prosecutor's office, the probation office, batterer intervention programs, the health care system, the religious community, other social services agencies, and child welfare agencies.

There is evidence to suggest that coordinating councils play a role in encouraging interorganizational exchanges, developing more highly integrated service delivery systems (Foster-Fishman, Salem, Allen, & Fahrbach, in press), and enhancing communication among the agencies involved (Abbott, Jordan, & Murtaya, 1995). Although there is relatively little research on the application of this model to domestic violence intervention, there is some evidence that this vehicle may lead to increased coordination among agencies responding to domestic violence. In a study done in San Francisco, the presence of a coordinating council was found to facilitate interactions between agencies, promote broader institutional change, and increase the responsiveness of the service system to the needs of battered women (Clark et al., 1996). Although these findings provide early evidence of the usefulness of these councils, more rigorous large-scale evaluations are needed to identify whether they are working, how they are working, and how they can be improved and disseminated across communities.

EVALUATING SYSTEMS CHANGE

One of the goals of a CCR is to include in the effort all relevant systems and agencies that affect women's and children's lives (Carter & Schechter, 1997; Clark et al., 1996). Hence, to effectively evaluate a CCR to families in which both children and mothers are abused, one needs a multilevel analysis approach. Evaluation efforts must investigate the degree to which change has occurred on the community level and the degree to which these efforts are resulting in meaningful change in the lives of women and children. A multiple-level framework includes the individual or family level (i.e., the women and children who are receiving coordinated services), the community level (e.g., coordinating councils, criminal justice system, health care system, social services providers), and the state or federal level (i.e., laws and policies governing the response to violence against women and children). Multiple processes and outcomes within each level must be evaluated as well. This multilevel framework allows for an examination of accountability at both the community and state or federal levels while examining how these policies and practices affect the safety and well-being of women and children. Shepard (1999) pointed to the necessity of systemwide evaluations, noting that it is difficult to understand the efficacy of one component of a CCR without examining all interrelated components.

Systems evaluations must be relevant and responsive to the needs and efforts of a given community (Kelly, 1988). The following description of a multilevel evaluation approach provides suggestions for investigation at each level. However, the evaluation implemented by a community should reflect the needs of that community and should further that community's CCR efforts (Hart, 1995).

Individual or Family-Level Variables of Interest

Outcome Variables

On the individual or family level, a number of factors related to the well-being of women and children must be assessed when evaluating the effectiveness of a CCR (see Table 12.1 for a summary). The safety of women

TABLE 12.1
Evaluating the Effect of Systems Change on Individuals and Families

Area of inquiry	Sample research question
Outcome variable	To what degree did the CCR result in . . .
Women's safety (batterer accountability)	Increased safety of women with abusive partners (e.g., absence of physical and psychological abuse, harassment, threats and other tactics of power and control)?
Children's safety (batterer accountability)	Increased safety of children of women with abusive partners (e.g., absence of physical and psychological abuse, being a witness to this abuse)?
Women's health and well-being	Increased health and well-being for women (e.g., levels of social support, improved quality of life, basic needs being met)?
Children's health and well-being	Increased health and well-being for children (e.g., levels of social support, improved quality of life, basic needs being met)?
Process variables	To what extent did . . .
Experience with systems response	Women and children feel supported and respected by the CCR? Women feel blamed for the abuse against themselves or their children? Women feel the batterer was held accountable for his violence?

Note. CCR = coordinated community response.

and their children is of primary importance and has emerged as a shared goal of child welfare agencies and domestic violence programs working in partnership (Carter & Schechter, 1997). Safety should be defined more broadly than the "absence of physical abuse," and an evaluation of safety should include an examination of psychological abuse, harassment, stalking, economic abuse, and threats. It is important when assessing safety that mothers are not held responsible for whether such abuse has occurred (e.g., by "ending the relationship"). The perpetrator should be held accountable for whatever violence the family experiences, and the community must be held responsible for holding the perpetrator accountable.

In addition to safety issues, the mother and children's social support, quality of life, access to community resources, and basic needs being met should be assessed. These are indicators of the degree to which the CCR is contributing to the overall well-being of the women and children in the programs.

Process Variables

In addition to attending to individual or family-level outcomes, a systems evaluation should address process issues on this level. For example, one might assess the degree to which women felt they were blamed by the system, were treated respectfully (i.e., their ideas and needs were taken seriously), or felt the batterer was held accountable for his actions. Overall, evaluation at the individual or family level should provide a picture of how the CCR is affecting the women and children's lives and how they are experiencing the CCR efforts. They are the ultimate judges of the effectiveness of community efforts.

Community-Level Variables of Interest

Although it is important to examine individual- and family-level factors affected by a CCR, evaluations should also attend to community-level changes. Evaluation at the community level includes multiple components, including change in (a) the availability and accessibility of community resources, (b) the quality of community resources and community responses, (c) the infrastructure of the community response, and (d) the degree of community awareness and involvement in the issue (see Table 12.2 for a summary). Finally, at the community level, evaluation must attend to outcomes associated with successful coordination.

Availability and Accessibility of Community Resources

One would expect that an effective CCR would result in an increase in the availability and accessibility of community resources, advocacy and

TABLE 12.2
Evaluating the Effect of Systems Change on the Community Level

Area of inquiry	Sample research question
Availability and accessibility of community resources	To what extent are community resources available and accessible to women and children in the community?
Increased resources	To what degree does the CCR result in increased resources in the community?
Available resources	To what degree does the CCR result in increased accessibility to resources in the community?
Quality and integrity of services	To what degree are the resources available in the community of high quality and integrity?
Culturally competent	To what degree are the services provided in the CCR response culturally competent?
Knowledge, attitudes, and behaviors of service providers	To what extent do service providers understand the critical issues regarding the overlap of child abuse and abuse of women?
Infrastructure/mechanisms of coordination	To what degree does the community have mechanisms in place to support the development and implementation of a CCR?
Coordinating council or collaborative entity	What facilitators or barriers do councils face in attempts to collaborate? What impact does the presence of a council have on increasing batterer accountability and the safety of women and children?
Training and cross training	To what extent have training programs been put in place to educate women's advocates and child protection workers about the overlapping issues of woman abuse and child abuse?
Confidentiality	To what degree has a system been put in place to balance the need for information sharing with respecting confidentiality and women's and children's safety?
Inclusion and leadership of women with abusive partners and domestic violence advocates	To what degree do collaborative entities or community agencies involve women with abusive partners in the creation of a CCR to violence?
Screening tool and assessment	How are varied community organizations coming together to create a common screening tool and assessment to identify domestic violence cases?
Indicators of successful coordination	To what extent is the community response to violence against women coordinated?
Increased communication among organizations	To what degree are relevant organizations communicating with each other more often or more regularly?
Increased partnerships among organizations	To what extent do needed partnerships exist among organizations and systems?
Increased exchange and sharing of resources among organizations	To what degree are relevant organizations exchanging and sharing resources in their response to violence against women and children?

(continued)

TABLE 12.2
Evaluating the Effect of Systems Change on the Community Level
(Continued)

Area of inquiry	Sample research question
Decreased revictimization of women or children by the system	Are the child protection and criminal justice systems responding to allegations of abuse in a way that holds the batterer accountable and supports women with abusive partners and their children?
Decreased duration of families involved with the system	Are women and children involved for shorter periods of time with the child protection or criminal justice systems?
Decreased number of families returning to the system	Are women and children returning to the system as victims of abuse less frequently?
Presence of policies and practices that encourage batterer accountability	To what extent has the community adopted policies and practices that ensure batterer accountability?
Community awareness	To what extent is the issue of violence against women and children discussed or acted on in the community?
Community education	Are there currently community education or outreach efforts in religious organizations, schools, or community centers? Are they effective?
Media campaigns	To what extent are there media campaigns aimed at educating the public about abuse related issues? Are they effective?
Political support	To what extent do local politicians support organizations working to end violence against women and children?

Note. CCR = coordinated community response.

support services, and opportunities (e.g., availability of employment, education). An evaluation at the community level, therefore, could examine the absence or presence of needed resources and opportunities within a community and the degree to which these resources are accessible to women with abusive partners. This component of the community level of evaluation is sometimes referred to as a community audit (Gero & Fowler, 1997); it provides important information about the context in which the evaluation is taking place.

Quality and Integrity of Community Resources and Responses

Following an assessment of the availability and accessibility of community resources needed by battered women and their children, the quality and integrity of community resources and responses should be evaluated. Such an evaluation would establish the degree to which community responses have taken into account the diverse needs and cultural backgrounds of the women and children being served by the community, including the degree to which the system response has addressed issues of race, language, religious background, socioeconomic class, cultural norms, and physical ability (Hart, 1995).

The attitudes and behaviors of direct service providers should also be assessed. Examining this aspect of the community level is important because systems-level change is successful only to the degree to which it is being implemented by the individuals comprising the system (e.g., service providers, advocates, child protection workers). This may be particularly important in evaluations of the system response to the overlap between child abuse and woman abuse given the varied perspectives among relevant service providers (see Beeman, Hagemeister, & Edleson, 1999). In the implementation of collaborative endeavors between child protection agencies and domestic violence programs, there has been a need to cross-train providers to familiarize them with the practices and goals in both fields and to develop a common ground (Findlater & Kelly, 1999; Schechter & Edleson, 1995). A systems evaluation must attend to the degree to which front-line providers (i.e., those working directly with the families) have a basic knowledge of both domestic violence and child protection and the degree to which they endorse an approach that addresses the safety of women and the safety of children. The endorsement of this dual focus is an integral component of a cooperative response between child protection and domestic violence programs (Carter & Schechter, 1997).

Infrastructure of the Community Response

Considerable information can be gained from evaluating the presence and functioning of the infrastructure of a CCR. The central question here is, To what degree does this community have mechanisms in place to develop and encourage a CCR? Evaluating the infrastructure necessitates a focus on both the presence of these mechanisms of coordination and the outcomes associated with successful coordination.

Examining the mechanisms of coordination includes evaluating the presence (or absence) and functioning of a number of potentially important components of a coordinated effort. The first of these concerns the presence of a coordinating council or other collaborative entities (e.g., interagency teams) that facilitate the communication and cooperation of relevant stakeholders involved in the response to violence against women and children. Investigations of these collaborative entities should attend to both process and outcomes because coordinating councils vary considerably in structure and function, and it is not yet clear what contributes to their effectiveness (Shepard, 1999). In addition, there has been no investigation of what outcomes can be attributed to the presence of councils as opposed to other components of a CCR. Thus, it is critical to explore the role of coordinating councils as one vehicle for creating an effective CCR to violence against women.

A second mechanism of coordination is the provision of training and cross-training opportunities for domestic violence shelter staff, child protection workers, and other service providers and legal system personnel. In one early effort to coordinate services, a statewide cross-training program was developed for all family preservation program managers, supervisors, and workers as well as training opportunities for domestic violence service program staff (see Findlater & Kelly, 1999). Cross-training opportunities may provide a cornerstone of the development of common ground between child protection workers and domestic violence advocates, and their presence and effectiveness should be addressed in a systems evaluation.

Third, several issues related to protocol should be addressed in a systems-level evaluation. These may vary from one community to another, but a persistent and complex issue is confidentiality (i.e., protecting women's confidentiality while creating a vehicle for communication between relevant organizations; Carter & Schechter, 1997). It should be determined whether the CCR has addressed issues of confidentiality and whether efforts have increased communication between organizations while ensuring women's safety.

Fourth, an evaluation should attend to the systematic inclusion and leadership of domestic violence advocates, child advocates, and women with abusive partners (a) on coordinating councils and other collaborative bodies responding to violence against women and children and (b) in the design and implementation of the system response. Too often, efforts to address an issue fail to incorporate the input of those most directly affected by the issue.

Given the tensions that have emerged historically between child protection workers and domestic violence advocates regarding batterers' accountability (e.g., Beeman et al., 1999), an evaluation should include an examination of policies within organizations that encourage holding batterers accountable. This may include practices within child protective services that substantiate cases of abuse against the assailant for physical abuse, endangerment of the child, or exposure of the child to violence rather than to the mother's "failure to protect." Another indicator of change in the child protection system would include filing and tracking cases using the perpetrator's name rather than the mother's (Edleson, 1998).

Finally, evaluations should include examining the use of a common domestic violence screening tool across organizations. Carter and Schechter (1997) suggested that an effective partnership to protect both women and children must include screening tools that routinely assess whether women have been "hurt by their partner, as well as the identification of indicators that suggest the presence of domestic violence" (p. 5). Thus, interventions usually aimed at protecting children should routinely assess the presence of domestic violence and the danger to women and children as a result of this violence.

Degree of Community Awareness and Involvement

Another critical component of community-level evaluation is the degree to which the CCR is stimulating discussion of the issues related to the abuse of women and children or making attempts to include community members in addressing these issues. The involvement of community members (e.g., neighbors, friends, coworkers) may play an important role in ending violence against women and children (Carter & Schechter, 1997). This includes an assessment of any media campaigns, political support, community education, and community coalition building that is addressing violence against women and children.

Outcomes of Successful Coordination

Beyond an examination of the mechanisms of coordination (process evaluation), indicators of successful coordination at the community level should also be assessed (outcome evaluation). These include (a) an increase in communication within and among organizations, (b) an increase in the exchange of resources among relevant community organizations and agencies, (c) the development of shared goals among collaborators, (d) a decrease in the revictimization of women or children (by the system and by the assailant), (e) a decrease in the duration of families being "in the system," (f) a decrease in the number of families who return to the system, and (g) the presence of policies that encourage batterer accountability (i.e., proarrest or mandatory arrest policies, enforcement of probation conditions, effective prosecution, and improving the acquisition and enforcement of personal protection orders). Overall, the purpose of evaluating the infrastructure is to examine the degree to which a CCR is occurring and whether the efforts to coordinate are resulting in increased communication and partnership in community organizations and increased batterer accountability.

State and Federal-Level Variables of Interest

The focus at this level of evaluation is primarily on the presence of laws and policies that give child protective services mechanisms to hold batterers' accountable (see Table 12.3 for summary). Although policy changes at the agency level may have some desired effects regarding batterer

TABLE 12.3
Evaluating the Effect of Systems Change at the State and Federal Level

Area of inquiry	Sample research question
Laws and policies	To what degree do the laws and policies of the state and federal government allow for successful prosecution of batterers?
Batterer accountability	To what extent are there laws or policies in place to encourage batterer accountability in the child protection system?
Funding opportunities	To what extent are there funding opportunities on the state and federal levels to support the creation of a CCR to violence against women and children?

Note. CCR = coordinated community response.

accountability, state and federal laws that allow for criminal prosecution of batterers must be implemented. Thus, a systems evaluation must attend to the legal context and take this into account when evaluating local coordinated efforts. It is also necessary to evaluate state- and federal-level funding opportunities that support the development of a CCR to violence against women and children.

Mechanics of Evaluations

The choice of evaluation strategies is usually driven by the research questions under consideration. Evaluators interested in understanding the collaborative process involved in coordinated system approaches would likely use qualitative research methods, such as focus groups, open-ended interviews with key members, and open-ended participant observation techniques. These strategies are ideal for studying the nature of collaborative efforts involving multiple individuals, organizations, and settings (Bogden & Biklen, 1992; Kingry-Westergaard & Kelly, 1990).

Outcome evaluations will likely require more quantitative techniques to examine the actual change in such variables as arrest and prosecution of the assailant, sanctions against the assailant, child protective services case dispositions, sanctions against mothers whose children are abused by the perpetrators, and safety over time of the women and children. Even in outcome evaluations, however, qualitative techniques are useful in helping explain why and how events occurred as they did, and they provide much richer data than do pure quantitative strategies.

In any and all evaluations, it is important that the women's and children's voices are heard and that their experiences are honestly and comprehensively portrayed. This entails involving women (and their older children, if appropriate) as members of the evaluation team; they should help in shaping the design, implementation, and interpretation of the evaluation effort. At the same time, when planning any evaluation, the safety of the women and children is of utmost importance. It is critical to consider all ways in which their safety might be compromised by participating in the evaluation. The best way to maximize their safety is to involve the women in all stages of the evaluation. They can help make decisions regarding safety and are likely to bring up issues the other team members would not have considered.

CONCLUSION

Any community response to intimate violence against women and children is only as strong as its weakest link. Arrest of the perpetrator, for example, is not effective in protecting the women and children involved if it is not followed by prosecution, appropriate sentencing, and monitoring of compliance with sanctions (Edleson, 1991; Steinman, 1991). Sanctions against perpetrators may not be effective if they simultaneously victimize women and children (e.g., when payments for batterer intervention programs come from the family's grocery money, when perpetrators are deported against the family's wishes). It is laudable that an ever-increasing number of communities are working to provide a CCR to this issue. Some efforts, however, are ineffective or even counterproductive, necessitating ongoing evaluations of CCRs at multiple levels. This chapter provided guidelines for examining the impact of CCRs on public policy, public awareness, systems change, and, ultimately, the safety and well-being of women and children.

REFERENCES

Abbott, B., Jordan, P., & Murtaya, N. (1995). Interagency collaboration for children's mental health services: The San Mateo County model for managed care. *Administration and Policy in Mental Health, 22,* 301–313.

Beeman, S. K., Hagemeister, A. K., & Edleson, J. L. (1999). Child protection and battered women's services: From conflict to collaboration. *Child Maltreatment, 4*(2), 116–126.

Bickman, L. (1996). A continuum of care: More is not always better. *American Psychologist, 51,* 689–701.

Bogden, R. C., & Biklen, S. K. (1992). *Qualitative research for education: An introduction to theory and methods.* Boston, MA: Allyn & Bacon.

Carter, J., & Schechter, S. (1997). *Child abuse and domestic violence: Creating community partnerships for safe families* [Report by the Family Violence Prevention Fund]. Retrieved on October 23, 1998 from the World Wide Web: http://www.fvpf.org/kids/childabuse.html

Clark, S. J., Burt, M. R., Schulte, M. M., & Maguire, K. (1996). *Coordinated community responses to domestic violence in six communities: Beyond the justice system.* Washington, DC: Urban Institute.

Dill, A. E., & Rochefort, D. (1989). Coordination, continuity, and centralized control: A policy perspective on service strategies for the chronic mentally ill. *Journal of Social Issues, 45*(3), 145–159.

Edleson, J. L. (1991). Coordinated community responses. In M. Steinman (Ed.), *Woman battering: Policy responses* (pp. 203–220). Cincinnati, OH: Anderson Press.

Edleson, J. L. (1998). Responsible mothers and invisible men: Child protection in the case of adult domestic violence. *Journal of Interpersonal Violence, 13,* 294–298.

Findlater, J. E., & Kelly, S. (1999). Reframing child safety in Michigan: Building collaboration among domestic violence, family preservation and child protection services. *Child Maltreatment, 4,* 27–47.

Foster-Fishman, P. G., Salem, D. A., Allen, N. E., & Fahrbach, K. (in press). Facilitating interorganizational exchanges: The contributions of interagency alliances. *American Journal of Community Psychology.*

Gamache, D. J., Edleson, J. L., & Schock, M. D. (1988). Coordinated police, judicial, and social service response to woman battering: A multiple-baseline evaluation across three communities. In G. T. Hotaling, D. Finkelhor, J. T. Kirkpatrick, & M. A. Straus (Eds.), *Coping with family violence* (pp. 193–209). Newbury Park, CA: Sage.

Gero, A., & Fowler, B. (1997). *Community audit: A resource for battered women's advocates.* Harrisburg: Pennsylvania Coalition Against Domestic Violence.

Hart, B. J. (1995). *Coordinated community approaches to domestic violence.* Retrieved on January 18, 2000 from the World Wide Web: http://www.mincava.umn.edu.nij.htm

Kelly, J. G. (1988). *A guide to conducting prevention research in the community: First steps.* London: Haworth.

Kingry-Westergaard, C., & Kelly, J. G. (1990). A contextualist epistemology for ecological research. In P. Tolan, C. Keys, F. Chertok, & L. Jason (Eds.), *Researching community psychology: Issues of theory and methods* (pp. 23–31). Washington, DC: American Psychological Association.

Quinn, K., & Cumblad, C. (1994). Service providers' perceptions of interagency collaboration in their communities. *Journal of Emotional and Behavioral Disorders, 2,* 109–116.

Schechter, S., & Edleson, J. L. (1995). In the best interest of women and children: A call for collaboration between child welfare and domestic violence constituencies. *Protecting Children, 11,* 6–11.

Shepard, M. (1999). Evaluating a coordinated community response. In M. Shepard & E. Pence (Eds.), *Coordinated community response to domestic violence: Lessons from the Duluth model* (pp. 169–191). Newbury Park, CA: Sage.

Shepard, M., & Pence, E. (Eds.). (1999). *Coordinated community response to domestic violence: Lessons from the Duluth model.* Newbury Park, CA: Sage.

Steinman, M. (1991). Coordinated criminal justice interventions and recidivism among batterers. In M. Steinman (Ed.), *Woman battering: Policy responses* (pp. 221–236). Cincinnati, OH: Anderson.

Violent Crime Control and Law Enforcement Act of 1994, P. L. 103-322, 108 Stat. 1796.

Wehlage, G. G., & White, J. A. (1995). *Citizen, clients, and consumers: Building social capital.* Washington, DC: Office of Education Research and Improvement

Williams, S. D. (1995). Integrating the family service system from the inside out: A view from the bureaucratic trenches. *Journal of Family and Economic Issues, 16,* 413–424.

13

PREVENTION OF DOMESTIC VIOLENCE: EMERGING INITIATIVES

DAVID A. WOLFE AND PETER G. JAFFE

Some days it seems that little progress has been made in addressing the fundamental causes and consequences of domestic violence and its effects on children. The problem seems as serious as ever, and the major underlying causes, such as abuse of power, inequality, and modeling of violence in the home, have remained largely unchanged over the past three decades. The government response has been to manage adult domestic violence, which involves providing services on an individual basis only when absolutely necessary. A crisis management strategy makes sense when the intervention is critically needed and highly effective at a particular time (e.g., unforeseen medical emergencies), but this approach is poorly suited to address the full dynamics of adult domestic violence. As a result, people who work with abused women and their children too often are left with a task that is beyond the capabilities of the current system and resources— "too little, too late"—resulting in the well-known signs of stress and fatigue. Crisis management is a necessary part of the response to adult domestic violence, but more proactive strategies of prevention are also strongly needed.

The news is not all bad; in fact, encouraging progress has been made in less than two decades. Scientific, professional, and activist groups have played a prominent role in recognizing the links between domestic violence and child psychopathology, among other issues. The number of shelters for battered women and abused children has increased dramatically, more laws are on the books, and interest by health care and other service professionals to modify child abuse reporting laws is growing, so that suspected cases of

This chapter is from "Emerging Strategies in the Prevention of Domestic Violence," by D. A. Wolfe and P. Jaffe, 1999, *Future of Children*, 9, 133–144. Copyright 1999 by David and Lucile Packard Foundation. Adapted with permission.

children who witness domestic violence are receiving greater attention. Encouragingly, these efforts have led to a consensus that family members who are maltreated by other family members must be protected. The growing interest by researchers and clinicians in the field of domestic violence makes it possible to establish a scientific foundation for implementing prevention and treatment initiatives and public policy to end domestic violence. The field is in the process of finding alternatives to violence that can be activated in each community in a manner that stimulates interest, informs choices, and promotes action to decrease violence and abuse in the lives of children, youths, and families.

In this chapter, key issues in the prevention of domestic violence are previewed. Included are discussions of the goals of prevention programs and theories of the causality of domestic violence and abuse. Next, prevention efforts designed to address the needs of children and adults are viewed through a developmental, or life-span, lens. Critical issues for prevention programs are described for different age groups. Finally, research and policy implications are explored for violence prevention endeavors in a number of settings, from homes, schools, and neighborhoods to courts and the culture at large.

EMERGING GOALS OF PREVENTION EFFORTS

Emerging changes in public policy, legislation, and service delivery illustrate a commitment to finding ways to reduce the prevalence and harmful effects of adult domestic violence. Still, strategies that address the issue at a broader level need to be developed and evaluated. Such strategies must take into account the many factors that influence the likelihood of adult domestic violence and those that promote nonviolence. There are established precedents for such an approach, such as public health campaigns to eliminate health risks among adolescents and health promotion campaigns to encourage healthy (low-risk) behaviors among segments of the population (Hamilton & Bhatti, 1996; Sherman et al., 1998). These approaches, adopted primarily for known health issues, hold considerable promise for behavioral issues as well because they recognize that change occurs through finding positive ways to communicate messages about healthy families and relationships.

One way to envision the goal of prevention is to promote attitudes and behaviors that are incompatible with violence and abuse and that encourage the formation of healthy, nonviolent relationships. The implications of this paradigm are significant and far reaching: If attention and resources are primarily focused on the occurrence of undesirable behavior, such as identified acts of violence, prevention efforts are usually directed toward identification, control, and punishment. However, if the goal of prevention is the promotion of healthy, nonviolent relationships, attention and resources are more likely to be directed toward establishing and building trust, respecting others' thoughts and expressions, and encouraging and supporting growth in relationships. This perspective implies a different list of intervention and educational possibilities, such as school-based curricula, neighborhood-based health and social services, and family-based child and health care, which are described in greater detail later.

THEORIES OF CAUSALITY

The prevention of domestic violence at first glance seems impeded by a lack of theoretical consensus as to its fundamental causes. However, the foundation of prevention programs might include several important principles:

- Domestic violence has been ignored as a major health, criminal, and social problem until recently and remains poorly understood among the general population.
- Domestic violence is a complex problem that cannot be understood by a single variable. Explanations require a multifaceted approach that recognizes individual behavior within a familial and cultural context (Dutton, 1995).
- The significance of childhood trauma, including witnessing adult domestic violence, is common to all theories, even though there is disagreement as to the processes involved. In general, these processes include learning maladaptive behaviors through modeling and reinforcement by people in the child's family, neighborhood, and cultural environment (Emery & Laumann-Billings, 1998). In turn, prevention efforts may include efforts to prevent children from ever experiencing such trauma as well as community readiness to respond as soon as possible to children in violent homes.
- As long as domestic violence is seen as acceptable behavior or tolerated by silence through public attitudes, institutions, and the media, there is little chance of changing individual behavior. In other words, the prevention of domestic violence is everyone's business and is each human services provider's responsibility.

Although far from realized, domestic violence prevention efforts have begun to organize around the principle of building on strengths and developing protective factors in an effort to deter violence and abuse. Learning to relate to others, especially intimates, in a respectful, nonviolent manner is a crucial foundation for building effective prevention strategies for related forms of violence and abuse between partners. Some prominent examples of these efforts are considered below.

PREVENTION EFFORTS ACROSS THE LIFE SPAN

Because violence in intimate relationships is deeply rooted in early family experiences and in broader cultural and social influences, deciding where to focus prevention efforts for greatest impact is a critical starting point. In principle, prevention efforts should involve every aspect of social ecology. Societal, community, and neighborhood forces; schools and peer groups; family processes; and individual strengths and weaknesses have all been linked to adult domestic violence. Therefore, all of these influences play a role in the prevention of violence and care should be taken to ensure that the interventions are appropriate, beneficial, and harmless.

It is widely accepted in this field that any prevention efforts have to be broadly based within the social networks in which people interact. Accordingly, actual or potential victims can be provided with counseling and referral services, such as crisis centers, shelters, and foster homes. Most community efforts begin in this manner because advocates recognize the basic humanitarian need to assist these individuals. Once greater recognition has occurred, some communities have introduced additional services and resources, such as changing laws and policies, training professionals, and establishing abuse registries and telephone hot lines. The next stage of intervention involves coordinated, system-integrated approaches to enhance the quality of services already available. Once in place, prevention programs in schools, law enforcement agencies, and similar organizations can begin to promote healthy, nonviolent relationships in the true prevention sense. The following framework examines primary, secondary, and tertiary efforts across the life span, as summarized in Table 13.1.

Infants and Preschool Children

Ensuring that children receive a healthy start, including freedom from emotional, physical, and sexual abuse and the trauma of witnessing violence, is a fundamental step in preventing the intergenerational patterns of family violence, and one that is supported by 15–20 years of research on the causes of such events. This step begins by defining the principles of a healthy child rearing environment. Allowing for a considerable range in ability and resources among North American families, certain features of a child's environment should be fundamental and expectable (Scarr, 1992). Infants

TABLE 13.1

Prevention of Domestic Violence Across the Life Span

Life stage	Community effort level		
	Primary	Secondary	Tertiary
Infants and preschoolers (age 0–5 years)	Home visitation by public health nurse and trained paraprofessionals assisting new parents	Home visitation with high-risk families Targeted to people at risk because of such factors as income, age, marital status, with the using of screening tools	Home visitation with abused women and children Targeted to those identified by domestic violence and child protection specialists as having experienced violence
School-age children (6–12 years)	School-based awareness and skills development Collaborative efforts by schools and communities to teach violence awareness and alternative conflict resolution skills	Community-based early intervention Children exposed to violence are offered crisis support, individual counseling, and educational groups	Disorder-based treatment services Children who show emotional and behavioral problems are offered specific mental health services that address the underlying trauma
Adolescents and high school age (13–18 years)	School-based awareness and skills development Same as above, with an emphasis on issues related to dating violence and forming healthy, intimate relationships	Community-based early intervention Same as above, tailored for adolescents exposed to violence and emphasis on dating relationships	Disorder-based treatment services Same as above, with the additional involvement of the juvenile justice system as the access and identification point for treatment
Adults (18+ years)	Public education Media campaigns promoting awareness of domestic violence, local specialized resources, and helpful responses for concerned family, friends, neighbors, and coworkers	Community-based early intervention Domestic abuse victims and survivors are identified at the earliest opportunity by front-line professionals in health, education, social services, and legal systems and are offered appropriate coordinated services	Community-based intervention for chronic domestic violence Intensive police, court, and community collaboration to prevent severe injury and death to abused women and their children with ongoing safety concerns in high-risk, chronic, and traumatic circumstances

require protective and nurturant adults as well as opportunities for socialization within a culture. For older children, an expectable environment includes a supportive family, contact with peers, and ample opportunities to explore and master the environment.

Model programs in this area have developed from the field of public health and nursing and involve efforts to provide support for new parents by home-visitation programs. For example, in a recent review of crime prevention research (as part of a 1997 report to the U.S. Congress), home visitation programs were described as one of the few approaches that were scientifically endorsed (Sherman et al., 1998). Such programs are most likely to be found in countries that provide universal health care, such as Canada and Scandinavian countries, in which government-funded hospitals, doctors, and nurses ensure good prenatal, postnatal, and follow-up care. For example, in Finland, 98% of families with small children attend well-baby clinics (Aronen & Kurkela, 1996). The overwhelming majority of these families volunteer for comprehensive assessments and regular counseling regarding parent–child relationships and child development over 5 years. Preventive interventions from birth and the style of counseling (building healthy parent–child relationships and understanding child development) have been well-received and are clearly nonthreatening to members of the community.

For the most part, home-visitation programs have addressed issues affecting child development rather than adult domestic violence, yet they hold considerable promise for the latter because of the fundamental principle of a healthy environment for children. These programs vary in scope and duration and can include educational aspects that improve parenting skills, reduce child abuse, and prevent isolation of young mothers. Public health nurses or trained paraprofessionals in the home not only provide valuable assistance to the developing parent–child relationship but also may become familiar enough with the marital relationship and family circumstances to offer assistance and referral to prevent abusive and violent relationships. For example, in the Hawaii Healthy Start program, home visitors serve as links to the criminal justice system. When early warning signs of domestic violence surface, the home visitor encourages mothers to develop safety plans and helps abusers to register for specific treatment programs in the community (Earle, 1995). Such support and assistance can be delivered on a universal basis, whereby all new parents receive basic in-home services for a specified time period. Unfortunately, however, few such model programs currently exist in North America (Wekerle & Wolfe, 1993). Alternatively, they may be delivered to selective groups, such as families or neighborhoods that are more at risk for abuse and domestic violence, similar to current efforts in child abuse (Olds et al., 1998).

At the tertiary level, the idea of family support and home visitation is often applied by community programs as an essential strategy in supporting abused women and their children once the extent of their problems has been identified. For example, innovative collaborations between child protection and domestic violence workers have led to more outreach programs that empower abused women to become more effective parents and maintain safety plans for themselves. These efforts serve an important prevention link because they avoid the historical pitfall of the state simply labeling abused women as unfit mothers, thereby justifying removal of the children. The National Council of Juvenile and Family Court Judges (1998) recently completed a publication that outlines innovative programs for abused women and their children across the United States. These programs vary in their focus and location in the helping system but share the goal of preventing woman abuse and its effects on children. Families First, a domestic violence collaborative project in Lansing, MI, is one example of an intensive, in-home crisis intervention program. The program is implemented by caseworkers with no more than two active cases and is geared to promote safety, parent education, and social support and to address basic needs, such as food, shelter, and transportation. The program exemplifies child protection and domestic violence expertise working together at the point of residence in a shelter for abused women. It also features intensive follow-up to empower abused mothers to be self-sufficient and maintain their parenting responsibilities.

School-Age Children

School-age children can benefit from learning positive messages about family roles while being taught rules about family boundaries and knowing where to turn to for help, if needed. In a comprehensive review of model programs for battered mothers and their children across the United States, many community agencies report significant initiatives in the field of primary prevention by collaborating with schools (National Council of Juvenile and Family Court Judges, 1998). Such efforts vary in terms of their specificity and comprehensiveness, but they share common goals of awareness and education to combat cultural stereotypes and inequalities that foster relationship violence. For example, the Women's Center and Shelter of Greater Pittsburgh (PA) developed extensive violence prevention programs for public school children between kindergarten and Grade 12. Through the collaboration with evaluators in public health, a major study has been undertaken recently to assess the impact of these comprehensive programs on students (J. Scott, director of education, Women's Center and Shelter of Greater Pittsburgh, PA, personal communication, August 11, 1998).

Descriptive findings currently point to promising outcomes that support this initiative.

One of the first programs to document efforts to prevent the cycle of violence by promoting violence awareness and safety skill development with school-age children was implemented by the Minnesota Coalition for Battered Women (Gamache & Snapp, 1995). The program targeted elementary and secondary students throughout the state in an effort to ensure that all children knew about alternatives to domestic violence. The curriculum represented intense collaboration among battered women's shelter staff and educators, modeled by a coordinator with expertise in both areas. The goals of the curriculum, entitled My Family and Me: Violence Free, for children between kindergarten and Grade 6 include the following: raise awareness of the impact of family problems; define violence and its effects; develop safety plans; learn to express feelings and opinions based on the values of equality, respect, and the sharing of power; learn nonviolent conflict resolution; and gain a sense of worth regardless of family problems. The ideas from this curriculum have spawned similar efforts across North America. The evaluation of this program, although limited in scope, suggests positive changes and knowledge about domestic violence and equivocal results about attitude change (Jones, 1991).

In Canada, a comprehensive violence prevention strategy was developed through the collaboration of school districts and community agencies. This program, entitled A School-Based Anti-Violence Program (A.S.A.P.), includes a manual and video detailing how to engage school staff, students, parents, and community agents in addressing domestic and school violence (Sudermann, Jaffe, & Schieck, 1996). Three main components of A.S.A.P. are (a) educator and staff development and awareness, (b) community involvement, and (c) student programs. Special violence awareness events and curriculum integration of violence awareness, prosocial skills development, and promotion of attitudes favoring nonviolence are emphasized. Involvement of school-based committees of educators, parents, students, and community members to plan implementation of the program is central to the approach. Preliminary studies of this school-based strategy are encouraging, with positive results shown from pre- to posttest for both male and female students in Grades 9 and 10 and positive results for female (but not male) senior students.

One of the key values inherent in both of these programs is the belief that every student needs to be aware of domestic violence and related forms of abuse. Even if they are never victims or perpetrators of domestic violence, young people may need to assist their peers and future neighbors in learning ways to stop violence against dating and marital partners. Violence in relationships is described as a community and societal issue, so programs are designed to involve community members, parents, students, and educators in the school-based prevention of violence.

Adolescents

Adolescence is a time of important cognitive and social development, whereby teenagers learn to think more rationally and become capable of thinking hypothetically. At the same time, they must develop and use effective decision-making skills involving complex interpersonal relationships, including an awareness of possible risks and considerations of future consequences and balancing their own interests with those of their peers, family members, and dating partners. Conformity to parental opinions gradually decreases, and the tendency to be swayed by peers increases until late adolescence. By mid-adolescence, romantic partners increase in their importance as social support providers (Furman & Buhrmester, 1992). Thus, early to mid-adolescence offers a unique opportunity for learning healthy ways to form intimate relationships, and teenagers are often keen to explore this unfamiliar territory.

Youths, especially those who grew up experiencing violence in their home, profit from education and skills that promote healthy relationships and provide useful alternatives to violence and abuse. Clear messages about personal responsibility and boundaries, delivered in a blame-free manner, are generally acceptable to this age group, whereas lectures and warnings are less helpful. By offering youths the opportunities to explore the richness and rewards of relationships, they become eager to learn about choices and responsibilities. The initiation phase of social dating is a prime opportunity to become aware of the ways in which violent and abusive behavior toward intimate partners may occur, often without purpose or intention. This premise holds true not only for individuals from violent and abusive family backgrounds where negative experiences were prominent but also for other adolescents (Gray & Foshee, 1997).

A discussion of choice and responsibility for one's own behavior and how abusiveness has different consequences and meanings for young men and women is a critical step in enhancing youths' awareness and recognition of dating violence (Gray & Foshee, 1997). Moreover, facilitating discussions of the meaning of violent dynamics, violent acts, and woman abuse simultaneously raises awareness of these issues and provides an opportunity to deal directly with issues of blame, responsibility, and victim–victimizer dynamics within the context of teenage dating relationships. Programs delivered universally through the high school often involve activities aimed at increasing awareness and dispelling myths about relationship violence, such as (a) school auditorium presentations involving videotapes, plays, professional theater groups, or a survivor's speech; (b) classroom discussions facilitated by teachers and community professionals involved in domestic violence intervention, such as shelter staff, crisis center staff, law enforcement personnel, and victim–witness advocates; (c) detailed lesson plans, programs, and curricula that encourage students to examine those attitudes and behaviors that promote or tolerate violence(these exercises serve as an introduction to nonviolent alternatives in relationships); and (d) peer counseling and peer support groups to assist students in developing empowerment initiatives.

Community-based programs for the prevention of relationship violence have goals similar to those of school-based programs, although they are intended for a more selective population, such as teenagers who are at greater risk of dating violence because of their early childhood experiences or similar risk factors. An example is the Youth Relationships Project (YRP; Wolfe et al., 1996), which was developed to help youths understand the critical importance of the abuse of power and control in relationship violence and relate these to their own social and dating relationships. YRP involves young people ages 14–17 years referred from active caseloads of child protective service agencies who experienced violence and abuse in their family background. They are informed of the program by their child protection caseworker, counselor, or other community agent, with an emphasis on building healthy, nonviolent relationships rather than attending treatment per se (which they generally resist). Because YRP is a secondary prevention program, participation does not require evidence of dating violence. Youths participate in an 18-session, small-group program designed to assist them in understanding the dynamics of intimate relationships, especially the definition and expression of abuse in relationships.

Through group discussion and exercises, the youths learn how to select appropriate alternatives to abuse and violence with dating partners. This strategy builds on current strengths and identifies negative relationship factors at a time when teenagers are motivated to learn about intimate relationships. Specifically, it attempts to help youths

- understand the critical issues related to healthy versus unhealthy (abusive) relationships
- develop skills to build healthy relationships and to recognize and respond to abuse in their own relationships and in relationships of their peers
- consolidate learning of new attitudes and skills and increase competency through community involvement and social action.

Efforts to provide youths with such positive educational and cultural experiences in which power is understood, not abused, are very recent, and program evaluations are incomplete. Early findings, however, show that youths are responsive to such information, especially if they are involved in its design and delivery. Six dating violence prevention programs designed for high school teenagers have included evaluation components (Wekerle & Wolfe, 1999). Each program addressed specific skills and knowledge that oppose the use of violent and abusive behavior toward intimate partners. Positive changes were found across the studies in violence-related attitudes and knowledge as well as self-reported perpetration of dating violence. Although preliminary, such efforts indicate that adolescents are receptive to these learning opportunities.

Adults

Public awareness campaigns, such as public service announcements and advertisements, are common approaches to primary prevention of domestic violence with adults. These campaigns are usually directed to recognizing the warning signs of domestic violence and publicizing specialized community resources, such as shelters for abused women. A comprehensive campaign that included a research component was developed by the Family Violence Prevention Fund in collaboration with the Advertising Council. The campaign involved television ads that made clear that "there is no excuse for abuse" and offered local contacts for domestic violence resources. The evaluation involved public opinion data prior to the campaign in 1992 and follow-up data gathered between 1994 and 1996. Although the findings were complicated by the extensive publicity about the O. J. Simpson trial that dominated media outlets during this period, these data suggest that people in the United States see domestic violence as an important social issue that requires state (police) intervention. Interestingly, many Americans excuse domestic violence as being the result of alcohol or other circumstances, and they are uncertain and fearful about intervening.

Klein, Campbell, Soler, and Ghez (1997) made a compelling argument that prevention is not a homogeneous intervention because attitudes vary according to sex and race. Not surprisingly, women tended to be more informed and committed to the issue. Views about the public nature of domestic violence and appropriate solutions also varied by ethnic self-identity. For example, visible minorities were less trusting of police intervention in these matters because they felt vulnerable in making family violence a public matter. Clearly, primary prevention is not a "one size fits all" proposition.

An additional point made by a public opinion survey is the importance of community leaders or well-known survivors speaking to the issue of domestic violence. Thus, it is more meaningful to have an African American political or church leader speak to his or her community about solutions to domestic violence than someone from a different cultural background.

To motivate decision makers, survivors should address the fact that violence may occur in any neighborhood. Thus, the challenge is to get not just police officers to respond but also friends, relatives, and neighbors.

Primary prevention strategies should ensure that everyone in the community knows the seriousness of domestic violence. Such efforts announce the availability of specialized resources for abused women, abusive men, and child witnesses to violence. If such resources are not available, concerned citizens should be motivated through increased awareness efforts to fundraise and lobby different levels of government for these resources. Secondary prevention has to ensure an informed and sensitive response to abused women and children by all front-line service providers, including justice, health, social services, educational, and mental health systems. The availability of a disclosure protocol, for example, to help a teacher handle students who reveal witnessing violence in their home may be an essential form of secondary prevention.

POLICY AND RESEARCH IMPLICATIONS

As researchers and clinicians, we are currently at the starting gate of domestic violence prevention efforts in North America. Whether we make real progress depends on public and governmental commitment to making prevention a long-term priority, similar to campaigns to prevent injury through seat-belt use, encourage environmental protection, decrease drinking and driving, and reduce smoking and related health risks. Although it is encouraging to witness the rising number of innovative programs around the world that are attempting to prevent domestic violence or to reduce its consequences, shortcomings exist because of the early stage of development of the field, lack of resources, and research limitations. The challenge, therefore, is to move beyond the fledgling local programs scattered across various communities to ensure comprehensive evaluations and research to support the effectiveness of current and future efforts.

Regardless of their attractiveness, prevention and health promotions have not been popular strategies among professionals or the general public for addressing problems of domestic violence. This state of affairs exists perhaps because prevention requires policymakers and administrators to confront social and political factors that undermine lasting solutions to social problems. Prevention entails environmental and cultural explanations in addition to individual ones for causes of violence and similar concerns and a strong commitment to large-scale, proactive intervention using public resources rather than individually focused, private interests. Furthermore, prevention requires social and political action directed at achieving fundamental change. Nevertheless, we owe it to children, young people, and families to consider building other bridges that promote competency and adaptive behavior in an effort not only to prevent something unwanted but also to bolster potential and growth for individuals and society.

Many promising programs and ideas can be applied to the prevention of adult domestic violence. Although there is a paucity of evaluative data, there is general agreement that children and adolescents, especially those growing up in violent homes, are an important prevention focus. The following major prevention strategies and research issues stand out:

- Considerable promise exists in expanding home-visitation programs developed in the field of public health to address the promotion of safety and security for infants and young children on a universal basis. This conclusion was reached in a comprehensive report by the U.S. Department of Justice (Sherman et al., 1998)and in a review of best practices in crime prevention programs based on programs from seven countries (Waller, Welsh, & Sansafon, 1997).

- Based on the collective wisdom of family court judges, child protection agencies, and domestic violence programs, there is a need to expand existing collaborative efforts by child protection and domestic violence agencies and staff to a more comprehensive primary prevention program (National Council of Juvenile and Family Court Judges, 1998).

- There is a growing recognition that crime prevention needs to focus on homes and communities to the extent that both are recognized as risk factors in violent behavior. Many children are exposed to violence not only in their homes but also in their neighborhoods and schools, which requires extensive collaboration among service systems. Thus, initial efforts may have to target high-risk neighborhoods and communities rather than assessing one client (potential victim) at a time (Earls, 1998).

- Primary prevention programs should be available in all schools and be developed as a partnership among students, teachers, parents, and community agents with knowledge and expertise about domestic violence. For adolescents, the programs need to be relevant to their interests, such as dating violence, and actively involve counseling, such as peer support and peer models. A major challenge for the domestic violence field involves better collaboration with the more general crime prevention strategies that are being actively promoted in U.S. schools in response to horrific tragedies, such as the Jonesboro, AR, shootings. There are overlapping strategies (e.g., clearly naming the problem), and domestic violence is often an underlying issue and concern for children. Although many parents and teachers are worried about violence in general, most children are more likely to witness and experience violence among people they know and trust. Therefore, the domestic violence issues are more relevant for them.

- Public education campaigns must tailor awareness efforts to recognize different perspectives and needs related to demographics, such as gender, race, and social class. Survey results strongly suggest that society needs to move beyond awareness and offer practical strategies on what the average citizen can do about domestic violence. These strategies have to be specific enough to help a friend or coworker deal with a perpetrator or victim that they know in a manner that ensures their own safety. In addition, broader messages are needed to inform people what they can do for the domestic violence issue in their community from fundraising to writing letters to the editor of the local newspaper.

- Evaluation research should be a regular feature of preventive interventions to establish the effectiveness of programs, to identify best practices, and to allow for the promotion of the most effective solutions to preventing violence. Therefore, long-term funding should continue to be made available for researchers to document outcomes and to study prevention efforts across a range of settings, such as homes, schools, communities, and court systems.

- There needs to be a national policy on zero tolerance for domestic violence that could revitalize training and services for abused women and their children in all human services sectors. One of the authors (Jaffe) had the opportunity to be a part of a federal commission that traveled across Canada and visited 139 communities and heard from 4,000 men, women, and adolescents about their ideas on how to end violence against women. Major conclusions included addressing underlying issues, such as inequality and poverty as well as zero tolerance policies geared to every sector of the community. The ultimate goal is to hold various service systems (e.g., justice, health, social services, mental health) fully accountable for services, policies, and training in the domestic violence area.

In the prevention of adult domestic violence, a clear commitment is needed from all levels of government to address these issues comprehensively, with the goal of establishing a consistent, coordinated, and integrated approach for each community. Given the extensive nature of domestic violence and its accompanying human suffering, this commitment to prevention cannot be postponed.

REFERENCES

Aronen, E. T., & Kurkela, S. A. (1996). Long-term effects of an early home-based intervention. *Journal of the American Academy of Child and Adolescent Psychiatry*, 35, 1665–1672.

Dutton, D. G. (1995). *The domestic assault of women: Psychological and criminal justice perspectives*. Vancouver, British Columbia, Canada: University of British Columbia Press.

Earle, R. B. (1995, October). *Helping to prevent child abuse and future criminal consequences: Hawai'i Healthy Start* [Program focus] (NIJ 156216). Washington, DC: U.S. Department of Justice, National Institute of Justice.

Earls, F. (1998, September). *Linking community factors and individual development* [Research preview] (NIJ 170603). Washington, DC: U.S. Department of Justice, National Institute of Justice.

Emery, R. E., & Laumann-Billings, L. (1998). An overview of the nature, causes, and consequences of abusive family relationships: Toward differentiating maltreatment and violence. *American Psychologist*, 53, 121–135.

Furman, W., & Buhrmester, D. (1992). Age and sex differences in perceptions of networks of personal relationships. *Child Development*, 63, 103–115.

Gamache, D., & Snapp, S. (1995). Teach your children well: Elementary schools and violence prevention. In E. Peled, P. Jaffe, & J. Edleson (Eds.), *Ending the cycle of violence* (pp. 209–231). Thousand Oaks, CA: Sage.

Gray, H. M., & Foshee, V. (1997). Adolescent dating violence: Differences between one-sided and mutually violent profiles. *Journal of Interpersonal Violence*, 12, 126–141.

Hamilton, N., & Bhatti, T. (1996). *Population health promotion: An integrated model of population health and health promotion*. Ottawa, Ontario: Health Canada.

Jones, L. (1991). The Minnesota School Curriculum Project: A statewide domestic violence prevention project in secondary schools. In B. Levy (Ed.), *Dating violence: Young women in danger* (pp. 258–266). Seattle, WA: Seal Press.

Klein, E., Campbell, J., Soler, E., & Ghez, M. (1997). *Ending domestic violence: Changing public perceptions/halting the epidemic*. Thousand Oaks, CA: Sage.

National Council of Juvenile and Family Court Judges. (1998). *Family violence: Emerging programs for battered mothers and their children*. Reno, NV: Author.

Olds, D., Henderson, C. R., Cole, R., Eckenrode, J., Kitzman, H., Luckey, D., Pettitt, L., Sidora, K., Morris, P., & Powers, J. (1998). Long-term effects of nurse home visitation on children's criminal and antisocial behavior: 15-year follow-up of a randomized trial. *Journal of the American Medical Association*, 280, 1238–1244.

Scarr, S. (1992). Developmental theories for the 1990's: Development and individual differences. *Child Development, 63,* 1–19.

Sherman, L. W., Gottfredson, D. C., MacKenzie, D. L., Eck, J., Reuter, P., & Bushway, S. D. (1998, July). *Preventing crime: What works, what doesn't, what's promising* [Research in brief] (NIJ 171676). Washington, DC: U.S. Department of Justice, National Institute of Justice.

Sudermann, M., Jaffe, P., & Schieck, E. (1996). *A.S.A.P.: A school-based antiviolence program.* London, Ontario, Canada: London Family Court Clinic.

Waller, I., Welsh, B. C., & Sansafon, D. (1997). *Crime prevention digest 1997: Successes, benefits, and directions from seven countries.* Ottawa, Ontario, Canada: International Center for the Prevention of Crime.

Wekerle, C., & Wolfe, D. A. (1993). Prevention strategies for child abuse and neglect: Promising new directions. *Clinical Psychology Review, 13,* 501–540.

Wekerle, C., & Wolfe, D. A. (1999). Dating violence in mid-adolescence: Theory, significance, and emerging prevention initiatives. *Clinical Psychology Review, 19,* 435–456.

Wolfe, D. A., Wekerle, C., Gough, R., Reitzel-Jaffe, D., Grasley, C., Pittman, A., Lefebvre, L., & Stumpf, J. (1996). *The youth relationships manual: A group approach with adolescents for the prevention of woman abuse and the promotion of healthy relationships.* Thousand Oaks, CA: Sage.

AUTHOR INDEX

Numbers in italics refer to listings in reference sections.

Aaron, S. M., 104, *107*
Abbott, B., 271, *280*
Aber, J. L., 50, *63*
Abrahams, C., 144, *151*
Abrahams, H., 138, 140, 141, *153*
Achenbach, T. M., 37, 58, 97, 105, 249, *261*
Adamson, J. L., 118, *127*
Alenderfer, M. S., 73, *85*
Allen, N., 143, 145, *155*, 179, *186*, 251, *266*
Allen, N. E., 271, *281*
Amaya-Jackson, L., 123, *131*
American Association for Protecting Children, 71, *85*
American Psychiatric Association, 37, 58, 244, *261*
Ammerman, R. T., 71, *85*, *261*
Anada, R. F., 42, *60*
Anderson, G., 69, 70, 80, *86*
Andres, J., 45, *58*
Anglin, T., 101, *109*
Angst, J., 45, *60*
Anthony, E. J., 68, 77, *85*
Appel, A. E., 29, 91, *105*
Appel, E. W., 3, *9*
Appelbaum, P. S., 122, *127*
Apter, T., 111, *127*
Arbitell, M., 95, 101, 102, *106*
Arias, I., 20, 25, 29, *32*
Aronen, E. T., 288, *297*
Arroyo, W., 36, *63*
Atkins, M., 29, 30, 244, 257, *262*
Austin, G., 192, 194, *201*
Azar, S. T., 71, *85*, 255, *266*

Bachman, R., 102, *105*, 157, *184*
Baker, C., 251, *266*
Bala, N. M., *200*
Ballard, T., *164*, 167, *184*
Bandura, A., 35, *58*, 250, *261*
Barad, S., 204, *218*, 239, 243, 247, *264*
Barling, J., 25, 28, 30, *32*
Barnes, K. T., 71, *85*

Barnett, D. C., 73, *85*
Barnett, O. W., 70, 71, *85*
Barrera, M., 220–222, 225, *230*
Bartha, C., 190, *201*
Bartko, W. T., *89*
Baskerville, S., *165–166*, *184*
Bauer, W. D., 71, *85*
Beach, S., 20, *29*
Beals, J., 229, *234*
Beck, U., 139, *151*
Beeghly, M., 51, *59*
Beeman, S., 96, *105*, *106*, 226, 227, *230*, 276, 277, *280*
Bell, C. C., 100, *106*, *107*
Belle, D., 220, 221, 223, 224, *230*
Belsky, J., 71, *85*, 228, *231*
Bennett, R. T., 42, *61*
Bennette, L., *184*
Beriama, A., 29, 244, *262*
Berkowitz, L., 251, *261*
Bermann, E. A., 4, *9*
Berndt, T., 228, *231*
Berthelsen, D., 117, 121, *131*
Bertrand, L. D., *200*
Best, K., 68, 88, 219, 222, *233*
Bewley, S., 141, 142, *154*
Bhatti, T., 284, *297*
Bickman, L., 270, *280*
Biklen, S. K., 279, *280*
Binney, V., 142, *151*
Birmaher, B., 38, *61*
Blakely, E. H., 67, *88*
Blanchard, A., 224, *231*
Blankenhorn, D., 159, 163, *164, 166, 167*, *184*
Blashfield, R. K., 73, *85*
Blumenthal, D. R., 118, *127*
Bogden, R. C., 279, *280*
Boldizar, J. P., 100, *106*
Boney-McCoy, S., 41, *59*, *110*
Boot, B., 169, *184*
Borgen, F. H., 73, *85*
Boriskin, J. A., 71, *86*
Boruch, R., 29, 30, 69, *86*, 244, *262*
Boudrea, L., *200*

Bousha, D. M., 71, 86
Bowermaster, J., 193, 200, 200
Bowker, L. H., 95, 101, 102, 106
Bowlby, J., 223, 231, 261
Bradley, E. J., 127
Brassard, J., 220, 229, 231
Brescoll, V., 257, 258, 262
Bretherton, I., 223, 231
Bridges, M., 67, 79, 87
Briere, J. N., 37, 57, 59
Broadhurst, D., 3, 10
Brofenbrenner, U., 220, 231
Browermaster, J. D., 157, 169, 170, 174,
    176, 177, 184
Brown, L., 224, 231
Browne, A., 16, 31, 258, 265
Brumaghim, J. T., 50, 51, 63
Bruner, J., 207, 217
Brunnquell, D., 70, 86
Bryant, B., 228, 231
Bryer, J. B., 41, 59
Brygger, M. P., 20, 30, 96, 106
Buhrmester, D., 225, 228, 232, 291, 297
Bullock, L., 142, 151, 152
Burgess, A., 150, 152
Burgess, A. W., 251, 263
Burleson, B., 227, 231
Burt, M. R., 269, 270, 271, 281
Burton, S., 141, 152
Bush, A., 168, 185
Bushway, S. D., 284, 288, 295, 298
Bussell, D. A., 113, 122, 124–126, 127
Bybee, D., 143, 145, 155, 251, 266

Cadenhead, C., 101, 106
Caetano, R., 22, 24, 25, 32
Cameron, S., 224, 234, 243, 246, 247,
    267
Campbell, J., 28, 31, 142, 152, 170, 176,
    184
Camras, L. A., 51, 59
Canadian Panel on Violence Against
    Women, 192, 200
Cangiano, C., 72, 87
Cantrell, P. J., 43, 59
Capsi, A., 18, 31
Carlson, B. E., 22, 29, 120, 121, 127
Carlson, V., 47, 52, 59
Carnochan, J., 108
Carter, J., 271, 273, 276, 277, 280

Caspi, A., 20, 32
Cassidy, J., 52, 62
Caster, J., 61
Cauce, A., 224, 231
Cavanagh, K., 141, 152
Channels, N. L., 113, 127
Charney, D. S., 38, 39, 59
Chase, S. E., 113, 128
Cherlin, A., 159, 184
Chetwin, A., 140, 152
Child Abuse Prevention and Treatment
    Act, 93, 106
Children Act Sub-Committee, 139, 140,
    152
Children's Rights Council, 167, 184
Chodorow, N., 145, 152
Christopher, J. S., 44, 61
Cicchetti, D., 33, 40, 47, 50–53, 59, 63,
    64, 68, 86, 89, 117–119, 128,
    219, 222, 231, 255, 263
Clark, C., 22, 24, 25, 32
Clark, S. J., 269–271, 281
Clarke, K., 124, 125, 129
Coatsworth, D., 67, 68, 69, 71, 77, 78,
    80–83, 88
Cobb, S., 221, 231
Cochran, M., 220, 223, 226, 229, 231
Coffey, P., 42, 61
Cohen, D. J., 47, 59
Cohen, S., 220, 222, 232
Cohler, B. J., 77, 78, 80, 81, 86
Cole, R., 57, 62, 288, 297
Coletta, N., 232
Collazos-Spiller, L., 116, 117, 120, 129
Comstock, G., 100, 108
Conaway, L. P., 44, 61
Cook, S. J., 70, 88
Corbin, J., 80, 90
Cornell, C. P., 72, 86
Cortes, R., 33, 69, 89, 117–119, 131
Corwin, D., 169, 184
Cowen, E., 224, 232
Cox, G. M., 240, 243, 262
Craig, G., 124, 125, 129
Craven, D., 22, 30
Crichton, L., 70, 86
Crick, N. R., 48, 59
Crittenden, P., 220, 232
Crogman, R., 146, 152
Cross, W. E., 228, 232
Cumblad, C., 270, 281

Cummings, E. M., 18, 29, 119, *128*, 204, *205, 217, 255, 262, 263*
Curry, M., 142, *152*
Cutler, S. E., 242, 250, *263*

Dahl, N., 38, *61*
Daly, M., 15, *30*, 102, *106, 110*
Daro, D., *10*
Davidson, T., 121, *128*
Davidson, W., 28, *33*, 240, 244, 246, 248, *266*
Davies, L., 141, *154*
Davies, P. T., 18, *29*, 255, *262*
Davis, D., 91, *108*, 239, *265*
Davis, L., 104, *110*
Davis, M., 38, 39, *59*
Dawud, S., 69, 89, 117–119, *131*
Dawud-Noursi, S., 20, 21, *33*, 96, *109*, 229, *233*
Deer, W., 136, *152*
DeKeseredy, W. S., 18, 20, *29*
DeLange, C., 97, *107*
Delgado, M., 228, *232*
Demi, A. S., 114, 115, 124, 125, *128*
Denzin, N. K., 127, *128*
DePaola, L. M., 69, 70, 80, 86, 117, 118, 121, *128*
Deutch, A. Y., 38, 39, *59*
Devoe, E., 37, *59*, 174, *184*
Dill, A. E., 270, *281*
Dillenburger, K., 137, 143, *154*
Dishion, T. J., *265*
Divorce Act, 191, *200*
Dobash, R., 135, 140, 141, 144, *152*
Dobash, R. E., 15, *30*
Dobash, R. P., 15, *30*
Dodge, K. A., 48, *59*
Doernberger, C., *88*
Doherty, W. J., 158, 159, 160, 180, *184*
Dominy, N., 147, *152*
Doolittle, F. C., 161, *185*
Doyne, D. E., 157, 169, 170, 174, 176, 177, *184*
Doyne, S., 200, *200*
Duncan, S., 149, *154*
Dunn, J., 223, *232*
DuRant, R. H., 101, *106*
Dutton, D., 157, 169, 170, 174, 176, 177, *184, 200, 200*, 285, *297*

Earle, R. B., 288, *297*
Earls, F., 295, *297*
Eck, J., 284, 288, 295, *298*
Eckenrode, J., 288, *297*
Edelbrock, C., 37, 58, 97, *105*
Edleson, J. L., 3, 9, 20, 30, 91, 92, 96, 103, 104, *105, 106*, 115, 120, 124, *128, 130*, 195, 196, *201, 203, 217, 219, 232*, 243, 247, 265, 269, 270, 276, 277, 280, *280, 281*
Edwards, V., 42, *60*
Egeland, B., 60, 70, *70*, 86, 88, 250, *262*
Eisikovits, A., 204, *218*
Elder, G. H., 67, *86*
Elicker, J., 53, *60*
Ellis, R., 141, *152*
Emery, R. E., 3, 9, 38, 45, 46, 60, 285, *297*
Engelman, E., 67, *88*
Englund, M., 53, *60*
Enosh, G., 204, *218*
Enright, S. D., 114, *131*
Erel, O., 20, *32*
Erickson, J. R., 116–118, *128*
Erickson, M. F., 60, 70, *70*, *88*
Ernst, G., 45, *60*
Eron, L. D., 251, *263*
Eth, S., 36, *63*, 99–100, *106*
Etzel, J. C., 75, *87*
Everson, M. D., 169, *184*
Ezell, E., 25, *32*

Fagan, J., 18, *31*
Fahrbach, K., 271, *281*
Fairbanks, L., 36, *63*
Faller, K. C., 169, 174, *184*
Fantuzzo, J., 30, 69, 70, 80, 86, 117, 118, 121, *128*, 244, 257, *262*
Farmer, E., 137, *152*
Felitti, V. J., 42, *60*
Festinger, T., 67, *86*
Fick, A. C., *100–101, 108*
Fiering, C., 228, *232*
Fiese, B. H., 46, *64*
Figueredo, A. J., 102, *108*, 116, 118–121, *130*
Fincham, F. D., 17, 18, *30*, 98, 99, *107*, 194, *200*, 204, *218*
Findlater, J. E., 276, 277, *281*

Fine, G. A., 114, *128*
Finkelhor, D., 15, *33*, 41, 45, *59*, *61*
Finlater, J. E., 104, *106*
Fish-Murray, C. C., 44, 49, *60*
Fitzgerald, L., *16*, *31*, 258, *265*
Fitzgerald, R., *200*
Fitzpatrick, K. M., 100, *106*
Flitcraft, A., 95, *109*, 143, *155*
Foa, P., 38, *60*
Foldenyi, M., 45, *60*
Follett, C. A., 76, *87*
Folman, R., 67, *86*
Fonagy, P., 53, *60*
Forsstrom-Cohen, B., 42, *60*, 120, *128*
Foshee, V., 291, *297*
Foster-Fishman, P. G., 271, *281*
Fowler, B., 275, *281*
Fox, J. A., 22, *30*
Fox, L., 50, *60*
Francis, D. J., 21, *31*
Frederick, C., 36, *63*
Freeman, L. N., 100, *106*
French, M., *262*
Frey-Angel, J., 239, *262*
Friedrich, W. N., 71, *86*
Frierson, T., 101, *109*
Furman, W., 225, 228, *232*, 291, *297*

Gaensbauer, T. J., 51, *60*
Gaffner, R., 157, 169, 170, 174, 177, 180, *185*
Galashan, S., 192, *200*
Gamache, D., 270, *281*, 290, *297*
Gano-Phillips, A., 194, *200*
Garbarino, J., 228, *232*
Garfinkel, I., 159, 160, *184*
Garmezy, N., 67, 68, 77, *86*, 88, 219, 222, *233*
Gauthier, L., 251, *266*
Geffner, R., *185*, 191, 194, 195, *201*, *218*, 252, *264*
Gelles, R. J., 3, *10*, 13, 15, 18, 27, 28, *30*, *33*, 35, 65, 72, *86*, 101, *110*, 170, 179, *185*, *266*
Gentile, C., 67, 90, 254, *267*
George, C., 52, *60*
Gergen, K. J., 206, *218*
Gero, A., 275, *281*
Gershuny, B. S., 38, *60*
Ghez, M., 28, *31*

Gianconia, R., 44, *64*
Giles-Sims, J., 27, *30*, 45, *61*
Gilgun, J. F., 125, *128*
Gilliam, G., 228, *232*
Gleason, W. J., 117–119, *128*
Glendinning, C., 124, 125, *129*
Gleser, G., 100, *107*
Goddard, C., 94, *109*
Goenjian, A., 38, 47, *63*
Gondolf, E., 119, 121–126, *128*, 170, 176, 177, 179, *185*
Goodlin-Jones, B. L., 126, *131*
Goodman, L., *16*, *31*, 258, *265*
Goodson, B. D., 97, *107*
Gordon, L., 91, *106*, 142, 145, *152*
Gordon, R., 238, *262*
Gottfredson, D. C., 284, 288, 295, *298*
Gottlieb, B., 220, *232*
Gough, R., 243, 249, *267*, 292, *298*
Grace, M., 100, *107*
Graham-Bermann, S., 4, 9, 19, *30*, 37, 52, *59*, *61*, 67, 69, 76, 78, 81, 86–88, 98, 104, *107*, 120–122, *128*, *129*, 204, 218, 225, 227, *232*, 241, 244–247, 249–259, *262*, *264*
Grasley, C., 243, *267*, 292, *298*
Gravelek, J. R., 256, *263*
Gray, H. M., 291, *297*
Gray, M., 149, *154*
Green, B., 100, *107*
Greenbaum, C., *33*, 69, 89, 117–119, *131*
Greenfeld, L. A., 22, *30*
Gruber, G., *263*
Grych, J. H., 17, *30*, 98, 99, *107*, 204, 218
Guba, E. G., 112, 113, *129*
Gunnarsson, L., 220, *232*
Guo, S., 101, *109*
Gurman, A. S., 242, *263*
Gyurina, C. H., 105, *107*

Hagemeister, A. K., 96, *105*, 276, 277, 280
Hague, G., 136, 138, 140, 141, *152*, *153*
Hamby, S. L., 15, *33*, *110*
Hamilton, N., 284, *297*
Hampton, S., 157, 174, *186*
Hangen, E., 94, 105, *107*

Hann, D. M., *100–101, 108*
Hansen, D. J., 40, 41, 44, *61, 62*
Hanson, K. L., 69, 81, 89
Harkell, G., 142, *151*
Harris, S. D., 45, *61*, 70, 87, 141, *153*
Harrison, C., 150, *154*
Hart, B. J., *270–272, 276, 281*
Hartman, C. R., 251, *263*
Harvey, S., 142, *152*
Harwicke, N. J., 48, *61*
Harwin, N., 137, 143, *153*
Haviland, M. G., 53, *61*
Hegemeister, A. K., *105, 106*
Heidt, E., 22, *33*, 94, 99, *109, 233*
Heller, J., 105, *107*
Henderson, A. D., 116–118, *128*
Henderson, C., 220, 222, *232, 233*
Henderson, C. R., 288, *297*
Hennessy, K. D., 119, *128*, 255, *263*
Henning, K., 42, *61*
Herman, J. L., 258, *263*
Herrenkohl, E. C., 250, *263*
Herrenkohl, R. C., 250, *263*
Hersen, M., 85
Hershorn, M., 17, *30*
Hester, M., 136–150, *153, 154*
Hetherington, M. E., 67, 79, 87
Hiatt, S., 51, *60*
Hilberman, E., 101, *107*
Hill, J., 51, *59*
Hinchey, F. S., 256, *263*
Ho, J., 46, 47, *64*
Hochstadt, N. J., 48, *61*
Hodges, W., *233*
Hodges, W. F., 22, *33*, 94, 99, *109*
Hoff, L., 147, *153*
Holden, G., 3, *9*, 22, 29, *30*, 45, *61*, 70, 87, 91, 101, *105, 107, 128*, 141, 144, *153*, 194, 195, *201, 203, 218, 219, 232*
Holtzworth-Munroe, A., 15, *30*, 91, *107*, 177, *185*
Hood, E., 190, *201*
Hooper, C., 145, *153*
Horn, W., *168, 185*
Hornick, J. P., *200*
Howell, M., 119, *131*
Hoyle, C., 136, *153*
Huesmann, L. R., 251, *263*
Hughes, H., 19, *30*, 67–70, 72, 75, 81, 87, 89, 116–118, *128*, 204, *218*,
239, 242–247, 249, 253, *263, 264*
Humm-Delgado, D., 228, *232*
Humphreys, C., 138, 140, 141, 145, *153*
Humphries, J., 137, 138, 144, 146, *154*
Hunter, R. S., 250, *264*
Huston, A. C., 4, *9*

Illinois Coalition Against Domestic Violence, 91, *107*
Insabella, G., 67, 79, 87

Jacobvitz, D., 250, *262*
Jaffe, P., 45, 65, 70, 87, 117–120, *132*, 157, 169, 170, 174, 176, 177, 180, *184, 185*, 192, 194–196, 200, *200–202*, 204, *218*, 224, *234*, 243, 246, 247, 250, 252, 256, *264*, 267, 290, *298*
Janoff-Bulman, R., 258, *264*
Jenkins, E. J., *106, 107*
John, R., 20, *32*, 116, 118, *129*, 219, *233*, 255, *265*
Johnson, C., 42, *64*
Johnson, D., 193, *200*
Johnson, E., 161, *185*
Johnson, H., *201*
Johnson, J., 143, *153*
Johnson, M. P., 18, *30*
Johnson, S., 52, *63*
Johnson, V., 240, 246, 253, *267*
Johnston, C., 71, *88*
Johnston, J. R., 189, 190, *201*
Jones, L., 290, *297*
Jordan, P., 271, *280*
Joseph, H., 222, *233*
Jouriles, E., 19–21, 26–28, *30–32, 34*, 45, 46, *61*, 70, 87, 116–120, *129*, 141, *153*, 194, 195, *201, 218*, 241, 245, 249, *264*
Juras, J., 143, 145, *155*, 179, *186*

Kalmuss, D., 38, *61*
Kaplan, A., 112, *129*
Kaplan, N., 52, *62*
Karyl, J., 22, *33*, 94, 99, *109, 233*
Kaufman, J., 38, *61*, 250, *264*
Keita, G. P., 16, *31*, 258, *265*

Kelly, J., 226, *234*
Kelly, J. B., 194, *201*
Kelly, J. G., 272, 279, *281*
Kelly, L., *31*, 141, 144, *153*
Kelly, S., 104, *106*, 276, 277, *281*
Kemmelmeier, M., 43, *62*
Kendall, P. C., 258, *264*
Kendall-Tackett, K. A., 41, 45, *61*
Kendrick, C., 223, *232*
Kerig, P., 120, *129*
Kihlstrom, N., 250, *264*
Kilpatrik, K. L., 118, *129*
Kingry-Westergaard, C., 279, *281*
Kirkwood, C., 147, *153*
Kitzman, H., 57, *62*, 288, *297*
Klaus, P. A., 22, *30*
Klein, E., 28, *31*
Klorman, R., 50, 51, *63*
Knaggs, T., 140, *152*
Kniskern, D. P., 242, *263*
Knoppers, B. M., *200*
Koby, E. V., 44, 49, *60*
Kohler, B. J., 68, 77, *85*
Kolbo, J. R., 67, 88, *107*, 118, 119, *129*
Korol, M., 100, *107*
Koss, M., *16*, 20, *31*, 42, *60*, 102, *108*, 116, 118–121, *130*, 258, *265*
Kovitz, K., 71, *88*
Krispin, O., *33*, 69, *89*, 117–119, *131*
Kroll, P. A., 41, *59*
Kruger, R., 20, *32*
Krystal, J. H., 38, 39, *59*
Kuczynski, L., 71, *90*
Kuhn, T. S., 112, *129*
Kunkel, A., 227, *231*
Kurkela, S. A., 288, *297*

Lamb, M. E., 20, 21, *33*, 69, *89*, 117–119, *131*, 229, *233*
Lambert, L., 69, 70, 80, *86*, 117, 118, 121, *128*
Langhinrischsen-Rohling, J., 41, 43, *61*, *62*
Langlois, A., 50, *60*
Larner, M., 220, *232*
Lather, P., 111, *129*
Laumakis, M. A., 116, 118, *129*, 219, *233*, 255, *265*
Laumann-Billings, L., 3, 9, 55, *60*, 285, *297*

Layzer, J., 97, *107*
Lecklitner, G. L., 104, *107*
Lederman, C. S., 104, *107*
LeDoux, J. E., 48, *62*
Lees, S., 136, *153*
Lefebvre, L., 52, *65*
Lehmann, P., 117, *129*, 254, *265*
Leighton, B., 103, *108*
Leitenberg, H., 42, *61*
Leonard, A., 100, *107*
Lependorf, M., 223, *231*
Letko, C., 102, *109*
Levendosky, A., 37, 52, *61*, 70, 87, 120–122, *128*, *129*, 225, 227, *232*, *263*, 250, 253–257
Levesque, D. A., 179, *185*
Levine, A., 161, *185*
Levine, J. A., 162–163, *185*
Lewis, J., 148, *153*, 196, *202*
Lewis, M., 228, *232*
Lieberman, A. F., 240, 246, 251, 253, *265*, *267*
Lincoln, Y. S., 111–113, 115, *129*
Linder, C. W., 101, *106*
Lindsay, R. C. L., *127*
Liss, M. B., 125, *129*
Litzenberger, B. W., 242, 250, *263*
Liu, X. D., 52, *63*
Loefkowitz, M. M., 251, *263*
Long, S. H., 50, *60*
Lorey, F., *33*, 69, *89*, 117–119, *131*
Lorion, R. P., 100, *108*
Lovell, M., *233*
Lowe, P., 138, 140, 141, *153*
Lubetsky, M., *85*
Luckey, D., 288, *297*
Luke, D. A., 70, 73, *87*, *89*, 242, 253, *264*
Lundy, M., 111, 114, 115, 122–124, *130*
Luthar, S., 68, 69, 81–83, *88*
Lynch, M., 68, *86*

MacIntyre, D. I., 43, *59*
MacKenzie, D. L., 284, 288, 295, *298*
Magdol, L., 18, 20, *31*, *32*
Magnatta, M., 190, *201*
Maguire, K., 269, 270, 271, *281*
Mahon, A., 124, 125, *129*

Mahoney, A., *31*, 117, 119, *129*
Main, M., 52, 60, *62*
Maker, A. H., 43, *62*
Malik, N. M., 104, *107*
Malinosky-Rummell, R., 40, 41, 44, *62*
Mallah, K., 49, *62*
Malone, J., 25, *32*
Malos, E., 136, *152*
Mama, A., 136, *153*
Mandell, N., 114, *130*
Marcus, S., 29, 30, 244, 257, *262*
Margolin, G., 20, *32*, 48, *62*, 67, 81, 88,
    91, *108*, 115, 116, 118, *129*, *130*,
    219, *233*, 242, 253, 255, *265*
Marks, J. S., 42, *60*
Marshall, L., 239, *265*
Martin, D., 121, *131*
Martinez, P., 100, *108*, *109*
Martino, G. A., 117, 118, 121, *128*
Martino, S., 51, *59*
Martino, T., 69, 70, 80, 86
Mash, E. J., 71, 88
Massar, C. P., 111, 114, 115, 122–124,
    130
Masson, J., 150, *154*
Masten, A., 47, *62*, 67, 68, 69, 71,
    77, 78, 80–83, 86, 88, 219,
    222, *233*
Maston, C., 22, *30*
Mauthan, B., 46, 47, *64*
Mauthner, M., 123, *130*
Maynard, M., 149, *154*
McCarthy, P., 150, *155*
McCloskey, L. A., 102, *108*, 116, 118–
    121, *130*
McCollum, E. E., 179, *186*
McCord, J., 43, 44, *62*
McDonald, R., 19, 21, 26–28, *31*, *32*,
    34, 46, *61*, 116, 117, 119, 120,
    129
McFarlane, J., 20, *32*, 142, *151*, *152*
McFerron, J. R., 95, 101, 102, *106*
McGee, R. A., 97, 98, *108*, 257, *265*
McGonigle, J. J., 85
McKiernan, J., 142, *154*
McLanahan, S., 159, 160, *184*
McLoyd, V. C., *185*
McMahon, M., 14, *32*, 170, 174, 177,
    180, *185*
McWilliams, M., 142, *154*
Mead, G. H., 258, *265*

Medina, J., 48, *62*
Mehta, P., 21, *31*
Meloy, J. R., 157, 169, 170, 174, 176,
    177, *184*, 200, *200*
Melton, G. B., 124, *130*
Mercy, M. A., 203, *218*
Mertin, P., *154*
Meyer, D. R., 159, 160, *184*
Meyer, K. A., *61*
Mezey, G., 141, 142, *154*
Miblinyi, L., *106*
Miell, D., 146, *152*
Miklas, S. W., *200*
Miliotis, D. M., 67, 88
Miller, D., 244, 247, 248, *266*
Miller, D. B., 101, *109*
Miller, G., 52, *63*
Miller, J., *233*
Miller, J. B., 41, *59*
Miller, N., *265*
Miller, P., 222, 224, *233*
Miller-Hewitt, S., *265*
Miller-Perrin, C. L., 70, 71, 85
Min, K., 22, *33*, 94, 99, *109*, *233*
Minnesota Department of Corrections,
    91, *108*
Mirlees-Black, C., 141, *154*
Mitchell, J. C., 221, 229, *233*
Moffitt, T. E., 20, *31*, *32*, *265*
Mokros, H., 100, *106*
Molloy, F., 224, *231*
Mones, P., 200, *200*
Monies, P., 157, 169, 170, 174, 176, 177,
    184
Monson, C. M., *61*
Moore, T. E., *32*, 38, 45, 58, *62*, 118,
    121, *130*
Moreci, P., *61*
Moriarty, A., 88
Morris, P., 288, *297*
Morrow, V., 114, 123, *130*
Mortimore, P., 46, 47, *64*
Mullender, A., 137, 138, 140, 141, 149,
    153, *154*
Munson, K., 101, *107*
Murburg, M. M., 38, 39, *59*
Murphy, C. M., 17, *31*, 118, *127*
Murphy, L. B., 88
Murray, C. C., 49, *62*
Murtaya, N., 271, *280*
Musick, J. S., 77, 78, 80, 81, 86

Nader, K., 36, 63
Nash, M. R., 47, 65
National Center for Health Statistics, 190, 201
National Council of Juvenile and Family Court Judges, 4, 9, 92, 108, 191, 201, 289, 295, 297
National Fatherhood Initiative, 164, 185
National Research Council, 15, 32
National Research Council, Institute of Medicine, 248, 265
Neeman, J., 67, 88, 118, 127
Neidig, P., 41, 43, 61, 62
Nelson, B., 38, 61
Nelson, B. A., 41, 59
Newberger, C. M., 88
New Jersey Coalition for Battered Women, 91, 108
Newman, D. L., 18, 31
Nguyen, H., 143, 145, 155, 179, 186, 251, 266
Nixon, J., 142, 151
Noel, J.-F., 200
Nordenberg, D., 42, 60
Norwood, W., 19, 25–28, 31, 32, 34, 46, 61, 116, 117, 119, 120, 129, 194, 201, 243–245, 247–249, 252, 264
Nova Scotia Law Reform Commission, 199, 201
Nunez, F., 36, 63

O'Brien, M., 20, 32
O'Connor, I., 117, 121, 131
O'Hagan, L., 137, 143, 154
O'Keefe, M., 28, 32, 101, 103, 108, 118, 130, 201, 249, 265
Okun, A., 87, 225, 227, 232, 257, 263
Okun, L., 27, 32
Olafson, E., 169, 184
Oldham, M., 137, 138, 154
Olds, D., 57, 62, 288, 297
O'Leary, K. D., 17, 18, 28, 30–32, 96, 109, 250, 266
Oliver, C., 142, 152
Osofsky, J. D., 47, 62, 100–101, 108
Ouston, J., 46, 47, 64
Owen, M., 137, 152

Paetsch, J. J., 200
Pagelow, M. D., 169, 186
Pahl, J., 146, 154
Paik, H., 100, 108
Paniagua, F. A., 77, 88
Parke, R., 233
Parker, B., 20, 32, 142, 152
Parkinson, D., 68, 71, 87, 118, 129
Parkinson, X., 245, 264
Parson, R. G., 131
Parton, N., 149, 154
Patterson, G. R., 250, 252, 265
Pavlovic, A., 150, 154
Pearson, C., 137, 142, 143, 149, 153
Peled, E., 91, 108, 116–118, 120, 121, 123, 124, 130, 195, 196, 201, 219, 224, 229, 233, 239, 243, 247, 265
Pence, E., 14, 32, 155, 170, 174, 177, 180, 185, 272, 276, 282
Pendergrast, R. A., 101, 106
Pepler, D. J., 32, 38, 62, 118, 121, 130
Perel, J., 38, 61
Perkins, C. A., 22, 30
Perrin, R. D., 70, 71, 85
Perry, B. D., 39, 63
Petchers, M., 97, 109
Peters, B. R., 28, 31
Peterson, C., 43, 62
Peterson, M., 72, 87
Pettitt, L., 288, 297
Piaget, J., 49, 63
Pianta, R., 60, 70, 71, 88
Pierce, G., 222, 233
Piper, C., 140, 154
Pitt, E. W., 162, 163, 185
Pittman, A., 243, 267, 292, 298
Pleck, E. H., 91, 109
Plotnikoff, J., 136, 154
Pollak, S. D., 50, 51, 63
Popenow, D., 159, 186
Porter, B. K., 18, 32
Porterfield, K., 87, 225, 227, 232, 257, 263
Posada, G., 52, 63
Powers, J., 288, 297
Poznanski, E. O., 100, 106
Prescott, S., 102, 109
Price, J. M., 48, 63
Pynoos, R. S., 36, 38, 47, 63, 99–100, 106

Quinn, K., 270, *281*

Rabideau, G. J., 119, *128*, 255, 263
Radford, L., 137–141, 143–148, 150, *152–154*
Radke-Yarrow, M., 67, 89
Radovanovic, H., 190, *201*
Ragg, D. M., 240, 244, 246–248, 266
Rand, M. R., 22, 30
Rapkin, B. D., 73, 89
Reason, P., 111, 113, *130*
Reder, P., 149, *154*
Regan, L., 141, *152*
Reid, J. B., 265
Reinherz, H., 44, 64
Reitzel-Jaffe, D., 52, 65, 243, 249, 267, 292, 298
Reno, J., 3, 9
Reuter, P., 284, 288, 295, 298
Ribordy, S., 51, 59
Richards, M, 114, 123, *130*
Richardson, J., 141, *154*
Richey, C., 233
Richie, B., 145, *154*
Richters, J. E., 100, *108, 109*
Rieder, C., 50, 63
Riggs, D. S., 38, 60
Riley, D., 220, *232*
Ringel, C., 22, 30
Ritchie, K., 45, 52, 53, *61, 63*, 70, 87, 101, *107, 128*, 141, 144, *153*, 194, 195, *201*
Rizley, R., 219, 222, *231*
Robinson, J., 57, 62
Rochefort, D., 270, *281*
Rodgers, K., 192, 196, *201*
Rodway, M. R., 239, 267
Rogosch, F. J., 50, 63
Rogosch, R. A., 53, 59
Roosa, M., 118, 120, *131*, 195, *202*
Rosen, K. H., 179, *186*
Rosenbaum, A., 17, 25, *30, 32*, 42, 60, 96, *109*, 115, 120, 122, *127, 128, 130*, 250, 266
Rosenbaum, M., 47, 64, 105, *107*
Rosenberg, M., 17, 19, *32*, 69, 89, 119–121, *131*, 256, 266
Rosenberg, M. L., 203, *218*
Ross, S. M., 102, *109*, 192, *201*

Rossman, B. B. R., 17, 19, *32*, 37, 45, 47, 49, 50, *62–64*, 67, 69, 81, 89, 117, 119, 120, 121, *130*, 241, 243, 245, 247, 254, 255, 256, 259, 266
Rowan, 113, *130*
Runyan, D., 15, *33*, 123, *131*
Russo, N. F., 258, 265
Russon, N., *16, 31*
Rutter, M., 46, 47, 64, 67, 81, 89, 219, 222, 224, *233*
Ryan, N., 38, *61*

Sacco, V. F., *201*
Sachs, V., 51, 59
Saigh, P. A., 36, 64
Salem, D. A., 271, *281*
Saltzman, L. E., 102, *105*, 157, *184*
Saltzman, W., 100, *108*
Sameroff, A. J., 46, 64, 67, 89
Sanders, A., *61*
Sandin, B., 91, *107*
Sandler, I., 118, 120, *131*, 195, *202*, 222, 224, 229, *233, 234*
Sandstrom, K. L., 114, *128*
Sansafon, D., 295 *298*
Santostefano, S., 49, 64
Sarason, B., 222, *233*
Sarason, I., 222, *233*
Saunders, D. G., 102, 103, *109*, 157, 169, 170, 171, 174, 176, 177, *186*, 255, 266
Sayer, S., 139, 140, *154*
Scarr, S., 285, *298*
Schafer, J., 22, 24, 25, *32*
Schechter, S., 269, 271, 273, 276, 277, 280, *281*
Schieck, E., 290, *298*
Schneider-Rosen, K., 51, 64
Schock, M. D., 270, *281*
Schornstein, S., 142, *154*
Schubiner, H., 100, *109*
Schulte, M. M., 269, 270, 271, *281*
Schuman, K., 192, 200
Schwartz, M. D., 18, *29, 32*
Schwartz, W. E., 242, 250, *263*
Sclater, S., 140, *154*
Scott, K., 244, 256, 267
Scott, R., 100, *109*
Sedlack, A., 3, *10*

Seid, M., 98, *107*
Seifer, R., 47, *64*, 67, 89
Seltzer, J. A., 159, 160, *184*
Sevenhuijsen, S., 148, *155*
Shadish, W. R., 242, 246, *266*
Shalala, D., 3, *10*
Sharkey, K. J., 43, *59*
Sheeran, M., 157, 174, *186*
Shepard, M., *155*, 272, 276, *282*
Sherman, L. W., 284, 288, 295, 298
Sherman, T. L., 67, 89
Shinn-Ware, H., 116, 117, 120, *129*
Short, J., 222, 224, *233*
Shpungin, E., 251, *266*
Shupe, A., 93, *101*, *109*
Sidora, K., 288, *297*
Sieber, J. E., 113, 115, *131*
Silva, P., 18, 20, *31*, *32*
Silverman, A., 44, *64*
Silvern, L., 22, *33*, 94, 99, *109*, *233*
Simmons, C. H., *131*
Simons, R. L., 42, *64*
Simpson, B., 150, *155*
Simpson v. Brown, 191, *201*
Sinclair, D., 191, *201*
Singer, M. I., 98, *101*, *109*
Singh, L. S., 102, *106*
Slavens, G., 101, *106*
Sleek, S., 4, *10*
Slovak, K., 101, *109*
Smith, A., 46, 47, *64*
Smith, C., 35, *65*
Smith, J., 117, 121, *131*
Smith, J. P., 249, *266*
Smith, M. D., 20, *33*, 123, *131*
Smith, R., 47, *65*, 82, 90, 219, *234*
Smitson-Cohen, S., 100, *107*
Smutzler, N., 15, *30*, 91, *107*
Snapp, S., 290, *297*
Socolar, R. R. S., 123, *131*
Soeken, K., 20, *32*, 142, *152*
Soler, E., 28, *31*
Solomon, B. B., 113, *131*
Son, L., 49, *62*
Song, L., 98, *101*, *109*
Sonkin, D. J., 121, *131*
Sonne, J. L., 53, *61*
Southwick, S. M., 38, 39, *59*
Spaccarelli, S., 51, *59*, 118, 120, *131*, 195, *202*
Specht, H., 227, *233*

Special Joint Committee on Child Custody and Access, 193, *202*
Spiller, L. C., 19, 26–28, *31*, *31*, *34*, 46, *61*, 243, 244, 247–249, 252, *264*
Spitz, A. M., 42, *60*
Sroufe, L. A., 53, *60*, 250, *262*
Stacey, W., 93, *101*, *109*
Stack, C., *233*
Stagg, V., 119, *131*
Stanko, E., 137, 139, *155*
Stanley, J., 94, *109*
Stanton, M. D., 242, 246, *266*
Starek, J., 22, *33*, 94, 99, *109*, *233*
Stark, E., 95, *109*, 143, *155*
Statistics Canada, 190, *202*
Steele, H., 53, *60*
Steele, M., 53, *60*
Stefani, R., 51, *59*
Stein, J. D., 45, *61*, 70, 87, 141, *153*
Steinberg, A., 36, *63*
Steinberg, A. M., 38, 47, *63*
Steinman, M., 270, 280, *282*
Steinmetz, S., 22, 24, *33*, 35, *65*, 250, *266*
Stephens, N., 27, 28, *31*, 46, *61*, 243, 244, 247, 248, 249, 252, *264*
Sternberg, K., 20, 21, *33*, 69, 89, 96, *109*, 117, 118, 119, *131*, 229, *233*
Stets, J. E., 169, *186*
Stith, S., 179, *186*
Stott, F. M., 77, 78, 80, 81, *86*
Straus, M. A., 3, *10*, 15, 18, 27, 28, *33*, 35, 41, 42, *64*, *65*, 71, 89, 94, *101*, *110*, 169, 170, *185*, *186*, *218*, 245, 250, *266*
Strauss, M., 80, *90*
Stuart, G. L., 15, *30*, 177, *185*
Stumpf, J., 243, *267*
Sudermann, M., *265*, 290, *298*
Sugarman, D. B., *110*
Sullivan, C., 28, *33*, 143, 145, *155*, 179, *186*, 240, 244, 246, 248, 251, 253, *266*
Sultana, M., 244, 247, 248, *266*
Sutton, S., 69, 70, 80, *86*, 117, 118, 121, *128*
Swank, P., 19, 26, 27, *31*, *34*, 116, 117, 120, *129*
Sydney, R., 20, *32*
Szinovacz, M. E., 20, *33*, *110*

Tammivaara, J., 114, *131*
Target, M., 53, *60*
Tellegen, A., 77, *86*
Temiko, S., 157, 169, 170, 174, 176, 177, *184*, 200, *200*
Terr, L. C., 254, *266*
Te Wairere, A., 140, *152*
Thoennes, N., 22–24, *33*, 169, *186*
Thompson, B., 100, *107*
Thompson, L., 113–115, 123, *131*
Thompson, R., 222, 223, 229, *234*
Thompson, R. A., 114, 118, *127*, *131*
Thompson, V., 43, *59*
Tjaden, P., 22–24, *33*, 169, *186*
Toedter, L. J., 250, *263*
Tracy, E., *234*
Trickett, P. K., 71, *90*
Turner, T., 42, *61*
Tutty, L. M., 240, 243, 246, *266*
Twentyman, C. T., 71, *85*, *86*
Tyree, A., 25, *32*
Tzelepis, A., 100, *109*

Urquiza, A. J., 126, *131*
U.S. Department of Health and Human Services, 71, *90*, 163, *186*
Utah Criminal Code, 92, *110*

van der Kolk, B. A., 38, 44, 49, 60, *65*, 255, *266*
Van Hasselt, V. B., *85*
Van Horn, P., 240, 246, 251, 253, *265*, *267*
Van Slyke, D., 48, *63*
Vargo, M., 68, 71, *87*, 118, *129*, 245, *264*
Vary, M., 100, *107*
Vaux, A., 222, *234*
Vaux, W. G., 164, *168–169*, *186*
Velicer, W. F., 179, *185*
Vincent, J. P., *31*, 117, 119, *129*
Violent Crime Control and Law Enforcement Act of 1994, P. L. 103-322, 108, 269, *282*

Waelde, L., 22, *33*, 94, 99, *109*, 233
Wagar, J., 239, 240, 243, 246, *266*, *267*

Waksler, F. C., 114, *132*
Walder, L. O., 251, *263*
Walker, J., 150, *155*
Walker, L., 121, *131*, 143, *155*
Waller, I., 295, *298*
Wallerstein, J., 196, *202*, 226, *234*
Walsh, R., 223, *231*
Wang, C.-T., *10*
Warchol, G., 22, *30*
Ware, H. S., 25–28, *31*, *32*, 34, 46, *61*, 243, 244, 247–249, 252, *264*
Warren, N. A., 114, 115, 124, 125, *128*
Waters, E., 52, *63*
Watson, L., *265*
Weeks, R., 42, *65*
Wehlage, G. G., 270, *282*
Wekerle, C., 52, *65*, 288, *298*
Wellman, B., *234*
Wells, W., *61*
Welsh, B. C., 295, *298*
Werkerle, C., 244, 247, 248, *267*
Werner, E., 47, *65*, 82, *90*, 219, *234*
West, J. C., 49, *65*
Wewers, S., *100–101*, *108*
White, J. A., 270, *282*
Whitehead, B. D., *187*
Whitney, P., 104, *110*
Whittaker, J., 233, *234*
Widom, C. S., 42, 44, 48, 55, *65*
Williams, J. G., 249, *266*
Williams, L. M., 41, 45, *61*, 118, *129*
Williams, O. J., 170, 171, 176, 181, *184*, *187*
Williams, S. D., 270, *282*
Williamson, D. F., 42, *60*
Wills, G. D., 119, *131*
Wills, T., 220, 222, *232*
Wilson, M., 15, *30*, 102, *106*, *110*
Wilson, S., 45, *65*, 70, *87*, 97, 98, *108*, 117–120, *132*, 170, *185*, 195, *202*, 204, 218, 224, *234*, 239, 243, 246, 247, 249, 250, 256, 257, *264*, *265*, *267*
Winstok, Z., 204, *218*
Wolchik, S., 222, 224, 229, *233*, *234*
Wolfe, D., 45, 52, *65*, 67, 70, *87*, *90*, 97, 98, *108*, 117–120, *132*, 170, *185*, 195, *202*, 204, 218, 224, *234*, 240, 243, 244, 246–250, 254, 256, 257, 258, *264*, *265*, *267*, 288, 292, *298*

Wolfe, V. V., 67, *90*, 254, *267*
Woodfield, K., 137, 138, 144, 146,
    154
Woods, L. R., 53, *61*
Woolfson, R., 136, *154*
Work, W., 224, *232*
World Health Organization, 142, *155*
Wraith, R., 38, *63*
Wright, J. C., 4, *9*
Wyatt, G. E., 126, *131*

Ylló, K. A., 16, *34*
Young, P., 140, *152*
Yuen, S. A., *108*

Zak, L., 45, 65, 117–120, *132*, 195, 202,
    250, 256, *267*
Zelkowitz, P., 229, *234*
Zigler, E., 69, 81–83, 88, 250, *264*
Zorza, J., 193, *202*
Zwiney, O. A., 47, *65*

SUBJECT INDEX

Abuse
    See also Child abuse
    emotional, 121
    legal obligation to report, 121, 126
    marital. *See* Marital abuse
    moral obligation to report, 122
    perpetrator of, removal from home,
      138
    physical. *See* Physical abuse
    psychological. *See* Psychological
      abuse
    sexual. *See* Sexual abuse
    vulnerability to, 71–72
Abuser
    biological relationship with child vic-
      tim, 102
    fear of, 172–173
    letter from victim of, 171–172
    use of court and legal system against
      partner, 171, 172, 173
Abusive fathers
    adult children of, 175–176
    child contact with, 140
    relationship with
      after divorce, 190–192
      quality of, 150
    rights of, 157–158
Academic performance
    exposed vs. nonexposed children,
      45, 46
    resilience and, 76, 77
Accommodation in cognitive develop-
    ment, 49
Accountability of batterer
    at community level, 275, 277
    family law–child protection pol-
      icy conflict and, 137
    at state and federal level, 278–
      279, 279
Adjustment
    See also Maladjustment
    after exposure to violence
      conceptual model for, 197, 198,
        199
      interaction of factors in, 199

      outcomes in, 198, 199
      protective factors in, 197, 199
      risk factors in, 197
    after parental divorce–separation,
      189–190, 194–195, 197, 198, 199
    of children in shelters, 238, 242
    correlation with domestic violence,
      22
    custody and visitation arrangements
      and, 198, 199
    following child abuse, 70
    marital conflict effect on, 194–195
    in resilience studies of children of
      battered women, 73
      cluster analysis in, 73, 74
      discussion of, 75–76
      distress in, 74
      factor variables in, 72–73
      methodology in, 72–73
      results in, 73–75
    of sheltered children, 238, 242
Adolescents
    defense of mother from abuse, 175
    prevention of violence in
      community-based early interven-
        tion, 292
      in dating relationships, 292, 293
      disorder-based treatment services
        and, 287
      school-based awareness and skills
        development in, 291–292,
        295–296
    response to adult domestic violence,
      55
    as victims of physical, sexual, multi-
      ple abuse
      reality distortion by, 53
Adult children of abuse
    interviewing of, 180
    memories of abusive fathers,
      175–176
Adversity, long-term consequences of, 78
Aggression
    after physical abuse, 40
    after sexual abuse, 45

Aggression, *continued*
  fear and, 251
  gender and, 249, 250
  intergenerational transmission of,
      250
  and interpretation of social situa-
      tions, 48–49
  intervention for
    group programs, 239–241, 252
    parenting programs, 253
    social learning paradigm in,
        252–253
  in intervention programs
    assessment of, 247
    research findings, 249–250
    theoretical explanations for,
        250–252
  maternal toward child, 251
  premarital against partners, 18
  in psychodynamic drive theory, 251
  in sibling relationships, 249–250
  in social learning theory, 250
  in social relationships, 249
  toward parents, after victimization
      by, 41–42
  verbal, in mothers of resilient chil-
      dren, 74
Alienated parent syndrome, 174
American Psychological Association
    definition of violence, 16
Antisocial behavior
  relationship with marital conflict
      and harsh parenting, 42
Antisocial personality disorder
  association with childhood abuse, 44
Anxiety in children of batterers, 253–254
Assimilation in cognitive development, 49
Attachment
  insecure
    in abused and neglected children,
        52
    criminal behavior and, 54
    social competence development
        and, 54
  resilience and, 76
  secure, social competence and self-
      confidence and, 53
Attentional capacity, and exposure to
    marital violence, 48
Awareness in child's construction of real-
    ity, 210

  of master child, 212
  of uprooted child, 213
  of vanquished child, 213

Battered women
  See also Mothers, battered; Women
  choices of, 179–180
  domestic violence advocates and,
      269
  in dual or coparenting relationship,
      180
  identification in pediatric clinics,
      57–58
  physical and emotional care of child
      by, 143, 144
  prevalence of, 170, 192
  protection of, systems-based response
      to. *See* Coordinated community
      response (CCR)
  protection of child by, research on,
      147
  types of, 170
  as victims, 143, 147
  victim status vs. exercise of choice,
      143–144
  violence in self-defense, 170
Batterers. *See* Men who batter
Behavior problems
  after multiple abuse, 53
  of exposed children in shelters, 45–
      46, 242
    correlation with posttraumatic
        stress disorder symptom scores,
        37
  trauma view of, 37
  from witnessing domestic violence,
      219
Beliefs in intergenerational transmission
    of violence, 42
Best interest of child
  in divorce legislation and policy,
      193–194
  social welfare agencies and, 269
Brain development, traumatic stress in-
    fluence on, 39

Causality
  in child's construction of interparen-
      tal violence, 207

in child's perception of parental expectation, 216
in resilience, 82
theories of, 285–286
Child abuse
See also Abuse; Child maltreatment and woman battering
by battered and nonbattered women, 144
birth order and, 102
categories of, 93
during contact visits, 138–139
in contact visits, 138–139
co-occurrence with exposure to domestic violence, later violent behavior and, 40
co-occurrence with wife–partner abuse and marital violence, 27–28, 176, 177, 270
duty to report, 121
and exposure to domestic violence, 192
false allegations of in custody battles, 191–192
by father or mother's partner, 191
gender differences in, 102
juvenile delinquent prevention study and, 43–44
by mother, 101–102, 149–150, 169
by mothers, 149–150
privitization of response to, 137
research participation as trigger for, 121
risk for, with mother battering, 170–171
Childbirth, abuse effect on, 142
Child maltreatment and woman battering
adult violent behavior and, 40
co-occurrence of
adult domestic violence definitions and measures in, 94
birth order in, 102
with childhood victimization, 98–99
children in cross-fire of, 101
with community violence, 99–100
dominant husband in, 102
evolution of, 101–103
gender in, 102
legislation and policy for, 92

maternal reciprocity in, 101–102
with media violence, 100
with multiple exposures and victimizations, 100–101
new initiatives and, 103–105
number of children in, 102
with other forms of violence and exposure, 98–103
policy and practice developments in, 92
prevalence of, 3
programs for, 92
with relationship discord, 99
research in, 92–105
step-parent in, 102
data on overlap
in archived case records, 94–95, 96
from client self-reports, 96
exclusions in, 94
problems of shelter children in, 95–96
from studies of violence against mothers, 95
study samples, 94–96
definitions and nomenclature in, 93–94, 94
evolution of, 99–100
Children
adult bias toward, 114
exposure to family violence. See Exposure to domestic violence
maternal ambivalence toward, 150
in published studies
as participants, 117–118
as subjects of investigation vs. partners to it, 118
safety of. See Protection; Safety
shelter residence effect on, 45–46
as social actors, ethical research with, 114
support of mothers, 147
as witnesses of violence
counseling programs for, 104–105
of nonmarital violence, 17
prevalence of, 3
state programs, 104–105
Children's Rights Council
custody reform and, 167
maternal abuse of child and, 169

Child's best interest
    in custody determination, 191
    legislation and policy and, 193–194
Child support
    bias toward women, 166
    current system for, 162
    father involvement programs and,
        161, 162
Cognition, approaches to
    cognitive control theory, 49–50
    Piagetian assimilation and accommo-
        dation skills, 49
    processing of survival information, 48
    social information processing theory,
        48–49
    problems in, from witnessing domes-
        tic violence, 219
Cognitive control theory
    leveling in, 49–50
    in management of arousal levels,
        49–50
    sharpening in, 49, 50
Common couple violence, inconsistences
    in literature for, 19
Community
    evaluation of coordinated commu-
        nity response in, 274–275
        awareness and involvement in,
            278
        batterer accountability in, 277
        common screening tool, 277, 278
        community awareness and
            involvement in, 278
        direct service providers in, 276
        infrastructure and, 276–278
        outcomes of, 278
        resources and, 273, 275–276
    exposure to violence in, 99–100
    and prevention of adolescent vio-
        lence, 292
    and prevention of school-age child
        violence, 287, 289–291
Compensating factors, in resilience, 78
Competence in child's reality construc-
    tion, 210–211
    of master child, 212
    of uprooted child, 213
Comprehension, impaired after child
    abuse and neglect, 50–51
Confidentiality, obligation to report and,
    123–124

Conflict
    constructive, 18
    interpersonal, 194–195
    marital
        antisocial behavior following, 42
        as constructive, 18
        vs. violence, 17–18
        witnessing of, 99
    violence and
        as cause of, 169
        in resolution of, 170
        as result of, 166
        vs. violence, conceptual distinctions,
            17–18
        witnessing of, 99
Conflict Tactics Scales
    in classification of families as vio-
        lent, 15–16
    Physical Aggression Scale, criterion
        for partner violence, 23
    in selection of violent and nonvio-
        lent groups, 21
Contact services, for father's rights and
    prevention of abuse, 139–140
Contact visits, child abuse in, 138–139
Coordinated community response (CCR)
    components of, 270
    coordinating councils in, 270–271
    evaluation of systems changes in,
        271–280
    mechanics of, 279–280
        coordinating councils in,
            276–277
        cross-training in, 277
        inclusion of providers and clients
            and, 277
        protocols in, 277
        qualitative methods for process
            evaluation, 279
        quantitative techniques for out-
            come evaluations, 279
    in mother and child abuse in same
        home, 270
    multilevel evaluation of, 271–280
        community-level variables of in-
            terest, 273, 274–275, 275–278
        individual or family-level vari-
            ables of interest, 272,
            272–273
        state- and federal-level variables
            of interest, 278–279, 279

for protection of battered women
and their children, 269–270, 280
in protection of women and children
victims, 280
and safety, 272–273
social services organizations in, 270
Coordinating councils, in coordinated
community response
evaluation of, 276–277
goal of, 271
membership on, 271
role of, 270–271
Coparenting
See also Joint custody; Shared parenting
with men who batter, 180, 181–182
Costs
mental health and social, of domestic violence, 143
of resilience, 78
Courts, abuser's use of against partner,
170, 171, 172
Crime
domestic violence as, 136
feminist support of, 136–137
domestic violence exposure as, 43
insecure and distorted attachment relationship and, 54
nonviolent relationship to abuse, 44
Culture
of childhood, acknowledgment of,
114
and mothering experience and activity, 143, 147
prevention of domestic violence
and, 293
resilience and, 77
and social networks, 228
and social support, 228
Custody
court award to abusive father, 180
domestic violence and, principles in,
191
false allegation of abuse and, 169
hidden children and, 167
labeling of battered women and, 174
maternal vs. paternal, 160
men who batter vs. nonviolent fathers, 193
reform of, 167
safety in, psychological, 150

socioeconomic status of father and,
177–178

Data analysis, writing and dissemination
of, in ethical research, 126
Data collection
distress with procedures for, 120–
121
guidelines for ethical, 124–126
Dating violence, prevention of, 292, 293
Death threats, by abuser, 173
Debriefing, in research, 125
Depression
in battered women, 143
in children of batterers, 253
in college women, after childhood
exposure to violence, 42
in mothers of resilient children, 74
parental abuse and, psychological
and physical, 43
Development
adverse effects on, 27–28
emotional
aggressive bias and, 51–52
in physically abused children,
51–52
reactions to emotions of others
and, 51–52
tasks in, 51–52
exposure to adult domestic violence
and, 91
exposure to severe, repetitive spousal
violence and need for instruments to assess violence-
supporting mechanisms, 56–57
need for multidomain assessment
of, 56
stages and social networks, 228
stages and social support, 228
Developmental factors, in resilience, 76–77
domains of, 76
over life course, 77
Developmental task(s)
attention, 48, 50
cognition, 48–50
comprehension deficits and, 50–51
emotional, 51–52
interpersonal relationships, 52–54
perception, 47–48
traumatization and, 46–47, 46–54

Distress
    in children of battered mothers, 74
    with data-collection procedures, in
        published studies, 120–121
Divorce
    See also High-conflict divorce
    abuse following, 170
    best interest of child and, 191,
        193–194
    child protection and, conflict of pub-
        lic law and private law in,
        138–139
    children's adjustment following, 190,
        194–195, 197, 198, 199
    domestic violence following, 157
    fathers and, 157, 158
    incidence of, 190
    labeling of battered women in, 174
    noncustodial fathers and, 159, 160
    nonresident fathers and, 159, 160
    social and legal policy on, child ad-
        justment and, 189–190
    social network changes following, 227
Divorce literature
    domestic violence in, 194–195
    interpersonal conflict in, 194–195
Domestic violence
    See also Interparental violence; Vio-
        lence
    among welfare recipient women,
        182–183
    criminalization of
        feminist support of, 136–137
        police practices and, 136
    and ethnicity, 28
    exposure to. See Exposure to domes-
        tic violence
    fatherhood movement and, 166–69,
        170–171
    mothering and, 135–155. See also
        Mothering and domestic violence
    prevalence of exposure to
        in combination with other fac-
            tors, 27–28
        concepts and definitions and,
            25–27
        conceptualization and operational
            issues in, 14–20
        documentation of, 13–14
        estimates of, 22–24, 23
        ethnicity and, 28

future research, policy, and prac-
    tice, 25–29
measurement of, 20–22
in special populations, 28–29
prevention of. See Prevention
screening for, 200
    need and training policy for, 58
    outcomes of, 103–104
social work responses to, 137
terminology for, 4–5
wife abuse vs. marital violence and,
    14–15
witnessing as child maltreatment, 104
Domestic violence advocates
    alliance with father involvement ad-
        vocates, 182
    concerns of
        adult children's memories of abu-
            sive fathers, 175–176
        batterers' impact on children,
            175
        creation of safe, stable environ-
            ments for battered women,
            170–175
        fatherhood advocate beliefs,
            169–170
Domestic violence movement, influence
    on fatherhood movement, 158
Duty to protect
    See also Failure to protect; Pro-
        tection
    in ethical research, 125–126
Duty to report abuse, 121, 126

Emotional abuse
    See also Marital abuse; Physical
        abuse; Psychological
        abuse; Sexual abuse
    depression following, 43
    emotional development and, 51–52
    exposure to domestic violence as,
        121
Emotional problems
    of children in shelters, 242
    from witnessing domestic violence,
        219
Empowerment
    defined, 113
    of research participants, 113–114,
        116–117

through safety planning with mothers, 149
of vulnerable and oppressed participants, in ethical research, 113–114
of vulnerable participants, in published studies, 116–117
Equifinality principle, 40
Ethical research
examination of current ethics and, 115–122
benefit to participants, 118
child participants as social actors and, 117–118
ethics as integral to research methodology, 116
prevention of harm to participants, 119–122
research as relational and empowering of vulnerable participants, 116–117
in studies published since 1970, 115–122
guidelines for
in data analysis writing and dissemination, 126
in data collection, 124–126
in design, 122–123
in recruitment of participants, 123–124
guiding principles in, 112
benefit to individual participants, 115
children as social actors, 114
empowerment of vulnerable and oppressed groups, 113–114
ethics as integral to research act, 113
prevention of harm to participants, 115
researcher–subject partnership in, 113
Ethnicity
domestic violence and, 28
prevention of domestic violence and, 293
Expectations
See also Parental expectations
of parents, 208–210, 209, 212–214, 215

of significant other, presentation to child, 216
Exposure to domestic violence
cognitive problems, 67
conceptual issues in, 19–20
data from children at women's shelters, 27
developmental tasks and, 46–54. See also Developmental task(s)
development and, 91
as emotional abuse, 121
emotional dysfunction and, 67
extrapolation from studies, 25
long-term effects of
definition of, 35–36
prospective studies of, 43–45
retrospective studies of, 40–43
maladjustment risk with, 26
need for multisite prospective studies of, 55–56
occupational status and, 44, 45
pathological outcomes of, 67
posttraumatic stress disorder from, 37, 67, 254
retrospective studies of adult experience of trauma, 40–43
short-term effects of
on children exposed to spousal violence, 45–46
prospective studies of, 45–46
social relationships problems and, 67
Exposure to family violence, research in
classification of abuse in, 196
correlation between exposure and negative effects, 195
discrete knowledge bases in, 195–196
interaction of risk and protective factors, 196
multivariate statistical techniques in, 197
outcome variables in, 196–197
prospective and longitudinal studies, 196
representativeness of child samples in, 196

Failure to protect
See also Duty to protect; Protection by abused mothers

Failure to protect, *continued*
   learned helplessness and,
     143–144
   research in, 149–150
  of nonabusive mother, 104
Families First domestic violence prevention program, 289
Family
   assimilation of violence by, 206–208
     causality in, 207
     continuum of emotionality in,
      207–208
     dimensions of process in,
      207–208
     moralization, meaning in, 207
     recollection in, 206–207
     from specificity to generalization,
      207
   coordinated community response ef-
    fect on, 272
     outcome variables in, 272–273
     process variables in, 273
   social supports of, 224
   structure of, gender-based and re-
    sponsible-fatherhood organiza-
    tions, 163–164
   violent, 15–16
Family Law Act, 1996, 138
Fatherhood advocates
   beliefs of
     battered women allege partner
      abuse, 169
     domestic violence as result of con-
      flict, 169, 170, 171
     failure to assess abusive behavior, 170
Fatherhood movement
   call for, 160
   characteristics of, 160
   and concerns of domestic violence
    advocates, 169–176
   domestic violence perspectives and,
    166–169
    father involvement advocates
     and, 166
    fathers' rights groups and,
     168–169
    responsible-fatherhood groups
     and, 166–168
   emergence of, 159–166
   father involvement programs in,
    161–163

   fathers' rights groups in, 164–166
   federal government involvement in,
    159, 160
   influence on domestic violence
    movement, 158
   responsible-fatherhood groups in,
    163–164
Fatherhood programs
   domestic violence as subject in,
    180–181
   for men who battered, 181
   peer support in, 181
Father involvement programs
   child support enforcement systems as
    barriers to, 162
   social welfare and social policy issues
    in, 161, 162
   strategies for promotion of, 162–163
   supporters of, 161
   U.S. Department of Health and Hu-
    man Services research project,
    163
Father(s)
   See also Fathers' rights groups; Par-
    ent(s); Responsible-fatherhood
    groups
   absence of, and dysfunctional fami-
    lies and society, 164
   abusive. *See* Abusive fathers
   access to child vs. battered women's
    safety, 177–178
   and divorce, 157, 158, 159, 160
   involvement of
    advocates of, 166
    violence potential in, 183
   married, 166–167
   noncustodial, 161, 159, 160
   relationship of, with victimized
    child, 103
   relationships of, with child's mother,
    181–182
   relationships with, after divorce,
    190–192
   resident, noncustodial, 162
   responsible, 163–164. *See also* Re-
    sponsible fatherhood groups
   role in child's life, 159, 160
   as victim, 138
   violent. *See* Abusive fathers
   in welfare families, 167–168
Fathers' rights groups

bias against spouses, 165–166
characterization of, 164–165
collective, 165
domestic violence and, 168–169
individual, 165
lobbyists as special interest group, 165
of noncustodial fathers, 164–165
visitation centers and, 178–179
vs. father involvement programs, 165
vs. responsible-fatherhood organizations, 165
Fathers' rights movement, false abuse allegations by malicious mothers, 191–192
Fear
of abuser, 172–173
aggression in, 251
assessment in intervention programs, 247
of loss of child to foster care, 138
misinterpretation of social situations and, 49
naming of, in The Kids' Club, 256
Federal government
See also Government; State government
accountability of batterer and, 278–279, 279
in evaluation of coordinated community response, 278–279, 279
and fathers' role in families, 169, 170
legislation for removal of perpetrator from home, 138
Female-to-male violence, 24
child adjustment and, 15
Feminists
and criminalization of domestic violence, 136–137
theory of violence toward women, 15, 18
Foster care, mother's loss of child to, 138

Gender
and aggression, 249, 250
physical abuse and, 71
prevention of domestic violence and, 293

response to marital conflict–marital violence and, 195
and social networks, 228
and social support, 228
Gender entrapment
mothering through abuse and, 145
relationship of victimization, survival, identity and, 143, 147
Government
See also Federal government; State government
commitment to prevention, 296–297
in coordinated community response evaluation, 278–279, 279

Harassment, of abuser, personal account, 171–173
Harm
See also Risks
prevention of
in ethical research, 115
informed consent in, 124
in published research studies, 119–122
Health
problems in, relationship with childhood adversity, 42
social support and, 220
woman's, domestic violence and, 142–143
Helplessness, learned, in sustained domestic violence, 144
High-conflict divorce
abusive fathers postdivorce relationships and, 190–192
characterization of, 189
children's best interests legislation and policy in, 193–194
custody issues in, 192, 193
research on impact of violence and conflict on children, 194–195
correlation between exposure and negative effects, 195
next generation, 195–199
Home visitation programs, in prevention, 288, 289, 295
Husband-to-wife violence, 24
Hypothalamic pituitary adrenal (HPA) disturbances, abuse associated, 38–39

Infants and preschoolers, violence prevention and
  healthy child-rearing environment and, 286, 288
  home visitation programs for, 287, 288–289
Informants
  questioning of, for presentation of expectations to child, 216
  in violence assessment, 20–21
Informed choice, in research participation, 114
Informed consent
  in research, 124
  and right to refuse, 119
Internalizing problems
  intervention for, research findings for, 253–254
  social learning theory and, 255
  trauma theory and, 254–255
Interparental violence
  See also Domestic violence; Violence
  children's constructions of
    causality in, 207
    dimensions of process in, 207–208
    moralization, meaning in, 207
    negotiations in, 206–207
    recollection in, 206–207
  correspondence of parental expectations and child's construction of reality, 215, 215–215
  research in children's experience of children's constructions of, 206–208, 210–214
    cognitive–contextual processing of, 204
    conceptualizations in, 204
    consequences of, 203
    extrafamilial influences in, 214–215
    operationalization of parental and other's expectations in, 214–215
    operationalizing conceptual framework, 215–216
    parental expectations in, 208–214
    terminology in, 203
    theoretical assumptions in, 205

Interpersonal relationships
  See also Social relationships
  of adolescents
    childhood abuse and, 53
    physical abuse and, 53
  attachment status of exposed children and, 52
  developmental tasks in, 52–54
  in divorce, 194–195
  in friendship and dating, 52–53
  reciprocity of, 226
  in secure vs. anxious-avoidant children, 53
  sexual abuse and, 41, 53
Intervention programs
  attrition in, 246
  for children of batterers, 238, 239–241, 242
    indicated, 238
    selective, 238
    sheltered children and, 239, 242
  comparison groups in, 245–246
  definition of exposed child in, 244–245
  design needs for
    abuse overlaps, 259
    broader sampling, 260
    comparative studies, 260
    conditions for success in, 260
    co-occurrence of violence, 259
    extended follow-up, 260–261
    health insurers and health maintenance organization funding and, 261
    minimum criteria and standards for efficacy, 261
    outcome studies, 260, 261
    risk profiles, 259
  evaluation criteria for, 242–249
    assessment, 247
    basis of, 242
    data analysis strategies, 248
    design, 245–247
    inclusion, 243–245
    theoretical explanations for goals and results, 248–249
  for exposure to marital violence, 200
  follow-up assessments in, 246–247
  sample population, size and selection for, 243–244

theoretical explanations in, for goals and results, 248–249
Intervention(s)
    application of research and theory in, 249–253
        to aggression, 249–253
        to internalizing problems, 253–256
        to social relationships, 256–259
    community-based early, in prevention of adolescent violence, 292
    in exposure to emotional abuse, 121
    indicated, 238
    at pediatric clinics, 57–58
    selective, 238
    and strategies for resilience, 84
Interviewing methods, in violence assessment, 20
Intimate partner
    abuse by, 3
    definition of, 23
    violence of, in National Family Violence Resurvey, 23, 23–24

Joint custody
    See also Coparenting; Shared parenting
    with abusive partners, 191

Kids' Club, The, 241, 245, 252, 253, 255–256, 259

Legal policy
    for child maltreatment and woman battering, co-occurrence of, 92
    on divorce, child adjustment and, 189–190
    evaluation of coordinated community response and, 278–279, 279
Legal system and courts
    batterers use of, 171, 172, 173
    father's use of, socioeconomic status and, 177–178
    protection by, weakness of, 173–174
    safety of battered women and children and, 177, 178

Maladjustment
    of children in women's shelters vs. community, 28–29

risk for, domestic violence exposure and, 26
    of women, exposed vs. nonexposed to domestic violence, 42–43
Male-to-female violence, 24
    child adjustment and, 15
Malicious mother syndrome, 174
Marital abuse
    See also Emotional abuse; Physical abuse; Psychological abuse; Sexual abuse
    in combination with child abuse, 192
    in National Family Violence Resurvey, 24
Marital conflict. See Conflict, marital
Marital violence
    child's response to, 195
    in combination with child abuse, 27–28, 192
    exposure to, intervention for, 200
    following conflict, 166
    meaning of term, 15
    as predictor of child physical abuse, 192
    wife abuse vs., 14–15
Master child, interparental conflict and parent expectations and, 212, 215
Media violence, exposure to, 100
Memory(ies)
    of adult children of abusive fathers, 175–176
    in child's construction of interparental violence, 207–208
Mental health, of battered women, 143–144
Men who batter
    changed in treatment programs, 179
    characteristics of, 176
    coparenting with, 180, 181–182
    correlation of child and partner abuse by, 177
    group treatment of, 181
    impact on children, 175
    postseparation abuse by, 193
    prediction of continuing abuse by, 176–177
    role in children's lives, 176
Monetary awards, in published studies, 118, 120

Moralization, in children's construction of interparental violence, 207
Mothering
    activity of, in cultural and historical context, 143, 147
    cultural support in, 148
    experiences of, 143, 145, 146, 147
    identities in, 146
    impact of domestic violence on, 143–145
    meaning of, cultural and social mediation of, 145, 146
    theories, beliefs, public education on, 147–148
Mothering and domestic violence, 135–155
    policy and program issues in, 136–141
        child protection and, 137–139
        contact services, 139–140
        crime control, child protection and family law, 136–137, 139
        effect on children and others, 141
        parenting programs, 140
        safe-contact center movement, 139, 140
    research on, 141–142
        beyond mother blaming, 147–151
        identities and experiences of mothering, 145–146
        impact of domestic violence on mothering, 143–145
        women's health and, 142–143
    theories, beliefs, education campaigns and, 148
Mothers
    See also Parent(s)
    abuse of children by, 101–102, 149–150, 169
    abusive–nonabusive polarization of, 145
    battered
        reciprocity of relationship with child and, 226
        shelter residence effect on, 45–46
    as copers and survivors, evaluation studies of, 146–148
    disabling abuse of, 143
    fathers' rights group bias against, 165–166, 191–192
Mothers Empowerment Group Program, 253

Multifinality principle, 40
    in exposure-related traumatic response study, 55

National Alcohol Survey, of married and cohabiting heterosexual couples, 23, 24
National Crime Victimization Survey, annual prevalence of domestic violence in, 22–23, 23
National Family Violence Resurvey, 23, 24
    intimate partner abuse in, 24
    marital violence in, 24
    wife abuse in, 24
    women victims of violence in, 23, 24, 27–28
    use of women's shelters by, 26–27
National Violence Against Women Survey, 23, 23–24
    intimate partner violence in, 23–24
Neurotransmitter function, changes in PTSD, 38

Occupational status, relationship with physical abuse, neglect, domestic violence exposure, 44, 45

Parent as social support, 224
Parental expectations
    of child, 209
        acceptance continuum in, 208, 209
        framing of, 208
        interactions between frames and scripts, 208, 209
        scripting of, 208
        types of parent–child interactions, 208–210
    in child's construction of reality
        awareness and, 210
        child profiles in, 212–214, 215
        competence and, 210–211
        interaction between expectation and construction, 211
        self-perception and, 212
        worldview and, 212
    presentation to child, 216

Parenting
    intervention program effect on, 247
    maternal
        in abusive environment, 144
        cultural support of, 148
    nonabusive behavior toward partner
        and, 183
    programs for
        for abusers, 140
        aggression reduction in, 253
        for violent parents, 150–151
    in women-headed households, 164
Parent(s)
    See also Father(s); Mothers
    abusive, characteristics of, 70–71
    protective function of, 70
    risk of abuse from, 71
    as social support, 223–224
    victimization by and aggression to-
        ward, 41–42
    violent, parenting programs for,
        150–151
Participation in research
    benefits of
        coerced, 119–120
        in published studies, 118
    choice to participate, 125
    control of, 124
    partnership of researcher and subject
        and, 111–112, 113, 118
    protection from abuse and, 125
    referral to treatment and, 118
Partner
    abuse by
        battered women allegation of,
            169
        of child, 191
        child abuse correlation with, 176,
            177
        and child sexual abuse, 142
        mother and child, gender and,
            102
    nonabusive behavior toward and par-
        enting, 183
    physical aggression against, premari-
        tal, 18
    violence of, 23
    women's violence against in self-
        defense, 103
Patriarchal terrorism, vs. common couple
    violence, 18–19

Pediatric clinics, as intervention sites,
    57–58
Peers as social support, 224
Perception of parental expectation, causal-
    ity and meaning in, 216
Physical abuse
    See also Emotional abuse; Marital
        abuse; Psychological abuse; Sex-
        ual abuse
    of children of battered women, 91
    co-occurrence with marital conflict
        exposure, 41
    co-occurrence with spousal abuse, 53
    depression following, 43
    developmental tasks and, 54
    emotional development and, 51–52
    follow-up from childhood into adoles-
        cence, 43
    gender and, 71
    interpersonal relationships and, 53
    perpertrators of
        characteristics of, 70
        occupational status and, 44, 45
    reality distortion in adolescence and,
        53
    resilience and, 70–72
    in retrospective studies, and physical
        aggression–violent behavior in
        adulthood, 40
    self-injurious behavior following, 41
    visual-motor performance delay and,
        48
        early vs. later-onset abuse and,
            47–48
Posttraumatic stress disorder (PTSD)
    from exposure to domestic violence,
        37, 67, 254
    from exposure to natural disasters, 36
    neurotransmitter function changes
        and, 38
    symptoms of
        correlation with problem behav-
            ior scores, 37
        following sexual or aggravated as-
            sault, 41
Pregnancy
    abuse during
        public health consequences of,
            142–143
        reasons for, 142
    battering during, 170

Preschoolers. *See* Infants and preschoolers

Prevention

    See also Intervention programs

    across life span, 287, 296–294

    in adolescents, 287, 291–293

        community-based early intervention, 292

        in dating relationships, 292, 293

        discussions of choice and responsibility for behavior, 291–292

        disorder-based treatment services, 287

        school-based awareness and skills development, 291–292

    emerging goals of, 284–285

    government commitment to, 296–297

    in infants and preschool children

        healthy child-rearing environment in, 287–288

        home visitation programs and, 288–289, 295

        at primary, secondary, tertiary levels, 287

    in infants and preschool children, 287

        collaboration of child protection and domestic violence workers, 289

    policy and research implications of, 294–297

    principles in, 285–286

    professional and public reaction to, 294–295

    promotion of healthy, nonviolent relationships, 284–285

    public education campaigns and, 284

    in school-age children, 287, 289–291

        collaboration of community agencies and schools, 287, 289–291

        Minnesota Coalition for Battered Women, 290

        promotion of awareness and safety skill development, 290

        A School-Based Anti-Violence Program, 290

        Women's Center and Shelter of Greater Pittsburgh program, 289–290

    strategies and research issues

        collaboration of child protection and domestic violence agencies, 295

        collaborative school-based programs, 295–296

        crime prevention and, 295

        evaluation research, 296

        home visitation programs, 295

        national policy on zero tolerance, 296

        public education campaigns, 296

Protection

    See also Duty to protect; Failure to protect

    of battered women, challenged, 175

    of child

        conflict of public law and private law, 138

        in divorce or separation, 138

        family law and, 137

        inability of battered mother and, 143–144

        legislation for, 137

        as mother's responsibility, 137–138

        in perpetrator programs, 141

        practices in, 148

        research in

            on effective practices, 149

            outcomes, 148

    of women and children victims

        coordinated community response in, 269–270, 280

        responsible-fatherhood groups and, 168

Protective factor(s)

    in adjustment, after exposure to violence and direct abuse, 197, 198, 199

    for overcoming adversity, 69–70

    relationship to development, 77

    social support, 219, 230

    in studies of development, 55

Protective orders, weakness of, 173

Psychobiology, following exposure to violence, 38

Psychological abuse

    See also Emotional abuse; Marital abuse; Physical abuse; Sexual abuse

depression following, 43
emotional development and, 51–52
PTSD. *See* Posttraumatic stress disorder
Public education
    on impact of children's exposure to
        domestic violence, 199–200
    in prevention of domestic violence,
        284

Race
    intersection of fatherhood and domes-
        tic violence issues and, 177–178
    and safety of battered woman, 178
Reality
    child's construction and negotiation
        of, 206
    distortion by abused adolescents, 53
Recollection, in children's construction
        of interparental violence,
        207–208
Refuges. *See* Battered women's shelters
Reporting abuse, in research
    breach of confidentiality and,
        123–124
    legal obligation to, 121, 126
    moral obligation to, 122
Research
    child participants in, risk–benefits
        for, 122
    ethical. *See* Ethical research
    participants in
        benefits to, 115, 123
        and data analysis writing and dis-
            semination, 126
        empowerment of, 113–114,
            116–117
        inclusion of voice and perspec-
            tive of, 123
        prevention of harm to, 115
    partnership of subject and researcher
        in, 111–112
Resilience
    in children of battered women, 72–84
        assessment issues and, 76–79
        cultural factors in, 77
        developmental factors in, 76–77
        future study needs and, 79–83
        heterogeneity in psychological ad-
            justment and, 72–76. *See also*
            Adjustment

costs of, long and short term, 78
definitions of, 68
emotional self-regulation and, 76
factors in protection from negative
    experiences, 219
future study needs for
    causal factors in, 82
    comprehensive models, 82–83
    individual differences in, 81–82
    measurement scales for outcomes,
        79–80
    methodological diversity, 80
    multiple domains, 79
    outcomes, 79–80
    protective factors in, 81, 82–83
    resilience over life course, 77–78
    risk factors in, 80–81, 82–83
    sample diversity, 80
general vs. domain specific, 77
identification criteria and practices
    for, 68–69
intervention strategies for
    process focused, 84
    resource focused, 83
    risk focused, 83
nomenclature and, 68
in physically abused children, 70–
    72
    mediators and moderators of,
        70
protective factors in, public policy
    strategies for, 84
social support in, 222
studies of children in stressful–high-
    risk environments, 67
Responsible-fatherhood groups
    Institute for American Values,
        163–164
    National Fatherhood Initiative, 163,
        164
    vs. domestic violence perspectives
        hiding children from, 167
        loss of family values and, 166
        married fatherhood as inhibitor
            of, 166–167
        protection of women and chil-
            dren in marriage, 167–168
        welfare families and, 167–168
Rights
    children's, 139, 167, 169
    fathers', 157–158

Risk factors
 for abuse, 71–72
  parents, 71
  relationship factors, 71
  societal, 71–72
  socioeconomic, 71
 in adjustment, after exposure to violence and direct abuse, 197, 198
 in studies of development, 55
 for vulnerability, 69
Risks
 in divorce and separation, 138–139
 in ethical research, management protocol for, 122
 independent of research procedures
  child abuse, 121
  women abuse, 121–122
 in research procedures
  coerced participation, 119–120
  distress from data-collection, 120
  participation as trigger for abuse,
   121

Safety
 of battered woman, father's access to
  child and, 177–178
 of battered women and children,
  157
  challenge to their advocates, 175
  legal system and courts and, 177,
   178
 of children and mothers, psychological, 150
 as common goal of domestic violence prevention and father
  involvement, 182
 custody, visitation, contact and, 150
 definitions of, 273
 in divorce and separation, 138–139
 evaluation of coordinated community response and, 272–273
 planning for
  mother's participation in, 149
  in social work and child protection practice, 149
  for traumatized child, 255
 safe-contact center movement and,
  139, 140
 of visitation centers, 178

 of women, fatherhood advocates
  and, 169, 170
School-age children
 accommodation skills of, 49
 violence prevention in
  awareness promotion and safety
   skill development in, 290
  collaboration of schools and community agencies in, 287,
   289–290
  programs for, 289–290
Self-injurious behavior, following co-
 occurrence of marital conflict
 exposure and physical abuse,
 41
Self-perception in child's construction of
 reality, 212
 of master child, 212
 of uprooted child, 213
 of vanquished child, 213
Separation, parental
 abuse following, 170, 193
 child adjustment following, 194–
  195, 197, 198, 199
 domestic violence following,
  138–139
Serotonergic system, in depressed abused
 and nonabused children, 38
Sexual abuse
 See also Emotional abuse; Marital
  abuse; Physical abuse; Psychological abuse
 of child, link with woman abuse,
  142
 and emotional and relationship problems as adults, 41
 follow-up from childhood into adolescence, 43
 history of, juvenile delinquent prevention study and, 43–44
 interpersonal relationships and, 41,
  53
 reality distortion and, in adolescents,
  53
 symptoms following, 45
Shared parenting
 See also Coparenting; Joint custody
 and high-conflict, violent families,
  193–194
 postdivorce, 190
 vs. custody and access, 193

Siblings
    abusive in American families, 17
    aggressive, 249–250
    as social supports, 224
Significant other
    expectations of child, 216
    social relationships and, 256–257
Social cognition theory, 258
Social competence
    development of
        attachment and, 54
        in maltreated vs. nonmaltreated
            children, 53, 54
    in resiliency, 76, 77
Social embeddedness,definition of, 221,
    222
Social information processing theory, cog-
    nition and, 48–49
Social learning theory
    in aggression intervention, 250,
        252–253
    internalizing problems and, 255
Social networks
    after divorce, 227
    characteristics of, in women's shel-
        ters vs. community, 225
    of children, 222–225
    cultural, gender, and developmental
        differences in, 228
    in definition and communication of
        social norms, 228
    definition of, 221
    fluidity of, 226–227
    practice and policy recommenda-
        tions, 229–230
    research on, 223–228
    social support vs., 220–222
    studies of characteristics of, 221
    violence effect on, 227
Social policy
    on divorce, child adjustment and,
        189–190
    and father involvement programs,
        161, 162
Social relationships
    See also Interpersonal relationships
    interventions for enhancing, cogni-
        tive–behavioral therapies, 258
    research findings, 256–257
        adoption of harmful schema and,
            256, 257

compromised support from sig-
    nificant others and, 256–257
feminist theory and, 258
social cognition theory, 258
theoretical explanations for,
    257–258
Social situations, hostile aggressive bias
    toward, 48–49
Social skills
    in access to social support, 227–228
    intervention program and, 247
Social support
    conceptualization of, 221
        research recommendations and,
            225–226
    cultural, gender, and developmental
        differences in research on, 228
    definition of, 221
    enacted, 221, 222
    functioning of, 222–223
        developmental view, 222–223
        situational view, 222
    influence on children, 219–220
    linkage with social network, 221
    mutuality with well-being, 227–228
    of parents, 223–224
    of peers, 224
    perceived, 221, 222, 223
    practice and policy recommenda-
        tions, 229–230
        coordination of formal–informal
            social supports, 230
        interventions for recipients and
            providers, 229–230
        interventions to enhance mater-
            nal support, 230
    research on
        methods and measures in, 229
        as multidimensional concept,
            225–226
        violence effect and, 227
    short- and long-term, 230
    of siblings, 224
    vs. social networks, 220–222
Social welfare agencies, best interest of
    child and, 269
Social welfare policy
    domestic violence and father involve-
        ment advocates, 182
    and father involvement programs,
        161, 162

Social work practice
    and domestic violence, 137–138
    and safety planning, 149
Socioeconomic status
    of father in custody and divorce is-
        sues, 177–178
    of mother, violence and, 103
Stalking by abuser, personal account,
    171–173
State government
    See also Federal government; Gov-
        ernment
    accountability of batterer and, 278–
        279, 279
    child witness counseling programs
        of, 104–105
    and evaluation of coordinated com-
        munity response, 278–279, 279
    response to violence, 148
Substance abuse, by battered women, 143

Training
    cross-training in coordinated commu-
        nity response, 277
    for domestic violence screening, 58
    in ethical research, 122, 126
    of professionals, in high-conflict di-
        vorce and domestic violence, 200
Trauma
    See also PTSD
    children's responses to
        behavioral, 37
        sensitization and, 39
    neurophysiological response to,
        and developmental tasks, 54
    research needs in
        physiological, cognitive neurologi-
            cal, imaging studies, 57
        symptom screening devices for,
            57
    symptoms of
        in exposed children, 46, 254
        in exposed children in shelters,
            46

Uprooted child, interparental conflict
    and parent expectations and,
    213, 215

Vanquished child, interparental conflict
    and parent expectations and,
    213, 215
Victimization
    in abuse vs. witnessing of abuse,
        98–99
    of child
        causes of, 71
        co-occurrence with woman batter-
            ing, 98–99
    gender entrapment and, 143, 147
    multiple, and exposures to violence,
        100–101
    by parents, and aggression toward
        parents, 41–42
    of women, 23, 24, 27–28, 143, 147
    of youth, multiples forms of, 41
Vigilance in exposed and victimized chil-
    dren, 50
Violence
    See also Domestic violence; Interpa-
        rental violence
    assimilation in family unit, 206–208.
        See also under Family
    awareness of, 19
    common couple vs. patriarchal terror-
        ism, 18–19
    in current peer relationships, domes-
        tic violence exposure and, 43
    definitions of, 94
        narrow vs. broad, 15–17
    domestic. See Domestic violence
    family, nonmarital, 17
    interparental. See Interparental vio-
        lence
    marital. See Marital violence
    measurement issues in
        accuracy of child reporting of, 21
        child's perception of, 21
        client disclosure and, 20
        disagreement about occurrence
            of, 20
        interview context and, 21
        multiple informants and, 20–21
        vocabulary in reporting, 21
    media, 4, 100
    nonawareness while living with, 19
    observation of, 19
        direct and indirect, 19
    ordinary or common, vs. wife abuse,
        18–19

partner, criterion for, 23
on television, 4
types and number experienced,
 women in shelters vs. in community, 27
of war, 4
witnessing intrafamily, 101
Violence against women
 definitions of
  disregard of women's beliefs and
   experiences in, 16
  focus on physical violence, 16
  nonphysical violence and child
   behavior problems, 16
 incidence of, 192
 meaning of term, 15
Violence Against Women Act, 269
Violent Crime Control and Law Enforcement Act of 1994 (P.L. 103-
 322), 269
Visitation
 issues in, 178
 safety in, psychological, 150
Visitation centers
 fathers' rights groups and, 178–179
 limitations of, 174
 safety of, 178
Vulnerability
 to abuse, predictors of, 71–72
 risk factors for, 69
  relationship to development, 77

Welfare recipients, domestic violence
 among, 182–183
Welfare system, responsible-fatherhood
 groups and, 168
Well-being
 social support and, 220–221
 enhancement of, 222
Wife abuse
 children's exposure to, in families in
  social services and criminal justice agencies, 28

co-occurrence of child maltreatment
 and. See also Child maltreatment
 and woman battering
meaning of term, 15
in National Family Violence Resurvey, 24
violence vs., ordinary or common,
 18–19
vs. marital conflict, 17–18
vs. marital violence, 14–15
Wife-to-husband violence, 24
Women
 See also Battered women
 abuse of, 121–122
 exposed vs. nonexposed to adult domestic violence, distress and maladjustment and, 42–43
 as head of household, 159, 160
  inadequate parenting by, 164
 as victims, 23, 24, 27–28
 violence against partner, in self-
  defense, 103
Women's shelters
 children in
  behavior problems of, 45–46
  data on, 26–27
  maladjustment of, 28–29
  study samples from, 26–27
  trauma symptoms of, 46
 funding needs and, 57
 in United Kingdom, 140
 victim use of, 26–27
Worldview, in child's construction of reality, 212
 of master child, 212
 of uprooted child, 213
 of vanquished child, 213

Youth Relationships Project, 240, 258
Youth victimization, multiples forms of,
 retrospective studies of, 41

ABOUT THE EDITORS

Sandra A. Graham-Bermann, PhD, is an associate professor of psychology and of women's studies at the University of Michigan in Ann Arbor and serves as the codirector of the Interdisciplinary Research Program on Violence. Her research on the impact of family violence on children's social and emotional adjustment includes studies of children in shelters, the community, schools, and clinical populations (http://www.sandragb.com). She is currently studying the effects of young children's exposure to multiple forms of violence. To study sibling violence and abuse and to assess the effects of domestic violence and child abuse, she developed several measures of family relationship qualities. With funding from national and local sources, she has studied the efficacy of an intervention program she created for children exposed to family violence and their mothers. As a clinical psychologist and researcher, she has consulted for the U.S. Department of Justice, the National Institute of Mental Health, and the U.S. Department of Health and Human Services, as well as for local shelters, nursery schools, and community programs. Her work has been recognized with awards for the prevention of domestic violence, research, and teaching excellence. She is the author of *Violence in the Lives of American Children: Epidemiology, Impact, and Intervention* (2000) and *Fostering Resilience in Young Children Exposed to Violence* (with Chantal Follett, 2000).

Jeffrey L. Edleson, PhD, is a professor in the University of Minnesota School of Social Work and director of the Minnesota Center Against Violence and Abuse (http://www.mincava.umn.edu). He has published numerous articles and six books on domestic violence, group work, and program evaluation. Dr. Edleson conducted intervention research at the Domestic Abuse Project in Minneapolis for over 16 years and has provided technical assistance to domestic violence programs and research projects across North

America as well as in several other countries including Germany, Australia, Israel, Cyprus, Korea, and Singapore. The recipient of several national awards, he has served as a consultant to government departments, foundations, and national professional organizations. Dr. Edleson is an associate editor of the journal *Violence Against Women* and has served on a number of other editorial boards. He is the coeditor of the Sage Book Series on Violence Against Women. His own books include *Working With Children and Adolescents in Groups* (with Sheldon Rose, 1987), *Intervention for Men Who Batter* (with Richard Tolman, 1992), *Ending the Cycle of Violence: Community Responses to Children of Battered Women* (coedited with Einat Peled and Peter G. Jaffe, 1995), *Future Interventions With Battered Women and Their Families* (coedited with Zvi Eisikovits, 1996), *Evaluating Domestic Violence Programs* (1997), and *The Sourcebook on Violence Against Women* (coedited with Claire Renzetti and Raquel Kennedy Bergen, 2001).